Gypsies
The Hidden Americans

Gypsies
The Hidden Americans

Anne Sutherland
Macalester College

Waveland Press, Inc.
Prospect Heights, Illinois

For more information about this book, write or call:

Waveland Press, Inc.
P.O. Box 400
Prospect Heights, Illinois 60070
(312) 634-0081

Cover: Shrecha and her sister. Older women are powerful forces in the *vitsa.*

Contents

Figures and Tables

FIGURES

TABLES

Preface

This study of the Rom has been in progress since 1968 of which two years were spent in continuous contact with American Rom. During this time I developed an admiration and respect for the Rom people that goes deep and will remain with me always. I feel a strong sympathy with their lives – at times tragic, at times humorous, but always fulfilling, and I hope that they and other readers will see this book as an appreciative understanding of them. In order to protect individuals, I have changed all personal names, but have drawn from a stock of common names used over and over by them. Consequently, though there may be fifty Gypsies in America using any single name in this book, it is not the name used by the individual I am referring to. I have also given a fictitious name to the particular community I studied. The readers are warned that no Rom they meet can be positively identified as any character in this book.

Besides the general support and stimulation of my family, I owe a special debt to my father for introducing me to the Rom and for sharing with me his insights into their character and into my own. I am very grateful to Jan Tompkins for her invaluable assistance in the field, where I benefited enormously from her experience and perceptiveness. I also wish to thank Ian Hancock, Harry Brunner, Brian Schwimmer, and Dr Walter Starkie for their encouragement and advice.

The preparation of this manuscript has come about as a result of the blind faith and encouragement of my husband Charles who set a standard for me that I have tried to fulfil. I have also benefited greatly from the intellectual stimulation and support, which long precedes this effort, of my teachers Peter Riviere and Rodney Needham. In an odd way I am also grateful to Stanford University for their hostility because it left me entirely without the taint of anthropological contact in the field.

The writing of this manuscript has been supported by a grant from the American Association of University Women. A grant from the Children's Hospital of San Francisco assisted in setting up the Romany School in the field.

1986 Preface

For centuries, Gypsies have been the object of much fascination and little understanding. My primary objective in writing this book was to dispel the misconceptions (i.e., Gypsy as metaphor for freedom; Gypsies as thieves) and to bring some objectivity to the subject of Gypsies. The more I learned, the more I began to appreciate the reasons for the elusiveness and complexity. I eventually became certain of only one fact: the Gypsies survive. The question I then posed for myself was simply: How? How has an ethnic group adapted to a constant flux of languages, countries, economic systems and environments; how did they become so flexible. The answers, I felt, would be found in the cultural construction of their world view—their understanding of reality—and the moral force that understanding carries with it. There I would find the secret to their ability to manipulate the outside world.

In 1968 when I first started the field work for this book, no major ethnography of an American group of Gypsies existed; I found myself in the position of having to undertake a basic ethnographic study in order to address the question of adaptation and survival. Most of the book is devoted to describing the particular group of Gypsies I knew. A major task was to locate the key factors of internal social organization as a basis for understanding how Gypsies deal with external forces.

One of the problems with focusing on internal social relations is that Gypsies must constantly counter negative stereotypes in their contacts with the outside world. These stereotypes often show Gypsies to be disintegrating, demoralized, illiterates and thieves. To the contrary, I found them to be intelligent, flexible, and resourceful survivors. To understand how a group thrives in such an adverse ethnic environment, one must look not only at internal social forces but also at the way Gypsies manipulate stereotypes and sometimes even cultivate the image of themselves as a demoralized group. This book is an analysis not of the external constraints which act upon the Gypsies but of how the Gypsies are active agents of their own situation. That situation includes deeply held prejudices, negative stereotypes and legal constraints. Persecution of Gypsies in the past has been severe and there is abundant evidence that they continue to be subjected to prejudice and discrimination. It is also disturbing that no matter how often these negative stereotypes are dispelled, they do not go away. I have often hoped my book would show the subtlety, complexity and genius of Gypsy culture, but not everyone reads it that way. A detective in the Vice Squad of a midwestern police department recently told me that he was glad I emphasized what strong family ties the Gypsies have and how much they love their children. Now that he knew their major weakness he would be able to keep them in the state long enough to prosecute them if he could have their children taken into custody! Even a reviewer of this book noted and experienced the problem of misinterpretation when writing about Gypsies:

> I was sitting in the emergency room of our local hospital, waiting for my three-year-old daughter to have the results of a recent adventure repaired, when I noticed a commotion at the desk behind me. A thickly accented voice was saying, "His name is Mitchell and we will pay in cash." Just as I turned to get a better look, the emergency room was inundated with Gypsies; real, live Gypsies. I had just finished reading Anne Sutherland's book for this review, and these people seemed to have walked in right off the pages. The use of American-sounding names; the readiness to deal in cash; the way they intimidated the staff without really upsetting things — all of these were typical of the Gypsy behavior reported by Sutherland.
>
> *Gypsies: The Hidden Americans* is definitely not an "apologia for why gypsies steal a lot," as it was described in the *New York Times* book review of November 8, 1975. In fact the opposite is true. Sutherland goes to great pains to explain that much alleged Gypsy stealing is mythical and exaggerated. In the incident mentioned above the Gypsies were reputed to have taken three crucifixes from the hospital during their brief stay. Subsequent inquiries failed to verify the fact; people see what they expect to see.

(William McCready, *American Journal of Sociology,* Vol. 82, No. 2, 1977, p. 476).

The Gypsy world view and part of their strategy for dealing with the outside world is to use an elaborate moral code of their own based on complex rules of purity and impurity. This code is used to relate to each other as a group as well as to maintain the boundary between themselves and outsiders. The code is based on the idea of Marime. Marime is a concept of moral impurity and can be applied to numerous situations. It is used to order people by age, gender, and kinship. It is a fundamental quality of power relationships, economic status and political authority as well as general fortune, health and moral state of being. It is an amazingly flexible code, widely encompassing but with a strong moral impact, adaptable to anything new while preserving a sense of tradition.

The extent to which this code has operated in Gypsy groups was only hinted at in work previous to this one. Apart from Carol Miller, few dealt with it at all. This book established without doubt the prevalence of such a system among the Vlax Rom in the United States and opened up the analysis of similar pollution systems in other groups (e.g. Judith Okely's *The Traveller-Gypsies* and M. Salo, ed., *The American Kalderash: Gypsies in the New World*). Both my own fieldwork and subsequent field work by others have demonstrated that it is women scholars who have the best access to information of this kind as this information is lodged mainly with *romni* (women) who have the major responsibility for maintaining the rules. This may account partly for its late arrival on the scholarly scene.

Gypsies taught me to question everything. As time went by, I wondered if the analysis I presented here was more important to me, the anthropologist, than to a Rom. I wanted to find out what they might think of it. The chance to do so came in 1978 when the BBC approached me about making an ethnographic film on the Gypsies as part of a series called *Face Values* (BBC, 1978). I had carefully protected the identity of the group I studied with name and place changes. I was certain they would refuse to agree to be identified so publicly, but the BBC was willing to send me merely to ask. I couldn't resist the chance to return to my friends, catch up on their news and show them the book I had promised. Contrary to my expectations, Stevan was elated to hear of the film, but we had a hard time coming to an agreement on style. "You want to film us, Annie, you go right ahead. You want a wedding—I can arrange it. Just tell me when, I find the bride, a nice-looking one too. Pinky would be good and she could marry George—he's a nice boy."

After I explained the BBC wanted a real wedding and real life scenes, he thought it lacked a sense of showmanship but agreed to do it my way, shaking his head at the incomprehensibility of the *gaje*. Then I brought out my book and showed it to him. To be frank, I was worried. Would they grab it and demand I account for every word? Would I be chastised for what I left out? Would they feel I betrayed secrets?

"This is the book I told you about Stevan." He was busy momentarily with grand-children's demands.

"Schrecha, this is the book about all of you." I tried again.
"What book, Annie?" she asked. And again attention turned to other more important issues. Was Johnny coming in tonight? Did I know why Yana had left her husband?

"Stevan, the book I wrote, remember?" I was desperate. "I want to read it to you."

"Why? I already know that stuff," he said, but seeing the disappointment on my face he agreed to humor me.

I started by telling this secretive crowd in a high ethical tone that I had disguised all their names and even where they lived to protect them. They looked at me as if I were crazy. I knew immediately that my protection was patronizing and an insult to them. But to be polite, they became mock-indignant. "Now, we'll never be famous," they screamed, laughing.

As I read key passages, I could tell they were getting restless and bored, so I quickly pushed on to the last chapter where I summarized the idea that *marime* is a key concept that allows them to talk metaphorically about categories of people within and outside the group, relative moral worth, social and economic status, and even general health and fortune. As I read and paraphrased madly, I began to doubt myself. This analysis was a tall order. How can such a system really work? Does it mean to them what I said it meant? Suppose they laugh and think this is really stupid. Everyone was quiet and thoughtful, as what I had written sank in. "What do you think?" I asked.

"Well," Stevan said, finally serious, "I wouldn't have put it that way. But...yes...I think you got it right."

There are 10 million Gypsies in the world. The variety of languages, countries, and customs represented among them is enormous. Even within the United States, sorting out the different groups is confusing. The total number of Gypsies is hard to estimate; one million or more is a common figure.

In the ensuing eleven years since this book was published our knowledge of the diverse groups inhabiting the United States has grown considerably. The Gypsies in this book are from only one of many groups. Although other groups (the Boyash, the Romnichal and Hungarian musicians) also had contact with the Vlax Rom in the Bay Area, I had no information on the location of these groups and certainly nothing on their social organization (pp. 14-18). Unfortunately, the title has created the false impression that the Gypsies in this book represent all Gypsies.

Recently I was called to task on this matter by Bill Duna, a professional musician and Hungarian-Slovak Gypsy who now lives in Minneapolis where he runs his own music business. He had just read my book and was incensed. "Not *all* Gypsies are fortune-tellers. My family has been musicians and professionals for generations." And with that he whipped out an album showing hundreds of his relatives all in the throes of playing violins. "Why doesn't anyone ever write about them?"

The Gypsies in this book are the Vlax-speaking Rom. There are many groups (nations and *vitsi*) within this category and each one differs somewhat from the other. Even within the different nations of Rom, there is considerable variety of kin groups, occupations, and area of location. The Vlax Rom are the largest group of Gypsies in the United States, numbering about 500,000. They live throughout the country, mainly in big cities. Chicago, for example, has approximately 23,000 Rom and Los Angeles 15,000 Rom.

The Romnichals, at between 80,000 and 100,000 are the second largest group and also live in all parts of the United States. Romnichal families in Texas figure 10,000 in that state alone. There are also many Irish and Scottish travellers. The Romnichals, Irish and Scottish travellers are sometimes lumped together because they all have come from the British Isles. Although there is some inter-marriage between them, they should be considered three separate groups.

Smaller groups of Gypsies include the following: the Hungarian-Slovak, some 15,000, including musicians as well as other professionals such as bankers, psychiatrists and neuro-surgeons; the Ludar are well-represented here but generally have not been studied; the Boyash, also known as Slovak-Hungarian are located mainly in the North; a few Lovara and some Sinti live in New York and Chicago. These are more recent arrivals on the whole and are not numerous. Most Lovara were killed during the war.

Finally, a word about political action among Gypsies. After the initial flurry of local pressure groups in different countries in the late 60's and early 70's (see page 291), Gypsies have now become more internationally aware. Professor Ian Hancock, a linguist at the University and author of many scholarly works on Gypsies is himself a Romnichal/Lovara Gypsy. He is a United Nations Representative for Gypsies. A major issue for him has been recognition of the fact that Gypsies were the first group targeted for genocide in Nazi Germany. As a result, over one-half million Gypsies in Europe died during World War II. This one issue of recognition in the Holocaust has galvanized Gypsies from all over the world. Various groups, including the Romani Union, have been pressuring the United States Holocaust Memorial Council, a federal agency created by Congress in 1980, to include Gypsies in the Holocaust memorial.

Gypsies are on the move again... move over, let them through!

Anne Sutherland
May 1986

Introduction

Approximately every twenty years someone predicts that the Gypsies are a dying culture and laments that the old ways have gone and that the future is bleak for the Gypsy. Usually, these predictions are based on events that make traditional occupations difficult or impossible, and the cultural repercussions of the economic situation are felt to be far-reaching. First it was 'education' that would bring the end of Gypsies, then the radio, and now television. What next?

Some have pointed out that the children are wearing American-style clothes, and that the men are no longer wearing earrings and a red bandanna on their heads; such observers have mistakenly interpreted differences in clothes by age group, sex, or country as evidence of assimilation. Some listen too closely to the vanity of the old men who assert convincingly that they are the last 'Gypsy King'. My own most valuable and knowledgeable informant assured me that 'there will be no more Gypsy Kings'.

Some of the more informed observers of American Rom[1] have been more specific in their predictions. In 1938, Victor Weybright stated in an article titled 'Who can tell the Gypsies' Fortune?' that because the Gypsies had turned to welfare they were now 'at the end of the Gypsy trail', and he described Steve Kaslov as the last spokesman of his people (see also Weybright 1945). But when Kaslov went to jail in 1942, New York Gypsy leadership became, if anything, more consolidated, and the Gypsies poured into New York (Cotten 1968: 1053–5). In 1949 Stephen Murin, writing on Hawaii's Gypsies, said, 'there is, at this moment, *nothing* to be optimistic about regarding the future of the Gypsies in Hawaii' (36, italics mine), and he lamented a law banning fortune-telling in Hawaii in July, 1949 that caused the exodus of the entire population of Gypsies. By December of that year they had returned, and in 1962, Mrs Ann Coleman of the Hawaii Welfare Department found that the colony had increased in numbers and confidence to such an extent that in a desperate 'final entry' to her report she added, 'the number has grown to the point where it is no longer possible to control the group' (Coleman 1962: 6).

In 1942, writing on the Rom in Philadelphia, Arlene Bonos declared that the basis of Gypsy culture is fortune-telling by women and predicted, 'Gypsies would become *more assimilated* if the men were forced to assume financial responsibilities for their families. This would cause the *basic family pattern to change*' (274, italics mine). As in many cities in the United States, fortune-telling was made illegal in Philadelphia, but in 1966, Coker reported that although the men were contributing more to the family income, 'whether men or women are the main financial providers in the household shifts according to circumstances' (87). These circumstances are basically economic necessity, but it appears that this has had little effect on family patterns.

Perhaps the most lengthy and thorough attempt to document the downfall of American Rom is Rena Cotten's PhD thesis entitled 'The Fork in the Road: a Study of Acculturation among Kalderash Gypsies'. She describes three acculturation periods: (a) pre-acculturation, 1910–25; (b) transition, 1925–33; and (c) acculturation situation, 1933–?; based on the change from camping to setting up winter headquarters in cities to 'inability to leave the city at will' (Cotten 1950: 25–6). In her preface, she states: 'The original intention of the writer was to attack the problems of resistance to acculturation among this very interesting group, but the material also lent itself to a different approach, the disintegration of the band.'

She also bemoans the weakness of the *kris* court system (207). But eighteen years later we find that she refers to the Rom as 'urban nomads' and concludes that 'It is the particular combination of miniaturization of the socio-political units and the hub-patterning of the *kris* that has proven so effective in implementing Romany resistance to assimilation for over half a millennium' (Cotten 1968: 1055).

Even Ronald Lee, who is himself a Gypsy, has lately taken a very pessimistic view of the future. He predicts the 'Canadianization' of the 'real' Gypsies who are becoming 'hoodlums, dope addicts, prostitutes and alcoholics following the natural process of the Canadianization of off-white minority groups' (1971: 233), and he states about his old patriarch 'when he died, the last link with the Gypsy past would go with him except for the manuscripts of folklore, laws, customs and traditions that I had documented' (234). Yet these words of foreboding contradict his earlier views when he wrote that the Gypsies remain 'as a people apart, since they have re-adapted themselves to the modern conditions of North America' (1967: 39). Re-adapted is the key word; the Gypsies always have and probably always will be re-adapting themselves to new conditions.

Certainly changes – in life-style, dress, occupations, and customs – have taken place among the Gypsies. Economic adaptability, combined with the inflexibility of certain basic rules, is the Gypsy's *forte*, and the consequence of flexibility is often change. A man, who began life by trading horses or hammering copper, might then move on to trading used cars or hammering car fenders or repairing copper boilers and drills; women tell fortunes when and where they can, but when they cannot, they move into farm labour or welfare with their families. Most of them do a little of everything. Like hunting and gathering peoples, it is not so much one particular skill that is important as the ability to extract a living somehow from the natural environment. For the Gypsies what counts is to be versatile in exploiting the available human and technological environment in which they find themselves. This versatility has changed relatively little.

The Gypsies have faced dramatic technological changes since they left India and began wending their way into Western Europe. To most anthropologists, technological change without social change seems inconceivable; yet the descriptions of the most basic economic and social behaviour from the earliest accounts to the present day, from Russia, Greece, North Africa, and Western Europe, to North and South America, are easily recognizable as 'Gypsy'. There are great differences, of course, but these are attributable just as often to tribal differences as to changes over time. No doubt individuals, and even large groups of Gypsies, have become assimilated throughout history, often through coercion. One of the most famous and apparently successful attempts to 'integrate' the Gypsies into the wider society was when they were made serfs in Rumania between the fifteenth and nineteenth centuries (Kenrick and Puxon 1972: 49–56). Even this drastic measure failed to some extent, for the Rom in America are probably descendants of those 'serfs'.[2]

The Rom in America are fully aware that changes have taken place among them. There is little an old person likes more than to talk of the good old days, the days of 'life on the road' when 'we didn't need no doctors or no schools'. Of course, they fail to add that they still spend almost the entire summer travelling (just as when they camped) and on average travel 42 per cent of the time; the young families over 50 per cent of the time. Mobility is a major method of problem solving and of social control, and as long as there is conflict there will be mobility. They also fail to mention that in those days their occupations did not require even a minimum of literacy which they now find very useful for dealing with the welfare system.

Sceptical as I am about assimilation of American Rom, I must repeat that social change does take place, and I might venture here to comment on some of the recent social changes that have been occurring. There has been an increase in the proportion of endogamous marriages, that is, marriages contracted within the *vitsa* or within related *vitsi* relative to those contracted with unrelated *vitsi*.[3] There has also been an increase in conflict for resources, and this has brought about a new emphasis on territoriality. The most economically viable *kumpania* is the one that has become more restricted to one *familia* or one *vitsa*. These tendencies are associated with an increase in the population density of the Rom in the United States, which means a relative saturation of their resources, that is, exploiting non-Gypsies by means of certain occupations. The biggest problem for the Rom has been the illegalization of fortune-telling, which has not ended fortune-telling but has made it less viable an occupation for large groups and correspondingly more suitable for a smaller tightly controlled group (like the *familia*) that can operate with police protection in one place. In some areas this is pre-determined by the authorities who may give licences only to one family. Conflict over territory is related to conflict over marriage bonds, and in order to counter the pressures put on marriage bonds by *Xanamik*, who are in competition with each other, marriages between related persons has increased.

I suspect that future demographic and economic pressures combined with the increase in conflict in certain areas may bring a tendency towards more strict patrilineal recruitment in the *vitsa* and away from the expressed cognatic principle of recruitment in order to restrict the size of the *vitsa* given the relative scarcity of resources. What has already happened in this area of social relations is the very rapid division of the *vitsa* along sibling lines into *familiyi* branches that eventually become new *vitsi*. But an assimilation of the Rom into the wider society seems unlikely, and if this is so, the question we must ask is: how have they remained socially distinct?

There are many examples in the literature of ethnic groups or sub-cultures that live within a wider culture, face tremendous pressures to assimilate, but have resisted this course. The Mapuche Indians of Chile, for example, in recent times have effected a successful adaptation to reservation life within their traditional social framework. Although they have had to change considerably in order to cope with new economic conditions, they have been able to do so in such a way as to retain their social integrity (Faron 1961: 62–5; 219–26). There are, however, ethnic groups that have a long history of interaction with a wider culture whose values and social institutions they reject. The Anabaptist groups in North America – the Hutterites, Mennonites, and the Amish– like the Rom, are very aware of outside pressures that threaten their existence, and also like the Rom, have suffered persecution for hundreds of years because of their way of life (Hostetler and Huntington 1967; Hostetler 1968). Moreover, they have to cope with internal social pressures, either as a result of external conditions or demographic growth, which they resolve by periodic migration. Because of these pressures, the most important issue that these Anabaptist groups face is the continuous maintenance of social boundaries between themselves and the wider culture (Hostetler 1968).

Barth (1969: 9–38) has proposed that the study of ethnic groups should concentrate on the analysis of social boundaries and how they are maintained. He points out that for groups that do not live in isolation, boundary maintenance is neither a simple nor a static issue. In fact, the very continuity of the ethnic unit depends on boundary maintenance. The study of social boundaries, he suggests, should be centred on an analysis of how the categories (ethnic labels) of a group are interconnected with their actions. If we take Barth's suggestion and look at boundary maintenance for one ethnic group or sub-culture in American society, the Amish,

we see certain interesting similarities with the Rom. Both the
Amish and the Rom are discrete societies that nevertheless inter-
act in many ways with persons from American society. The
groups are perhaps extreme cases among minority groups both
because they are such separate cultural groups and because they
have worked out very effective methods of boundary maintenance
over a long period of time.

The Amish have a set of beliefs, moral values, and rules for
behaviour based on Christianity as presented in the Bible but
with their own interpretation, usually unwritten, which is called
Regel und Ordnung (rules and order). Behaviour according to the
Ordnung must be accepted by each and every Amish, and any
person rejecting this set of rules, any person demonstrating
erring ways, is subject to *Bann und Meidung* (excommunication
and 'shunning'). *Meidung* consists primarily of denying commensality and applying social ostracism to the shunned person. The
families of the shunned also suffer ostracism and often ask the
shunned member of the family to leave so they can return to
normal lives (Hostetler 1968: 47–69). Shunning is not permanent;
a person may accept the *Ordnung* and the church once again by
mending his ways. The Amish, therefore, have a very effective
method of ensuring that membership in the group and conformity
to the Amish way of life are synonymous. The strict boundary
between membership (acceptance of *Ordnung*) and non-member-
ship (subjection to *Meidung*) is reflected also in inside–outside
categories of persons. *Unser satt Leit* (our sort of people) and
anner satt Leit (other sort of people) define distinct differences in
dress, sexual roles, language, and custom. With one's own people,
cooperation, generosity, mutual aid, and respect for elders is the
norm. The sense of community is very strong, and members do
not usually suffer from alienation or loneliness. With outsiders
all social relationships must be kept within certain bounds and
strong affective bonds are avoided. There is also a general avoidance of outside social institutions – schools, armed forces, and
other bulwarks of American values and socialization.

When we look at the question of boundary maintenance for the
Rom we find many similarities with the Amish. As an ethnic
group, the Rom represent a somewhat exceptional case for two
reasons. Not only do the Rom have a fairly separate social organization, and therefore could be considered a culture in its own right,
but they also have been labelled a 'pariah group' (Cohn 1970;

Barth 1955, 1969: 31) because of the attitude of the 'host population' towards them.

> These [pariah groups] are groups actively rejected by the host
> population because of behaviour or characteristics positively
> condemned though often useful in some specific, practical way.
> European pariah groups of recent centuries (executioners,
> dealers in horseflesh and leather, collectors of night soil, gypsies,
> etc.) exemplify most features: as breakers of basic taboos they
> were rejected by the larger society. Their identity imposed a
> definition of social situations which gave very little scope for
> interaction with persons in the majority population, and simul-
> taneously as an imperative status represented an inescapable
> disability that prevented them from assuming the normal
> statuses involved in other definitions of the situation of inter-
> action. Despite these formidable barriers, such groups do not
> seem to have developed the internal complexity that would lead
> us to regard them as full-fledged ethnic groups; only the
> culturally foreign gypsies clearly constitute such a group.
> (Barth 1969: 31)

I have not found that classifying the Gypsies as a pariah group
has been useful for understanding their social processes and
structure. At best, it has resulted in 'partial ethnography', which
can often be very misleading. For example, Cohn (1970: 21) in his
study of the Canadian Rom as a 'relatively stable pariah group'
remarks:

> The Gypsies translate *vitsa* to mean tribe, and there are many
> of these among the Rom. However, all intermarry rather freely,
> and it is almost impossible to find anyone who can identify
> himself purely and simply with only a single *vitsa*. When asked
> about his affiliations, a Gypsy may give a long account of the
> different associations of his mother and father, going on to the
> various connections he has through the marriages of his
> children, ending up with a statement such as 'I guess I'm all
> mixed.' Nevertheless, for certain purposes, Gypsies do identify
> themselves and one another as belonging to a given *vitsa*; for
> any given individual this identification tends to vary according
> to the convenience of the circumstances. (Cohn's translation.)

These statements give the reader an impression of confusion, an
absence of meaningful social units, and a lack of social ordering

altogether. The *vitsa* is presented as a unit with no clear structure, no clear method of recruitment and completely fluid intermarriage. Although he correctly points out the element of freedom in choice of *vitsa*, Cohn both dismisses the cognatic principle of descent and underrates the importance of the *vitsa* as a unit of social organization. In fact, as we shall see, the *vitsa* has a definite structure, *vitsi* intermarry according to a specific pattern, and although *vitsa* membership does vary according to the circumstances, it is possible to delimit these circumstances. The root of the problem lies in the approach. Simply by defining the Gypsies as a pariah group and viewing them from the outside, internal social organization is obscured. Again, by producing only a partial ethnography, the interconnection between the various units of social organization cannot be fully understood, and the impression of confusion remains. If only because for the Rom, non-Gypsies are a pariah group, this approach is bound to have irresolvable problems.[4]

However, it is interesting to look at the question of boundary maintenance once one has a more thorough understanding of social processes. For the Rom, the maintenance of boundaries between themselves and the *gaje* (non-Gypsies) is a continuous, almost daily, concern. It is based on two factors: (a) social contact with *gaje* is limited to specific kinds of relationships, namely economic exploitation and political manipulation for advantages. Purely social relations and genuine friendship are virtually impossible because of the second factor; and (b) a whole symbolic system and set of rules for behaviour (*romania*) which place the *gaje* outside social, moral, and religious boundaries in a multiplicity of ways, the most important being their *marime* status. The relationship between these two oppositions: Rom/*gaje* and *romania*/*marime* is the key to their maintenance of a distinct way of life. An explanation of the behaviour that is implied by these categories is a major purpose of this book.

The Rom are also aware that they live within a society that generally despises them and erects its own boundaries against them. Because they are always trying to improve their economic position by manipulating *gaje*, not only to earn a living but to gain political advantage over other Rom, they must often counter the prejudices and erroneous labels which are given to them. On the other hand, their sense of moral superiority is not threatened by their position in American society or by the attitudes of *gaje* towards them, and their separateness, which they covet, is actually protected and enhanced. Therefore, while on the one hand, they often find it useful to counter *gaje* attitudes, these same attitudes help to maintain the boundaries and reinforce Rom ideas about the foolishness of the *gaje*.

Finally, boundary maintenance is also contingent on their ability to adjust to change. The Rom have developed an economic system that allows great flexibility and a moral system that is very inflexible. They can adapt to numerous cultural, technological, and economic changes while maintaining very rigid ideas of *romania* and *marime* (inside and outside) enforced by the authority of the elders. The literature on Gypsies indicates that this combination of economic adaptability and moral or ideological solidarity is common to all Gypsy groups. A recent, as yet unpublished, ethnographic study of British Travellers who, of all Gypsy groups, are perhaps the most distinct from the Rom, has shown that their pollution ideas are in fact very similar to those described here and are the basis of their system of boundary maintenance.[5] A comparative study of several Gypsy groups would be necessary to test this hypothesis, but such a comparison must be based on thorough and detailed ethnographies. The present work is a step in this direction.

Methodology

This book is an ethnographic description of a group of American Rom living in Barvale, California. It is based on two years fieldwork in this community or *kumpania* (pl. *kumpaniyi*) and is supplemented with intensive interviews with one Rom leader. Since the literature on American Rom is paltry and unreliable in general, very little written material has been used. However, when certain kinds of data were unobtainable, either because of my particular role in the community, or because of my sex, published material has been used to supplement the field notes, welfare records and reports, newspaper articles, and taped interviews.

The Rom are the largest group of Gypsies and exist in every part of the world. They recognize the existence of other Gypsy groups but consider these people to be morally and socially inferior to the Rom. The Rom are divided into four nations or tribes called *natsiyi* (sing. *natsia*). These are, in order of social status, the Machwaya, Lowara, Kalderasha, and Churara. This work deals with persons from all but the Lowara *natsia* who occupied the *kumpania* in Barvale, but since this area was dominated by certain Kalderash families, most information could be said to be derived from them. The distinctions between the various *natsiyi* include dialect differences and certain variations in custom and appearance, but these differences are not significant in terms of the social structure except that they are manifestations of the status of each *natsia*. The difference in social status is an extremely important term of reference for behaviour especially in conflict situations when these statuses are most openly expressed. The different statuses are symbolized in myth by the sun (Machwaya), moon (Lowara), stars (Kalderash), and a knife (Churara).

The Barvale *kumpania* is only one of a large number of *kumpaniyi* in California and the rest of North America. This *kumpania* is dominated by a Kalderash *vitsa* called Kashtare but is open to other Rom who obtain prior permission from the leader or *rom baro* ('big man') or who are relatives of members of the *kumpania*. There is no economic monopoly in Barvale as the main sources of income are welfare and summer farm work. Not all *kumpaniyi* take this same form, however. Some are tightly controlled by one *familia* or *vitsa* who have a monopoly on fortune-telling establishments either through exclusive licences or bribery. This kind of closed *kumpania* is typically Machwaya. Other *kumpaniyi* are quite open and loosely organized and people come and go freely, utilizing any economic resources in the area. The *kumpania* is the most important economic group. A *kumpania* has the right to safeguard the economic resources of its territory and make rules about how and how much they are to be exploited. Trespassers can be expelled through recourse to American law, if necessary.

The *kumpania* is also the area of residence and is composed of so many households or *tsera* (tents). Barvale has thirty-three households with approximately three hundred Rom, the average family size being seven. However, because there are households in residence, it should not be assumed that these are stable or permanent units. The mobility of each household is quite considerable. Some travel as much as 60 per cent of the time, coming and going so frequently that it is difficult to know if they belong to the *kumpania*. The majority of households stay in Barvale over the winter and leave to camp and work in nearby fields during the summer months besides additional trips to attend rituals and visit relatives during the year. The average amount of travelling time in Barvale was 42 per cent of total time. Some households, especially those headed by very elderly and infirm persons, travel only when absolutely necessary, such as for a funeral feast (*pomana*) or an illness. Travelling is a social imperative on many occasions, and it is a major form of social control. When there is a conflict, the families involved leave town for a period of time until the gossip has quietened down.

Politically, the *kumpania* also has a very important role. Each large extended family (*familia*) is headed by the eldest functioning adult who has considerable power over family members, and together, through discussion and consensus, these elders make important decisions on matters of social, economic, and moral concern to the *kumpania*. In a *kumpania* such as Barvale, there is also a *rom baro* or leader who, besides controlling his family, has claim to some authority over other families in the *kumpania* and represents them to outside agencies and officials (*gaje*). The *rom baro* claims to have influence with these important *gaje* and uses this influence both to establish his authority with the Rom as well as to obtain economic benefits for his people and ease legal difficulties. The *rom baro* also has another role and that is to arbitrate in fights and solve internal conflict as well as see that moral and social rules are upheld. He may also, with the support of the *kumpania*, punish infractions of these rules. Sometimes mobilization of opinion and arbitration are not sufficient and recourse to stronger legal methods, the *kris romani* (Romany trial), is necessary. The strongest leader in an area will also be the judge at these trials. Thus the *kumpania* is also the smallest *public* moral and political unit which can make decisions on matters beyond more personal family concerns.

The Rom have a cognatic terminology and trace descent through both males and females. An extended cognatic family covering three to four generations is called a *familia* and is headed by the eldest member who may be either male (*phuro*) or female (*phuri*). Members of a *familia* feel a very strong loyalty to each other, often live together, though there may be five to ten households, and cooperate economically, sharing with and aiding one another at all times. There is also a larger unit of cognatic kin composed of several *familiyi* (headed by brothers and cousins) called the *vitsa*. Membership in a *vitsa* is cognatic by right but restricted in practice primarily to descendants of males. Since post-marital residence is normally patrilocal, males generally choose to call themselves by their father's *vitsa*, and females eventually call themselves by their husband's (and children's) *vitsa*. However, no one loses the right to join the *vitsa* of his or her mother. Like the *natsia*, each *vitsa* has a status and a name; this status is partially determined by the status of the *natsia* to which the *vitsa* belongs and partially by its own reputation, size, power, and wealth. Because these latter four factors fluctuate over time, the status of a *vitsa* is not as immutable as the status of a *natsia*, and a considerable amount of information is required to be able to evaluate its position. This information, plus the name of a person's father (and therefore *familia*), is used to identify another Rom and determine what attitude and behaviour is appropriate with him. Members of one's own *vitsa* are relatives (*niamo*), and behaviour towards relatives is appropriately cooperative and friendly.

Marriage can take place between any two Rom; however, there is a preference for marriage with a second cousin of one's own *vitsa* or the *vitsa* of a female ancestor (mother or grandmother). This preference for endogamous marriage is consistent with a suspicion of *streyino* Rom (those whose *vitsa* is not familiar) and the loyalty and mutual aid expected between kin. Affines are persons to whom one owes certain obligations and respect rather than affection, but affines who are also kin are said to create stronger marriage bonds. This is particuarly emphasized in the *Xanamik* (co-parent-in-law) relationship which is fraught with tension and the source of much internal conflict. The stated preference for endogamous marriage is not merely an ideal but is practised in approximately half the marriages.

Marriage is prohibited between cognatic members of a *familia* which includes kin up to the first cousin. It is also prohibited with non-Gypsies (*gaje*) who are the social and moral opposites of the Rom and is highly frowned upon when with members of non-Rom Gypsy groups. However, this prohibition is more strictly interpreted for women than for men. Women are outcast (*marime*) from the group if they have sexual relatons with a *gajo*, whereas men are only temporarily *marime* (polluted) on condition that they incorporate their non-Gypsy woman into their family and teach her proper rules of submission to her mother-in-law and cleanliness behaviour. Even so, these Rom-*gaji* marriages constitute only 5 per cent of all marriages.

Not only marriage with *gaje* but all social relations with them are in a sense *marime*. The only truly acceptable relations with *gaje* are situations of economic exploitation or political manipulation. *Marime* is a very broad concept (meaning both pollution and rejection from the society) which is an effective form of coercion. The ultimate punishment by the society is when a person declared *marime* in a trial is denied commensality and normal social intercourse even with his own relatives. The effectiveness of *marime* in political and coercive contexts is due partly to its broad application to many other categories of persons, concepts, and beliefs that are evil, lowly, rejected, harmful, or negative in some way. *Marime*, its opposite concept *wuzho* (purity), and a third, intermediary concept of dirt, *melalo*, form the basis of a whole system of related categories which include social boundaries and status, body symbolism, sex, age, health, luck, and supernatural beings. This symbolic system has an enduring quality and may be the key to Rom survival as a group.

Definition of a Rom

There are many distinct groups of people who are brought together under the word 'Gypsy' or who in some way refer to themselves as 'Gypsy' or 'Romanies'. In America some of these groups are the Kalderasha, Machwaya, Lowara, Xoraxai, Roman-itchal (English Gypsies), Gitanos (*Kale*), Boyash, Ungaritza (Hungarian Gypsies), and so on, and in Europe there are also the Rudari, Sinte (or Manush), Aurari, Ursari, Churara, Irish and Scottish travellers (Tinkers), and others.[1] Besides these groups there are also references to Gypsies according to a certain area such as French Gypsies, English Gypsies, Italian Gypsies (*Zingari*), Spanish Gypsies, Hungarian Gypsies, Russian Gypsies, Mexican Gypsies, and so on. Designations by country actually tell one very little and do not necessarily identify the group, since there may be Kalderasha in Italy, Russia, or Sweden with very little difference between them, except that their second language is the one of that country.

There is a great deal of debate among gypsiologists over who should and who should not be designated a 'true Gypsy' and several criteria have been suggested for doing so. Some are inclined to include all 'travellers' or 'nomadic' people in western society as Gypsies, others look for Romany origins or 'blood' and extent of intermarriage with non-Gypsies, and others (including many Gypsies) feel that knowledge of some dialect of the language is the best criterion. While I do not wish to become involved in a general definition of 'Gypsy', since it is a fairly arbitrary choice where one draws the boundaries, it is very important here (1) to place the people I shall be describing into some broader classificatory system in relationship to other groups of Gypsies and (2) to present their own classification of other Gypsies.

Although the general term 'Gypsy' is very ambiguous it is relatively easy to single out the Rom as a group. They are basically those people who call themselves O Rom and who speak an inflected, Sanskrit-based language which they call *Romanes*. The Rom are divided into four tribes which they call *natsia* (nation) or *rasa* (race). These are the Kalderasha, Machwaya, Lowara, and

Churara.[2] Each tribe is further divided into sub-units called *vitsi* (or *tshera* by the Lowara) and each *vitsa* into *familiyi*.

Based primarily on linguistic evidence, it has been postulated that the Rom left India approximately AD 1000 (Clébert 1963: 38–46), and entered Western Europe at the beginning of the fifteenth Century (Clébert 1963: 54–62). Upon entering Western Europe, they represented themselves as 'Egyptians' and from this word, the name 'Gypsy' has been derived. It is also speculated that some nomadic Rom have mixed with other nomadic or travelling people and have altered their society considerably (for example, the travellers of Great Britain). Some Rom settled in one place and changed considerably, forming sedentary groups such as the Hungarian Gypsies, who are often musicians, or the *Gitanos* (*Kale* speakers) of Spain who are flamenco dancers. These sedentary groups have changed so much that they are no longer considered Rom, though still 'Gypsies'. The nomadic Rom themselves have spread throughout the world, and though they may occasionally bring in women who are outsiders, they have remained Rom and still keep the tribal and *vitsa* organization of the Rom. They consider themselves a distinct group, culturally and racially, from other Gypsy groups.

The Gypsies with which this study is concerned, call themselves Rom, which they translate as 'the Gypsies', 'the people', or 'the public', and all of which mean 'we the Rom' as opposed to the *gaje*, which is normally translated as 'Americans'. The use of Rom to refer to themselves as a people must be distinguished from *o rom* meaning adult man or husband, and I have indicated this in the spelling.

In general, these Rom classified other Gypsy groups on the borderline between themselves and the *gaje* (non-Gypsies). While they recognize that these people are not *gaje*, because they have certain things in common with the Rom, they also feel that they are somehow not the same either and not Rom (in English, they would say 'not real Gypsies'). However, in certain individual cases, some members of other Gypsy groups were accepted as a 'real Gypsy' depending on the situation. For example, a boy who wanted to marry a Romanitchal girl was likely to insist that she was a 'real Gypsy'. Consequently, it is often difficult to know how an individual in any one context is classified though it may be fairly clear how the group he comes from is classified.

It is possible for a group of Rom to become a borderline group (according to other Rom) by taking up a sedentary life, by losing the *Romanes* language, or by marrying too frequently with *gaje*. It is also possible for individual families in a borderline group to become assimilated with the Rom through marriage over several generations. For example, certain families of Romanitchal in America have so intermarried with Kalderasha Rom that they are dying out as a distinct group and have effectively become Rom. The opposite is also possible. Families who marry frequently with *gaje* and take up the *gaje* way of life will become *gaje* over a few generations.

In the strictest sense it is not possible for an individual Rom to 'become' a *gajo* or an individual *gajo* to 'become' a Rom as these are seen to be opposite racial and social categories. A *gaji* who marries a Rom and lives in the Rom community (*kumpania*) is called a *gaji romni* (non-Gypsy wife) and even her children in some instances may be called *gaje*. Other than the *gaji romni*, non-Gypsies do not generally enter the Rom community.[3] On the other hand, although a Rom never becomes a *gajo*, he may decide to leave the community, and if he does this he becomes *marime* (defiled, outcast) and it is said 'he went over to the *gaje*'.

The Barvale Rom have a very ambivalent and contradictory attitude towards other Gypsy groups, partly because they are generally ignorant of their ways and have very little contact with them. They had generally heard of most of the other Gypsy groups but knew precious little about them. The terms that they familiarly used to describe Gypsies other than themselves were: *Rom Ameriko* (American Gypsies), Boyash, and Romanitchal (English Gypsies). A sample of statements about these Gypsies includes:

> 'There is the *Rom Ameriko* which includes the Gypsies who have lost their language and the Boyash. They are not Gypsies any more.'
> 'American Gypsies, Boyash, and English Gypsies do not speak *Romanes* or go by our traditions (*romania*).'
> 'Scotch Gypsies and English Gypsies are not Gypsies. People just call them Gypsies. The Rumanian Gypsies (Boyash) are different too. They don't speak the language.'

I suspect that the term *Rom Ameriko* is a catch-all term for Gypsy groups that the Rom do not understand but consider

Americanized and for individuals who claim to be Gypsy but are not affiliated through their families with any Rom *vitsa*. The Boyash are a separate group of sedentary 'Rumanian Gypsies' and speak a secret language, Ruthenian (Lee 1968: 15). There are several Boyash families in California. Since they had been living there longer than the Rom they had the only fortune-telling licences in some cities. They rarely mixed with the Rom, came to any of their social functions, or intermarried. The three or four Boyash–Rom marriages that I knew of lasted less than one year, and as one *romni* remarked: 'It never works if you don't marry your own kind.' The English Gypsies or Romanitchal in America are also a separate group in their own right, but many are becoming assimilated either with the Rom, through intermarriage and through learning inflected *Romanes*, or with the *gaje*, through marrying *gaje*. According to Ronald Lee (1968: 13) the Lee-Adams family of Los Angeles, for example, is composed of Romanitchal families (Lee) who married with Machwaya Rom (Adams).

For the Rom use of the language *Romanes* and acceptance of *romania* (law and tradition), including shame (*lashav*) and *marime* as embodied in the *kris*, are the most important conditions for accepting someone as a Rom. Anyone failing this test is liable to be labelled Boyash, *Rom Ameriko*, or 'not Gypsy'. Therefore even though the Romanitchal and Boyash are groups in their own right, they are not considered 'true' Gypsies by the Rom.

It must be emphasized that these classifications rarely appear as clear-cut in conversation as I have presented them here. Statements by informants on classifications always depend on at least two factors: (1) how the informant himself is classified, and (2) the context being discussed; for example, whether the informant feels friendly towards the person he is classifying (in which case he is likely to be 'more Gypsy') or whether he is engaged in some disagreement (in which case the person is likely to be 'less Gypsy').

To illustrate, in a conversational context the following contradictory statements were given by the same woman, a Kalderasha *romni*, on the same day, but to two different Rom:

1 English Gypsy is not Boyash. Emma is English Gypsy, not Boyash. She is *gaji*. You take Boyash, they is something like us. They know what shame is. They know what's right and

what's wrong. Boyash knows a little of the language. Emma
is English Gypsy. She understands a little but she only knows
a few words.

2 Boyash!!! They're not Gypsies. They have no shame.

In the first statement the speaker was involved in a conversation
with another old lady whose daughter-in-law was causing her much
grievance, and she blamed this on the fact that the daughter-in-
law's grandmother, Emma, is an English Gypsy, even though the
daughter-in-law's father and grandfather are Rom. The speaker
did not want to displease the old lady and wanted to show that
she took her side against the daughter-in-law. Her emphatic
and disdainful description of an English Gypsy and defence of the
Boyash was all the more necessary since the old lady herself had
married a Boyash and the married son in question was himself
half-Boyash. It is quite apparent that without all this background
information the statements, taken at face value, would be very
misleading.

In the second statement, the same speaker was discussing the
Boyash in Barvale who have fortune-telling licences whereas the
Rom do not, and she was disgusted that they should have obtained
them although they were 'not Gypsies'.

The Literature

The literature on Gypsy groups is extremely large. 'Gypsy',
loosely defined, may include any group of people who are or were
nomadic and who speak or did speak some form of Romany
language. Strictly defined, it usually refers to the nomadic Rom.
In most sources on Gypsies the word is never defined.

A Gypsy Bibliography, published in 1914 by George Black,
contains 4,577 items but claims that 'a complete bibliography of the
subject, it is needless to say, is almost impossible, the indirect
material being so abundant' (Black 1914: v). The Catalogue of the
Romany Collection at the University of Leeds (1962) lists 1,234
items, and the Catalogue to the Scott Macfie Collection at Liverpool is similarly large. There are also two journals that deal
exclusively with material on Gypsies. The Gypsy Lore Society
has been publishing a journal more or less continuously since its
foundation in 1888, and the French journal *Études Tsiganes* has
been published since 1955.

There are several reasons for the immense quantity of publications on Gypsies. First, they live in almost every part of the world; consequently, there is something written about Gypsies in almost every language, including several dialects of Romany. Second, they clearly hold a tremendous romantic appeal to most people. This commonly held view of the Gypsies as an exotic and romantic people, combined with their own secrecy and elusiveness in relations with non-Gypsies, also partly accounts for the problem that a great deal of what has been written is misleading, false, vague, exaggerated, or mystical.

I spent the best part of a year reading the literature on Gypsies, primarily on the Rom, and although this exercise was helpful in providing insights into how to approach the groups I studied and what kinds of general behaviour to expect from them, it has been disappointing in terms of providing reliable data for comparative purposes. When reduced to the reliable sources the literature is actually quite paltry.[4]

The most reliable and detailed sources on European Rom[5] are Maximoff's novels *The Ursitory* (1949) and *Savina* (1957) and other articles on his fellow Kalderash in France. His work is particularly interesting because he writes as an insider. Tillhagen's series of articles on Swedish Kalderash published in the *Journal of the Gypsy Lore Society*, though based on information from only one informant, is also quite useful. But perhaps the best European source is Jan Yoor's *The Gypsies* (1967), which is an account of his experiences with the Lowara Rom as a young boy.

The literature on North American Rom is also extremely small when reduced to the few reliable sources, and a major work on the American Rom is yet to be written. The most thorough and detailed descriptions of Rom are to be found in a handful of unpublished theses.[6] There are also several useful articles. Ronald Lee's The Gypsies in Canada (1967-9) is perhaps the most informative since, according to his own statements, he is of English Gypsy parentage but has taken the path of the Kalderash in order to survive as a Romany (1968: 14). Unfortunately, his descriptions of Kalderash customs do not provide any great detail, and several of his statements were challenged by my own informants. Nevertheless, I have used some of the information to supplement my own data.

There are, in addition, a few articles that take an anthropological approach to the subject.[7] But like everything written on

Gypsies, all these sources must be approached with scepticism and caution in order to separate the wheat from the chaff.

Even in these few more reliable sources, the information gained is meagre and the depth of analysis disappointing. There is a tendency to generalize about 'Gypsies' from the little information gleaned from a few informants or friends. Even Cohn's recent analysis of the 'Gypsies' as a pariah group generalizes to all Gypsy groups information gained basically from a few Canadian Rom informants (Cohn: 1970). Worse still, only a few sources actually identify which group they are talking about. This may be because they wish to protect the secrecy of their contacts, but often it is because they are confused about the relationship between various groups. This confusion stems, of course, from the very contradictory and confusing picture that the Gypsies present of themselves and other 'Gypsies' to an outsider.

For all these reasons I have preferred to avoid the use of written sources when possible and rely primarily on my own ethnography for the major part of this thesis. I could only be sure of the existence of a belief or practice if I observed it myself. Even in the Barvale *kumpania* there was much discussion about different customs among my informants, and it was particularly difficult to generalize a certain fact to all the *natsiyi* and *vitsi* represented in the *kumpania*. When it came to the use of printed sources, the problem was even greater, and often I would read something out to them to see if they agreed with the statements or not.

In general, reliability, whether of written sources or one's own informants' statements, is the major problem in a study of the Rom or any other Gypsy group. This problem is due to the nature of the people themselves, their skill at deception, and their disdain for outsiders. However, if one has at hand all the circumstances in which a piece of information was obtained – the group membership of the informant, his position in his community, the role of the *gajo*, etc. – then it is possible to judge more accurately the veracity of the statements.

Field Conditions

As a general example of how to study a secretive, closed group hostile to outsiders, for the interest of others who wish to work with Gypsies, and so that my own work can be judged fairly for

its failures as well as its achievements, it is important to understand the field conditions that I faced in this study. The first
Gypsy I met was a young woman of my own age who smiled at me,
talking soothingly and ingratiatingly, but when I asked to speak
with her father, she lunged at me, grabbing my face with her
fingernails, screaming and cursing, 'WHAT DO YOU WANT?'.
The second Gypsy I talked with vehemently denied that he was a
'Gypsy' (what better technique for not answering questions!),
and the third feigned imbecility, mumbling to herself and staring
wildly into space. From this and subsequent experiences – such
as polite imperviousness, pretence of mental retardation, deafness
or blindness, mocking lies, to simply disappearing from sight – I
concluded that the question–answer approach was unprofitable if
only because the Gypsies do not consider it a reliable means of
communicating with each other, much less with the *gajo*. Attempts
to employ questionnaires, formal interviewing schedules, testing
(even tests that account for illiteracy), eliciting word pairs, and
other standard techniques of gathering information would be met
with even less success. The sight of a tape recorder in most
instances was liable to provoke panic and close channels of
communication.

It soon became clear that these are people who, through
centuries of experience in avoiding the prying questions of curious
outsiders, have perfected their techniques of evasion to an effort-
less art. They delight in deceiving the *gajo*, mostly for a good
reason, but sometimes just for the fun of it or to keep in practice.
Ambiguity and unpredictability surround their behaviour with
the *gajo*, hence the attraction to the romantics. For example, the
further I penetrated into their customs and habits, the more at
ease they felt in my presence, but the more conscious they were of
having to conceal. My relationship with them was in one sense a
constant fluctuation between pleasure that I 'understood' them
and fear that I was learning too much. My position as an outsider
(*gaji*) was never forgotten.

I underwent many disappointments and discouragements
trying to get to know the Rom and needed much perseverance to
overcome their natural suspicion of an outsider. My first important breakthrough was through an acquaintance, whom the
Gypsies called Bruno. Bruno had worked as an investigator for the
New York City Welfare Department on the Gypsy caseload and
had made many friends among the Gypsies.[8] He has as suspicious

an approach towards the Gypsies as they have towards the *gaje*, and perhaps for this reason he is well liked by them. He had also painted a very flattering portrait of an old matriarch now living in Fort Worth, and her son John Marks was grateful.

John Marks is a highly intelligent and able leader, very well informed on Romany law and tradition. He is also very skilled at dealing with the *gaje* and has a well-established *kumpania* in North Texas due to his excellent diplomatic relations with the authorities. He is very proud and vain, and he decided that he wanted to have his life's story told and that I was to be the one to do it. His life history is a fascinating one and his dealings with other Gypsies and other *vitsi* are representative of many Rom leaders of his era. His peculiarity was that he would only talk when he was on the move and with something to quench his thirst so that every interview I had with him was spent driving around in his car while he talked and drank beer from cans that he would pitch onto the roadside every few miles. Usually we drove all day and averaged about 300 miles, nine pints of beer, and four hours of tape. His car, though only six months old, had done 18,000 miles, but he used to lament the good old days when he was 'on the road'. Because of his insight into his own people and because he was concerned to have the 'truth about the Gypsies' written down, John is by far the best single informant I encountered, though I was too green at the time to appreciate fully everything he said or to question him intelligently. This may have been an advantage since, unlike other informants, he let me record his descriptions on tape, and everything he said is relatively uninfluenced by me.

Among the most valuable data I received from him were complete descriptions of two *kris* (trials), beginning with the origins of the conflict to the payment of the last fine (Appendix A); therefore, although I have never attended a *kris* (and as an outsider and a woman this would be very difficult), I have very detailed evidence of how it works. The drawback is, of course, that it is not backed up by observation.

Though my conversations with John were very valuable, the field situation was not satisfactory for several reasons: (1) I could make no observations for myself as I was isolated from the community; (2) the situation was a temporary one based only on the highly selected opinions of one person; and (3) my relationship with my informant was secretive because of his political position in the Rom community. It became clear that the only way I would be able to establish long-term relationships with several Rom would be to establish myself as a respected[9] ally of a Rom community with no allegiance to one particular person.

Besides the two months of interviews with John Marks, the largest part of my data derives from the nine-month period during which I was Principal of the 'Romany School' set up for Gypsy children in Barvale, California. Although my analysis is based on the field work in Barvale, the intensive interviews with John Marks supplement many gaps in the data (due partly to my role as teacher) and provide a broader perspective. In general, the combination of the two sets of data makes it easier to know what was and was not unique about the Barvale *kumpania*.

The Romany School was set up with the assistance of Mrs Janet Tompkins, a social worker who has, in her own words, 'had the dubious pleasure of matching wits with the Barvale Gypsy colony for over six years' (1971). Mrs Tompkins was also an extremely valuable source of information as she had over the years developed great insight into the ways of the Rom. She also had a record of the history of the *kumpania* since she observed it from the beginning and has taken a great interest in trying to work out their social organization. She kindly made available to me much information, not least of all her reports on the community (Tompkins 1965a; 1965b; 1967).

The community itself was very keen on the idea of a 'Gypsy School'. They had been plagued for years by the welfare department and the police to send their children to school, and while they felt there was some advantage in gaining basic literacy for their children, they have always been strongly opposed to 'American Schools', which they believe are corrupting and threaten their way of life. A school of their own that could be arranged according to their own rules and at the same time eliminate the pressure from the truant authorities was welcome.

I spent five months (September 1969 to February 1970) setting up the school, which is still in operation at the present time, though I left in October 1970. During this time I had contact with the families involved and began to establish rapport with them. The school was situated in an almost abandoned church and run on donations and a grant from the Children's Hospital of San Francisco. From the beginning the elders and parents of the Rom community had absolute authority in the school, and they 'elected' school board officers who were the three leaders of the three *vitsi* of the *kumpania*.

From the very beginning I worked very closely with the leaders and later on with several families with whom I developed special friendships. The politics involved in running a 'Gypsy School' are the same as the *kumpania* politics since the school simply became an extension of general social relations both within and without the group. For example, when two adults of different *vitsi* had an argument, it was carried over into the school by their children, and in order to continue classes it became necessary for me to follow the discussion, listen to all sides, and participate in the outcome. Therefore, although I was 'teaching' from one to four every afternoon, I generally spent each morning before school and several hours afterwards visiting families and discussing the daily events. In general, I spent ten hours per day with Rom. In addition, there were special occasions, *pakiv*, *slava*, *pomana*, weddings, baptisms, and other events which I had to attend. As the head teacher it was essential for me to be involved in the daily life and problems and participate in the rich social and political life. Therefore, although I never lived with a family (and this would be unthinkable to them), I followed daily news. The school itself was a further source of information because I could observe the children, work on the *Romany* language, and, as part of the teaching, collect stories and essays from them on various topics.

Even though I was in the community almost all the time, many events were still initially kept secret from me; however, eventually either a child or an offended adult would reveal the secret and once I had heard one side of a story, usually everyone was very anxious to present his own point of view. There was very little that went on of which I was not eventually aware. Sometimes informing became a problem since the informer often repented later on and the whole community would be wary that I knew too much. Another problem was that, like the social worker and the police, I became an important *gaji* political figure in the bid for power among the three leaders. Therefore I had to be very careful not to side with one or the other during some crisis (and there were, on average, three crises a week) as my opinion could be interpreted to mean one of the leaders was out of favour and must leave town until things cooled off. In effect I became part of the political structure, insofar as it includes the *gaje*, and this put a strain on my ability to keep an objective position. Objectivity, of course, does not form part of Romany vocabulary. I should add that my position meant that certain facts, such as income outside welfare, crimes, etc., were consistently kept from me, but this sort of information was easily obtained outside the community where my role was less clearly defined.

Language

Perhaps the most difficult problem was that of the use of language. There are several linguistic studies that facilitate the task of learning Romany.[10] Besides these aids, I was later able to use the Romany correspondence course 'Learn Romani' compiled by Ronald Lee (1969a). In addition, I had the help of one family for a month before they disappeared. But other than this, I had to rely on the children around me and the general conversation that I was hearing. Although the community showed an initial interest in teaching me a few words of Romany, they became very suspicious and upset when they found I was learning 'too much'; therefore, in order to keep the good relations I had established with them, it became necessary for me to cease all appearance of learning their language. Consequently, although I understand a good deal of Romany, I was never able to speak it with them, demonstrate that I was understanding, or ask questions about the language. Therefore, a lot of the conversations and information I have were given to me in English, which is the language they use for outsiders, although a good deal of it is from the Romany conversation that I overheard. Since conversations in Romany were carried on in my presence with no inhibitions (because it was assumed I could not understand) all the time, this situation had its advantages. I often sat for hours listening to conversations in Romany that I made notes on later.

Finally, I think it is important to define the implications of being a woman among the Rom. Most social occasions, conversations, and activities require the separation of the sexes, and the Rom have clearly defined sexual roles. The leadership of the community, the laws, and political matters are generally handled by men and sometimes a few old women. A young woman, especially a *gaji*, is not permitted to interfere in these internal affairs, though as I have mentioned I did participate in the external aspects of political relations. Men also work in separate groups from women; therefore, male occupations and cooperation were another area of relations that I could not observe but had to rely on statements of the men for data. For these aspects I have drawn on written sources for supplementary information. On the other hand, many female activities such as menstruation, pregnancy, childbirth, and female knowledge, such as pollution concepts, illness, medicines, and supernatural beings, were easily available, and I believe the depth of understanding and knowledge of these aspects compensates for the deficiency in male data.

Names and Appearance

Anonymity and invisibility combined with intense secretiveness are keys to the ability of the Rom to adapt and survive in an alien culture. Most are not registered at birth, in school, in a census, or with draft boards. Outside police records and welfare departments officially they do not exist. Even when they do have a name officially registered, it is usually not their own, and they may claim to be Mexican, Indian, or anything else besides Gypsy.

All Rom have at least two names, and perhaps several birthdates since they may not know the real date anyway and certainly do not care what it might be. They may have several *nav gajikano* (non-Gypsy names) such as Steve Adams, Pete John, or Johnny George. They also each have a *nav romano*, their true name which may be *Tinya le Stevanosko*, (Tinya, the son of Stevan) or *Mara o Spirosko* (Mary, the daughter of Spiro). They also have a *vitsa* name for further identification, but they are not called by this name. Finally, there is usually a nickname which relatives and friends use (for example 'Blue Eyes', *Kali* (Blackie), Flicka (Clever one), etc.). A Rom can usually tell how well a person knows him by the name he uses. I could usually tell how much I was trusted by the name I was given to use. The *nav gajikano* is used only for *gaje* and never among Rom. The number of non-Gypsy names a person has is more or less correlated with the number of difficult situations he has encountered with the law or the number of records there are on him. The non-Gypsy names are used over and over again since they do not matter anyway. I know personally three Miller Georges of the same generation, four Rosie Costellos in Barvale alone and at least three George Adams within one extended family. This is convenient for invisibility because even if one wanted to tell a non-Gypsy how to locate a person, it is very difficult given the *gaje* name alone. In one area there might be fifteen Rom by that name.

In appearance men are almost indistinguishable from the rest of the population. Men generally wear either dude cowboy clothes, or, among older men, the 1930s style large-lapelled suits are common. Older men sport a handlebar moustache, a hat, and tie. The neckscarf (*diklo*) was not commonly worn except among a few young boys. Some old men dress very colourfully. Miller George wore a faded brown suit with chalk on the lapels, a wide colourful tie, and was always found leaning on a pool cue. Most older men are overweight and have gold teeth or a few snaggle teeth left. Many men wear gold rings, diamond tie clasps, and other jewellery, such as a gold sheriff's badge (for the *rom baro*) or a diamond studded gold buckle on their cowboy belt.

Young married men often like flashy clothes such as shiny metallic blue or green suits and unmarried boys may wear purple bell-bottom trousers and fancy shirts or dress like their fathers. Boys wear the same clothes as American children though some may be seen dressing like their fathers either in a suit and felt hat with a feather, or in ranch clothes.

Women are much more easily distinguishable from the population although when in public places they may switch to 'American clothes' so as to go unnoticed. Before menstruation, girls wear shop-bought clothes, usually dresses. This changes dramatically after their first menstruation. The traditional 'Gypsy' dress worn by most women, is a long pleated skirt which contains seven to twelve yards of material. The length of the skirt varies with the age and the occasion but is always below the knee. Older women wear ankle- or ground-length skirts, and younger women like them down to the calf. For parties and rituals all ages wear them long though young marriageable girls like to have their skirts as short as they can get away with, which is just below the knee. A sleeveless blouse with a very low *décolletage* is almost always worn. This may button in front but more often it is the traditional style which wraps around the waist or is a loose overblouse. Sometimes it is a kind of sleeveless vest, pinned with a gold brooch between the breasts. When it is cold a sweater or fur coat may be donned, always leaving the cleavage exposed.

A woman's brassière is usually used for her handbag. One woman kept all light things such as documents, money, cigarettes, and a lighter in her brassière, and then kept heavy items in a huge front pocket which was hidden in the folds of her skirt. Most skirts have pockets sewn into them in various places for carrying items unnoticed. All women wear some jewellery, the more the better. Gold coins made into necklaces, brooches, or pendants are coveted. A very popular necklace is one made of gold teardrops on a chain. This necklace is traditionally given to a girl when she becomes engaged. Tear-drop or other dangling gold earrings are also worn, and ears are pierced. Some women have very impressive jewellery. Yana wore an enormous necklace of huge gold balls which hung to her waist; at the end was a sheriff's star in gold with a gold Indian head soldered onto the middle and little gold hearts hanging off each point of the star.

Shoes are usually high-heeled sandals made of gold or some other shiny or patent leather material. Dress material is preferably bright. Red chiffon and metallic or gold lamé material is often used. Sari materials are becoming very popular, and only the best silks with gold braiding are used. Old women rarely use cosmetics, but the younger women generally make up their faces quite heavily for parties. The hair is always tied up in some way and is considered uncombed if left loose. Old women wear braids tied back and covered with the traditionally long *diklo* and perhaps a flower in the hair, but younger married women wear a smaller band of cloth or *diklo* (scarf) with their hair pinned up in a bun. Unmarried girls do not wear a *diklo*, and some married women only wear it when they dress up. Women do not usually cut their hair and must have it long enough to put up.

In men, and particularly in women, aggressiveness, a loud and dominating voice, ability to argue well – to out-reason, out-shout, and out-trick an opponent – intelligence, cunning, and quick-wittedness are exalted virtues. A shy, retiring, or slow-witted person is pitied, especially if she is a woman, for she will never make a successful wife, and her husband will have to support the family. A girl who is aggressive and clever is always highly desired as a wife. Shouting is the only way of making oneself heard in a crowd of Rom, and the shy and squeamish child learns quickly that he is ignored; consequently, competition among children is intense and encouraged by parents. Cleverness is highly rated and the child who is out-going, aggressive, tricky, and illusive, even when the victim is his parents, is praised and rewarded by everyone. A child who cannot tell when his parents are lying to him is considered hopelessly stupid. Versatility is also very important, and the ability to switch tactics, for example, from aggression and threats to humble submission, tears and supplication, is valued.

Ethics and Reliability

The Rom are extremely secretive and suspicious of non-Gypsies and on the whole do not want anything known about them by the outside world. Some secrets have practical reasons behind them, such as hiding extra income from welfare workers, concealing illegal activities from the police, and so on, but many times secretiveness is simply a protective barrier for their group against a more powerful outside society. Often, I have been told, 'It's against my religion to tell you . . .', and although 'religion' may seem a strange translation of *romania*, there is a kind of religious intensity about being a Rom. The Rom are deeply committed to their own self-preservation; each person is a vital force to the group, and ideally his life is an open book to the others. Respect with 'the public', as they refer to themselves in English, is the most important attribute a man or woman can have and therefore *marime* (which they translate as 'rejected') is the most severe punishment. Each death is not only a personal loss but a loss to the whole group and requires intensive participation in mourning. As an anthropologist, of course, I found none of this to be new or unusual in kind, but only in degree. The Rom are deeply and intensely aware of their own self-preservation.

On the other hand, they are also aware of the many misconceptions about themselves in the eyes of outsiders. Sometimes they enjoy a good laugh on the *gaje* for being such fools and encourage the misconceptions for the enjoyment of the irony, but at other times these misconceptions can be very inconvenient to them. They become understandably irate when they are harrassed or arrested every time a child in their neighbourhood disappears, especially considering that there has never been a single proven case of child theft by a Gypsy. At these times they have told me to 'write the whole truth about us' and although I think that this is a difficult task, and that they are likely to change their minds sooner or later, this is what I have attempted to do. At the same time I have also tried to protect as many secrets as I possibly could without abandoning the project altogether. Nevertheless, when one describes a society whose existence depends in part on the ignorance of outsiders to their ways, one has by definition violated something.

On the other hand, truthful and realistic information about the Rom could be very helpful to them. Much of their persecution in society has been based on ignorance, unfounded prejudice, and a belief in many of the pervading myths of the wild, irresponsible, sexually immoral, earringed Gypsy. Many Gypsies in Europe and in America have published serious accounts of their own people for this very reason. They are tired of distasteful and harmful misconceptions about them (see Lee 1967–9, 1971; Maximoff 1949, 1957, 1960, Hancock 1973, 1974; and Wood 1973).

Because of their general mistrust of outsiders, building up a relationship of trust with the Rom is a very slow process. Explaining that I was a 'social anthropologist' at the outset was difficult since, like most people, they had not the slightest notion what that might be and further explanation meant either 'journalist' or 'detective' to them, two categories of persons they have had little reason to trust – the one providing the misconceptions for the other to use against the Rom. My primary role in the community was as a teacher to their children, but I was able to explain to the elders eventually that I wanted to write a book about them (although my original intention was not a book, but a PhD). Reactions to this varied. John Marks, a believer in the importance of dispelling false notions in print, and elderly women who wanted dying customs preserved, were enthusiastic and spoke openly to me. Some agreed that I should write about how wonderful the Gypsy people are but not tell any 'bad' things about them. Others mistrust the written word so much that they fear anything that goes into print about them.

A major outcome of the secretiveness is the problem of ascertaining the reliability of one's data. The Rom often lie to each other about everyday matters, but they almost always lie to the *gaje*. There is no particular shame attached to lying to each other (except in specific circumstances, such as when one swears in front of the 'public' in a *kris*, swears on a dead relative, or proclaims 'may I go home to find my father dead at this very moment if I am lying . . .'), but to lie to the *gaje* is certainly correct and acceptable behaviour, and even one's dead grandfather might forgive a broken oath in this circumstance. Consequently, from the very beginning I decided to cross-check three times every piece of information that I received, no matter how trivial or unimportant it might seem. I might challenge several people at different times with the same piece of information or try alternative stories to test their reactions, and usually the contradictions could be ironed out and the most plausible solution gained. Since being unpredictable and elusive is part of the code of behaviour with *gaje*, it was not considered odd for me to act the same, and of course, I was also not burdened with having to stick to the absolute truth. For example, one of the most common misrepresentations is in giving ordinary kin and affinal relationships, but by using my method of cross-checking, eventually every relationship sorted itself out, and I was able to draw up an accurate genealogy. I kept a daily list of items that I had not checked and generally threw in one or two in any one conversation. Most people were at least not up to date on other people's lies, and in this way eventually most things leaked out. Spur of the moment lies were, of course, more easily uncovered than systematically planned ones.

My cross-checking technique was all the more acceptable since the Rom employ the same tactics with each other. They rarely accepted a statement from me or any other Rom without some kind of corroboration from someone else. When 'caught out' in this way, I never saw anyone show embarrassment. They enjoyed it when a good story was put over on them as much as they enjoyed putting one over on someone else. Therefore, when I doubted their veracity, or tricked them into admitting something, or lied to them myself, they were just as cheerful about it as they would be with each other and respected me all the more for it. Even with these measures, I have no doubt that various facts were still kept from me, and probably there will be details in my data that are not correct; however, I do not think that the general patterns would be much changed.

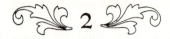

The *Kumpania*

According to Jan Yoors, who travelled with the Lowara as a boy in pre-World War II Europe, a *kumpania*[1] referred to a group of Rom who travelled together in wagons or with tents, who may or may not be related, but who joined together temporarily for economic reasons and for security. As Yoors describes it, the *kumpania* is an extremely flexible unit but even though individual members, relationships, and leaders may change in a particular *kumpania*, the *kumpania* keeps its form and its rules of organization. One of the rules is that newcomers to the territory of a *kumpania* must get permission to work in that area and perhaps pay something in compensation since they will be exploiting the economic resources, the *gaje* (non-Gypsies). In exchange, the *kumpania* will help acquaint the newcomer with local conditions, laws, and authorities. A newcomer who does not respect the territory of a *kumpania* may find himself in trouble with non-Gypsy authorities (Yoors 1967: 121–3, 135). We can conclude, therefore, that the European *kumpania* was, before the war, a travelling group that moved within a certain area and protected its right to exploit the economic resources of that area.

In America the *kumpania* has become more bound to a territory an1 less fluid in composition than among pre-World War II Lowara. The most important change is not that it is connected to a territory but that the territory is almost entirely urban rather than primarily rural. Ronald Lee, a Canadian Gypsy, points to a 'Gypsy Map' of North America:

The Gypsies of each town and city of the U.S.A. and Canada are organised into what we call *kumpaniyi* or 'unions'. Each *kumpania* is composed of all the male members of the community inhabiting that particular town or city, and they, together with their families, are under the supreme authority of the *Kris Romani* (tribunal of Gypsy elders) which is their only authority in matters of Gypsy law and ceremonial behaviour (*Romania*). (Lee 1967: 42).

Though Lee emphasizes the males of the community, most Rom described the *kumpania* as composed of so many *tsera* (tents) or households. As among the Lowara, the *kumpania* maintains a monopoly, or tries to establish a monopoly, on the economic resources of the area (fortune-telling licences, welfare, etc.), and the families in a *kumpania* cooperate with each other as *wortacha* (partners) in exploiting these resources and protecting them from other Rom.

A *kumpania* should not be confused with *wortacha* or 'partners' (Lee 1967: 42) which refers to an alliance of men or women for a specific job such as fixing fenders. I believe Cotten has made this mistake when she defines *kumpania* as a 'temporary grouping of people for the specific and exclusive purpose of accomplishing a given job, after which its members break up, returning to their individual *tserhas* and going their own separate ways' (Cotten 1955: 22). The *kumpania* does not exist for the purpose of executing one job, but is a much more durable social, political, and ceremonial unit. What she means by 'returning to one's *tserha*', (or *vitsa* as other Rom call it) I cannot say, since the *vitsa* is a category of kin and not a spatial grouping. This kind of confusion of terms is very common among Gypsiologists and is not entirely absent among Gypsies themselves.

In addition to being an economic territory, the *kumpania* is the public unit of moral, social, and political behaviour which comes under the authority of the *kris romani*. Individual families, extended families (*familiyi*), and even the *vitsa* do not have the authority to make public verdicts and decisions on questions of law and social behaviour (*romania*). Since these are units of kin they are expected to support their relatives. As Yoors has emphasized, the *kumpania* is not a kin group; it contains a cross-section of various kin groups. Important questions of morality and trials (*kris romani*) on these questions will usually involve several *kumpaniyi*. For example, two *familiyi* may arrange a marriage, but it is not a binding contract until it is sealed in the presence of the *kumpania*. If, however, a *kumpania* in fact only contains one extended family (*familia*), as some small and tightly controlled *kumpaniyi* do, then it is not a sufficiently broad cross-section of persons to hold a *kris* by itself or make decisions beyond those which are family matters.

The members of a *kumpania* often celebrate life-cycle rituals and other feasts together. They solve personal conflicts and problems, disagreements over economic matters, and questions of morality. To solve these problems they hold discussions (*diwano*), and if the issue is important enough or if a breach of *romania* has occurred, they may call a trial (*kris romani*) for a final decision. They take up collections to help needy families, to pay fines, bail or funeral costs, or to contribute to a newly married couple. Thus, the *kumpania* is not only the largest economic group occupying a specific territory, it is the largest viable social and ceremonial group.

Kumpaniyi on the west coast of America generally take one of three forms. These forms are more points on a continuum rather than separate types. At one end of the continuum there is strict control of the economic resources such as a monopoly on fortune-telling licences. In this case the *kumpania* usually is small and consists of one *familia* (in several households) who allow only their close relatives to join the *kumpania*. The leader of the *kumpania* will be the head of the *familia*, and there is no one in the *kumpania* who can challenge his or her position. In the middle of the continuum is a fairly open *kumpania* which contains several *vitsi* although it is dominated by one. It fails to have a strict monopoly of the economic resources, for these are often areas where welfare is the main source of income. Welfare, theoretically, is available to anyone whereas a fortune-telling licence is more difficult to obtain. Where a licence is not required to tell fortunes, such as in Hawaii or Texas, again it is very difficult to have a strictly controlled *kumpania*. In this kind of *kumpania*, families of different *vitse* and *natsiyi* co-reside more or less peacefully under the leadership of the *rom baro* who is a liaison with the authorities and arbitrator for any problems that arise. The *rom baro*, who is most likely to be from the largest *vitsa* in the *kumpania*, will have challengers for his position, but if he is an effective and just leader, he will keep the support of the *kumpania*.

At the end of the continuum of least control is open territory both in terms of who can live there and what they can do for a living. Strictly speaking it is not a *kumpania* for there is very little sense of a united community. Each group of extended families will have their own patriarch or matriarch to whom they look for leadership, but there is no generally recognized leader for the whole *kumpania* (although there may be contenders for leadership). This is a very unstable situation, and the current tendency is for the open territories eventually to become dominated by a leader of a large *vitsa* and develop into the second type of *kumpania*.

An example of a very strictly controlled *kumpania* is the Los Angeles *kumpania* as it was under the leadership of the late Big George Adams (*Joji Baro*) who monopolized fortune-telling establishments in southern California until his death in 1964. He controlled entry into his area through force and with the help of the police, and his monopoly made him very wealthy and powerful. He shared his wealth with his relatives and friends by setting them up in fortune-telling, and they in turn gave him a certain cut for his protection from outside competition. The same situation existed in San Francisco under the rule of Barbara Miller prior to 1966. When these two leaders were gone, both *kumpaniyi* became open territory and until now no one has been able to establish the kind of control that existed formerly.

It is the *kumpania* of the middle of the continuum, a group unable to enforce an economic monopoly, organized under one leader who has only limited control, which is probably the most common on the west coast of America. The specific *kumpania* that I shall examine here, falls into this area. Within it, the Kashtare *vitsa* has the largest numbers of people and most influence. One Kashtare family elder is the acknowledged leader of the *kumpania*, but he has several rivals for his position and he lacks a great deal of control over families outside his *vitsa*. A history of the development of this *kumpania* will illustrate the nature of the group and its composition.

The Barvale Kumpania

Barvale is a depressed town of substandard housing in a large metropolitan area, its most noticeable feature being the maze of railway tracks that form natural boundaries for the various ethnic groups, Blacks, Mexican-Americans, Indians, and poor whites, most of whom subsist through social welfare.

Before 1964, there were only a few isolated Rom families in Barvale and several Boyash families who had managed to obtain fortune-telling licences before the illegalization of fortune-telling by the Town Council (Ayres 1966). In 1964, several events changed this situation and brought about a sudden influx of Rom families. First, Big George Adams, the powerful leader of the Machwaya in California, died in August. His death was a great blow to his people because no one was strong enough to take control of his empire and maintain the monopoly the Machwaya had enjoyed until then. This meant that, apart from San Francisco, which was still run by Barbara Miller, California had become open territory. Besides, Big George's funeral attracted thousands of Rom from all over the country, and many of these people drifted up to Barvale.

The second change was that in February 1964 the welfare programme expanded to include employable fathers. Before 1964, a family with an employable father was ineligible for welfare. For most Rom families, welfare support had been difficult to obtain unless they could prove that one or the other parent was incapacitated. One Rom family had managed to do this for several years by disguising their identity, the mother claiming to be insane. It took two years for the welfare department to realize they were a 'Gypsy' family and not 'suffering from wanderlust' and 'schizophrenia'.

A third factor which changed the ethnic composition of Barvale was the increasing amount of automation in farm labour, a major source of income for most Rom families in California. This meant that families who depended on summer farm work to tide them over the winter were forced to look for other alternatives, such as welfare.

A fourth factor which made Barvale more appealing than other towns in California, was the availability of cheap housing there. Before urban renewal in Barvale, there were a large number of houses doomed to be torn down within months. The landlords of the houses wanted to get some rent from them, and they did not care who rented them, or what they did to them. This was ideal housing for the Rom since it was cheap, they could knock out all the walls to make it into one big room, and they were not likely to to get evicted for violating garbage regulations. When one house was torn down they were quite happy to move to another condemned one. Some of them even took advantage of a fund for re-locating families forced to move by the renewal project. Each family got $500 for 'moving expenses'.

Finally, the Rom who came to Barvale after 1964 immediately began cultivating good relations with the police. They invited the police to their feasts and weddings, and the heads of family agreed to keep their people from stealing and committing petty crimes. Of course, they could not be responsible for the 'riff-raff' who come to town (i.e. families not of the leaders' *vitsa*), and these the police were encouraged to move on. The police responded favourably to this cultivation of good relations since in general they face extremely hostile ethnic groups who feel mistrust and contempt towards them. The Gypsies were the first and only group in Barvale who actually made friendly overtures to the police, and the police were both flattered and sympathetic to the Gypsies' problems. They consider the Gypsies their biggest success story.

Apart from the isolated families prior to 1967, the first big families to come to Barvale were the Mikailesti[2] headed by 'Big Mick' who soon emerged as the leader. After testing out the welfare and police departments, and establishing an informer relationship with them, 'Big Mick' began bringing in relatives and establishing his own power over the area. He immediately gathered information on how he could manipulate the welfare department. His social worker described one interview in this way:

> 'Big Mick' is now recognized as the leader of the Gypsies in this area, and they both respect and fear him. We suspect that it is 'Big Mick' who is encouraging and assisting Gypsy families to settle in this community. His motives are not known, but it is possible that he has a desire for power and is empire-building in his own small way.
> . . . (he) has close contact with the police and I suspect that he is an informer on occasions when he wishes to punish someone. He as much as told me this during the interview.
> . . . During the home visit, I had the feeling that (he) was interviewing me just as much as I was interviewing him . . . and I had the feeling that he was 'playing dumb' on many occasions to find out how much I knew about the Gypsies. He also asked many policy questions. One of the questions he asked was, 'if more Gypsy families come here, will it spoil it for the rest of us?'

Then, in the beginning of 1965, there arrived a large number of Kuneshti families led by five siblings and their spouses and at the end of the summer of 1965 six or seven families of Gurkwe arrived (*Figure 1*). By December, 1965, the welfare office had approximately sixty-five Gypsy cases numbering about 455 people.

To handle the sudden influx of Gypsy families coming in under 'Big Mick's' encouragement, the welfare department put all Gypsies under one social worker, and formed a Gypsy team composed of an intake worker, a field worker, a public health nurse, a

FIGURE 1 Number of (a) Kuneshti, (b) Gurkwe, (c) Machwaya, and (d) Kashtare households in Barvale: 1964–70.

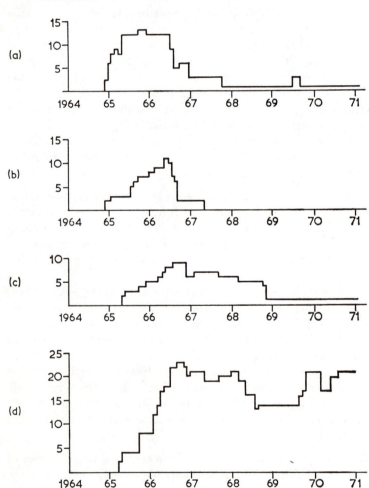

medical social worker, a school guidance worker, and a fraud investigator. The Gypsies also had their own team to handle the welfare department, composed of 'Big Mick', the leader of the Gurkwe, and three or four Kuneshti leaders (Tompkins 1965b: 1).

Then in February 1966, 'Big Mick's' wife died. Since she had been a powerful force in his leadership, there was a struggle for power among the various leaders, including the leaders of the new Kashtare families, Stevan and Spiro. 'Big Mick' kept control, but not for long, because:

A most devastating thing occurred in the Spring of 1966, . . . – 'Big Mick' (our local 'king') ran off with another man's wife! What made this doubly shocking was that Mick's late wife was barely in her grave three months when he did this shameful deed. I have never seen such outrage among any group of people. His closest friends and even his relatives joined in the chorus of vilification. They swore that if he ever returned they would black both his eyes, force him to return the wife, and pay the husband damages. One woman exclaimed: 'He has disgraced his family and has brought shame to all of us!' (Tompkins 1967: 1.)

With 'Big Mick' gone and disgraced, a bitter struggle for control ensued for three months. Each of the major patriarchs approached the welfare and police departments requesting that they appoint him 'king'.

Meanwhile, the Kashtare *vitsa*, who had recently lost a family elder, had swelled their ranks with relatives attending the *pomana* feasts, (*Figure 1*) and their family head, an impressive 350-pound man named Stevan emerged as leader. When this happened in the autumn of 1966, the Gurkwe and Kuneshti families began to leave (*Figure 1*), their leaders disgruntled.

During 1965 and 1966, several Machwaya families had also come to Barvale, but some were only distantly related to each other, and they had no strong leader. Mostly they represented the replacement of Machwaya throughout California since the death of their leader. In 1966, Machwaya families began gathering awaiting the death of an old Machwano patriarch named Budo who at eighty-five could no longer travel. Approximately ten families gathered around Budo; when he died in November 1966, gradually they drifted off, the largest exodus being in the Autumn of 1968 during civil disturbances. There are still a few Machwaya families in Barvale of which only one is not closely intermarried with Kashtare.

Since 1968, the largest and most powerful *vitsa* in Barvale has been the Kashtare *vitsa*. There are five distinct Kashtare *familiyi* in Barvale and though they do not always agree about everything, they generally accept Stevan's leadership. Many of the families are more or less permanently based in Barvale, but others frequently travel back and forth to Oregon, Alaska, Los Angeles, and Texas. Besides the Kashtare there are a few Machwaya and Kuneshti families, but they do not form a large cohesive group.

The exact composition of a *kumpania* is very difficult to determine since it is in a constant state of flux. Since I finished field work there have been a number of changes. For example, one Kuneshti family has been thrown out and returned several times. During these periods of absence, Stevan ordered all the Kuneshti to stay in their own Kuneshti-dominated *kumpania*.

But Stevan sees the Machwaya as his main rivals. 'The Machwaya don't like us to have Barvale. They always run people out of town. This isn't right. Now we run them out of town and they don't like us.' He has been at loggerheads with an educated Machwano for a long time, and before that he threw out another Machwano who tried to move in from Santa Rosa. At the same time it seems that Stevan is bringing more families of his own *vitsa* and that Barvale is more and more becoming an exclusively Kashtare town.

Ignoring the movement of families to and from the *kumpania*, *Table 1* gives an indication of the number of households and people in each *familia* during one period of time as a sample of the composition of the *kumpania*.

Apart from the large majority of Kashtare *familiyi* (1–5) and the three Machwaya *familiyi* (6–8), there are only a few isolated *familiyi* in Barvale consisting of an extended family occupying one household each. These isolated families have no other relatives in the *kumpania* to turn to for support and aid. The only exceptions are families 12 and 13 who say they are 'cousins' and who have arranged a marriage between two of their children. The Kuneshti head of family also has a weak link with Kashtare family 2 whose matriarch is his sister, and he is trying to arrange a marriage with *familia* 3 to establish affinal ties there.

The Kashtare *vitsa* on the other hand is represented by five large *familiyi* and is closely intermarried with Machwaya *familia* 6.

TABLE I *Population and households – Spring, 1970*

vitsa	familia	head	households	no. of persons
Kashtare	1	Stevan	6	44
Kashtare	2	Spiro	5	44
Kashtare	3	Sonia	5	38
Kashtare	4	Mary	2	19
Kashtare	5	Rosie	1	12
Machwaya/Kashtare	6	Ruby	4	33
Machwaya	7		3	26
Machwaya	8		1	5
Romanitchal	9		1	6
Gurkwe	10		1	3
Lameshti	11		1	8
Micheleshti	12		1	11
Mineshti	13		1	11
Kuneshti	14		1	6

TOTAL: 33 266

Average household size: 8 persons

Kashtare and Machwaya/Kashtare	23	190
Machwaya	4	31
Kuneshti	1	6
Miscellaneous families	5	39
	33	266

FIGURE 2 The five Kashtare *familiyi*.

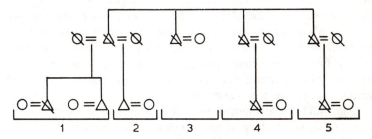

Only the heads of *familia* are shown here. Each *familia* includes two to three generations of descendants.

The heads of *familiyi* 1 and 2 are half-brothers so that their descendants are half-first cousins. The heads of *familiyi* 4 and 5 are both the widows of first cousins (FBS) to the heads of *familiyi* 1 and 2 so their descendants are also cousins. The head of *familia* 3 is Aunt (FBW) to the head of *familia* 1; therefore her descendants are cousins both to him and his *familia* (*Figure 2*).

Furthermore there are marriages between these *familiyi*. Two second generation members of *familia* 2 are married to two second generation members of *familia* 4 (*Figure 3*). The Machwaya

FIGURE 3 Marriages between two Kashtare *familiyi* in one *kumpania*.

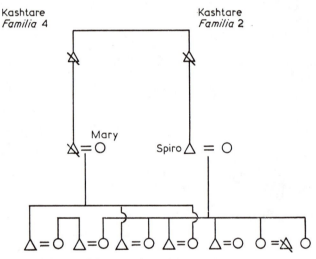

There are four genealogical levels of living persons of which two are not shown here.

Kashtare *familia* 6 is headed by an old matriarch who is the elder sister of Stevan's wife. Her elder brother was at one time married to Stevan's sister and a younger brother is married to Stevan's first cousin (FBD) and she herself was once married to a Kashtare. As a result of these four marriages, these two groups of families are very closely linked and have arranged marriages in the next generation as well (see *Figure 4*).

Data such as contained in *Table 1* represent only a short moment in the history of the *kumpania*; however, they serve to exemplify its composition. For, although the *kumpania* occupies a specific territory and residents generally live in houses, these

FIGURE 4 Kashtare and Machwaya intermarriage.

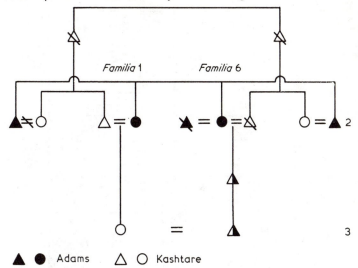

▲ ● Adams △ ○ Kashtare

households are very mobile. Since there has been much speculation on just how mobile American Rom are, it would be useful to determine more precisely the amount of travelling undertaken by families in the *kumpania*.

Travelling is undoubtedly extremely important for the Rom for a large number of reasons. However, because they no longer travel in groups of caravans or pitch their tents in the fields of America, many Rom claim that they are no longer nomadic, and they speak with nostalgia about the 'good old days' when they were 'on the road'. They have been supported in this conclusion by non-Gypsies who feel they are on their way towards assimilation (see, for example, Weybright (1938), Murin (1949), and Cotten (1955)). Assimilation, however, is not necessarily inevitable when nomadic peoples move into houses.

Travel

Figure 5 is a record of time absent and time present in the *kumpania*, by household, during a nine-month period. It does not include, (a) daily travelling for work when the person returns to Barvale the same night or next day, (b) visits to or from relatives and friends in nearby *kumpaniyi*, or (c) weekend fishing trips or camping trips.

FIGURE 5 Time absent from the Barvale *kumpania*.

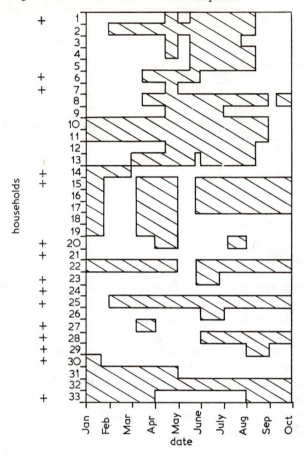

+ households headed by an old person

[hatched] time absent   [blank] time present

See *Table 3* for key to households

In the Spring of 1970 there were thirty-three households more or less permanently residing in Barvale. Transitory families and occasional visitors have not been included, since they do not form part of the *kumpania* proper. From *Figure 5* it can be calculated that on average households were travelling outside the *kumpania* 42 per cent of the time.

Figure 6 gives the fluctuation in the amount of travelling by months. April and June were peak travelling months because of the special events at those times. In March, many families left for a time because of a big fight which occurred at Easter. In April, a *pomana* (death feast) was held in Oregon and most Kashtare relatives from Barvale attended, returning at the end of April. At the end of May, when school ended, Stevan, along with the welfare

FIGURE 6 Amount of travelling per month.

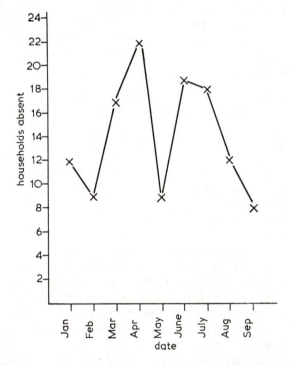

authorities, gave the families a free hand to leave and work during the summer months. By September most families had returned since the summer harvest was over, and this month showed the least number of absentee households. It is possible that this range of fluctuation in periods of two to three months occurs year-round as this seemed to be the usual time families would stay in one place before they became restless and wanted to travel. It also seemed to be an optimum length of time for relative harmony between families, before a major conflict would occur.

Certain households travelled more than others. A breakdown of households by age indicates that households headed by an elder who was over fifty and usually infirm travelled considerably less than households composed of young working-age families headed by a person between thirty and forty years of age. Households with elders as heads of household (see *Figure 5*) travelled 26 per cent of the nine-month period and households headed by young families travelled 56 per cent of the period (see *Table 2*). Of all the travelling done by the *kumpania* as a whole, households composed of younger families did 73 per cent of the total. Old people often claim they do not like the rigours of being on the road all the time, and usually they are quite ill and in need of medical care. Many families settle into a *kumpania* when their patriarch or matriarch becomes old and infirm, but when he or she dies they will travel

TABLE 2 *Amount of travel according to age of head of household*

	households	months of travel	average amount of time travelling
households with elderly person or couple at head:	15	35	26%
households with young couple at head:	18	91	56%

for at least several months, often up to a year because the place of death is *prikaza* (bad luck). In Barvale there were two exceptions to the general decline in amount of travelling by old people. Households 12 and 13 (*Figure 5*) are composed of young families who care alternatively for a very elderly and senile old lady. Although they are constantly complaining that they cannot travel because of her, they spent 50 per cent of their time travelling. The head of household 15 is also the head of an entourage of households (16–19) and often this old lady, who is quite agile, is the very one who is anxious to be on the move. These families (15–19) travel as a large group and are extremely mobile. They were absent 60 per cent of the nine-month period.

Family groups (*familiyi*) varied according to the percentage of time that they spent travelling. Certain family groups were much more mobile than others. *Table 3* gives a breakdown of the family groups according to the amount of time spent travelling.

There is no typical *familia* in terms of travelling. Some, such as the Machwaya, were fairly settled, travelling about one-third of the time. The four *familiyi* who travelled the least, are all small, single household *familiyi* headed by an old person or couple. At the top of the scale, *familiyi* 12, 13, and 3 travelled extensively and these *familiyi* were not stable members of the *kumpania* but were generally on the move from one *kumpania* to another. *Familia* 2, on the other hand, is more permanently settled in the *kumpania*, and the old couple who head this large *familia* (household 7) do not

TABLE 3 *Percentage of travelling time by families*

familia (on *Table 1*)	households (*Figure 5*)	% time travelling
12, 13	31–32	66
3	15–19	60
2	7–11	55
8	33	55
4	12–13	50
9	28	44
1	1–6	37
7	24–26	33
6	20–23	31
5	14	22
14	27	11
10	29	11
11	30	6

travel extensively any more, though their children (households 7–11) travelled to and from Barvale during the whole nine months (*Figure 5*). In general, it can be said that *familiyi* 2, 8, and 3 travel considerably, but they do have Barvale as their base and eventually come back to it whereas *familiyi* 12, 13, and 5, which I shall call travelling family groups, have no definite base and travel from *kumpania* to *kumpania*.

Travelling family groups who have not chosen one *kumpania* as their base generally have two patterns of travel. They may travel within a certain area such as the west coast, or the southern states of America, or they may set up a winter–summer circuit between two places or areas. Though I could not calculate what proportion

of American Rom are travelling family groups and what proportion live more or less in one *kumpania*, I suspect that a majority of
families are associated with a *kumpania*.

Travelling family groups may be composed of one extended
family and may be very small, or they may be very large and composed of several extended families led by the elderly parents.
However, no matter how large they become, they should not be
confused with a European *kumpania*, as described by Yoors, for
they are merely a large group of closely related families on the
move; whereas a *kumpania* refers to a group of several *familiyi*,
not necessarily related, occupying a certain territory.

Travelling family groups have several schemes for making a
living, but the one they used most often in Barvale is what the
welfare department calls the 'pending transfer system'. They
establish a residence for a few weeks, receive their first cheque,
and then transfer to a new place before a social worker can visit
them. It takes two months to transfer their case, and meanwhile
they can receive their cheques for these months. Before the two
months are up, they transfer to another place. One social worker
told me she had several cases in which a year passed before the
family was visited by a social worker the few times necessary
to write up a social study. In this way, they not only avoided the
questions and interference of a social worker, but they were able
to keep their income from welfare cheques while working on the
move. Alternatively, they may come to town, hide their cars and/
or trailers, stay with friends or relatives in order to have an address
long enough to get their first cheque, and then move on to the
next place. For large families this can be a profitable and quick
way to get money.

Other travelling family groups adopt a slightly different pattern
of travel. These families establish a regular circuit, usually spending the winter in one area, involved in a certain occupation, and
the summer in another place doing something else. By combining
two occupations and two areas they are able to make a better income. In Barvale many families were on welfare the year round but
spent several months in the summer camping in fields and picking
crops, along with other migrant labourers, for extra income. One
group of Kuneshti families set up a circuit between San Francisco
and Hawaii. They spent the summer in San Francisco where they
established residence and received welfare cheques supplemented
by occasional trips to engage in farm labour. In the autumn they

would fly to Hawaii where they were able to make a good living at fortune-telling. The occasional *bujo*[3] helped them to get their tickets back to the mainland. In one lean year they did not earn enough in the fields to get to Hawaii and were forced to spend the winter in San Francisco.

Reasons for Travelling

Travelling family groups must have a source of income which they can rely upon while on the road. There are many schemes which they have developed to cope with this problem such as the 'pending transfer scheme' and a summer–winter work circuit. The amount a particular market has been tapped in one area is a factor in travelling. For example, families who travel around picking up auto-body work, tarring roofs and driveways, fortune-telling, or selling plastic flowers may find an area overworked by other families, and this will make them move on to new areas. In almost any area, they may still supplement their income with a welfare grant.

Families who choose one *kumpania* as their base of operations travel for short periods to pick up extra income. They may take off several months in the summer to work in the summer harvest or to pick up body and fender work. In Barvale, for example, they have so overworked the auto body repair market that young men will travel fifty to a hundred miles per day seeking jobs in nearby towns. These trips are limited in duration because after a certain absence they will be likely to have their welfare cheques discontinued; therefore, they tend to return at regular intervals.

Families in the Barvale *kumpania* travel for a variety of reasons besides economic ones. Travelling is socially imperative and is incorporated into the whole structure of law, social control, morality, and religious beliefs. Specifically, illness or death requires the presence of close relatives. Families will travel thousands of miles to New York, Mexico, or Alaska, to be near a sick relative. If death occurs they will stay for the three-day and nine-day *pomana* (death feast). Later they may take another trip to attend the six-week *pomana*, usually in a different area to allow friends and relatives there to attend. One family, for example, was in Hawaii when the father of the family died. The whole family (fourteen persons) returned to San Francisco with the body since it was more expensive for all the relatives to fly to Hawaii, and after the nine-day *pomana* they went to Texas for the six-week *pomana*, accompanied by several relatives from Barvale. Relatives of the deceased will travel long distances at great cost to attend a *pomana*, out of respect to the *mulo* (spirit of the dead). They may also flee the *mulo* if they feel they are being plagued by him, and they believe they can 'outrun' a *mulo* by keeping on the move constantly.

Though families will travel for economic or religious reasons, travelling is also a social occasion. Some families travel to visit relatives, to contract a marriage for a son, to attend a wedding, a baptism (obligatory for the godparents of course), a *slava* (a Saint's day feast), or *pakiv* (party in honour of a visitor). At times several of these social events may be combined in one trip, or a family may visit several *kumpaniyi* on a trip. Women often visit their parents when they are about to give birth and return to their husband's family with the new baby after confinement.

Travelling also may have political implications. When there is a *kris romani* (trial), families who are closely involved will travel far to attend. They will also attend a *kris* nearby even if only peripherally involved. Many conflicts, of course, do not necessarily result in a *kris*, but relatives will go to each other's aid in difficult times. If a conflict develops in a *kumpania* over leadership, or a new leader emerges, families will leave and join another *kumpania* according to their standing in the new situation, and new families may take their place.

In general, the most accepted and common way to solve any problem arising between two families is for the families to leave the *kumpania* until they can come back in peace. Travel is a major method of social control and is a time-honoured solution to pressures from both the outside and inside. Demands from school authorities that parents send their children to school, demands from vocational authorities that young men take a job or attend vocational training, harrassment from the police, or any pressures from the welfare department, police, government authorities, neighbours, or irate landlords, usually are solved by an exodus of the family for as long as is necessary.

It is surprising how well this technique works. A diligent truant officer has no authority or concern for a family once they have left town, and when they return he will generally have to begin all over again applying pressure to the family before threatening prosecution. Once the threat is made, the family takes off again.

Of course, a person who is wanted for welfare fraud or a crime, whether innocent or guilty, is unlikely to return to the same place, at least under the same name.

Any scandal that arises in the *kumpania* requires that the offender (and sometimes the offended as well) leave town. An illegitimate pregnancy, a wife who leaves her husband, a case of adultery, or any such breach of morality will result in a re-sorting of the families in the *kumpania*. A person who becomes *marime* (rejected) will almost certainly leave town until his case is sorted out or his sentence completed.

Travel is a very effective way of problem-solving for the individual and a form of social control for the community. Any person who is a source of trouble, whether or not he is to blame, must leave town until the community decides to accept him again. In any fight between families, all parties disperse for a certain period of time and then return to town, usually with a compromise solution to the situation. For example, at the Easter *slava* a fight broke out among several young men over shared payments for a body and fender job. The fight soon involved two large *familiyi* of the same *vitsa* (descendants of half-brothers) numbering five to six nuclear families on each side. When it was finally stopped by the police, the nuclear families immediately involved left town for several weeks until their fathers (the half-brothers) could work out a solution. The problem of the money was finally settled and a broken car window was paid for by collections from both *familiyi*. The charges made by the police were dropped and in a few weeks the fight was forgotten.

Finally, a word on the symbolism of travelling. Travelling for the Rom is associated with health and good luck whereas settling down is associated with sickness and bad luck. Old ladies who feel ill will take a trip 'to recover', against their *gajo* doctor's advice. One young mother remarked: 'I am tired and run down. I want to get away, have a rest, travel.' She took off with her seven children and came back looking rested. One old lady took a trip whenever she got depressed or felt sick, and another who was too ill to travel, would just go and sit in her car for hours with the door open when she became low or depressed. Another young girl remarked that the Rom used not to fight when they were travelling, but now that they have settled in cities, they fight continuously. All Rom agreed that when they were travelling all the time they were healthy and never needed doctors, but now that they live in houses they are subjected to many *gaje* diseases.[4]

We have seen that a *kumpania* is a territory where various families live together primarily for economic reasons. But families in a *kumpania* reside there only in the sense that it is their base from which they travel out for a variety of reasons. Some closely related extended families, which I have called travelling family groups, travel so much that it is difficult to say whether they 'live' in a *kumpania*. The Rom usually adopt one of three patterns of travel. They may choose a *kumpania* to live in and travel only occasionally for necessary social reasons. They may adopt two *kumpaniyi*, making their living in one in the summer and in the other in the winter. Finally, they may travel in large family groups continually between various *kumpaniyi* where they have relatives and will be allowed to settle for short periods of time.

Households

The Rom refer to households as *tsera*[5] which also means 'tent' (G. & L: 365). The Kalderash Rom were tent-dwellers until the 1930s when the depression forced them into houses and on welfare. At that time a *kumpania* contained a certain number of *tsera* in each camp, much in the same way that the Lowara *kumpania* described by Yoors (1967) was composed of a certain number of caravans. Now that they have moved into houses, on the whole the Kalderash still refer to a *kumpania* as consisting of so many tents or houses. When I asked Tanas Stevenson how many 'Gypsies' there are in San Antonio, he answered, 'Twenty-five houses, twenty-five tents'. During the Easter *slava* in Barvale the ritual of visiting each household in the *kumpania* was still referred to as '*tsera a tsera*' or 'going from tent to tent' (their translation). Similarly, when a woman marries it is said that she goes to live in her husband's tent ('she's gone to his tent, his home'), and to divorce him is to 'break up the tent'.

The *tsera* or household is the basic residential unit of the *kumpania*. In other words, each *kumpania* may be broken down into a certain number of households called *tsera*. The household usually contains an extended family covering three generations: grandparents, children, and grandchildren. Twenty-three of the thirty-three households in Barvale were composed of extended families. The ideal size of a household is twelve to fifteen persons.

It may be smaller, but then the residents tend to join another household, and it may be larger, sometimes as large as four nuclear families or about thirty-two people; but usually when it gets over fifteen there is a tendency to split the units. Some families, such as *familia* 3 in *Table 1*, might occasionally live in one household when working the crops or travelling, and they almost always congregate in one household during the day, but usually try to arrange several houses to live in because of their large numbers. When there is a large *familia* such as this, young couples

TABLE 4 *Family size*

age of parents	average number of children
50–60	9
40–50	7
30–40	7
20–30	5

This is based on a sample of forty-five families (eleven per age group). It may appear that family size is diminishing but it must be remembered that the 20–30 and often the 30–40 age groups are still producing children. Informants state that families are smaller since the depression (1930s), but they fail to account for the decrease in infant mortality which has been considerable in the last ten years. Families in the older generation often had twelve to fourteen children but lost perhaps four to five of them.

and their children may seek their own house as long as at least one couple is residing with the parents.

Households with nuclear families occur at a certain point in the developmental cycle of the family. Ten of the thirty-three households in Barvale contained nuclear families *most* of the time (at times they joined with the parents' house), and these were mainly nuclear families with many small children. Rom families generally are large, with an average of seven children per family for all age groups (see *Table 4*), and when this peak is reached they live as nuclear family households until the arrival of grandchildren shortly thereafter.

Nuclear family households also occur when a family is living in a *kumpania* in isolation from close relatives of its own *vitsa*. However, if they cannot find a house, are without money to pay rent, or have some other difficulty, they can almost always move in with a less closely related family for a short time. A homeless family cannot be refused shelter if it can be provided. Some families who are only distantly related or 'just friends' may live together for a short time (several months), but this is an unusual situation. In Barvale, two families joined households when one was evicted. Although they were only distantly related cousins, they had no other closer relatives in the *kumpania* and looked to each other for support.

The household is the basic economic and residential unit. Members of the same household eat together, share house-cleaning duties, cooking, caring for an elderly person, and often work together, sharing the income. If the house is an *ofisa* (fortune telling parlour), the women will share the fortune-telling, with the older women training the younger ones and the income being shared for living expenses. If the family is on welfare, the women will join together as a team imploring the social worker to meet their special needs, or increase their cheque. Sometimes the income is pooled and handled by the elder of the household. Several married men and women were known to give over their entire cheque from welfare to their parents. More often, individuals handle their own money but contribute to household expenses as necessary, always under the supervision of the eldest. Women generally handle the welfare cheques and give money to their husbands when they ask for it. Daughters-in-law in a household are expected to pay most household expenses such as rent, telephone, utilities, and food, as well as provide spending money for their husbands and necessities for their children.

The usual residence rule is for a couple to live with the husband's parents when they marry, travel with them, and care for them until the couple has had several children. By the time the couple have five to seven children of their own, they often move to their own house, provided the parents have a younger son or daughter to take care of them. Even then, their teenage daughters may be required to live with the old parents to provide housekeeping services or care for any young grandchildren that the old parents have adopted. As soon as the couple's eldest son gets married, he will bring his wife (*bori*) to live with his parents. Occasionally, a daughter may bring her husband or return from her husband's family with small children and join her parents' household. Given this usual developmental cycle, the nuclear family in a single household is a short, temporary arrangement.

There were thirty-three households in Barvale in the Spring of 1971 with a total of 266 people, or an average of eight persons per household. Households in Barvale took one of the five forms given below:

1. old parents, their unmarried children, if any, a married son/ daughter with his or her spouse and children (six households);
2. a widowed man or woman, his/her unmarried children, if any, and a son/daughter, his or her spouse and children (nine households);
3. a middle-aged couple, their unmarried children, one married child, his spouse and children (five);
4. an old couple and their unmarried children and one or more grandchildren (three);
5. a nuclear family – parents and unmarried children (ten).

Some households will have nieces, nephews, cousins, and friends staying with them, but this situation is always temporary, unless they are adopted as children. However, it is considered mean to refuse to house anyone who is homeless. Shrecha, for example, once had a fight with her landlady over the number of homeless Gypsies she was taking in. She said she could understand her landlady's point of view; however, 'Gypsies must always help one another', and 'I could never deny food or shelter to Gypsies who need it if I can possibly provide it'. She herself has lived with various friends for periods of time. Examples of actual households are listed according to their form:

HOUSEHOLDS – CASES FOR EACH FORM

Form 1 Stevan and his wife Yana have two married sons and two married daughters living in their own houses in Barvale with their families. They also have an unmarried son and an unmarried daughter living in their own house besides a married son, his wife, and their four children. During one month a niece came to live with them until her marriage was sorted out and occasionally several of their teenage granddaughters living in Barvale will stay for weeks at a time.
Total: ten people

Form 2 Old Rosie is a widow, living with her son, his wife, and their seven children. She also has an unmarried daughter

C

who stays with her and helps her son's wife with the housekeeping, care of the old lady and care of the children.
Total: eleven people
Katherine's husband died at a young age and left her with three young children, a married adopted son and his wife, and their daughter and another daughter who left her husband and has a young daughter as well.
Total: nine people

FIGURE 7 Sketch plan of location of households in 1966 before re-development.

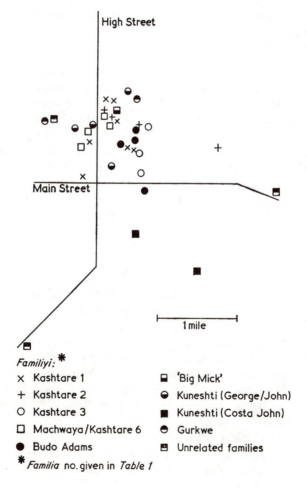

Familiyi: *

× Kashtare 1	◖ 'Big Mick'
+ Kashtare 2	◑ Kuneshti (George/John)
○ Kashtare 3	■ Kuneshti (Costa John)
□ Machwaya/Kashtare 6	◒ Gurkwe
● Budo Adams	▣ Unrelated families

Familia no. given in Table 1

Form 3 Harry and Rosie had eleven children, nine living, though they are still only in their early forties. Their eldest son is married, and he and his wife live with them, including their children.

Total: fourteen people

Form 4 Miller and Mary have several married children living elsewhere, two unmarried sons living with them, and a granddaughter who is six years old.

Total: five people

Spiro and Rosie have two sons and daughters living in their own homes in Barvale with their children and grandchildren (the old couple's great grandchildren). Spiro and Rosie are ill and prefer to live in their own

FIGURE 8 Sketch plan of location of households in 1968 after redevelopment.

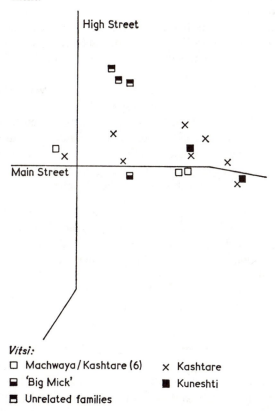

Vitsi:

☐ Machwaya / Kashtare (6) ✕ Kashtare

◨ 'Big Mick' ◼ Kuneshti

◧ Unrelated families

trailer with their five-year-old granddaughter. Their teenage grandchildren take turns living with them and caring for them.

Total: three people

Form 5 John lives with his wife and six unmarried children. He is trying to arrange a marriage for his eldest son who is fourteen.

Total: eight people

Though some families had house trailers, most families lived in houses in Barvale. These families have certain requirements. First, they prefer houses located on the main streets. Before urban redevelopment they would choose dilapidated houses as near the central streets as possible. Now that all these houses have been demolished, they have moved to residential side streets as close to main streets as possible (see *Figures 7* and *8*).

Second, closely related families tend to congregate in one area if they can. If this is difficult they wait until a house nearby comes up for rent and move. *Figures 7-9* for 1966, 1968, and 1970 show that families congregate in down-town areas and that one *familia* tries to get houses in the same areas.

Unrelated Rom do not like to live too closely together. The Machwaya and Kalderasha are especially careful to avoid each other's neighbourhoods (see *Figure 9*). One Machwaya family described how they tried to prevent a Kalderash family from moving into a nearby house by telling them that someone had died in that house and that they could hear ghosts there at night; they were hoping to keep the house for other Machwaya.

We don't let tribes move in next to us. If someone who is not Machwaya wants to live in our neighbourhood, we tell them no and they do the same to us. Nikola's family wanted to move into the house next to us and my brother told them that a man had died there and the house was haunted. They moved in anyway but one day the old lady found the toilet lid down when it had been left up and she knew there were ghosts there and moved out.

It is now very difficult for the Rom to find a suitable house to live in and the shortage of housing is one factor in limiting the numbers of families who can come to Barvale. Landlords do not like to rent to Gypsies and once they do, they find the place only

FIGURE 9 Sketch plan of location of households in 1970.

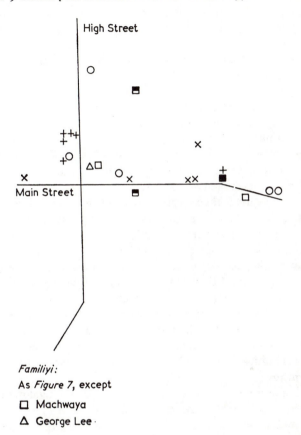

Familiyi:
As *Figure 7*, except
□ Machwaya
△ George Lee

suitable for Gypsies. But also once they do rent to Gypsies they often get used to their ways and become more tolerant of them. Nevertheless, evictions are frequent because landlords cannot tolerate the rubbish, the large numbers of people, the frequent loud noise, and damage to the house. In 1966, the police, in support of landlords, made a list of fifty-two Gypsy 'garbage offenders' whom they threatened to prosecute if they did not clean up. Besides the problem with landlords there is also a shortage of cheap, run-down housing which they can afford.

Third, they prefer to live in a house which has been occupied by a Rom family previously. The Hawaii Welfare Department refers to these houses as 'The Gypsy Trail' because the same addresses crop up for all the Rom families (Coleman 1962: 3). If a house has not been occupied previously by a Rom family, it must be purified by scrubbing with strong astringents and cleaners and then purified by incense burnt in each room 'to remove the smell' of the *gaje* who were the previous occupants. It is believed that one is more prone to *gaje* diseases if one occupies a house recently occupied by *gaje*.

Fourth, they prefer to live as close together as possible. If they can, related Rom will share a duplex (a house divided into two self-contained flats), rent neighbouring houses, or houses as close to one another as they can find them. There was one famous house divided into four flats which was gradually taken over by Rom families and occupied constantly until it was torn down. The families who lived there were closely related, visited constantly, shared cooking, and at times it was difficult to know who lived in which flat. The furniture as well as the occupants in the house changed daily from one flat to another.

New families who come to town will immediately move in with a close relative until they can find a house of their own. Houses of the leaders and patriarchs are, of course, the most frequented reception centres. In 1966, for example, the four houses of the four *vitsa* leaders were the most frequent addresses given to the welfare department by families getting their first cheque. Some of these families were simply picking up extra cash as they breezed through town.

The houses are mostly two-bedroom wooden bungalows in poor condition, with small bare gardens around them. The rooms are small and cramped, and because families are large and visitors frequent, open spaces are preferred to privacy. The Rom will tear down as many inside walls as possible and remove doors, leaving only the bathroom, kitchen, and possibly one bedroom intact. Landlords are prone to object to this reorganization of their houses, but once a family has made the necessary alterations, they have little option but to rent to Gypsies in future. When storefronts are available, these are highly coveted by the Rom because of the larger space and one-room arrangement. Spiro's favourite dwelling, until it was condemned by the City and he was evicted on a court order, was a former bar and dance club with a neon sign on top saying 'The Owl Club'. This consisted of one enormous room covered in drapes and tapestries with two luxurious canopy beds near the front and the household shrine on the bar.

Besides housing twenty-eight members of his family, it was the favourite meeting place for local and visiting Rom.

The houses are usually decorated in bright colours and patterns with the walls covered in tapestries or drapes, the windows by more drapes, and the floors carpeted with thick, deep pile carpets. Some homes are extremely tidy and luxuriant with double beds covered in red velvet, huge sofas lining the room, and enormous gold or silver ceramic lamps and bowls of plaster fruit on metallic coffee tables. Others are very bare and may contain only a sofa, double bed, coffee table, and a few drapes.

Whatever the wealth of the family, the spatial arrangement is usually the same. The front part of the house, which is usually the living room and a few bedrooms with walls knocked out to make one big room is the more public area where visitors are greeted and past which *gaje* are not usually allowed to go. The back room is almost always the kitchen, and this is the private area of the house reserved for family, relatives, and close friends, whether Rom or *gaje*. In one house, the back garden was made into a family room, complete with four large patterned red carpets on the grass, a sofa, coffee table, and a huge eating table. Here I was served coffee only after I became quite intimate with the family and after much discussion on their part.

The family sleeps in the biggest room. One family who had a private front bedroom never slept there and used it only to pile clothes and junk because, they claimed, they were too 'afraid' to sleep closed up in a room near the street. Often there is at least one double bed reserved for the eldest in the house, the grandparents, and one bed for the parents. Older boys and girls will get next preference and sleep on the sofas which line the walls, but they always sleep, separated by sex, on opposite sides of the room. Young couples may sleep on the sofa until they can get a bed of their own. Children and anyone left without bed or sofa, sleep on the floor covered with blankets or large eiderdowns (*perina*) which the young girls and *bori* (bride) make. Once a girl menstruates, she must not sleep with the young girls anymore and during her menses sleeps by herself in a corner of the room, facing the wall with her legs crossed or clamped together. Small children and babies may sleep with their parents in the bed. In one family the two boys slept with their parents and the girls on the other side of the room on the floor. When travelling, families either sleep on the floor in someone's house or in their cars.

Most homes have a household shrine especially if there is an old person (*phuria*) in the house. In one home this was on a buffet, in another, on the mantelpiece, and in another, on a table in the corner of the room. The shrine contains pictures and statues of saints, a resurrection plant (*genus selagenella*), candles, and perhaps some holy water and a spoon (where it is sometimes possible to see the saints). There may also be pictures of deceased relatives lying in state in their coffins or pictures of the gravestone reserved for an elderly parent. One woman has a full size statue of a male saint in her home, and despite her mobility, which was considerable, she carried this fragile object wherever she went.

Cooking in the household is usually the duty of the daughter-in-law in residence, the mother, or sometimes the eldest daughter. When families live in nearby homes or in flats within one house and are closely related, they generally share the cooking and eat together. Even when not living nearby, families within one *familia* often eat together. If there is food in the house, relatives come to eat. There is no specific mealtime; when food is available and prepared, people eat, otherwise the larder is usually empty. In some houses, a pot of stew can always be seen on the stove, and the family, relatives, and friends visiting eat when they feel like it.

The Rom like hot, spicy, greasy food, high in carbohydrate, very fattening, and very constipating; consequently most suffer from overweight and haemorroids. Most dishes are cooked in one pot on the stove as in campfire days and with a great deal of chili peppers. They are especially fond of stews which they make with green and red peppers, tomatoes, potatoes, onions, garlic, and some meat. There are various kinds of *paprikash* stews (not made with paprika). One *paprikash* is called *puyo* and is made with chicken. Others are *Xaimoko* made with rabbit, *Xabe* with beef, and others with fish or lamb. There are also several spicy soups: *fusui eski zumi*, butter bean soup often made with ham and *pertia*, jellied pigs feet and ears. Meat is usually whole pig or lamb roasted on a spit for rituals or huge hams or lamb steaks bought wholesale and barbequed with hot sauce called *chile mole*. The fat crust of the ham is the favourite part of the meat, and when a guest does not want to eat but must take a small amount, he asks for this. Baking is rarely done, and often sweet breads will be bought from the bakery, but the Rom have bread of their own as well which is eaten more as a staple. *Xaritsa* (fried cornbread) is sometimes made, but the favourites are flour breads (*pufe* which is fried and *bogacha* which is baked). The favourite desserts are *pirogo*, a kind of noodle and cheese pudding and *saviako*, a rolled pastry made with fruit, cottage cheese, and raisins in the middle. They also have their own method of making coffee and tea. Coffee (*kafa*) is boiled with the groats and dipped off the top with a spoon. Tea (*chao*) is made with sugar and poured over fruit (strawberries, peach or apple slices, or lemon), Russian style, in a glass.

The most celebrated dish is *sarmi* which is made with cabbage leaves stuffed with pork, onions, peppers, rice, and tomatoes. This dish is essential at any ritual and is so important that women may not cook it when menstruating, pregnant, in confinement, or in mourning. A woman's ability to cook is judged solely on her success at making *sarmi*. At a ritual feast *sarmi*, meats, hot sauces, celery sticks (for virility), salads, *pirogo*, *saviako*, and perhaps a stew or two are usually served. Bread always accompanies a meal. Only at the *pomana* feast is fruit put on the table.

Conclusions

The *kumpania* is a group of Rom families who live together in a specific territory, share in the economic exploitation of this territory, and cooperate with each other economically. It is also the basic political unit and members of a *kumpania* can make decisions on moral, political, and economic questions which are considered public rather than family matters. The degree of political cohesion in the *kumpania* varies from an area strongly controlled by the leader of one *familia* to an uncontrolled, open territory. Most *kumpaniyi* fall somewhere in between these extremes and have a leader who comes from the largest *vitsa* with authority but no absolute control.

Barvale has been occupied by various *vitsi* since 1964, and at that time it was led by 'Big Mick'. As more and more families moved in his leadership was challenged and when he left, Stevan, the leader of the Kashtare gained in authority and other *vitsi* began leaving. At the present time Stevan, now the *rom baro* of Barvale, is attempting to consolidate his position by working with *gaje* authorities, opposing rival Kuneshti and Machwaya leaders and bringing in more Kashtare families. Thus he is working towards creating a more restricted and controlled *kumpania*.

Although the *kumpania* occupies a specific territory and the residents live in houses, it must always be remembered that these households are very mobile and are absent from the *kumpania* on average 42 per cent of the year. Some groups of families travel so much that it is difficult to say whether they live in any *kumpania* for very long at all.

In spite of the extreme mobility of most families, nevertheless residence takes a specific pattern in the *kumpania*. Households generally contain a large extended family covering three generations, headed by an old couple or widowed grandparent. Families prefer to live together until the numbers grow so large that it becomes uncomfortable for the elderly; then large nuclear families set up their own household. Families who are related to one another, but do not share the same household, try to rent houses as close together as possible in specific areas of the town. A family that moves out of these areas, but remains in the *kumpania*, is demonstrating that it is ostracizing the community and will be questioned on its behaviour (see *Figures 7* and *9* – unrelated families). Finally, the Rom choose houses lived in previously by other Rom because they are more likely to be pure (*wuzho*), to be arranged into one large room, and to have more tolerant landlords.

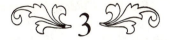

3

Economic Relations

In the area of economic relations, we must look at relations between Rom and *gaje* because the *gaje* are the source of all livelihood and a certain amount of political power, and with few exceptions, the Rom establish relations with *gaje* only because of some economic or political motive.

The Rom have developed one set of rules for behaviour in obtaining economic or political gain from the *gaje* and another set of rules for the same behaviour with their own people. The *gaje* – the policemen, social workers, politicians, newspaper reporters, landlords, shopkeepers, doctors, teachers, neighbours, and social anthropologists – on the other hand each have their own motives and self-interests in their contacts with the Rom (for example, getting their children to school, getting their votes, making them comply with garbage regulations, preventing them from stealing, finding out how they live); the Rom understand these motives and rather than ignore them play an active role in controlling and manipulating these necessary *gaje* contacts in such a way as to diminish the threat of control from them. For example, harrassed police community-relations officers, despised by most minority groups, feel flattered to be invited to a Gypsy *slava*. Imagine their pride at being able to say to their fellow police officers that through their friendship and understanding the Gypsies are practically free of crime.[1]

These relations with *gaje* are of an opposite nature to their economic relations with each other. Economic relations between Rom are based on cooperation and mutual aid, and it is generally considered immoral to earn money from other Rom. The *gaje* are the only legitimate source of income and skill in extracting money from them is highly valued in Rom society.

There has been much written on 'Gypsy occupations' and the problems that arise in trying to list Gypsy occupations illustrate the pitfalls of approaching Rom society from the outside. Rena Cotten (1954: 113–16) has made a four-page list of Gypsy occupations without beginning to exhaust them all. Clébert's is typical of attempts to give some order to Gypsy economics. In his chapter on occupations (1963: 129) he generalizes: 'With a few variations, the Gypsies are first and foremost smiths and workers in metals, musicians and mountebanks, horse-copers and dealers, exhibitors of animals and fortune-tellers.'

He explains that all these occupations were condemned by the Laws of Manu (*Manava Dharma Sastra*) in India and that the 'Gypsies have followed precisely those occupations that were cursed by Manu' (129). This explanation of traditional occupations, which Clébert links with the suggestion by Eliade (1959) that there is a close bond between the art of the smith, the occult sciences, and the arts of song, dance, and poetry, is interesting for an historical perspective; however, it does not explain the many changes in occupations that have occurred among all Gypsies, and it leaves out many recent skills and schemes (peg-makers, basket weavers, travelling movie showmen, not to mention farm labour and welfare). Also, it does not provide an understanding of what all these occupations have in common.

To analyse 'Gypsy occupations' merely by listing the numerous occupations and dividing them into categories such as 'musician' or 'workers in metals' is not only inadequate, it is misleading. To understand Gypsy occupations, or better, Gypsy economics, it is necessary to outline the jural rules for economic relations. The first and most basic rule is that the code of economic relations among Rom must be viewed in opposition to the code of economic relations with *gaje*. The opposition is simply that between co-operation and exploitation. Within the limits set out by this code, there are a large number of ways to make a living available to the Rom in America, and new sources of income are always being sought within these limits. The first step is to understand the nature of economic relations between Rom.

Economic relations between Rom

In the *kumpania* men and women cooperate with each other in exploiting the economic resources of their area. Any job, scheme, or source of income may be exploited individually, but the Rom prefer to work in groups rather than on their own. These groups are called *wortacha* or partners, and are always formed between members of the same sex. Men work in teams of men, and women work in teams of women, though women often take along children of either sex. *Wortacha* also include young unmarried males (or females) who learn the skills of the adults.

Adult partners work as equals and divide the expenses and the profits from a job equally; however, an elder person may be given a small amount extra as a token of respect for his age, and unmarried trainees do not get a full share but receive what the others will give them. The Rom do not work under the employment of another Rom for a wage, even if one person has located and organized a job. If a man wishes to 'hire' someone to do parts of a job he has no skill for or does not wish to do (for example, a 'dirty' job), he hires a non-Gypsy labourer (Lee 1967: 42–43). This distinction is crucial, for a man may be honoured to join a group of men as a partner, but he would lose his self-respect if he were being employed as a labourer for them.

All the men in Barvale worked with partners most of the time although occasionally a man went out alone. Some men worked with adult sons, but often partners were cousins of the same age. For example:

a. Nicky usually did body and fender repair jobs with his second cousin Billy and his first cousin Jimmy. All three men are just under twenty years of age and are recently married.
b. Harry and Tom are brothers with large families and usually work as partners with Toma, a cousin of similar age. On one job they each got $50.

Women also worked in groups when telling fortunes around town or dealing with the social worker for welfare in the home. Women in the same household generally team up and do not work with women of other households unless they are close relatives. The most usual team is headed by an elderly woman and includes her adult daughters and daughters-in-law. Katherine, for example, always works in collaboration with her daughter Mary and daughter-in-law Rachael. Her social worker described the team thus:

Rachael, Mary, and Katherine are a formidable trio and they usually travel together. They are all experts at wheedling and begging. Sometimes they will work in relays, and at other times they employ siege tactics, that is, they all talk at once and it is very difficult to separate their needs from their desires.

The *wortacha* in each *kumpania* (and partners are usually formed with members of the same *kumpania*) have the right to exploit the territory that their *kumpania* covers. Rom from another *kumpania* are not allowed to move into their area without prior permission, and they do not go to the territory of another *kumpania* unless it has been approved there. Rom who do infringe this rule will be severely criticized by the local *kumpania*, and if they ignore this criticism they may find that they have been turned in to the local police for fixing fenders or fortune-telling without a licence. Informing to the local *gaje* authorities on a person who infringes on the economic resources of a *kumpania* is generally considered acceptable; however, the objective is only to harass the person and not to get him arrested. Only just enough information is given to the authorities to arouse their suspicions, but not enough to warrant a conviction. Welfare is included in the resources of a *kumpania* and in Barvale a stranger coming to town has to get approval from some prominent and respectable *phuro* (elder) and the *rom baro* in order to get on welfare.

The Rom in a *kumpania* not only work together but they cooperate economically in several other ways. Though ideally all Rom should help each other, in practice, apart from relatives, it is the Rom of the same *kumpania* who come to each other's aid. This is accomplished by means of collections (*kidemos*) among the *kumpania* members, and the idea is to pool enough money for the needy without any single family being too debilitated by the expense (see also Lee 1967: 44). Collections are a kind of insurance scheme because a Rom who gives freely in collections can expect to get help himself at some time in his life. Those who are mean with their contributions lose respect in the community.

Collections are made for a number of reasons, usually on ritual occasions. For example, a collection is taken at the *pomana* (death feast) to help the family of the deceased pay the funeral expenses, and a collection for the bride and groom is a standard part of the wedding ritual. A *slava* may be given in the *kumpania* with the help of a collection, though more often it is several relatives who join together to give a *slava* rather than the *kumpania* as a whole. At the Easter *slava*, everyone in the *kumpania* gave his own *slava* and each family visited the *slave* of the other families. Collections taken up in Barvale over a period of three to four months included:

1 *Pomana*

   a. A collection was taken to send Stevan and Yana to the *pomana* of Stevan's nephew in Oregon because they did not have the money to get there.
   b. At the *pomana* in Oregon three collections were made to pay for the food and expenses. The first brought in $2,600, the second $1,500, and the third (from people arriving later) about $2,000. Each adult gave about $5.
   c. When Marco died his body and his wife, mother, children, and daughters-in-law and their children were flown from Hawaii to San Francisco, paid for by a collection taken among relatives in the Bay area and the *kumpania* in Hawaii.

2 *Wedding*

   a. When Sandra and Steve married, there was a collection at the wedding table. Each man gave $10 to $20 and about $600 was collected.
   b. At a wedding in Fort Worth $255 was collected for the bride and groom and at a wedding in Oklahoma $1,350 was collected.

3 *Slava*

At the 28th August *slava* to St Anne, four families pooled funds in order to give the *slava*.

The *kumpania* will also make collections on non-ritual occasions. If someone needs a private doctor's care or hospitalization, and the immediate family cannot afford to pay for it, the *kumpania* will take up a collection to help. The person's relatives in another *kumpania* will also send money. If someone in the *kumpania* is arrested and needs money for bail or must pay a fine, again a collection will be made. If there is a fight or disagreement in the *kumpania* and property is damaged, the *kumpania* will make a collection to pay for the damage and settle the fight. Finally, if a genuinely destitute family arrives, the *kumpania* will help them out not only by sharing some home with them but with a collection to get them started again. Spiro once said that any Rom who comes to Barvale and is desperate can expect help and that he

personally knew of four or five collections being made on such
occasions.

It is the leader of a *kumpania* who handles the collection. In
Barvale, both 'Big Mick' and Stevan have been responsible for the
collections. Examples of these collections include:

1. The Rom will often prefer to pay for private medical care
   with a collection rather than be cared for by a welfare doctor
   if they feel this care may be better (Tompkins 1965b: 8). In
   1966, Marcia needed an operation for mastoids. A collection
   of $50 was made as a deposit on her operation; the balance
   ($400) was never paid.
2. Fines and traffic tickets are paid promptly in Barvale by the
   Rom. Stevan personally takes up a collection and pays the
   fines (usually for breaking garbage regulations) about once
   a month (Tompkins 1967: 11).
3. At the Easter *slava* fight, Spiro's car was smashed and no one
   would claim responsibility for it. Stevan, to end the argument, took $10 from each person involved in the fight to pay
   for the damages to the car and everyone was satisfied with
   this solution.
4. When a couple and their four children arrived in Barvale,
   expecting their fifth child and completely out of cash, they
   were taken by Stevan to get their first welfare cheque and
   were given the rent and a full house of furniture through
   donations from relatives and friends.
5. When Dorothy decided to leave her husband, his relatives
   demanded $150 for her return to compensate for the loss of
   their *bori*; her relatives in Barvale and New York made a
   collection to pay for her ransom.

In summary, the men and women of a *kumpania* cooperate
economically in several ways in order to ensure a living. They not
only share economic resources, homes, and income, but through
this system of sharing, they avoid extreme want and the necessity
to abandon their way of life and take employment from the
gaje.

Although men and women work in separate unisexual groups as
partners and although men generally take up certain occupations
and women others, basically men and women use the same techniques to make a living. They rely on their wits and a forceful

personality to make the *gaje* give them money. This requires considerable skills which must be learned from elders over a long period of time. The techniques used[2] are based on close observation and knowledge of the income, status, and aspirations of a given *gajo* combined with behaviour from the Rom that is most likely to break down the non-Gypsy's resistance to the pressure put on him by the Rom. This behaviour includes creating a loud commotion to embarrass the non-Gypsy, switching from flattery to hostility to confuse him, or begging and pleading to invoke sympathy. To earn money with one's wits is highly valued and admired while to be a slow-witted or shy person is considered extremely bad luck.

The Kalderash in Barvale maintain that women are primarily responsible for supporting their husbands and family. This does not mean that men do not work, only that the primary moral responsibility to provide for the family falls on the women of the household. The ability to make money is still a major criterion in choosing a daughter-in-law for one's son and a major obligation of a wife. On the whole, this ideal corresponds with practice. Women still provide the largest amount of income in Barvale though men may earn most of the money when the family is travelling. Even on summer work in the fields, women generally work the hardest (Tompkins 1965a: 3), and in welfare, with few exceptions, the woman handles everything. In case after case in welfare records the wife has also provided the major support of the family before welfare, whether by telling fortunes, working in the fields, selling flowers, or begging. A woman who fails to provide for her family is in a sense a failure as a woman, wife, and mother. A family that rises economically generally invests in the woman's occupation rather than the man's, even if their wealth was originally acquired through his efforts. Men do not value their occupations over the woman's but consider it more as a temporary measure in bad times. Except in the few cases where a man takes a pride in some skill such as coppersmithing, it is felt that a rich man would be foolish to work.

It is difficult to divide occupations strictly into male and female work. Basically, the women are fortune-tellers and handle welfare negotiations. In some cases, the man always dealt with the social worker. In these cases, the wife generally was considered a 'bad' wife, that is, shy and unable to hustle for more money from the social worker; but the man was not condemned for taking over this role, only pitied for having a bad wife. Occasionally, men will tell fortunes as well, though they do not set up an *ofisa* (fortune-telling premises) or make a regular practice of this. They do participate in their wife's business by building the booth in a carnival or setting up the *ofisa*. Both men and women also engage in farm labour, though again some men will leave this mostly to their wives and children. Male occupations are more exclusive and most male occupations are never done by women. Coppersmith work, tarring roofs and driveways, body and fender car repairs, trading cars and trailers, are all men's jobs.

Economic relations with Gaje

We have seen that the Rom cooperate with each other in a number of ways including extracting money from the *gaje*. Both men and women use similar techniques to achieve this aim, techniques that require the ability to convince a non-Gypsy to part with his money. This technique might be called 'hustling'. Whatever the method used to achieve this aim, it is always one that does not require the Rom to undertake employment from a non-Gypsy and that allows him freedom to travel. The preferred arrangement is to charge a fee for a service (such as fortune-telling) or to obtain a contract from a non-Gypsy for a specific piece of work (such as fixing a fender).

In times of extreme want, it is not always possible to avoid employment, but in this case it is taken for a few days in order to get enough cash to reach a relative who can then help the needy family. Some men will take short-term jobs with construction companies, or gardening work. Some women have taken piece work in a factory, but only when they can work in groups together and physically removed from non-Gypsy women. In general, any employment that requires close contact with non-Gypsies or puts a person under the direction and authority of a non-Gypsy is avoided. This kind of employment is considered *marime* because it requires some kind of commitment to American society and contradicts important values of Rom society. For example, most regular employment would interfere with the mobility required of any Rom. A Rom who does take employment is considered 'Americanized', and his behaviour is taken to mean that he 're-jects' Rom society and therefore is *marime*. One girl who took a position with the Job Corps (a programme for training young people) was treated as if she had committed a breach of the sexual code and she and her family became *marime*.

Though money must be earned from *gaje*, but not by employment, it is immoral to earn a living from other Rom. However, at certain times money exchanged between Rom is considered legitimate and is not viewed as money earned. The brideprice should not be considered a method of financial gain (when this does happen it is highly unethical) but is an exchange between two families. The extra amount given to an elder *wortacha* in the *lovoro* (division of the take) is not viewed as money earned but a sign of respect for his age and experience. When a leader gets a certain cut from new Rom coming into a *kumpania*, whether it be for welfare or fortune-telling, this also is considered a token of respect to the *kumpania* for the use of its resources; however, here the line between respect and earning money becomes very fine.

The legality of a scheme or occupation is not an important consideration for the Rom except when this is an inconvenience to them or when they are likely to be arrested. Avoiding arrest is extremely important; jail means being denied social contact with one's own people and being forced to live among the *gaje* (which is *marime*). Stealing from other Rom is wrong, but it is not necessarily wrong when it is from the *gaje*; although one should not be too greedy. 'The story of God' is a myth which provides an explanation and justification for stealing for the Rom and there is no man, woman or child who does not know it.

> Jesus was going to be crucified and a Gypsy blacksmith, who was a slave, was ordered by the Roman soldiers to make four nails, three to go into his hands and feet and one through his heart. The Gypsy stalled and stalled but the soldier whipped him so he made the four nails. He asked God to help him and to help the Gypsies. God cried and the Gypsy cried. When he was to deliver the nails he swallowed one and told the soldiers he had lost it. When God saw that he had swallowed the nail for Jesus' heart, he said, Gypsy you are free to go and travel anywhere and you can steal your food and take what you need to live. And that is why Gypsies travel and why they steal.

Actually the Rom in Barvale are relatively crime-free compared with the rest of the city. They are not involved in felonies, armed robbery, rape, or murder, and their most serious offences have been traffic and garbage violations and stealing from shops. An old crone once said to me: 'Gypsies never kill someone. It is the worst crime. The next worst crime is betraying one of your own people.' Although they are mostly involved in questions of fraud, in three years the welfare department found only ten instances of welfare fraud. Nine of these instances of welfare fraud were cases of failure to report possession of a car that is more valuable than welfare regulations allow (Tomkins 1967: 11).

Murder is so serious a crime that there is no specific punishment against it since no Rom will admit that it can happen. However, there is no doubt that the person who committed such a crime would be a total outcast (*marime*); though this would hardly be effective since if he were socialized properly enough to fear *marime* he would never have committed the crime in the first place.

Extortion, blackmail, or coercion of other Rom, are strongly prohibited but not unheard of. When they occur, it is always a method, though considered an immoral one, of getting or keeping power among Rom. The late Tinya Le Stevanosko used these techniques to relieve the powerful Machwaya of some of their wealth for his poorer relatives and increase his own power. The Machwaya themselves may not be entirely ignorant of these tricks as a recent newspaper article indicates:

CRIME FIGHTERS OR EXTORTIONISTS? The National Gypsy Crime Investigators' Inc. claims the first; other Gypsies claim the second.

Boto Adams claims his organisation is dedicated to 'clearing the names of the Gypsies' and to exposing certain con-artists who are 'extortionists in the guise of fortune-tellers'. But the Corporation's dedication to the routing of the 'renegades' has placed its own actions in the spotlight of illegality. Since its founding in February, 118 extortion charges have been filed against the group.

Some observers have voiced the opinion that the NGCI Corporation is just a way in which Boto and Mike Adams can better their [power] position in the Gypsy nation. But the two Adams deny this accusation. 'We're out to prove to the courts', Boto Adams said, 'that the self-appointed [Gypsy] kings, or rulers, are in the confidence game.' (Jones 1970)

Within the general principles of economic cooperation between Rom and economic exploitation of *gaje*, the number of schemes for making money and the number of occupations is very large and very flexible. In Barvale, the most important source of income is welfare.

Welfare

It is the obligation of the woman to get welfare and to protect her husband from any interference from the welfare department in his life or activities. She must use her skills as a 'hustler' and her knowledge about welfare policy acquired by word of mouth from other Rom in order to be effective in her job. The women have many techniques for keeping the men out of welfare negotiations and for convincing the social worker to deal only with her. She may claim her husband is deaf, mentally retarded, senile, or physically disabled, or she may simply take over all negotiations while he stays in the background. A few examples of intake interviews in 1965–6 show the effectiveness of this policy by the attitude and conclusions of the social workers.

1. 'The —— are a Gypsy family and take full advantage of the fact in trying to avoid questions put to them. They have supported themselves largely as fruit pickers but in the seasons, Mr —— does body work and Mrs —— a little sewing. Mr —— allowed his wife to dominate the interview and at times she said he could not hear, but it seemed more his custom of allowing her to be the spokesman for the family than his failing to understand what I was saying. If anyone is hard of hearing, it would seem that Mrs —— was the one because every question I asked her had to be repeated. I felt this was in order to give herself time to think of an answer rather than because she did not understand the question.'

2. 'Mrs —— is truly the leader of this family. She is a rather aggressive 25 year old woman. She makes capital of the fact that she is a Gypsy and that Gypsies have a much more difficult time in life than other people. She seemed extremely protective of her husband and evidently has accepted her family pattern that the woman, not the man, is the breadwinner and the agency representative for the family. Mr —— appeared to know nothing or to be unwilling to say anything. He conversed with his wife several times in a language which I think is Romanian. As far as the family was admitting he

has never worked one day in his life for any organized employer. Mrs —— kept saying that Mr —— was extremely nervous and that he couldn't work because he had bad nerves.'

3. 'Mrs —— has a very cloying, wheedling personality and it is difficult to interview her. She is very grim and serious when she is performing; has no sense of humour unlike most of the other Gypsy women I have had dealings with lately. Mr —— has a pleasant, undemanding personality, but he gives free rein to his wife and he usually sits in the car while she takes one of the children to bombard an agency with pleads and threats. He has, I believe, always lived with (his mother) and it sounded like she supported him more than he supported her.'

4. 'Mrs —— is the most powerful procurer. When she wishes to perform, the others stand back with awe and admiration. She never gives up. If three blankets are approved, she wants four. Mrs —— has been successful earning money in Hawaii as a fortune-teller. Mr —— seems ineffectual and simpleminded in contrast to the women. He is usually not around during contact with the social service and will not show up at all unless you specifically insist. According to his own statement he has never worked more than two or three days for any employer. It does not appear he would be capable of earning the thousands it has taken to transport his family so many times to Hawaii.'

As an occupation for the women, welfare requires the same skills as fortune-telling: she must convince the *gaje* to give her money. Although the Rom are informed of their legal right to welfare by their social workers and have an amazing knowledge of the very complicated bureaucratic procedures involved, most Rom do not believe that simple legal entitlement to welfare is the only condition necessary for them to get their 'little cheque'. Of course this is perfectly true since welfare procedure is so complicated and changes so frequently that often the social workers themselves are not sure of the legal conditions.

To the Rom, personal contact and influence with the social worker is the most important condition for getting welfare. They believe that the way the social worker feels about them and the amount of pressure or flattery they give to her will affect the expediency and availability of their cheque. Some believe that she can cut them off any time she desires, and they often recommend that she do this to punish someone who has breached their moral code. Consequently, they are cautious never to offend her. If someone does offend her, the others hasten to apologize for him adding that he was *dilo* (crazy). Many newcomers to Barvale believe that they will not be able to get a cheque without Stevan's influence since it is well known that he and the social workers are on friendly terms.

For example, one family came in with Stevan and applied for welfare. When the worker got their case from another county she found great discrepancies in the birth-dates and called them up to question these. The man immediately said, 'you mean Stevan doesn't want us to get welfare'. The worker explained this had nothing to do with it, and she was sure they could straighten things out. He replied, 'I thought Stevan had it fixed'. He must have concluded Stevan was against him because he left town without ever getting his cheque. In one intake interview, a woman who was nine months pregnant offered to get down on her knees if the social worker would issue her a cheque that day.

All of these beliefs have a certain basis in fact. Many social workers are strict about establishing eligibility and can delay or deny welfare because forms are not filled out properly and information not given correctly. Since most Rom cannot read or write (and certainly cannot read the forms given to them) they often give very contradictory and incomplete, sometimes false, information to the welfare department, and an unsympathetic social worker can deny them assistance. Generally, they also lack many of the documents required by a bureaucracy such as birth certificates, driver's licences, credit cards, and draft cards. This means that residence requirements must be gleaned from pawn tickets, traffic tickets, and landlords' or shopkeepers' statements. In Barvale the social worker is very sympathetic to them and as she has had years of experience in sorting out their confusing statements, she speeds up their applications by filling out the forms for them.

In counties where 'special needs' such as bedding, furniture, refrigerators, and washing machines are issued, the sympathy of the social worker is essential for obtaining these items. Some families get more special needs than others, and the ability of the women to hustle the social worker can make an important difference. In Barvale, 'special needs' are only issued to the old people (which all the Rom accept as fair) because it created such competition in hustling the social worker. However, this is only the policy of an individual social worker and has little to do with legal entitlement.

Acquiring welfare, therefore, entails the same kinds of skill that other occupations require; that is, the ability to understand, convince, flatter, cajole, pressure, and manipulate the social worker. Welfare is not considered a hand-out; it is money that they convince the *gaje* to give them. The legality or illegality of their position in welfare is contradictory and arbitrary to them, but as in other occupations, they learn to avoid arrest.[3] They do not consider themselves a depressed minority having to beg for charity from the middle-class majority. On the contrary, welfare is to them an incredible stroke of luck, yet further proof of the gullibility of the *gaje*. Of course, there are problems connected with it. The *gaje* want them to send their children to school, the young men to vocational training, and the *gaje* in general want a lot of information which the Rom do not wish to divulge. However, as long as these pressures can be delayed or avoided, welfare is a reasonably good occupation for the Rom.

Perhaps the best illustration of their attitude towards welfare is the English names that they use for social workers (who in *Romanes* are simply *gaje*). Since they cannot read, the Rom rely on the spoken words in English, and this, plus perhaps a good sense of humour, is possibly the reason for the homonyms which they have substituted. Most Rom in Barvale refer to 'welfare' as the 'world's fair' and hence a welfare worker becomes the 'world's fair worker'. Sometimes they may use the expression 'the wealthy worker' and some skip the difficult pronunciation (for a *Romanes* speaker, 'w' is very difficult to say) and call the social worker simply 'the money lady'. Whether these substitutions are conscious or unconscious, they concisely express the general attitude of the Rom towards welfare. Once, when I asked a young girl of eighteen what she wanted to do with her life she replied, 'go on welfare'. She could not see why she should take up any other occupation and risk failure when there was a perfectly secure and reasonable one at hand.

Income is generally very difficult to determine since most Rom will not discuss what they earn; however, income from welfare is available from welfare records. Welfare cheques depend on what category of aid the recipient is eligible for and, if a family receives

'Aid to Families with Dependent Children' (AFDC), how many children they have. Welfare rules fit amazingly well with Rom family patterns. When a family receives AFDC a child will be cut off welfare at age sixteen if he or she is not in school and at any age if married. The Rom will not send their children to school but prefer to marry them at a young age; therefore a young boy or girl can marry at sixteen (since they would be cut off anyway), and once the wife becomes pregnant she can begin getting her own cheque. The Rom also have large families and of course this gives them a larger cheque. They share houses and meals and therefore they are able to make their money go further. They pay very low rent, are not interested in acquiring the usual material possessions an American family is accustomed to, although they do have other big expenses such as *pomana* and *slava* feasts, gold, new cars, and travel expenses. They also know how to find jewellery bargains and stretch their money further by buying food and supplies at wholesale prices.

On AFDC the average Rom family of seven children and two parents received $373 per month. This figure seems small, but it is deceptive because most households do not contain so few persons. An older man or woman in the house may be eligible for Old Age Security (OAS), Aid to the Totally Dependent (ATD) if he is physically disabled (as most old people are), or the Blind Aid programme if he can convince a doctor that he cannot read an eye chart. Consequently households that pool their funds can manage fairly well. The following income from welfare by household gives a more accurate picture of the financial situation:

1. $114 ATD to head of household for obesity
    80 AFDC for her two minor daughters
    148 AFDC for her adult daughter and child
    148 AFDC for an adult daughter-in-law and child
    114 ATD for an adult son with cerebral palsy

    total $604 per month

2. $142 ATD to head of household for obesity, diabetes, and heart trouble
    172 AFDC to wife and two children
    221 AFDC to a daughter-in-law with three children

    total $535 per month

3. $180   to wife for Blind Aid
        221   AFDC for her husband and three children (one
                an adopted granddaughter)
        ─────
total $401   per month

4. $173   ATD and OAS for head of household
        172   AFDC for her two dependent children
        221   AFDC for her son and three dependent children
        ─────
total $566   per month

These figures do not include income from able-bodied adult men
in the household. Welfare policy requires that an able-bodied man
must at least be seeking employment. Only three Rom in Barvale
are considered employable by the Welfare Office. The rest have
been able to claim some kind of exemption, either a physical disability or the physical disability of a wife or parent, for whom they
are caring. Most men are quite ill and can get a legitimate doctor's
exemption. Those who cannot often prefer to 'desert' their wives
(i.e. keep away from the social worker), not to avoid work which
they are doing anyway, but to avoid the kinds of employment that
the employment office might force them to take and sometimes to
avoid reporting their own income. It is also quite common for a
married son living with his parents not to be claimed at all, and his
wife (usually said to be an unmarried or divorced daughter with
children) therefore has all the contact with the welfare department
and the man is free to come and go as he pleases. If the man
cannot claim any physical disability, and it is already known that
his wife is not a sister, he can arrange intelligence and psychological tests to 'prove' he is of moronic intelligence and not capable
of taking a job anyway. An example of such a test is the following:

DESCRIPTION AND BEHAVIOUR

Mr —— was a short, slight, pallid, aged looking man, with
pockmarked skin and a weak voice. He arrived clutching his
chest and looking as though he were about to expire. Asked
about retraining he shrugged with helpless resignation and said
farm work was 'all I've done all my life'. Cooperation with
testing was good and scores appear valid.

TEST FINDINGS

An IQ score of 64 was obtained. This is in the retarded range (69 and below), ranks in the lower 1 per cent of the general population and represents a mental age of about ten years. Thinking was markedly concrete with the lowest scores in phases of testing requiring abstract thinking. Visual motor performance was also poor. These results raise the question of organicity. Other phases of testing such as vocabulary, general information, long and short term memory, judgement, etc., were consistently in the retarded range.

Personality tests do not reflect severe pathology such as psychosis. Responses suggest a semi-plastic childlike view of the world, lack of maturity, and a moderate ego weakness. Diagnostic impression is inadequate personality and possible non-psychotic organic brain damage in a retarded person. Re-training does not seem feasible. Instruction of the subject and his wife in birth control methods is strongly recommended. This man has nine children.

This kind of report is typical of test results on Rom. They always appear extremely cooperative with the tests and always are declared mentally retarded with a 'childlike' personality or a 'passive-dependent' personality. It is fairly obvious that the Rom, who are generally extremely intelligent, extroverted, and aggressive, are simply acting in a manner that is the opposite of their usual behaviour. I am always amazed at the consistency of the results, and although I could see what kind of act this particular man was exhibiting in the interview, I asked him how he was able to manage such advantageous test results. He told me proudly:

The trick is never to protest anything but act like you are doing everything right and are, you know, simple-minded and good hearted about it. Anything she asks me I just give some wrong answer. For instance there was a picture of this doll, and I was supposed to connect the arms and legs. Well I put the legs in the armholes and the arms below. She kept trying to help me but I stuck with that like I was sure it must be right.

Of course, the fact that he could not read or write was also an advantage since this immediately classed him in a sub-normal intelligence group. One crafty lady went to Sacramento for a few months where she convinced her social worker that she was a retarded Cherokee Indian and obtained this psychological evaluation:

> . . . her manner was childlike, mental age of about eight years. Personality tests suggest a simple, childlike, not very competent person who is anxious and self-preoccupied. Diagnostic impression is passive dependent personality and probably organic brain syndrome in a retarded person.

The fact that this result is so similar to the other (the two people are not consanguineally related) suggests some kind of similar technique on how to manage the tests. This 'Cherokee Indian' was able to get such sympathy from her social worker and keep her so occupied in providing special needs (which require a large number of forms and estimates) that she was unable to get any information on the family or observe them long enough to find out their true financial situation. When the social worker began to see the light, the family left Sacramento and returned to Barvale.

If, however, all other methods fail and a man is unable to have himself or his wife declared physically or mentally disabled, then he can try passive resistance.

Stevan's son-in-law is one of the three 'able-bodied men' in Barvale who have to either be looking for a job or training themselves so that they are employable. (Illiteracy counts as a social disability, but the person involved must go to night school.) He first said he had back trouble, but the doctor found him perfectly fit. Then he had to go to night school, but he missed most of the classes and only went just enough to keep them from dropping him. Then the employment officer said they must find him a job. He always missed the first appointment with them and then went to the second. Finally when they were ready to discontinue his cheques he moved away, but he stayed less than two months so his case was not transferred, and when he came back, the pressures on him to get a job had to begin all over again.

Most of the families were on Aid to Families with Dependent Children (AFDC), but all the old people not yet sixty-five, and therefore ineligible for a pension (OAS), generally had obesity related illnesses and could get disability aid (ATD). Physically fit elders always had at least one adopted grandchild and therefore were eligible for AFDC. One lady who had no adopted grandchild (which is quite rare) immediately had one flown out from New York City so that she could have a means of support. One woman was able to prove that she was blind because she 'could not read the eye chart' and was eligible for the Blind Aid programme. Several were able to get ATD simply for obesity which they considered a wonderful joke since to them obesity indicates health and prosperity; thin people are thin because they cannot afford a good meal or else are extremely ill. In most cases obesity, heart trouble, and diabetes went hand in hand, and the disability was genuine.

1. Tom and his wife came to Barvale with their son Johnny who they claimed was fifteen (he is probably about eighteen). They produced a midwife's certificate from Tom's sister who said he was 'born in 1954 or 1955 but I know he is 15'. This gave them a year of AFDC until they could get through an application for ATD. At sixteen Johnny would be discontinued because he was not in school.

2. Ruby, Tom's eldest sister, was on AFDC for her grandchildren until the last one became sixteen. Then she brought in an affidavit from Lalie, the only person old enough who could have delivered her, stating that she was midwife at Ruby's birth and giving her age as sixty-five. Consequently, Ruby qualified for OAS and her cheque went from $138 to $173.

Young people who have just married, are therefore discontinued from their parents' cheque, and have no way to get a cheque of their own, are eligible for General Assistance (GA) of $30 per month until they conceive their first child, usually within the first year of marriage. Even this short interlude between being on one's parents' AFDC cheque and getting one's own can be avoided by keeping the marriage a secret or calling it a betrothal until the girl has conceived.

We can see that practically all Rom can claim some aid from the Welfare Department. Besides the normal support programmes, AFDC, ATD, OAS, and GA, there are also special funds and programmes in the Welfare Department which the Rom make full use of. These special funds are more difficult to get, require special application by the social worker and special approval in Sacramento. Of all the people in Barvale on welfare (and a large number of non-Gypsies are on welfare in Barvale) the Rom are by far the most effective at acquiring these special funds. One large factor in their favour is their social worker who is very helpful and always informs them of funds that are available. The way in which the Rom make use of these funds is unique, however, and even their social worker can never predict what scheme they will come up with when they get the information. Every law has a loophole and the Rom seem particularly good at ferreting out these loopholes.

1. *Urban Renewal*

When the urban renewal programme began, a fund was established to aid families being forcibly moved from their homes to a new area. Each family was given $500 for the expenses and psychological disturbance of moving. The Rom, who preferred the condemned housing in the centre of town, would move into one of these houses, which, of course, had very low rent and which they could alter to fit their needs, knocking out all the inside walls. Approximately six families received their $500 compensation.

2. *Special Housing Needs Fund*

This is a fund established to help welfare recipients to buy their own house if they have problems in getting a house to rent (usually because of racial discrimination). The welfare department provides a certain portion of the down payment if the recipient can get a loan. Stevan put in a claim on this fund on the basis that he was constantly being evicted for 'garbage problems' and 'noise' and that he was being discriminated against because of his cultural pattern of life. He had now bought two houses with this fund, negotiating a personal loan from the owner of the house. Since he is the only Rom in Barvale who owns property, his prestige has been considerably enhanced and his leadership reinforced.

3. *Travel Money*

A welfare recipient who finds himself stranded away from his 'state' and applies for welfare in another state can usually convince the welfare department there to send him back 'home' because it is cheaper for them than supporting this person for a long time. The Rom, who travel constantly, often use this system when they are low on funds and want to return to the *Kumpania*.

    a. Anna attended Big George Adams's funeral in Los Angeles in 1964 and had to leave Los Angeles when the welfare department threatened to take away her children because of 'neglect'. She arrived in Barvale and went to the welfare office with the story that she and her husband were driving along the highway and he unhitched their trailer and left her pregnant with seven children. She wanted the welfare department in Barvale to return her to New York (where she would join her husband presumably). They decided it was cheaper to send her back, even though she had to fly because a doctor declared she had a stillbirth in her womb. They bought shoes and clothes for the children (who could not fly in 'rags'), took them to the airport, bought their tickets, and sent them on their way.

b. One family claimed to the Cleveland Welfare Department that they were from Barvale although the Barvale Welfare Department did not know them. The Cleveland Department was so anxious to get rid of them that they bought all six people bus tickets and gave them $50 in cash to send them to Barvale.

c. Another woman went to Chicago twice to visit relatives. Each time, when her money ran out she went to the Chicago Welfare Department and created such a scene they sent her back. The second time 'stretched' welfare policy considerably.

Fortune-Telling

I shall not give a detailed description of fortune-telling practices, (a) because this has been done adequately in written sources (see Brown 1924: 94–122; Mitchell 1955: 43–4, 71–89; MacDonald 1939; Levy 1962: 47–52) and the Rom in Barvale have basically the same techniques, and (b) fortune-telling is not an important source of income in Barvale, nor is it practised very often since it is illegal.

Fortune-telling is the traditional occupation practised by women. All women and most young girls are trained as fortune-tellers even though they could not often use their skills. Many told fortunes on the street, at fairs or flea markets, and other special events. Most also told fortunes during their travels in places where it was possible to do so, that is, where the police were unlikely to harass them and where they were not infringing on the territory of another *kumpania*. Many families went to Hawaii and Alaska primarily to tell fortunes, and they claimed to be able to make a fair living from it. Several families spent the summers travelling with carnivals and operating fortune-telling concessions. These were always the same families, and most of them grew up working in carnivals. One man referred to the carnival as the 'college of canvas' in which he was educated. John Marks described how carnival fortune-telling worked:

> In the summer the men go out and work in carnivals and do boiler repairing in between. They usually clear $5000 to $6000 for the summer after living expenses for the family, but sometimes they get only $500 to $1000. The carnival is a big racket. They charge $25 to $200 for a fortune telling concession and then charge for lights, a watchman, and garbage. Then they tell you if there is a complaint you are on your own. In a carnival you can only make money if you steal and cheat people.

As with all fortune-telling set-ups, the men handle all the negotiations and arrangements with the carnival, build the fortune-telling booth, prepare advertisements or handbills, and the women tell the fortunes.

Local laws on fortune-telling vary considerably. In Barvale there are several Boyash families who have licences to tell fortunes and operate palmistry parlours (Ayres 1966) because they had already set up their places before the law prohibiting fortune-telling was passed in the city. The Rom resent this privilege very much since they consider that the Boyash are not 'real Gypsies', and they are constantly trying to get licences of their own. In San Francisco, fortune-telling is also illegal; however for years the police turned a blind eye to Barbara Adams who had the only fortune-telling parlour in the city. Because of this monopoly, she is reputed to have made a fortune, and she still operates a palmistry bookstore now that she is out of jail. Most fortune-telling *kumpaniyi* in northern California are controlled by the Machwaya who have been able to secure licences for their families alone. One very wealthy and powerful Machwano convinced the city council to reduce the prohibitive fortune-telling fee from $9000 per annum to $500 per annum for members of his family. Instead of prohibiting fortune-telling by an exhorbitant fee, the council simply made a limit on the number of fortune-tellers per head of population; consequently, one family has the area completely under its control (*Richmond Independent*, September 1966: 3). In Texas fortune-telling is illegal but 'readers and advisors' can hang out their shingles, and John Marks and his *kumpania* control that area through his friendships with the police, who are happy to keep the number of readers and advisors limited to members of his family.

Fortune-telling in itself is not very lucrative; however, the *bujo* is very profitable. The *bujo* is a confidence trick whereby a person (always a fortune-telling customer) is cheated out of a large savings. There are many ways to pull a *bujo*, but the most common is what the Rom call in English 'switch-the-bag' because the money (which is cursing the unfortunate person) is sewn up in a piece of cloth and switched for an identical bag containing cut up newspapers. *Bujo* is the *Romanes* word for 'bag'.

The Barvale Rom claim that they will not pull a *bujo* because it causes too much trouble. They would have to go on the run, and it would spoil their good relations with the police. Apparently since the FBI have cracked down on the *bujo*, and the Rom cannot flee to another state, the number of *bujo* frauds has dropped considerably. John Marks had a very pessimistic view of the future of fortune-telling:

> Fortune-telling is dead. The women are now doing legitimate fortune-telling. To make money you have to take people and be on the move all the time. I never did go for that. I can make a good living without any scheme. Some women don't bother to tell fortunes now because there's not much in it if you don't steal.

However, John, like other Rom, protects his fortune-telling area zealously and will not allow others to move into his territory. The new kind of scheme for fortune-telling seems to be like the one explained by this Machwaya fortune-teller.

> I once had a long discussion with a Machwaya career fortune-teller regarding the ethics of her trade. She made a point of distinguishing between the boojo (*bujo*) which was a 'swindle' and simple overcharging which was 'fair'. She never practised the boojo, not because it was against her principles, but because it was 'bad business'. One had to be continually on the run if one practised the boojo. It is safer and more profitable simply to overcharge an occasional well-heeled customer. She claimed that she had once gotten $800 from one woman for three sessions. She felt that the woman had gotten her money's worth because she had been given good advice (along the lines of the 'Power of Positive Thinking'), and had been greatly

helped as a result. This fortune-teller said that most of her customers were depressed women who needed someone to talk to. She compared her services to those of a 'psychological doctor'. (Tompkins 1967: 10–11)

Fortune-telling is always a method of making money, the *bujo* being the spectacular take. Irving Brown has described it aptly:

Nine-tenths of all fortune telling is an exhibition of skill in extracting money rather than in rending secrets from the future. It is also an exhibition of character reading, which in the case of certain Romanies I know is nothing short of miraculous. By long practice they have cultivated their powers of observation and sub-conscious reasoning to a degree that makes an open book of the entire person to whom they are giving a 'reading'. As they themselves are not always conscious of how they do it they attribute their remarkable powers to supernatural causes; and thus a few *dukkerers* believe that if they so desire they can tell 'true' fortunes. Likewise, many gypsies believe in the truth of dreams, though they use them also to hoax. (Brown 1924: 95–6)

Actually, all female occupations – welfare, fortune-telling, selling plastic flowers, picking pockets, begging – are methods of extracting money that require powers of observation and skill in evaluating personalities.

Farm Labour

Farm labour was a major source of income for many Rom families until five years ago when automation in the fields made this area of operations increasingly more difficult. Most families still do farm labour in the summer, but they are unable to save enough to live for the winter; therefore they return to Barvale in the autumn and apply for welfare again.

Many families applying for welfare for the first time stated that formerly they had been supporting themselves with farm labour the year round. Several also had given up farm labour because of illness or incapacity to do the strenuous work. The Kashtare families claimed that they never needed welfare until farm labour failed to provide enough support for the whole year.

When families are engaged in farm labour the year round, they

camp in the fields or stay in 'fruit shacks' provided by the employer. One girl of twenty-five told me that she had lived all her
life in camps in the fields, with occasional residence in Los Angeles
in the slack winter months. Camping and moving from field to
field following the crops is attractive to many Rom families who
like to be on the move and work together in family groups; however, they all agree that it is a hard life.

The present pattern of farm labour is for the patriarch (*phuro*)
of each family to lead his families to the agricultural areas where
he has arranged a contract with a local grower. In 1965 and 1966,
Spiro George made a contract with a grower for five of his families,
and he himself got two cents for every crate of tomatoes picked by
the younger members of his *familia*. Welfare records show that at
least six *familiyi* were led by their patriarchs to work while the
patriarch supervised the arrangements and presumably got a
pakiv for his services. One social worker described a Kashtare
family in this way:

> I got quite a bit of information about their routine while the
> families are on the road. They travel about in cars and live in
> tents, cooking their food communally. Stevan arranges for the
> jobs and the camping space. He does not, however, actually
> work himself and has not done so for about eight years. While
> the families work (including his own wife and children) Stevan
> will go fishing in a nearby stream. Occasionally he will bring
> water and refreshments to the workers and he will negotiate
> with the employer any problems which might arise. I assume
> that there must be some kind of shared income arrangement.
> I assume also that Stevan scouted out the welfare department
> and approved it for his family just as he would an agricultural
> employer. In fact, the family recently gave him a station wagon.

In 1967, Stevan personally contacted the employment office,
located jobs for his relatives but, because of poor health, was unable to lead them to work as usual. However, in the summer of
1970 when his families went to Oregon to pick green beans he
went with them for a few weeks, presumably to supervise negotiations.

When working in the fields, the whole family participates. They
live in their own camp or set of shacks and keep separate from the
other *gaje* workers. Farm labour does not conflict with their desire
to maintain control over their own way of life since their employers

do not care how they live or what they do so long as they pick the fruit or vegetables. Their only contact with the *gaje* is through the employer, and this contact is handled by the patriarch. The mobility they are able to have is so desirable that most able-bodied families will do farm labour in the summer even when they earn less than their welfare grant provides.

Male Occupations

Although women do most of the work that brings in an income, men generally handle the aspects of the women's work that is required to set them up in business. Men arrange for an *ofisa* or a fortune-telling concession in a carnival; they advertise the business in the local newspapers, hand out printed handbills, and make the sign to go outside. They also protect her from the amorous advances or irate threats of her customers. They arrange farm labour contracts and negotiate pay and conditions, although women and children reputedly do the most work. Men scout out a welfare department to find out the rules and conditions – who to see and what sort of line is most likely to be effective – but it is the women who handle the negotiations. If a woman is wanted for a crime they handle her disappearance, and if she is arrested they arrange bail and lawyers.

There are many occupations that only men pursue and that are not auxiliary to the work of the women. However, I shall limit this description to work that was done at various times by men in the Barvale *kumpania*. The most common occupation of the men was auto body repairs. One man described how they solicit jobs.

> We drive around up and down the streets until we see a car with a dent in it. Then we approach the owner and offer to fix the dent for a few dollars. If the owner says yes, then we do the repair job. I always carry three tools: a dolly, a screwdriver, and a tapping hammer.

The men do not take jobs with local garages. One young boy went to the Oakland Skills Center for two years and learned the trade quite successfully, but he would not take a job with a garage because he preferred to hustle jobs with the other boys.

Sometimes in the summer the men take off for longer journeys, seeking body and fender work in more lucrative and less tapped areas. One man gave an amazing description of how he was able to make a living for his family of nine during a three-month trip covering 1400 miles.

I went to Ventura County, pitched a tent in the state park and applied for welfare. But they said it would take two weeks to get a cheque and it was raining hard so we couldn't stay that long. So we went to Salinas, picked brocoli and got $40, $80 for fender repairs, and stayed in a motel. Then we went to Redwood City for two days and got $20 for a fender repair but were kicked out of town by the police. Then we went to Eureka, got no work and were told to leave. Then we went to Red Bluff, no work, and left after three hours. In Redding we got $30 in car repairs and lived two days in the car; then to Marysville and got $35-40 in fender repairs and stayed four days in a motel. Then, to Yuba City, no work, kicked out of a government camp. No work in Portersville, but in Bakersfield I earned $30 and stayed one week in a cabin for $18. Then in Fresno I got $10 from a Mitchell family (relatives) and in Sacramento another $10 loan from another Mitchell family. Then to Delano where I got $30 for fixing a fender, and when I arrived in Barvale the people (Rom) took up a collection to pay our first month's rent and I applied for welfare.

Some of the men who were more experienced coppersmiths still do re-tinning and repairing copper-bottomed pots for restaurants or repair the copper in steam drills and copper boilers. John Marks was fond of spending four to five months in the summer travelling around with other men soliciting these contracts. According to his statements he was able to make a good living legitimately. Here is a description of one job that was not so legitimate.

My brother Steve and three or four men went out to Alpine to the public schools and got the job of working on the boilers, about twelve of them in total. They re-built the fire pots and the oil burners and re-installed the boilers. They charged $6000 for the job and hired Mexican labour to do the unskilled work. Every night they would go into Mexico and drink too much tequila and had a hangover the next day so they didn't do too good a job. Also they used poor materials and lied about how much material they had used. They did this job in the summer, and in the fall, when the custodian fired up the boilers, the insulation started to peel away after a few weeks.

Some groups of men travel around in trucks and camp in parking lots. They tar roofs or spray asphalt on driveways. Some of them have developed quite a racket from this by diluting the tar so much that it never dries, but it costs less to them and therefore their profits are higher. By the time the home-owners discover their dilemma, the men have packed up their trucks and moved to another city. According to John Marks they can make $50 to $200 a day at this trade. No one in Barvale went in for this line of work because the police were wise to this scheme; however, several groups of these roof tarrers passed through Barvale each year.

Whatever their trade, men operate independently of any firms, going from place to place soliciting a contract and carrying their tools with them. Occasionally men did take employment from a *gajo* for two or three days, but they never did so on a long-term basis. I was not allowed to accompany the men on their work, nor was it discussed with me in any great detail. Income from the men's labours was never revealed either since it was not reported to their social worker.

Older men generally have some debilitating illness and do not practise a trade, much preferring to leave this to their young sons, their wife, and their *bori*. Most of them claim to be coppersmiths (among the Kalderash) though many had not done any coppersmith work for years. One old man gave the following job history which illustrates the changes which have taken place in the occupations of men over the last fifty years.

date of job	duties	reason for leaving
1915–25	horse trading, driving horses from Montana to east and west coast cities	emergence of auto
1925–41	coppersmith, re-tinning pots and pans	skill became obsolete
1941–5	shipyard work	end of war
1945–64	farm labour	seasonal work, disability
1965–70	welfare	

It should not be assumed that welfare is the final and ultimate occupation for the Rom. During the 1930s, many Rom went on welfare only to leave when the economic situation improved. Young men work nowadays even when they are unable to make much. In places where fortune-telling is illegal, welfare is often necessary, but in places where it is possible to do fortune-telling, such as in Texas, Hawaii, and Alaska, the Rom will flock there to tell fortunes. I suspect that if the ban on fortune-telling were lifted in Barvale, most women would prefer to work.

Other Schemes

There are several other less legitimate ways of making a living, such as stealing and picking pockets, though in Barvale the Rom keep away from this owing to their relations with the police. Most Rom prefer to convince the *gaje* to give them money rather than have to steal it. As in other occupations, women work in teams (*wortacha*) and often take along children who are a great advantage since they are small, quick, and cannot be thrown in jail.

> Officers report that five local housewives have reported being victimized by a heavily built Gypsy woman in her mid-forties, a second Gypsy woman ranging from sixteen to twenty years and a four-year-old Gypsy girl. Other cases are on file from San Pablo, Oakland, and Berkeley housewives.

> Here is how the bunco game works, police say: One of the adults will knock on the door and plead to be allowed to enter. The excuse will be that they wish to heat a baby bottle or that the child must use the bathroom. Once inside the house, the adults will split up. While one engages the householder in conversation, the second will take the child either to the kitchen or bathroom where apparently both take anything of value they find. In some cases, the Gypsy women laid their hands on the victims under the pretence of massaging them or curing their ills. Actually, according to police, the women were searching them for valuables – or distracting them while another member rifled through a purse. (*Richmond Independent*, 22 May 1968: 35)

‘GYPSY WOMAN’ HIT-RUN THEFT
A hit-run thief, described as a young gypsy woman, propositioned an El Sobrante man, then ran away with $100 she

plucked from his shirt pocket. When he refused her proposition, Heim said the woman reached in through the open window, grabbed the money that was sticking out of his shirt pocket and ran away. Heim attempted to follow when a male accomplice 'appeared out of nowhere' and warned the robbery victim to leave the girl alone. He then struck Heim several times and fled. (*Richmond Independent*, 20 May 1968: 21)

There are several more imaginative schemes than stealing. Children with cerebral palsy make effective beggars, besides making them feel useful and economically independent. Families often ignore telephone, gas, and electricity bills, preferring simply to use another name in another place. At one *pomana* a family ran up a $778 telephone bill calling relatives to the funeral and then left town.

There are several schemes for travelling cheaply. Tickets are bought at half price by telephone and when a 'matured' child turns up at the airport, the Rom make a scene, and the airline is glad to put them aboard the plane. One man ordered over $10,000 in tickets by telephone, had them sent to relatives and never paid for them. When he was convicted, his relatives paid the airlines back the money on condition that he not be jailed. Several Rom have been able to get new Cadillacs for the price of the down-payment only by purchasing it on someone's credit card and then changing the licence plates into those of a State that does not require papers in order to register it. As long as they do not sell the car, it is virtually untraceable.

It always amazes me that illiterate Rom are able to work a highly complicated bureaucratic system to their advantage. False insurance claims, travel schemes, money from redevelopment, and all the complications of welfare bureaucracy are only challenges to them and they never tire of working out a new method for turning the *gaje* system to their advantage.

I should conclude with a reminder that these schemes are not necessarily practised by all Rom and that many of them are done only because these particular Rom have not been able to make a living in their traditional ways. The Rom in Barvale are very poor, and their economic relations, occupations, and income cannot be generalized to all Rom, some of whom are quite wealthy and successful businessmen in fortune-telling or the used-car business.

Conclusions

The Rom in Barvale are engaged in a large variety of schemes and
jobs in order to make a living; however, the basic income is from
welfare and auto-body repairs, supplemented by farm labour in
the summer. Both their basic work and the other peripheral earnings such as fortune-telling require a great deal of imagination,
aggression, and intelligence, as well as utilizing techniques in
'hustling' which they have developed from childhood.

The occupations which the Rom engage in have certain characteristics in common. First, an occupation must allow mobility and
flexibility. As noted in Chapter 2, mobility is not only essential as
a form of social control, but the freedom to travel is imperative
for a large number of social and religious reasons. This rules out
regular, full-time employment. Second, occupations must allow
Rom to work with other Rom either in family or household groups
or as partners in the *kumpania*. Occupations that require continuous contact with *gaje* are avoided and are *marime* (polluted).

Most families are able to thrive within these limitations to
earning a living; however, when a family fails to obtain a minimum
income for subsistence and for any reason cannot get aid from
relatives, the *kumpania* is a source of support. Through a collection,
the *kumpania* will help any family in good standing over hard
times. Generosity is a virtue and a form of insurance, for who
knows when he also will need economic assistance from the
kumpania. Generosity, mutual aid, and daily economic cooperation are normal patterns of behaviour between relatives and are
ideals of behaviour between all Rom; however, these ideals do not
extend outside this social boundary. Economic relations with *gaje*
are based on extraction, not cooperation and are governed by
ideals entirely different from those expected between Rom. These
ideals include cleverness and effectiveness in extracting money
co nbined with freedom from *gaje* influence and values.

4

Leadership and Conflict

This chapter has two disparate aims. The first is to give examples of situations of stress and conflict. This will provide a basis for later discussion of social categories and relationships, namely relationship terms, the *vitsa* and *natsia*. The second aim is to describe certain aspects of the political organization of the *kumpania*. These aspects are, (a) the role of the *rom baro* (leader), the power basis of leadership, and how leaders operate in situations of conflict, and (b) the social (gossip), legal (*diwano* and *kris romani*), and outside (*gaje* authorities) mechanisms which are used to solve disputes and enforce the laws (*romania*).

Four illustrations of conflict situations are described. The first two, the Easter *slava* fight and the Devil incident, which took place in Barvale, are concerned primarily with political rivalry and problem-solving within the *kumpania*. The second two, given in Appendix A exactly as they were described, are concerned with legal mechanisms of problem-solving which are necessary in cases of conflict between leaders of two *kumpaniyi*. One important factor that emerges from these cases of conflict is that they cannot be fully understood without an understanding of certain social categories, the relationship terms, the *vitsa*, the *natsia*, and the relative status between several *natsiyi*.

This discussion of political and jural matters is not an exhaustive study of Rom politics, which could be a major topic in itself, but is intended to illustrate political facets of social categories. I have had to limit the number of conflict situations described because the actual number recorded is too large to include here. In fact, one of the most apparent characteristics of the Rom is that they are almost constantly involved in conflict with each other, a factor that masks their equally intense solidarity as a group.

Although their expressions of solidarity may be less obvious than their expressions of conflict, the solidarity of the Rom is proportionally as intense as the degree of in-fighting.

Solidarity is perhaps best manifest when death or a serious illness occurs. The death of an adult male or female is treated as a loss to the whole group as well as a personal loss to relatives. Mourning by cognatic relatives, friends, and Rom from the area is extremely intense. As one man explained it: 'When there is a death or an illness, all Gypsies get together, whether they have to walk, sell everything, no matter what. It's a sign of respect. You can't understand how strong we are about sickness, about operations and the rest.' I was present on one occasion when a family, on being told of the death of a relative 500 miles away, dropped what they were doing and left within fifteen minutes for the funeral.[1]

Death is not the only time when the Rom come together as a group. Any serious trouble, such as an arrest, will unite everyone in a collective effort to help. If necessary, fines, bail, lawyer's fees, and bribes will be paid by a collection in the *kumpania*. This cooperation is more than a method of self-protection as a group against outsiders, it is also a measure of the value that is placed on group membership. Imprisonment, like death, means the loss of a member of the group. To go to jail is to have to live among the *gaje* and to be denied the fellowship of one's own people. Jail is a *marime* place in the sense that it requires separation from the Rom.

The Rom say that *marime* means being 'rejected' from the Rom as a group and being 'dirty' or polluted. For the moment, it is the sense of rejection that is most relevant. When a person is declared *marime* publicly, whether by a group of people (such as families in the *kumpania*) or more formally in a *kris romani* (trial), he is immediately denied commensality with other Rom. Anything he wears, touches, or uses personally is polluted (*marime*) for other Rom, and he is generally avoided in person as his *marime* condition can be passed on to others. *Marime* in the sense of 'rejected' from social intercourse with other Rom is the ultimate punishment in the society just as death is the ultimate punishment in other societies. For the period it lasts, *marime* is a social death.

Marime is a very effective punishment for several reasons. First, almost all social interaction among the Rom involves eating together. To be denied commensality is to be barred from the most enjoyable and important social contact. Second, a *marime* sentence always includes the family of the *marime* person so that an individual must consider the consequences of his actions for his family as well as for himself. Third, *marime* forces a person to 'associate' with the *gaje* in a way that he would not normally do. Finally, *marime* means a loss of respect and status in the group (even when re-instated) and contains the onus of uncleanliness and moral defilement.

Marime is the public rejection of a Rom by his society, however, even voluntary separation or separation imposed from outside is associated with *marime*. Jail, as I have mentioned, is a *marime* place because it means a long separation from the group and association with *gaje*. Relatives will make great sacrifices to protect each other from jail. When they do not, it is always because the individual has committed some offence which is difficult to punish, and it is convenient to let the *gaje* do it for them. Voluntary exile from the group is also a *marime* crime. This rarely happens because of a conscious choice to leave the group. More often it is because a sexual offence has occurred and the person involved leaves rather than face the consequences. I was able to verify only one case of a genuinely conscious choice to leave the group. This involved a young woman who left the *kumpania* and took up *gaje* employment. Within a year she was found and returned to her family by relatives. In the ensuing trial she and her family were given *marime* sentences for a specific period of time in order for her to be reinstated. Suicide is also viewed as extremely shocking and incomprehensible and may result in a *marime* sentence on the family of the suicide victim. The point which is important here is that the same intense emotion which is expressed against a person who has been declared *marime*, emotion which includes the horror of pollution, is also expressed in support of a person who is threatened with loss of physical or social life whether it be by illness or from American laws.

Part of the painfulness of being denied contact with one's own people, whether it be in a jail, a hospital, or a job, is that of being alone.[2] To be among a group of Rom is the natural everyday context within which a person lives, learns and expresses his personality; to be among a group of *gaje* is to be alone. Wherever he travels or lives, a Rom is rarely alone. More often he is surrounded by large numbers of relatives and friends. Only when he is rejected by the community or chooses to be by himself is the individual alone. Loneliness is perhaps the rarest condition an individual experiences in his lifetime.

As might be expected, visiting and gossip are major pastimes and it is rare to enter a home that does not have visitors or to find a group of Rom anywhere who are not discussing the recent events in their own or in other *kumpaniyi*. Just as the Nuer love to talk about cattle (Evans-Pritchard 1940), the Rom love to talk about each other. Of course the frequent marriages, baptisms, parties, feasts, and funerals, are always occasions for visiting and gossip.

Besides being a major pastime, gossip is also a major form of social control. It is the primary means of pressuring an individual. Once word gets around that some people consider another person's actions to be *marime*, others will not wish to risk contamination and will avoid him. Consequently, no individual can afford to ignore anyone's statements concerning his reputation no matter how unfounded in fact they may be. Gossip can make or break a person's reputation, and when it occurs it must be fought immediately. To ignore gossip would be tantamount to admitting guilt. This does not mean there are no curbs on gossiping. One man in Barvale was declared *marime* for six months for malicious gossiping.

Naturally, visiting and gossip take place among Rom who are living in close proximity, that is in the same or a nearby *kumpania*. People in nearby *kumpaniyi* are constantly in touch with each other and maintain an intense system of communication among themselves. They generally know what is happening, what is being talked about, and where people are. During travels, more distant relatives and *vitsi* members are contacted, and every traveller to an area brings news about people in the area he just left. Since there are always people coming and going from the *kumpania*, contact is maintained with many areas of North America. This enhances their sense of solidarity as a people since without communication, they could not maintain their social and moral system.

Of course, not all Rom meet each other in travels, and sometimes it is important to contact relatives or friends who are far away. For example, when there is a serious illness or death, relatives must come to the side of the stricken person. For these emergencies, the Rom have an amazing system of communication which makes it possible for one person to contact any other in a very short time. Even if the person has deliberately gone into hiding, he can often eventually be found. Although letter and telegraph are often used, the telephone is the main instrument of communication and it has been a great boon to communications in the last thirty years. In times of an urgent matter, I have known a telephone bill to total $700 in a few days.

The communication system works through the *kumpania* and *vitsa* units. Every *kumpania* leader has a list of key telephone numbers of other *kumpania* and *vitsa* leaders. They must have the number since it could be listed under any name. If they do not have a number for someone in the *vitsa* they want to contact, they can contact someone in the *kumpania* where he is likely to be and get a message to him. Since people are constantly on the move, and numbers go out of date quickly, a list of non-Gypsy telephone numbers is also required. A social worker well known by Gypsies describes how she became part of this communication system:

> In every Gypsy knapsack there is a scrap of paper somewhere containing a list of telephone numbers of key people in various parts of the country who can be relied upon to relay messages. These people are not Gypsies, but are policemen, social workers, undertakers, pawnshop operators, etc., who are known to be stable, reliable, and in constant contact with Gypsies in their area. I have received calls from all over the United States from people I don't know to transmit messages to people I usually don't know either. The caller always gives just as little information as possible; however, from the various names given, I can figure out which *vitsa* is involved, contact the leader of that group and the message gets through. (Tompkins 1967: 9)

When I myself became a link in the communication system, I found I also was receiving calls from people whom I did not know, to help locate someone thought to be in the vicinity.

Gossip, visiting, and other forms of communication are informal expressions of solidarity and means of social control. The formal system includes, (a) a code of tradition and rules called *romania*, (b) a legal body that makes decisions and enforces the rules (*diwano* and *kris romani*), and (c) punishment by fine or *marime* to enforce the legal decisions. *Romania* is the highest authority of the Rom, is accepted by all those who consider themselves Rom, and is given a kind of sacredness demanding obedience.[3] *Romania* is a set of moral codes and rules of behaviour known by all but interpreted primarily by elders. Disagreement about proper behaviour, takes the form of denying accusations or presenting contradictory statements of fact; the moral rules themselves are not usually questioned. Occasionally, they may be changed. A meeting of *vitsa* heads from all over the country was once held in Los Angeles to discuss 'new rules' for elopement, settlement of brideprice, and informing. *Romania* is an all-inclusive, obscure concept and is very difficult to define, but in a single context it is usually quite clear. In a sense this whole book is a statement of *romania* because *romania* includes traditions, customs, ideal behaviour, morals, beliefs, rituals, and attitudes. In practice, the force of *romania* is the general consensus of opinion on a particular question.

When a consensus of opinion cannot be reached, then the interpretation of *romania* must be taken to a final decision-making body, the *kris romani* which is said to be composed of a man and wife from each *vitsa* in the vicinity (which may be a very large area comprising five or six States) led by one or more judges. It is said that the '*vitsi* assemble' in a chosen place to hear both sides of the case and make a decision. Their decision is final and a man pledges to accept it before the *kris* convenes. Not to accept the decision would be to deny *romania*.

Punishment itself is rejection from *romania*. Punishment is to become *marime*, to be denied physical contact and social intercourse with one's own people, to be forced to 'live among the *gaje*', and to be polluted. *Romania* is social life; *marime* is social death. With these oppositions in mind – *romania/marime*, belonging/rejection, purity/pollution – we can now examine the political organization of the *kumpania* beginning with the basic principles of authority, sex, and age.

Secular Authority and Mystical Authority

An individual becomes increasingly more powerful with old age, a large *familia* following, a good reputation, and the establishment of effectiveness with *gaje* authorities in the *kumpania*. If a man has a strong and aggressive wife, is wealthy, and shows an ability and desire to help other Rom who come to him for aid, then he may become a leader, a *rom baro* or 'big man'.

The sexual division of authority is more difficult to define than it first appears. In general, the authority of the men is based on secular, political knowledge, such as manipulating *gaje* officials, using 'strong men' to scare or coerce opponents, and speaking and arguing well, especially in a *kris*. The authority of women is based on their knowledge of the *mule* (spirits of the dead), medicines and their innate ability to pollute (*marime*) a man. Men may appear dominant in many instances, but fear of mystical reprisals is not taken lightly by the Rom. Old Paraskiva was feared because 'when her brother died he said he would always take care of her'. Her dead brother was true to his word one day when she became involved in a fight once with her *Xanamik*. When they threatened to curse her, her brother appeared to the four of them, lying in a coffin with candles around him. After this vision, she was never crossed or contradicted again. The distinction between the power of men and the power of women is illustrated in the belief that death, the final authority, is a man, but a woman can scare him away by cursing him and threatening to lift her skirts over him to make him *marime*.

The division of male secular and female mystical authority has parallels in many other societies so it is not surprising to find it among the Rom. However, a simple opposition of secular and mystical authority would be very misleading of Rom politics. Whatever the basis of their authority the effect is that old women have a great deal of influence and secular power. There are many examples of old women who become the ruling force in a *kumpania* and control access to economic resources and *gaje* authorities. Barbara Miller of San Francisco is the most obvious case in northern California. Not only do women occasionally run a *kumpania*, but an old widow will undoubtedly be the ruling force in her *familia* and perform all the duties of a *familia* head normally performed by men. There is no difference in potential power of a *phuro* or *phuri*, but since widows are more common than widowers, this can have a great effect even on a male-headed *kumpania*. Of the five Kashtare *familiyi* in Barvale (who are powerful only if united, as they well know) two were led by men and three by women. And as far as effectiveness with *gaje* authorities is concerned, the most important *gaje* official in Barvale, the social worker, found:

> ... the oldest women in the families, in most cases, hold the power. The old men are respected and catered to, but the old women are feared, probably because of their occult reputations. Old Gypsy women understand the spirits and know all the

charms and healing potions. It is not wise to run afoul of them. (Tompkins 1965a: 3)

More than sex, age is the crucial factor in authority. Power and old age diminish sexual separation. Powerful old men and women can sit and talk with each other. In Barvale, this privilege was exercised mainly by the *rom baro* Stevan and his wife Yana. They were the only two old people who actually joined conversation circles of the opposite sex for longer than a few minutes.

Old people have more knowledge and authority than young people. The older one becomes, the more one knows about *romania*. Knowledge of *romania* is a great source of power, for *romania* is an absolute and final authority. Since an individual generally only learns about behaviour as the situation arises (cf. Rena Cotten 1950: 141, on learning) – for example, a woman knows nothing about procedure at birth until she herself has a baby – it is only the very old who can claim to know everything about life, beliefs, customs, and expected behaviour. In their persons, they embody the force of *romania*.

As men and women get older, more and more respect and authority is given to them. In *Romanes*, respect and authority are expressed by the word *pakiv* (or *dav pakiv*) which means to 'obey, respect, esteem or honour' (G. & L.). *Barearav* (which is the verb formed from *baro* (big)) is also translated as 'to honour, respect, and obey'. This concept is connected with the terms normally used for leaders who are *rom baro* ('big man') and *romni bari* ('big woman'). To be *baro*, means to be obeyed and respected and, by implication, to be old.

Although old age is essential for authority, not every *phuro* (old man) or *phuri* (old woman) becomes a *rom baro* or *romni bari*. The difference is that a *rom baro* heads his *kumpania* or his *vitsa* and *kumpania* whereas the eldest patriarch (*phuro*) or matriarch (*phuri*) has authority over a limited number of families who are their descendants. John Marks claimed to be *rom baro* for his *vitsa* as well as his *kumpania*, and judging from the examples of cases he handled, the places he had to go, and the numbers of *vitsa* members from other *kumpaniyi* who came to him for guidance, this claim is probably true. According to him, he was 'picked' for leadership by his father and father's brothers (*vitsa*) because he knew English well, had learned something about the law (American law), and 'word got around that I was able to help people with the law'.

Stevan at times claimed leadership for his *vitsa*, for example in the statement 'my father's people (*vitsa*) always send their girls (with marital problems) to me', but I doubt if his influence extended much farther than his own *kumpania*.

In any case, the *rom baro* has authority that goes beyond his own *familia* whether it is his *kumpania* or his *vitsa* and *kumpania*. At the same time a *rom baro* has the same duties to his *familia* as any other head of *familia* (*phuro*), and in any *kumpania* there may be several *phuro* or *phuri* whose word is law for their kin. In most cases, there is only one *rom baro* for a *kumpania*.[4] Stevan's position as *rom baro* in Barvale was fairly weak in the beginning but has become consolidated in the last few years. His two main contenders are a Kuneshti (Miller George) and a Machwano (Joe Adams) who claim they do not recognize his position (primarily because they do not want to accept leadership from a person of another *natsia*), although like everyone else, they rely on him in times of trouble.

Stevan has several advantages over them. Both Miller and Joe have authority over only a small family whereas Stevan not only has a large *familia* which includes six married children and their spouses, but also has numerous other *familiyi* of his *vitsa* in Barvale. They will usually support him when his opponent is of another *vitsa* or *natsia*. He also has established himself as a leader with the police and with the welfare department, the two most important *gaje* official bodies for the *kumpania*. They have accepted him as the liaison between themselves and the *kumpania*. This position is also accepted by newcomers to the *kumpania* who seek his recommendation with the social worker to apply for welfare. Newcomers who by-pass him are immediately visited by him and his wife and must get his stamp of approval. Those who challenge his position are deemed 'trouble makers' or 'bad Gypsies' with the authorities and are eventually forced to leave the *kumpania*.

Stevan is very able at dealing with the *gaje* who usually find him a personable man. He is extremely large (350 lb) and is an impressive speaker with a loud voice. His wife is also very respected and has an even louder voice and imposing appearance. On the other hand, Miller George is small, weaselish and very unimpressive, and Joe Adams is married to a *gaji*, facts that make their chances of assuming leadership unlikely.

Roles of the Rom Baro

Some of the duties of a *rom baro* to his *vitsa* or *kumpania* are the same as the duties of a *phuro* to his *familia*. The role of the *phuro* is very important because he has strong control over his *familia* and may be a contender for *kumpania* leadership. Basically, the *phuro* or *phuri* is responsible for handling only problems that arise in his *familia*, although he may enlist the aid of the *rom baro*. These include marital and legal problems, contracts for summer work, and arrangements for ritual feasts. The difference between a *rom baro* and a *phuro* is basically (a) realm of authority, which is correlated with (b) amount of authority. For example, the strength of Stevan's authority was greatest as *phuro* for his own *familia*, less as *rom baro* for the five Kashtare *familiyi* in Barvale, less again as *rom baro* for the *kumpania* as a whole, least for his *vitsa*, and non-existent for his *natsia*. It must be stressed that it would be very difficult for a *phuro* to become *rom baro* without the following of a large *familia* which congregates under his authority. For this reason, one of the first tactics of a leader is to bring as many relatives as possible into his *kumpania*, smooth over difficulties for them, and help them to get set up economically. In return, they can usually be relied upon to give support for his leadership. On the other hand, he is also anxious to keep out non-relatives who will not support him and whose loyalty is to their own *phuro*. This is one reason why a *kumpania* generally tends towards consolidation under one leader and one *vitsa* until some event occurs to shift the balance of power.

Basically the duties of a *rom baro* fall into two major sections: (a) to handle all internal problems that arise in the *kumpania* or in the *vitsa*. These include disagreements in work, marriage, family relations, trials, funerals, etc.; and (b) to handle all affairs with *gaje* authorities in the *kumpania*, help anyone who is in trouble with American law, arrange work contracts, establish relations with the authorities which are advantageous to the goals of the Rom community, and deal effectively with outside pressures to conform to American society. This description by his social worker of 'Big Mick's' role in Barvale gives a fair idea of the range of duties.

'Big Mick' now freely admits that he is the regional Gypsy leader and says his territory extends as far north as Santa Rosa and as far south as Oakland. He officiates at weddings and funerals, negotiates with the police on behalf of Gypsies who are in trouble, and takes up collections for funerals and to bail someone out of jail. He has unsuccessfully attempted to set up a fortune-telling business in this area by negotiating with the police. Fortune-telling here is illegal. 'Big Mick' has close contact with the police, and I suspect that he is an informant on occasions when he wishes to punish someone.

A Rom who can claim to have 'influence' with non-Gypsies who are themselves in a position of authority (police, social workers, judges, district attorneys, lawyers, politicians, civil servants, etc.) can use this influence or threat of influence to coerce other Rom. Other Rom fear his ability to get them arrested or harassed by these authorities. Often this influence is highly exaggerated, but sometimes it is based on fact, such as when bribing does take place. A more subtle approach is to gain knowledge of the laws and manipulate them for one's own political advantage. Both these methods are used to handle internal as well as external problems. The law may be used to get a daughter returned from a *Xanamik* by claiming she has been 'kidnapped' or claiming that 'statutory rape' has taken place. A fight may be stopped or a brideprice returned by taking out a warrant for someone's arrest and then dropping the charges when the money is paid. Finally, there is always the threat of getting someone cut off welfare. Yana claims she can have anyone 'kicked out of the *kumpania* because she and Stevan have influence with the police and welfare'. All these methods of coercion require a knowledge of law, police, and welfare procedures. They represent one way in which *gaje* support the internal political system by enforcing rules which the Rom themselves have difficulty in enforcing. Tompkins (1967: 6) writes of two examples of the use of the police to solve internal conflicts:

Since Gypsies have no jails of their own, they will sometimes use our civil law enforcement agencies to satisfy personal grudges. These episodes usually involve false reports of theft or kidnapping. The irate Gypsy will go to the police and claim that another Gypsy has taken a large sum of money from him. He will keep pestering the police until they apprehend the accused thief. Sometimes the 'thief' will even be extradited from another State. After he is brought within the jurisdiction of the local Gypsy court (*kris*), civil charges are usually dropped and the police are apprised of the fact that they have been used.

Also the police have been, on several occasions, very helpful in collecting brideprices. Many of the girls are married very young, in non-recorded Gypsy ceremonies. If the husband's family reneges on the agreed upon brideprice, the bride's father has the recourse of going to the police and swearing that his minor daughter has been kidnapped for immoral purposes. He, of course, will not mention the fact that his daughter was married in a Gypsy ceremony with his consent. The daughter will be located and returned to her father, and the husband will be charged with statutory rape. If the husband's family then pays up, the charges will be dropped, the girl will be returned to her husband, and all parties will generally disappear, much to the mystification of the Police Department.

The two *kris* cases in Appendix A are detailed examples of the same procedure.

Influence with police or welfare authorities is not only used as a form of social control but is also used to help people in the *kumpania*. Through trial and error, the *kumpania* has built up a body of knowledge and experience with social workers so that they know exactly which story and type of behaviour reveals as little as possible about themselves yet still establishes their eligibility for welfare. They also know which stories the social worker is not likely to accept (even if they are true).

Stevan and other *phuria* advise new families on how to obtain welfare quickly, what to say and what not to say in the intake interview, and how to obtain the necessary documents. Birth certificates, for example, are usually provided by having some old lady make a midwife's statement. This means that ages can be accommodated to welfare regulations. Even if she were the actual midwife (and one local *phuri* seems to have delivered a large number of babies), it is very unlikely that she would remember the date; however, the welfare department is required to accept a midwife's affidavit. Therefore a new family can claim that a large number of children are 'under sixteen' so that they can be included on the cheque without being in school.

Problems over school attendance and medical examination (for ATD eligibility), psychological examination (see Chapter 3 on the techniques of behaviour with a psychologist), and employment (or adult education) for men, are also handled or advised by the *rom baro* or *phuro* who has experience and knowledge in these matters. Any problem which he handles for a family enhances his reputation for being effective at dealing with the *gaje* and re-inforces his leadership.

Once, when pressure from the welfare department was mounted on the community over school truances and violation of garbage regulations, and at the same time several leaders were vieing for authority in the *kumpania*, Stevan, who was trying to get police and welfare support of his leadership, took the following tactic:

> He promised me that he would round up all of the children [of his *vitsa*] and take them to school the following Monday morning. This is exactly what he did. His wife reported that he had gotten up early in the morning, had driven around from house to house forcing all the children to get out of bed, get dressed and get into his car. Approximately 10 a.m. he had them all rounded up and delivered them to Peres School. The School Secretary was very upset, and the School Principal was quite stupefied when this 350 lb. Gypsy in a big Stetson hat arrived with all these ragged children and demanded that the Principal take good care of them. What made the scene even more memorable was that he drove up in his big silver Cadillac which barely runs but provides an impressive front. (Welfare Record)

Needless to say, to the delight of the school authorities, he never did this again. But he took the following course with the police:

> Stevan has formed an informer relationship with the police department. The police call him whenever any of the families under his control misbehave in the community. He is constantly taking up collections to pay traffic fines; he has forced all of his relations to buy garbage cans and to keep their houses neat. The other families [of his *vitsa*] do not appear to resent Stevan's authority; however, those in the Kuneshti and Machwaya tribes (*vitsi*) are unhappy about his friendliness with the police and are concerned about his presumed influence with this department (welfare). Stevan, of course, makes the most of his position, and I'm sure he takes credit for the Gypsy cases which we accept or reject in our intake office. Although he is extremely insistent (in front of the social worker) that all of his relatives put their children in school, he is very resistant where his own

children are concerned. I think that he figures that if he goes on record as supporting education, we will overlook the fact that his own children are not in school. (Welfare Record)

There are other problems besides welfare which occur in the *kumpania*. John Marks dealt with arrests for swindles by his relatives and worked with the police, usually making a deal with them to pay the money back if they would drop charges. One leader in Oregon contacted the Oregon Rehabilitation Agency and suggested a scheme for 'rehabilitating' the men in his *kumpania* by training them in the auto sales business. Every male got a 'salary' during 'training' and the leader became an official 'aide' in the programme, taking an even better salary than the trainees. The whole programme cost $71 000.[5] Stevan has taken advantage of several schemes such as this in Barvale. Relocation money for families living in slum redevelopment areas was available at one time and several families who moved from one condemned house to another legally received $500 each. Some suggested doing this again, but the welfare department understandably refused. Stevan has also managed to buy a house with financial aid from the welfare department by claiming he has 'special housing needs' which is, of course, perfectly true since landlords frequently evict Rom families.

In Barvale, influence with the welfare department and the social worker who handles the Gypsy caseload is so important that when 'Big Mick' left the *kumpania*, one Kashtare elder simply came to her and asked her to make him the leader. Another contender went to the police with the same request. Both welfare and police told them they would have to work it out themselves (and implicitly the winner would get their support). This they did at the annual meeting of the *kumpania* with the police department. Every year the police call a meeting with the Gypsy community to tell them that they have to send their children to school, buy garbage cans, and in general comply with the law. That year (1968) after their usual vehement agreement with all these mandates from the police (those whose children are least in school agree most ardently), they asked to be left alone a short while. The police and social workers agreed reluctantly, and after fifteen minutes of tremendous noise and shouting, the Kuneshti, led by their contender Miller George, walked out looking disgruntled, and the Kashtare, led by Stevan, emerged victorious. Stevan shook hands with the police and social workers adding, 'we'll have this town organized now. You can come to me with any problems'.

Stevan's next step in consolidating his leadership was to 'get authority from Sacramento' (the State capital). At the time, a new law was being put before the Senate to raise the monthly amount of welfare cheques, and State Senator Nejedly was supporting the bill. He sent around a form letter asking all those on welfare to write to their representatives in support of the bill. As welfare recipients, the Gypsies received these form letters. Stevan took his letter to be a personal plea for the support of the *kumpania*. He was also probably the only welfare recipient who read it. He went to his social worker and asked her what he should do since he cannot write. She suggested they all sign a petition in support of the bill and send it to the Senator. He then went to every home, had tea with them, talked with them, and got the petition signed. This alone took several days. Instead of mailing it, he took it to Sacramento, told the Senator's secretary that the Senator wanted to see him personally, and somehow convinced her to agree to it. Nejedly appeared, had coffee with Stevan, and gave him a guided tour of the Capitol. Stevan came back to Barvale with his prestige greatly enhanced. His story of his 'friendship and influence' with the Senator was very impressive, and the other contenders for leadership lost their last hope. Of course, when the bill was passed, Stevan took credit for getting their 'little cheques increased'. Yana's version of this trip is interesting in that she makes it the key point in Stevan's rise to power:

> We went to see Nejedly in Sacramento. We told all the Gypsies to come with us to meet this man, but they said we were crazy so we went by ourselves. He gave us the authority. So then we went to Janet (the social worker) and we said, 'O.K. Janet, we'll build this town together', so Stevan did. See, he got Senator Nejedly's card (calling card), and he got his own house. These two things make everyone jealous. But we built this town. And we don't want no Machwaya on the school board (Romany School). They take advantage because they are more educated.

Building up 'influence' with *gaje* authorities is a major criterion for getting control of the *kumpania*. But a leader must also have 'influence' with his own people. He must have a large family and *vitsa* following in the *kumpania*, be well-respected, give impressive speeches, be large and strong, and have lots of grandchildren.

When he fulfils these conditions, he must then be clever and crafty enough to enlist the support of *gaje* authorities, smooth the path for his people with them, and be effective in getting them out of trouble. He is the bridge between the Rom and the *gaje*.

One might wonder what the police, social workers, and other officials think of Rom political manœuvres. The primary reaction is, I believe, confusion. I have no doubt that Senator Nejedly was entirely ignorant of the effect his calling card had on the Barvale *kumpania*. Most likely he thought of Stevan as a somewhat over-powering eccentric man rather than a crafty politician. The police and social workers in many cases, especially when their experience with Gypsies is limited, do not realize the full extent of their usefulness to the Rom community.

In Barvale where the Rom have been living in large numbers since 1965, the authorities have considerable experience in dealing with them. They often know that they are being used to settle a feud, enhance a particular leader's power, or to make money (the police in a neighbouring town still will pay a Gypsy informant, whereas in Barvale, they have learned to avoid this since the 'informant' is not informing, but using the threat of informing to coerce another Rom). However, even when they do know the full significance of the events, there is usually little they can do about it. Both police and social workers see their role as agents of the law. If a man takes out a warrant on another or gives even slight evidence of welfare fraud, it must be investigated, even if it is known that this is being done for another reason. Then if the same person drops the warrant or refuses to bring proof of welfare fraud, again there is nothing else to do but drop the case. Meanwhile the primary objective for the Rom has been achieved.

A policeman or social worker may not like the allegation that Stevan has 'influence' with them, but what can they do but deny it (which has little effect on the community since they know that an official could hardly admit it). For the people in the *kumpania* proof of Stevan's influence is that he is effective in dealing with *gaje*, and does solve their problems with authorities. Also Stevan invites *gaje* to social functions, gives them places of honour next to him, flatters them, and introduces them as 'my social worker'. One policeman in Barvale was known only as 'Miller's policeman' because of his quite obvious friendship with the Kuneshti leader. Stevan also shows his people cards, sheriffs' badges, letters of recommendation, cheques (for informing), photographs of himself taken with *gaje* officials – any visible proof of 'influence' with authorities.

Whenever photographs were taken, a round of political photographs was first necessary. Stevan once asked to have his picture taken with the head of the welfare department because 'she is the one who signs the cheques'. No doubt he was planning to take credit for getting everyone's cheque signed each month. However, although there is an element of bluff, it is quite true that Stevan does have the support of the police and social workers and that he is very effective at working out problems with them. If this were not so, his 'proofs' would soon become meaningless.

Dealing with the *gaje* in order to gain influence with them, make money from them, or get them to help solve *kumpania* problems is only one area of relations in which the *rom baro* helps his people and increases his authority and prestige. He is also a leader in internal affairs. He must solve problems and disagreements, not involving the *gaje*, that arise in the *kumpania*, and his fairness, judgement, and ability in these situations will be tested each time, either enhancing or lowering his prestige. His own behaviour and that of his family, is expected to be morally exemplary, and he often punishes those who defy the moral code. He must be generous and share any wealth and good fortune with his people. He may be expected to give a *pakiv* in honour of an out-of-town guest, not only to show his generosity to his people, but to enhance his prestige by hob-nobbing with illustrious men. He takes up collections for destitute people, handles marriages, trials, and *pomana* arrangements, and is expected to be generous in giving to any collection.

A *rom baro* who effectively handles problems that arise in his *kumpania* or *vitsa* gains prestige, but if he refuses to help people, his usefulness as a leader begins to wane. John Marks described his situation in this manner:

> I would not be the celebrity I am now if I had to do it all over again. People call me, and I have to handle all cases, divorce cases and all sorts of trouble and go no matter where it is. If I hadn't this position, I would not have gone to the extremes I did to prove I was a big man. That's where I made my mistake. It cost me a lot of money, a lot of money.

In Barvale most problems are brought to Stevan for a judgement, even by his rivals. However, several people were disgruntled with his leadership because they felt he did not do enough for them. At the Easter fight in which Stevan was himself involved, his opponents made deprecating statements about his position. His sister-in-law (BW) remarked:

> If he wants to be 'king', he has to help people. He didn't help Sonia when her house burned down. He is trying to kick me out of town and get my house for his son because I have no man to protect me. That is not what a 'king' does. If he wants to tell us what to do, push us around, and say our kids have to go to school, then he has to help people too.

And Spiro, whose car was smashed up, said:

> He should have a collection to pay for my car but look, he didn't even show up for the *kris*, and his sons are threatening my Nicky and Tommy.

Presumably every leader meets this criticism sometime. When 'Big Mick' was *rom baro* an old woman remarked: 'If he were really king, he would be rich and take care of all of us.'

One of the problems that always arises for a *kumpania* leader is the availability of work. Stevan has often organized summer farm work for other Kashtare, though he rarely extends this to other *vitsi*. Nevertheless, he claims that it is only with his recommendation that they can all get welfare and newcomers accept this prerequisite.

Another duty of the *rom baro* is to handle marriages, divorces, *pomana* arrangements, and enforce morals in general. Big George Adams, a respected and wealthy *rom baro* in the area, is usually selected as judge in a *kris*. He is not only the most powerful *rom baro* in the area but is also reputed to have high moral standards and to exercise *kris* judgements fairly. Stevan handles many divorces for his own *vitsa*, and often the women involved stay with him in hiding until the situation is settled. 'Big Mick' actually found a husband for one old lady in his *kumpania*:

> Shortly after she arrived, I was informed by the Gypsy leader 'Big Mick' that he had selected a husband for Rosie Brown. The prospective groom was a 63 year old bachelor who has been a house guest of 'Big Mick's' for the last few months. (Welfare Record)

When word got around that one lady had a 'friend' keeping his house trailer in her yard, 'Big Mick' was indignant and forced them to get married, performing the ceremony himself:

> 'Big Mick' mentioned a problem which was of utmost concern to the Gypsies in this area. He said that there was a certain old couple who were 'carrying on' and the Gypsies were quite upset because they were setting a bad example to the Gypsy teenagers whom the parents were trying to control. He said the Gypsy community was insisting that the couple either split up or get married. 'Big Mick' performed the Gypsy ceremony. [He] . . . 'phoned me to report the marriage and stated that the Gypsy community was now satisfied and that the old couple had regained status within the group. (Welfare Record)

At one time, 'Big Mick' had a woman committed to a mental institution because her behaviour[6] was disapproved of by the community. Her husband was furious that 'Big Mick' did this 'because he's no relative of mine'. Her husband died a few days later while she was still in the institution (Napa State Hospital). 'Big Mick' not only arranged for her to be released but organized the entire funeral arrangements for her husband. He contacted all the relatives of the husband and took up a collection for the funeral. Then he and several men went to Napa to collect the wife for the funeral, an accomplishment which caused her social worker to write: 'they managed something which no-one else has ever been able to manage, that is, getting a person out of Napa so soon' (after five days). The staff there explained that several 'burly uncles' had arrived, picked her up and talked the Director into releasing her (Welfare Record).

On one occasion, Stevan also demonstrated his ability to 'punish' someone for his behaviour, in this case, Miller, his political rival. Although Stevan did not say why Miller and his family were being ostracized by the *kumpania*, it almost certainly had to do with Miller's informer relationship with the police. Ostracism is extremely effective because it was agreed by all that 'he would have had to leave town if the people didn't visit them no more'. Miller repented his ways and Stevan called a meeting in the park where he publicly announced that the ostracism of Miller George and his family should end. Later Stevan explained:

> if you go to someone's house, they will take the chair and turn it away or fold it up to show that you are not wanted. If I tell

them to do this with someone they will. Then that person will have to leave town. That is the way it is. But this meeting is the way things should be done to get the people together. Now everybody will get organized, and we will keep Gypsies out of town who might cause trouble.

Public ostracism, which implies that the person is *marime* or unclean, is very effective; the shame (*lashav*) is so great that the family will leave town or as in this particular case, ask to be reinstated in a public meeting (*diwano*).

Symbols of Leadership

The term for leader, *rom baro* or 'big man' does not refer only to size in the sense of greatness, power, or authority, but also to physical attributes. To be large, tall, big in frame, fat, and have a large head are all physical ideals in general, but particularly for a *rom baro*. It is not accidental that of the three men vieing for leadership in Barvale, the most powerful was also the largest in physical size. In fact their physical size corresponds proportionally with the amount of influence they had in the community. 'Big Mick' was over six feet tall which is very large for a Rom and was very heavy set. Stevan weighed 350 lb, a fact that prompted John Marks to take along 'six of the Marks muscle boys' to Wichita, Kansas, to settle his son's divorce (Appendix A, Case 1). Stevan's wife once lamented that he used to weigh 400 lb, and she preferred him that way. In general, when speaking of the power of a *rom baro*, people refer to the man's size as if to prove their point.

A large head is particularly important, and this can be enhanced by wearing a large hat, usually a stetson, and having large moustaches. When recounting the greatness of ancestors, the largeness of his moustache is often included in the description, such as 'he had moustaches which went to the ground'. Stevan grew a moustache as he consolidated his position in the *kumpania* because, as one lady remarked, 'if he is going to be big, he must have a big moustache'. The head and hat are important symbols of authority and prestige. Just as a woman must remove her jewellery (her symbols of prestige) at a *pomana*, a man cannot wear a hat. This is the only time that it was prescribed that a hat be removed. There is one myth about the infamous Tiny Bimbo which explains that he got his power from the hat that he stole from the Devil's head while engaged in a fight with him. At the St Anne *slava* in Barvale, the head of the lamb was carefully preserved on the table and then taken home for Stevan and his sons to eat. Later, Stevan's *bori* explained the eating of the head: 'it's not for health (like the rest of the *slava*) but is good for the head man. It's like strength; we believe in that.' The word for head (*shero*) also means 'headman', leader, or chief (G. & L.).

Along with a large and impressive stetson hat, the rest of the Western clothing is a favourite outfit of authoritative men. Stevan generally wore a silver buckled belt, boots, a string tie with silver clasp, and a suit cut in the Western fashion. He also wore a sheriff's badge and when a rival got one he was furious and made him take it off. Stevan promptly went out and had one made in gold twice the size of the last one.

A very important factor in leadership is wealth. Wealth is displayed in specific ways, primarily in the gold jewellery which the wife wears, but also in a large and expensive car. Ownership of property is also being stressed recently, and I did not hear of an important leader who did not boast of owning property although very few other Rom were interested in property as it was detrimental to their mobility. Wealth is also shown by generosity, and a leader who is generous is highly respected by all. In August, Stevan gave an elaborate *slava* (which took all the savings from his sons' summer work) and conspicuously invited other prominent men from nearby *kumpaniyi*. Though formerly they had not taken Stevan seriously, these men did attend and eat with him, and this was taken as tacit acceptance of his position. As a result, Stevan's prestige was greatly enhanced by this *slava*. A man who is wealthy is almost certain to have authority and prestige, but it is possible to make a show of wealth to compensate for the lack of it. Stevan is not wealthy, and this is a drawback to his consolidation of authority, but he compensates for this by a demonstration of wealth. For instance, he can now claim that he 'owns property' although the downpayment was given by the welfare department, and the monthly payments come from his welfare cheque.

Finally, other symbols of power are needed as proof of influence with *gaje* officials. These may be calling cards, letters from *gaje* officials or any evidence of having 'worked' for them, such as a cheque from the police department. One man actually got his son to take a job as a policeman so he could ride around in a police car to the houses of intruders in the *kumpania* and scare them away. When the Romany school received a picture of President Nixon, a Machwano rival was very upset when Stevan took it home with him because 'he has too much power already. It will make him too big.'

Conflict

But what are the implications of leadership in a situation of conflict? In a dynamic context, how effective is the leader at problem-solving? There is another aspect of conflict which also must be considered. Recently, there has been a great deal of work on conflict as one 'arena' of the field of politics.[7] Political contests for access to and use of power are situations in which social process can be studied in relation to the social framework – the relationships, groups, values, and economic resources – of a particular society. The cases that are described here illustrate the operation of leadership, the role of *gaje* authorities, the meaning and value placed on social categories and groups (kinship relations, the *vitsa*, the *natsia*, and the *kumpania*), and the implementation of social control. We have already discussed the use and control of economic resources in the context of the *kumpania*, but have only briefly mentioned the categories that the Rom use to organize their social world. Two issues which arise from these cases of conflict are (1) the importance of a thorough analysis of these categories for an understanding of social process and (2) the way that these categories are manipulated in a particular context.

Most Rom felt that conflict was on the increase. 'Gypsies used to live together, all the tribes (*natsiyi*) around a camp-fire. They travelled together and got along. Now they fight a lot and don't associate [with other *natsiyi*] so much.' The general feeling was that fighting between *natsiyi* had increased, and this was one reason given for keeping other *natsiyi* out of the *kumpania*. Whenever possible, blame for a fight was shifted to members of other *natsiyi* or distantly related *vitsi* within the *kumpania*. Similarly, support and aid was generally for the more closely related persons. The increase in conflict was also the reason given for preferring endogamous marriages over marriages between unrelated *vitsi*. In general, a distrust of distantly related or unrelated Rom was prevalent.

Barvale contains three *natsiyi* though it is dominated by the

Kalderash. Visitors from neighbouring *kumpaniyi* (who admittedly should not be considered objective) often commented on the amount of conflict in Barvale and exclaimed that they preferred their own more homogenous restricted *kumpania* where everyone 'got along'. San Francisco, the most open *kumpania* in the area, also has this reputation for a great deal of fighting, and during the whole period of my field work, the families there were embroiled in one *kris* after another.

It is difficult to say how much conflict has actually increased. Certainly claims of harmony in the past cannot be accepted. Even a brief perusal of the literature indicates that in-fighting is a common trait of all Gypsy groups over time (see history of the New York Gypsies, for example, in Cotten 1968: 1053–1055). It does seem that as the population of Rom in America increases, so the fight for economic resources becomes more intense. Certainly the *kumpania* is becoming more exclusive in an attempt to decrease conflict and increase economic and political advantage. Whether or not conflict has actually increased, it is felt to be a problem among the Rom and was an issue of constant concern.

THE EASTER SLAVA FIGHT

The Easter *slava* in Barvale was the occasion for one of the many fights which took place there during my field work, but it was unusual in that the contestants were families of the same *vitsa*. Members of the same *vitsa* ideally should cooperate economically and should share good feelings with each other. When serious conflict between *vitsa* members does occur, it is seen as a threat to the unity of the *vitsa*, and reconciliation must be immediate and effective.

At the Easter *slava* each family visits the house of every other family to share food and drink, even if only a token amount, wish each other luck and good health (*baXt hai sastimos tiri patragi*), and exchange ritually prepared red and green coloured eggs. Visiting, gossiping, and drinking take place all day long, and this naturally leads to the airing of recent events and grievances. One of the issues under discussion among the men was a recent *lovoro* (division of earnings) between *wortacha* who shared a body and fender job. The job was shared by first cousins, George and Harry and their sons Mike and Johnny (see *Figure 10*). According to Harry and his son Johnny, the division of money (*lovoro*) was not

E

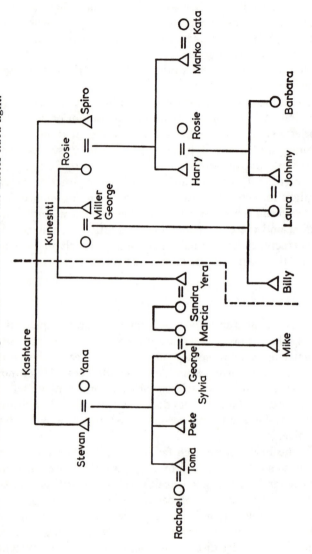

FIGURE 10 Genealogical relationship between contestants at the Easter *slava* fight.

- - - - - division of two factions

carried out fairly, and they claimed that George and his son Mike owed them $75. The more they drank, the more they felt the injustice, until finally they came to blows. Toma and Pete entered the fight to help their brother George. When someone 'cussed' Harry's mother, Marko entered the fight to aid his brother and defend his mother's honour. According to Marko, his mother Rosie was referred to as a 'dirty *Kuneshti*' and this was a 'very dirty thing to do because I couldn't cuss his mother because she is dead'. Because the fight could not be broken up, several women entered the arena. Laura defended her husband Johnny, and attacked George who was then in danger of pollution (*marime*) from contact with her skirts. Consequently George's sister Sylvia attacked Laura to protect her brother, and both Sylvia and Laura received the worst injuries, their faces being badly scratched. Finally, Barbara defended her father and brother, Harry and Johnny, and Billy defended his sister Laura. Rachael defended her husband Toma and Marcia her husband George. Marcia's sister Sandra was also involved and her husband Yera (a Kuneshti and brother of Rosie, Harry's mother), went to his wife's aid. Yera's role in the fight was never clarified, and to this day his true actions remain distorted. Finally, the police arrived, and everyone was arrested and taken to the police station.

Both elders of the two *familiyi*, Stevan and Spiro, were absent during the fight, visiting other houses. They were shocked that a fight could occur 'within the family' and they immediately went to the police station and had the contestants released. Some time after this, someone smashed up Spiro's car, and there were more scuffles and more arrests. Spiro immediately enlisted the aid of his brother-in-law Miller George and took out a warrant for George's arrest to force him to pay damages for his car. Miller also took out a warrant against George for striking his son Billy who is a minor. He also threatened to have his own brother Yera arrested. Harry and his family immediately left town 'till things cool off', and a short time later, George and his family also left town.

Stevan immediately began to seek reconciliation. His first concern was to have all warrants dropped. He tried to convince the County District Attorney to drop the case, but instead he was given notice to appear at the District Attorney's office with the other side to discuss the matter. This turned out to be Spiro's main threat to Stevan and his family. Both sides 'phoned the social worker several times to enlist her support for their side and suggested she cut off the other side's welfare. Finally a *diwano* (discussion meeting) was called 'to discuss the fight and arrange a *kris*, if necessary'. Spiro's family, convinced they had the upper hand because of the District Attorney's action, decided the *diwano* should take place at Marko's house, and they made preparations for food and drink. But Stevan's family did not show up and retired to Shani's house. Shani is a cousin to both Stevan and Spiro and was neutral in this fight, being related equidistantly to both sides. Meanwhile Spiro mobilized more support by sending for Kuneshti relatives from Los Angeles and San Francisco who arrived in time for the *diwano*. On the appointed day the whole *kumpania* gathered at Marko's house, ate, and discussed the issues, including the question of Stevan's fitness to be *rom baro*. Stevan's contingent were conspicuously absent which meant that the large numbers mobilized in Spiro's support could make no decisions. As the day ended Stevan showed up alone and held a discussion with Spiro. Both men expressed shock that their sons could fight and that the police were involved in the matter. They were very friendly with each other, almost jokingly so, and repeated regrets that this could happen between brothers and 'within the family'. They exclaimed that this was the first fight that they had had in their *kumpania* (certainly not true), and they agreed that 'the old man's car must be fixed'. Finally, they haggled over whether it would cost $20 or $500 to have it fixed.

After much discussion at the *diwano*, it was decided that the true blame for the fight belonged to Yera, 'that drunk Kuneshti from San Francisco'. They asked the social worker if there was anything she could do to prevent him from coming to Barvale because 'he's on welfare over there'. The *kumpania*'s reputation became the issue of much exclamation, and everyone reiterated their loyalty to the *kumpania* and their blame on the outsider. Even Miller George agreed that his brother should not be allowed in Barvale, but this only incensed the others who began remembering all the past deeds of Yera, Miller, and the Kuneshti in general. This feeling became so strong that Miller left town the next day for a few weeks until sentiment cooled down and an engagement between his son Billy and a girl from another Kashtare family (not involved in the fight) was broken off.

Stevan took up a collection in the *kumpania* and paid for his half-brother's car. In turn, Spiro dropped all charges against

Stevan's son George before the date to appear at the District Attorney's office. Miller George was forced to drop his charges for the assault on Billy before he left town. Everyone in the *kumpania* recalled indignantly how Miller had once hired himself as an informer to the police and how he had gone in a police car to threaten people to 'send their kids to school'. Most of the families involved (*Figure 10*) left town for a short while until things could 'cool off' and when they came back they could actually joke about the 'Easter fight'. In all, the fight covered a period of two weeks.

Several elements of this conflict must be discussed in greater detail in order to understand why events took the course they did. First, it should be noted that a *slava* is often the occasion of a fight. According to the Rom, that Easter there were 'fights all over the country', and Stevan mentioned several places where his relatives had been in similar brawls. At the next *slava* in Barvale, a fight was only narrowly prevented by keeping certain people away from the *slava*. Not only the *slava*, but other ritual occasions when large numbers of Rom congregate are the setting for open conflict.

Second, alliances took a specific pattern consistent with the stated ideal that while relatives can be trusted, unrelated persons cannot. Specifically, the closest kinship ties – father/son, brother/brother, brother/sister, sister/sister, and husband/wife – determined the partisanship of the persons involved. It can be concluded from the alignment of sides that closeness of kin relationship is the single most important factor in determining political alliance since all the persons involved were related to each other in some way. *Familia* obligations took priority over non-*familia* kin.

There was one important exception to this rule. Miller George defended his son, daughter, and daughter's husband in the actual combat. This was to be expected, but later on he helped his sister's husband (Spiro) and attacked his brother, Yera. Conversely Yera defended his wife and wife's sister instead of his brother Miller. Though I never heard Yera's explanation of this, since he was forced to leave town immediately, Miller admitted that turning against his brother was an unusual thing to do, and he felt somewhat sensitive about the stand he had taken.

The issue that overrode closeness of kin relationship was *kumpania* affiliation. For Miller these two affiliations were in direct competition. He was desperately trying to establish his

position in the *kumpania*. He was the eldest Kuneshti there and
had only a small family following while his brother was well
established in the Kuneshti-dominated *kumpania* in San Francisco. Miller had tried at one time to assert his leadership in San
Francisco through influence with his social worker, but this had
failed, partly because the social worker there disliked him and
partly, I suspect, because his brothers failed to support him. One
of his brothers, but not Yera, was himself vieing for leadership in
San Francisco. Miller was aware that his position in a Kalderash-
dominated *kumpania* was not strong, and he thought that by
defending the *kumpania* over his own brother he might strengthen
it. However, this tactic back-fired, and the result was that both
Kashtare families were annoyed at his involvement and blamed
him along with his brother, not accepting his unorthodox choice
of affiliation. They immediately fell back on accepted *natsia*
statuses to explain their actions – 'all Kuneshti are crazy'.

It was predictable, but unfortunate for Miller, that the method
by which the fight was resolved was to close ranks as a *kumpania*
and as *vitsa*. The fight itself was a threat to *vitsa* unity since
families within one *vitsa* are supposed to defend each other.
Therefore although it was a distortion of the facts, since the disagreement originally was between George and Harry, the whole
blame for the incident was transferred to Yera who was not only
an outsider to the *kumpania* but to the *vitsa* and *natsia* as well.
Beliefs about their superior status as Kalderash, and about the
unity of their *kumpania*, were reinforced by this tactic. The collection to repair Spiro's car not only brought the two *familiyi*
together again, but also as a gesture of economic cooperation,
demonstrated the unity of the *kumpania*.

Stevan's leadership, which had more than once been challenged
by both Spiro and Miller was reinforced by this incident. Although
Stevan was personally involved, he handled the *diwano* in such a
way that he could avoid direct confrontation and work primarily
at soothing feelings and at being a 'fair' judge. He not only solved
the immediate problem by paying for Spiro's car with a collection,
but also managed to promote unity rather than factionalism, by
transferring the primary blame on a *vitsa/kumpania* outsider. At
the same time he dealt a serious blow to the political position of
his rival, Miller George.

In the fight itself it is worth noting that the younger men, and
not the elders, engaged in actual physical violence. According to

the elders, if they had been present, they would have used their authority to prevent physical violence. The older man usually acts as judge and reconciliator, and he defends the traditions. In the *diwano*, Stevan arranged to confer with Spiro, calling upon their relationship as brothers, and the two elders solved the problem without the intervention of a wider group. Not only was Stevan outnumbered on this occasion, but his family were morally in the wrong both on the question of the *lovoro* and in having smashed Spiro's car.

Although the fight was centred around a question only involving men, the role of the women was crucial. The women were able to divert the violence of the men to themselves, through their polluting power, before anyone was seriously hurt. The police were also used to break up the fight before it got too serious since there was no one there who could be a neutral arbitrator. Later, the threat of arrest was a coercing force in getting the car paid for, and the shift of blame to Yera was reinforced by the suggestion that he was infringing on their economic resources because 'he was on welfare over in San Francisco'.

A man gives his first allegiance to his *familia*, then to his *vitsa*, and finally to his *kumpania*. Theoretically a fight should not occur between families of one *vitsa*. When it did, the fight was resolved by closing ranks (a) along *vitsa/natsia* lines (Kashtare against Kuneshti) and (b) along *kumpania* lines, putting the blame on an outsider. This glossed over the real differences – I never found out how they were resolved, since no one would talk about it – and drew the warring families together. At the same time, it increased Stevan's reputation as an effective leader, not only in solving internal differences but in his effectiveness with the social worker, police, and District Attorney (Public Prosecutor). In this conflict, the particular concepts that were rejected, that is, the other *vitsa* (Kuneshti) and the other *kumpania* (San Francisco) were embodied in the rival for leadership, Miller George, and his brother Yera.

The Devil Incident

The Devil incident was a conflict between political rivals of two different *vitsi* (Kashtare and Mineshti) for control of the Barvale *kumpania*. Stevan's rivals, John Nicholas and Ted Wanko, chose a rather interesting and unusual method of attacking his leadership.

John Nicholas has never been very much liked in the Barvale *kumpania*, therefore he is only a sporadic member of the *kumpania*. Usually when public opinion against him begins to rise, he leaves, only to return when he feels that gossip has lessened. None of his relatives live in Barvale though he has several in a nearby *kumpania*. Once when his relatives from nearby came to Barvale to hold a *kris* over a case of adultery, a fist fight broke out, John Nicholas brandished a pistol, and several arrests ensued. The Kashtare in Barvale were irate at this incident because they felt their good relations with the police were being jeopardized by these outsiders. Because of his action with the pistol John Nicholas had to flee so quickly that he was forced to abandon his possessions, and they were promptly stolen by his non-Gypsy neighbours. He blamed this misfortune on the Kashtare.

Stevan and Nicholas, as political rivals, have had verbal confrontations in public. One of these occurred at the annual police meeting with the Gypsies, and the police were forced to intervene. John had denied that Stevan was *rom baro* in Barvale and had declared that he was 'not afraid of him'.

John Nicholas did several other things which infuriated the *kumpania*. One day he publicly attacked the social worker, claiming that she was stingy and was withholding money from them. To make matters worse, he and Miller George, the Kuneshti contender for leadership, went to her superior officer and formally complained of her stinginess. Instead of supporting this ploy for more money, the other Rom in the *kumpania* were furious that he would risk jeopardizing their position with the welfare department, and they forced him to apologize to her. He complied, and with tears in his eyes, he claimed that he had had a nightmare about this incident (the *mule* told him he had done wrong).

A short time later, Ted Wanko, a Mineshti, landed in Barvale with his eleven children and two grandchildren in a destitute financial state. The *kumpania* could hardly refuse him aid, but they were not exactly happy about it. Wanko immediately joined forces with his 'cousin' John. They reinforced this relationship by arranging a marriage between their two children and began extending each other *Xanamik* privileges. Then Wanko announced that he possessed a devil (*o Beng*). Nicholas began a rumour (which he imputed to Stevan's brother Spiro) that there were in fact two devils, a live one and a dead one. Wanko kept the live one in his bathtub and the dead one in a coffin. The live one was alleged to swim around, eat rice, play with the children, watch television, and feed the baby its bottle. It was also said that it liked to travel but always came back when the family was ready to leave on a trip.

Spiro, along with several other elders, visited Wanko and demanded to see his devil. Wanko showed them the dead one, and they reported to the *kumpania* that it really was a devil and was very dangerous. The whole *kumpania* was thrown into a state of panic and fear, and several families prepared to leave town immediately. Adults were worried enough, but the children were petrified, not leaving their houses and suffering nightmares. Stevan was called upon to do something about the devil immediately. He appealed to the social worker to help him: 'All my peoples are worried, Jinnit. We gotta do something about this or they're gonna run away. They're scared. Everyone believes it's the devil. It has horns and everything.'

He made the sign of the cross every time the word 'devil' was said. He insisted that she must go to see the devil with him, and they would take a priest, who was a special friend of the Rom because he baptized the children. 'Then maybe we'll convince the people it's all right, or we can run Wanko out of town. This is important, Jinnit. There won't be no school with this devil loose in town.' Before she could go, Stevan went himself to see the devil, and he also saw only the dead one. He returned saying it was horrible.

Meanwhile there was a three-day *pomana* in an adjacent *kumpania*. Several hundred Rom were there, and they were very concerned about the Barvale devil. Stevan attended the *pomana* and reported, 'That's all they was talking about, that devil, didn't even think about the Gypsy who died, whose funeral they was at. They're afraid its a curse (*amria*). They're all going to die. We tried to find Tinka yesterday (a *phuri* renowned for her knowledge of the supernatural) to take a look at it, but she wasn't at the funeral.' Stevan repeated that he had to get a priest to look at it and ease everyone's mind. He told the social worker that it was too dangerous for her to go alone to look at it. There was a danger in just looking at it. (Wanko, it seemed, claimed it would harm the social worker, Stevan's main claim to authority.) Then Stevan added that Wanko couldn't be around too long because 'the boardahealth is after them, they're so dirty. Me and Yana didn't wanta drink coffee there, they was so filthy.'

Stevan went to the nine-day *pomana* which was held in Sacramento, and five hundred Rom were there. He was put in the position of having to defend his town. Everyone was afraid of the devil in Barvale, and they made it clear that it was his responsibility to see that no harm came to anyone.

The social worker also went to see the devil. She described it as a devilfish (stingray) cut up to look like a devil and put in a coffin with candles around. 'It was repulsive and convincing', she reported. Wanko and Nicholas, put on the spot, admitted to her that 'it was all a joke'. They said they had spread the rumours to make Stevan look foolish and make the Gypsies leave town. Wanko told her that when he heard that she had been told of the devil, he made an announcement in front of several men that he wanted to know who had 'informed' to her. He said that if the informer did not step forth by the next day, he would be blind, and the day after he would die. Lo and behold, Stevan and his wife dropped in that evening. Wanko had warned Stevan that he would get sick if he saw the devil. Stevan saw it anyway and said it raised his blood pressure.

The social worker reported back to Stevan that the devil was a stingray and showed them a picture of it in a book. Stevan and Yana were furious and claimed that they had never believed it was a devil. Yana, when she heard of the deceit, explained, 'they're so dirty', pulled her blouse away from her chest, and spat on her breast with disdain. They blamed Nicholas for the whole thing and repeated that he had no 'business coming to Barvale'. A few days later Nicholas met the Sheriff, got a deputy's card from him, and bought a badge twice the size of Stevan's. Stevan and Nicholas almost came to blows over this at a school board meeting.

Stevan, Spiro, and Miller George formed a coalition against Wanko, Nicholas, and Joe Adams, Stevan's Machwaya rival. Stevan began mobilizing his support. He visited everyone in the *kumpania* and talked about how he had tackled and thwarted the devil, not exactly single-handed, but with the help of the social worker. Together the two of them squashed Wanko's cruel prank on the children and averted a catastrophe.

This incident was an attempt by Wanko and Nicholas to take over the *kumpania* later with the help of Joe Adams, a Machwano who has always resented Stevan's leadership. The weapon they used was supernatural, and it would have devastated Stevan's reputation if it had not been exposed as a hoax so quickly. Stevan knew it was a challenge to his position, but he could not be sure that there was no real danger from the devil. The devil is believed to cause certain illnesses and is especially dangerous to children. Besides, the devil is a source of evil, an ill omen (*prikaza*), and is generally feared by Rom. Wanko's threats of harm from the devil were directed primarily at Stevan, so he attempted to prevent fear in the children by claiming that his devil was kindly to children.

When the story of the devil spread all over California during the *pomana* feasts, Stevan's reputation was at stake. Since it was his territory, he was called upon to resolve the danger. If he had failed, he and his relatives would be forced to leave. His first move was to enlist the support of the social worker, who generally recognized his leadership, and of a priest who is well known in the *kumpania*. He felt certain that the *gaje* would expose the devil since they would not believe in it. To convince the social worker to help him, he pointed out that the school would close down if this problem were not solved. This ploy was effective because Wanko was afraid to anger the social worker even though he wanted Stevan to appear foolish. Wanko was a newcomer, and his family's welfare applications, involving considerable financial gain to himself, were still being processed. The social worker exposed the hoax in time for Stevan to save his dignity and claim he never believed in it.

After the disclosure of the hoax, Stevan immediately attempted to destroy Wanko's reputation in the *kumpania*. He claimed that Wanko had scared all the children, and this was why Stevan was so concerned – not for himself, he never believed it, but because it was cruel to the children. Wanko had tried to avoid terrifying the children by insisting that the devil 'plays with them and feeds the baby its bottle'. But the children were terrified anyway so Stevan had an effective argument. Stevan also spread talk of how 'dirty' the whole Wanko family was. This was where Yana's role was crucial as she put a curse on Wanko and spat on her breast to protect herself from his pollution. She knew how to fight mystical danger with mystical power. Later, she also spread the rumour that Wanko committed incest with his two eldest daughters. This rumour had some basis, they said, because once the police were after Wanko for possible incest with his daughters.[8] Finally, Stevan boasted that he and the social worker were a powerful team and could expose even a devil. This was further 'proof' that the social worker supported his leadership and that he had influence with her.

The Machwaya family, led by Joe Adams, supported Wanko's 'prank' though of course they themselves would never 'believe' in the devil. They considered themselves educated and rational whereas 'the Kalderasha are an ignorant, superstitious lot'. Joe Adams generally supported anything that made Stevan look foolish or threatened his leadership, and he constantly reminded Stevan that the *Machwaya* are superior to the *Kalderasha*. One of the reasons he was so concerned to point this out was that he occupied a rather peripheral and powerless position in the *kumpania*. Besides having a *gaji* wife, he had only a few relatives in Barvale and so relied almost entirely on beliefs about Machwaya superiority in order to assert himself in the *kumpania*. During the devil incident he pointed out to the social worker:

> Kalderasha fight all the time. They're ignorant people. They can't represent the school board. You should pick someone who can write and pick someone who can explain themselves – make a good impression on the people. John Nicholas, what about him? He should be on it. The Micheleshti are a big tribe. The Kashtare, they want to take over. You tell them they can't. They gotta listen to the by-laws.

Wanko quite naturally allied with his cousin, his nearest relative in the *kumpania* and reinforced this relationship with *Xanamik* obligations. As has already been explained, he also enlisted the aid of the *Machwaya* who are always ready for an attack on Kalderash leadership. However, Stevan used this attack to his advantage, and every time he told the story, he put it that Stevan and 'his social worker' thwarted Wanko, Nicholas, the devil and the Machwaya in general. He also placed most of the blame on Nicholas and Joe Adams since they were *kumpania* members of long standing and posed more threat to his leadership than Wanko who was a newcomer. The ostracism by the *kumpania* (due to Stevan's efforts) of Nicholas and Wanko was so strong that both left town soon afterwards. One reason Stevan was effective at creating a climate of *kumpania* opinion against Wanko and Nicholas was undoubtedly that they posed a serious threat to the *kumpania*'s reputation. Other *kumpaniyi* were talking of avoiding Barvale as a dangerous place. In this way, Stevan turned a personal threat to his leadership into a wider threat to his whole *kumpania*.

There are certain similarities between the Easter *slava* and devil incidents. The first step, when a crisis arises, is to enlist the aid of the *gaje* to solve the immediate problem. In the first fight, the police were called in to stop the physical violence, and in the second, the social worker and a priest were asked to expose the hoax. However, useful as the *gaje* are to relieve immediate tension, the final solution to the problem is always an internal matter. In both cases this was accomplished by shifting the blame for the crisis to 'outsiders' whether they be outsiders by kinship, *vitsa*, *natsia*, or *kumpania*. Closeness of relationship, identity, and residence emerge as ideals of unity, and problems are shifted to outsiders even when this involves reinterpretation of the facts. In both cases this included ostracism and the actual physical removal of the outsider.[9]

Both these conflicts occurred between members of the same *kumpania*, and therefore the culprit could be removed to another *kumpania*. How then are problems solved between members of two *kumpaniyi?* Two cases of conflict between leaders of two different *kumpaniyi* (described in Appendix A) show the increased importance of *gaje* laws and authorities and of a higher body of law and procedure, the *kris romani*. The following discussion of these two cases will be primarily concerned with these two elements.

Both cases in Appendix A are cases of conflict which take place between *Xanamik* (co-parents in law) of different *kumpaniyi* over rights and obligations involved in marriage. The first conflict is resolved in a *kris romani*, and the second conflict is resolved by means of a *diwano*. In the first, divorce results, and in the second, the marriage is restored after two years of negotiations.

Both the *diwano* and *kris* are important mechanisms of decision-making and are employed whenever a problem cannot be solved by any other method. A *diwano* is a meeting that is called to sort out differences and problems and settle them in public discussion. The *diwano* has force and influence just as public pressure has influence, but the decision is not as morally binding as a *kris romani*. A *diwano* may precede a *kris*, and if a problem cannot be solved in the *diwano*, it may be decided that a *kris* is necessary. Though the *kris* is the final legal decision-making body on a particular case, sometimes a *diwano* involving many *vitsi* may be held to make policy decisions in general. Such was the case in the autumn of 1969 in Los Angeles when the leaders of the West Coast *vitsi* assembled to decide new policies on three problems

which were causing them much trouble. These were (a) relations
with a *gajo*, (b) informing on intruders to the *kumpania*, and (c)
divorce and return of brideprice. The rules were changed to be
more realistic and to avoid so many *kris* in future. For example, it
was decided that if a marriage fails, half the brideprice must be
returned, but no *kris* is necessary unless this solution is not
acceptable to both *Xanamik*.

The *kris romani* is a formal tribunal consisting of a council of
elders and one or more judges. The *kris* has a formal procedure
(described in Appendix A, Case 1) and its decision is final and
binding. The decision to have a *kris*, and the verdict of a *kris* is
made by the 'public' and not the individuals involved in a conflict.
The individual plaintiffs must place their fate in the hands of the
kris. A *kris* should only be convened for a very serious problem or
wrongdoing, and generally is concerned with divorce and return
of the brideprice or an act of immorality such as adultery, incest,
homosexuality, or sexual relations with *gaje*. Punishment is
generally by payment of money or a *marime* period for the guilty
family. Unless there is a serious injustice or an act that defies
important principles of *romania*, a *kris* is not called, for it is an
arduous and expensive process.

In the Bay Area there were at least five *kris romani* held during
my nine months of fieldwork and at least twice, perhaps three
times as many *diwano*. However, I shall limit my discussion
primarily to the cases in Appendix A.[10]

In both cases, American law enforcement procedure and
officers are used to coerce one's opponent, and this precedes any
internal settlement. In the first case, Stevan accused John Marks
of a serious moral offence that marred his reputation and required
an equally strong defence. To demonstrate his indignation and to
punish Stevan he had Stevan's daughter arrested for an American
crime. There followed a contest to see who could blackmail the
other most effectively. The person with the most 'influence' with
the police and knowledge of police procedure had the most power.
Police were used for coercion and revenge but were not accepted
as arbiters of the case. This can only be settled by Rom in a
legitimate way. In the second case John enlisted the support of a
detective, and this, plus his influence with the Fort Worth police
in general, prevented his arrest. His effective use of the police in
his *kumpania* is indicative of a closed *kumpania* under strong
control. In a more open *kumpania* this would be very difficult to do

since no one group has the support of the local authorities or control of economic resources. However, even though John was able to use the *gaje* authorities effectively, as he himself pointed out, this does not solve the problem. 'Even if you weren't (guilty) in American law, you have won nothing as far as a Gypsy trial is concerned. You see, he done it by force. He didn't do it legally according to Gypsy laws.'

In Case 2, it was quite clear that no moral crime had been committed. Normally, when there is a severe accident, relatives do stay with the hurt person, and Rita should have been allowed to stay. Her grandfather-in-law did not agree with this view, perhaps because this is not a *Xoraxai* practice or perhaps because he felt the opportunity was being used to keep Rita with her family. John claimed that he did not want to take away the man's *bori*, but, on the other hand, he was not going to be forced to send her back. Besides, the respect due to his dying mother made it a question of pride. The situation turned into a serious contest between *rom baro*, but since no 'injustice' had been committed, only a *diwano*, and not a *kris*, could be called to solve the difficulties.

However, in Case 1 a moral crime, that is, possible incest between a man and his *bori*, was claimed to have taken place. This taint on John's reputation was very serious. Not only would his reputation be ruined, and his family made *marime*, but he would be unlikely ever to get another *bori* for his son. For these reasons, his defence of his reputation was very exaggerated; he went 'crazy' (*dilo*) as he put it. From his point of view, he felt that a grave injustice had been committed. His *bori* was not having sexual relations with her husband, and he had a right to the return of the brideprice that her father was trying to avoid paying. Accusations on both sides were serious enough for a *kris romani* to be arranged to settle the matter.

In Case 1, a trial was called because suspected incest is a grave crime and because there can be no divorce without final resettlement of the brideprice. Generally, people discuss events until they are settled or until they decide there must be a *kris*, but any defendant may request a trial if he feels there has been an injustice. It is by no means certain that his request will be successful. Diane Marino, for example, has for several years been trying to bring her son-in-law to trial for bigamy with a *gaji*. Because of her accusation many people do avoid him and his family; however, she has never been able to get enough support for a *kris* because she is poor whereas his family is powerful, rich, and influential with the local judge of the area. When Rachael decided that her daughter-in-law was 'no good', it took her several months to convince Stevan to hold a divorce *kris*. As a last resort, and only as a last resort, a woman can bring a man to trial by throwing her skirts over his head, causing him to be defiled until the matter can be decided in a *kris*.

It is important that a trial take place in a neutral *kumpania*. The *kris* in Case 1 took place in New Orleans, just outside Texas, which is the boundary of John Marks's influence. Besides choosing a neutral place, there must also be several *vitsi* present to make the result a 'public' one. The *vitsi* must come from 'all parts of the United States', and 'a man and wife from each tribe (*vitsa*) must be there'.In case 1, both John Marks and Stevan shared the cost of the hall, but, in some cases, the cost is borne by the person who has been declared guilty.

The first duty of the assembled *vitsi* representatives is to pick the judge and jurors. Ideally, they should be respected men with reputations for being just, honest, and for up-holding law and tradition. In practice, they are also well known and powerful *kumpania* leaders. In Case 1, 'there were two judges and twenty-five jurors . . . it doesn't ordinarily take more than one judge and ten or twelve jurors, but in this particular case there was a lot of conflict' (Appendix A, p. 294). 'You base this choice on friendship, on people you know are reliable, that you know are your friends, that you know they won't go as friends against the truth. You can know a person for life, and you can ask him to a Gypsy trial, and he can be sworn in to give nothing but the truth, and he would do so even if he condemns me' (Appendix A, p. 302). Both sides have to accept the choice of mediators and give an oath that they will accept the verdict before the cases are heard. This is not difficult to achieve because if a powerful and respected man is chosen it would be unwise to cast doubts on his reputation and refuse to accept him without good reason. The 'jurors'[11] mentioned are those respected men who will discuss the case with the arbitrator and final decision-maker. They will influence his opinion, but his decision is final.

After the judges and jury are picked, the next step is for the men to swear to accept their verdict. This is a formal oath (*amria*) such as 'may my child die tomorrow (*te meral muri shey*) if I go back on my word' (see Yoors 1967: 169, for further examples). Such an oath before a large company of respected Rom is not easily broken, and it is believed that retribution will fall on that person if it is broken. Finally each side presents his story to the people present. One old lady said: 'they put the fighting parties one at each end of the room, and the other people sit along the sides. Each side tells its case and presents its arguments.' Oration and ability to speak well and convincingly are very important. An aesthetic use of the language is also beneficial to one's case, and if a man feels he is not a good speaker, he may get someone else to tell his story. His main aim is to try to get the sympathy and understanding of the people there, convince them that his actions were justified and that the actions of his opponent were not.

When the cases have been presented, the judges and jury go to one side to discuss the issues and come to a decision. The main body of jurors is almost always a group of men, but the women stand to one side (as is usual in gatherings of Rom) and interject comments and opinions. The two individuals involved in the case cannot be present at this discussion. Indeed in a case involving immorality of a young girl or man, the young person is not present at the whole trial but is represented by the adults of his or her family.

The verdict in Case 1 was only reached after considering many factors. John Marks was declared innocent of the seduction of his daughter-in-law, while Stevan was found guilty of fraud and of mis-using the institution of the brideprice. Even though he was acquitted of incest, the accusation alone marred his reputation. Added to this was the curse by his *bori* which was a bad omen (*prikaza*) for him. He mentioned elsewhere that the court advised him not to go to church and not to 'swear on bibles that it is not true (the accusation) because your *bori* condemned you'.

It was also decided that he should get back part of his brideprice, but since he had caused Stevan much expense and trouble with American law, he was asked 'as a favour to the public' to accept one fifth of his *daro*. Another factor taken into consideration was that Stevan was known to be very poor and could not raise more money. In order to get a settlement and to be able to remarry their children without delay, a decision agreeable to both sides had to be reached. John accepted this small repayment in order to get his son remarried and had to promise to incite no further arrests of members of Stevan's family.

Generally, each party keeps his word. 'Once any family or any person, even without a "background", gives his word to the public, they generally live up to it' (Appendix A, p. 296). 'The Gypsy court's decision is about 90% followed. I told you about Stevan who did not, but usually the decision is abided. If I went against the Gypsy trail, I would lose my life before I would lose my name' (Appendix A, p. 304). In some cases, security money must be put up to ensure that the word is kept. John once mentioned several large sums which had been given to him for safe keeping until someone had complied with the verdict in a trial. Keeping this money caused him considerable trouble with the internal revenue authorities who were loath to accept this explanation of the money. In this particular case, he did not trust Stevan and demanded that three respected men give their word to pay him if Stevan did not. As it turned out, they were instrumental in forcing Stevan to pay since he could not afford to incur the wrath of three such powerful men.

In Cases 1 and 2, the punishment was by fine or return of the brideprice for the bride. However, neither of these cases involved proven sexual immorality. In such cases the punishment may be a period of *marime* for the individual and/or his family. During this time they are considered unclean and are denied commensal privileges with other Rom. Because of the increasing number of elopements and 'runaway' girls, there has been an increase in *marime* sentences. One judge explained:

> Sentences are getting more lenient now. There is more compromise. The standard sentence is thirty days *marime*, but it used to be seven years. Then, cases were very rare so they could make an example of one person, but now it's more common, and you can't do that to so many people.

During fieldwork there were two *kris romani* involving immorality and *marime* sentences. In one case, which was not resolved by the time I left, a young 'tomboy' girl ran off with a man's wife. It took a year for the husband to find his wife, and when he did, the two girls were brought to trial but only after much fighting between the families, several hospitalizations, and arrests. First a *diwano* was held to hear the cases. Then women from each *vitsa* involved accompanied the girls to a doctor to get a certificate of health to check that they were 'clean'. They were examined for venereal disease and for pregnancy, and this report was brought to the *kris*.

Though I did not hear the verdict, everyone who discussed the case was very shocked by it and felt that they should get at least one year *marime*.

The second case involved a twenty-year-old girl who 'ran off to the *gaje*' – she joined the 'Job Corps' and worked at *gaje* employment for a year. When she was finally located, she also had to (a) be examined by a doctor to see that she was not pregnant or infected with venereal disease, (b) have a testimony from the Job Corps that it is not a penal institution and that she was a good and moral girl while she was there, and (c) have testimony from the social worker that she had never been in trouble. The trial was held in the local park in Barvale, and the result was that the family was *marime* for thirty days. The judge stated that the crucial factor was that the parents did not know that the girl was going to run away, but since they were responsible for her actions, they had to be given a penalty, though a light one, for not having proper control of her. After her thirty days, she was immediately married off. It was interesting that during the trial, her actions were referred to as her 'crime'.

Conclusions

We have discussed four cases of conflict, the first two as examples of how problems are solved in a *kumpania* by transferring blame to an 'outsider' who must leave the *kumpania* and the last two as examples of problems that arise outside the *kumpania* and must be resolved by a higher authority, the *kris romani*. All four cases also demonstrate the kinds of problems that *kumpania* leaders face and resolve and the resources that they call upon to aid them. It is clear that in each case *gaje* authorities are used to support the leaders of a *kumpania* and to stop or create trouble as the situation demands. The political relationships between *gaje* and *kumpania* leaders take a defined and consistent pattern for resolving conflict. The same pattern was observed for economic relations between leaders and *gaje*. However, an understanding of this pattern does not tell us what the issues and internal factors really are for Rom society. These internal factors are the kin and affinal relationships, the broaders social categories (*vitsa*, *natsia*), and other concepts, such as *marime*, which are crucial to an understanding of political relations and conflict. It appears that support in time of conflict is given first to one's *familia*, then to one's *vitsa*, and finally to members of the *kumpania*. Relations between members of different *natsiyi* are generally hostile. These units of social organization, the *familia*, *vitsa*, and *natsia*, can now be examined with the four examples of conflict in mind.

5

The Relationship Terminology

The Rom have a cognatic relationship terminology basically similar to the English kinship terminology, but with certain very important differences. In a cognatic terminology, sex is ignored as a criterion for tracing kinship links. There is no terminological distinction to indicate descent traced through the mother or the father's side. This creates an open-ended network of kin, and almost any Rom in North America could probably trace some relationship to any other Rom if he could go back far enough. In fact, when two strange Rom meet, this is the first thing they will attempt to do.

The inner core of this network of kin (Appendix B, terms 1–2, 5–8, 11–12) contains terms for very specific biological relationships: *papo* = FF MF; *mami* = FM MM; *dad* = F; *dey* = M; *phral* = B; *pey* = Z; *shav* = S; *shey* = D.[1] Outside this core of relations are terms that apply to a large group of relatives and cover more than one genealogical level (Appendix B, terms 3–4, 9–10, 13–14):

kak(o) = the brother's and sister's husbands of ego's parents and grandparents (uncle, great-uncle)
bibi = the sisters' and brothers' wives of ego's parents and grandparents (aunt, great-aunt)
woro = male cousin
vara = female cousin
nepoto = ego's grandsons and sibling's sons (nephews)
nepata = ego's granddaughters and sibling's daughters (nieces)

Since many relationship terms are similar to English ones, and since the Rom themselves constantly translate their own terms into English when they speak with *gaje*, it is very important to establish the differences between *Romanes* and English usages.

Consequently, a brief explanation of the terms is presented before proceeding to the behaviour expected between sets of kin.

1. *papo*, FF   MF   (mod. Greek *papos*)[2]
   mami, FM   MM   (possibly Indic)

These terms can be translated accurately as 'grandfather' and 'grandmother' as they correspond exactly to the English meaning of the words. According to G. & L., reference is made to the more specific biological relationship by the use of such constructions: *dadesko dad* 'my father's father'; *dadeski dey* 'my father's mother'; *dako dad* 'my mother's father'; *daki dey* 'my mother's mother'. The Rom in Barvale used this kind of explanation frequently when they wanted to be more specific both in English and in *Romanes*. I also heard *muro paposko papo* 'my grandfather's grandfather'.

2. *kak(o)*   (indic *kak*)   FB   MB   FZH   MZH
   bibi   (indic *bibi*)   FZ   MZ   FBW   MBW

These terms refer to ego's 'uncle' and 'aunt' again in the English sense of the terms, but they also include relatives in the second ascending genealogical level who are the siblings and their spouses of those one calls *papo* and *mami*. When the terms are used as terms of reference they are used largely for those kin named above.

Kako and *bibi* can also be used for an old person (as an address of respect) who is only distantly related even if the exact relationship is not known. In casual conversation the terms of address *kako* and *bibio* may be used by any younger person to an old and respected person. This is not meant to imply an exact kin relationship, but rather to indicate respect and deference to age. *Kako* may be used for example with any old and respected man who is a family patriarch or leader of the *kumpania*. In one case, a family always called their mother '*bibio*' because 'she is so old'. She was twenty years older than anyone else in the *kumpania*.

3. *dad*   (indic *dad*)   F
   dey   (indic *dei*)   M

These are terms of reference which are used for one's true (and adopted) parents. Terms of address are *mamo* or *dale* (voc. sing. of *dey*) for mother, and *tate*, *dade*, or *mova* for father. Children who have been adopted by their grandparents will not normally use these terms of reference or address but continue to call them *papo* and *mamio*. The grandparents, however, will usually call the child *shoro* (s) or *shori* (D) and not *nepoto* although they may refer to him as *muro nepoto* (my grandson). There is no stigma attached to adoption, rather the child gains from the prestige of their adopted parents (who are old) and therefore will keep the true relationship term; however, grandparents are inclined to use *shav* or *shey* for their children as well as grandchildren.

4. *phral*   (indic *p'al*)   B
   pey   (indic *p'en*)   Z

Phral and *pey* refer to ego's biological brother and sister respectively. Both terms may be used generally between persons of equal age and status in the same way that they might refer to a person of superior age and status as *kako* or *bibi*. As a sign of friendliness and equality, it is common to begin a statement with *phral*, but this is in no sense a confusion with the biological relationship, simply a statement of role and status.

5. (v) *woro*   (Rumanian *ver*); 'male cousin'
       vara   (not in G. & L.); 'female cousin'

(V) *Woro*[3] and *vara* refer to 'cousins of all degrees of relationship'. These terms cross genealogical levels, age, and status and imply no relationship of either hierarchy or equality. It is indeterminate of status, age, or roles and is a very open-ended category in terms of relationships. Cousins may either be raised as siblings in the same household and be very close, or they may never see each other, or they may marry one another.

Irving Brown (1929: 176) records that *vero* (cousin) was used as a term of affection and equality like *prala*; however, I never heard it used this way. Ackerley (1913–14: 212) recorded for the Kalderash in 1912: *tsatso vojro* (lit. 'true cousin') for first cousin and *duita vojro* for second cousin. I very much doubt that *duita woro* is now used, however, the Rom constantly referred to their 'first cousin' in English as opposed to 'just any cousin'. The difference has behavioural concomitants. For example, marriage with a first cousin is strongly frowned upon, whereas marriage with a second cousin is highly desirable.

6. *shav* (Indic *čiv*) s; young 'Gypsy' boy
   shey (Indic *čai*) D; young 'Gypsy' girl

Shav and *shey* refer to ego's biological sons and daughters and sometimes to any young pre-puberty child. Aunts, uncles, and grandparents frequently call their grandchildren or nephews/ nieces *shoro* or *shori*. The plural *shavai* means 'children'. *Shabaro* and *shebari* (lit. 'big boy' and 'big girl') refer to a young man or woman who has reached puberty and is of marriageable age but not yet married. These terms are also used during the betrothal and wedding to indicate the groom and bride. A non-Gypsy boy or girl of this age group is called *raklo* or *rakli*. One always distinguishes between a young 'Gypsy' boy or girl and a 'non-Gypsy' one. There is no term which can be used for both; therefore the distinction is always present in the categories themselves.

Again, although these terms may refer to biological progeny as well as in the general sense of 'child' this does not mean that there is no distinction made between one's own children and the children of others. The meaning is always clear in the context.

7. *nepoto*   (Rumanian *nepot*); 'grandson' 'nephew'
   nepata   (Rumanian *nepoate*); 'granddaughter' 'niece'

These terms refer to one's grandchildren as well as nephews and nieces. Cohn discusses this usage:

> The terms *nepoto* (masc.) and *nepata* (fem.), lump together the English terms 'nephew' (respectively 'niece') and 'grandson' (respectively 'granddaughter'). This particular crossing of two generations in a single term apparently occurred in Proto-Indo-European and in Latin (the Latin term is Nepos). So the Gypsies here seem to have maintained older usages. (Cohn, 1969: 478)

Cohn explains the usage as a way of distinguishing relatives to whom one has secondary responsibility from one's own children who are of primary responsibility. Particularly in the matter of arranging a marriage, this distinction is important, because while a man and his wife have the final responsibility in arranging their own childrens' marriages, they are also aided in the negotiations by their parents and siblings. Consistent with this idea is the practice of calling adopted grandchildren *shav/shey* rather than the more 'distant' sounding *nepoto/nepata*.

Besides these terms used for relatives, there are other ways of expressing a relationship. This method is not only extremely common when describing relationships but is used specifically when more detailed information than the terminology can supply is required. Some examples are:

1. *o shav paposko phral*	'the son of my grandfather's brother', i.e. 'my second cousin'
2. *muro dad, laki papo su phral*	'my father and her grandfather were brothers', i.e. 'we are second cousins'
3. *muri dey hai laki dey su pey*	'my mother and her mother are sisters', i.e. she is my first cousin through our mother's (*vitsa*)'

Marriage brings a change of status from youth to adulthood and is a condition of that change. To remain unmarried is to relinquish full adult status. The terms for husband (*rom*) and wife (*romni*) are also the terms used to indicate adult status (man, woman) so that terminologically the two changes are inseparable. A third aspect of the terms *rom* and *romni* is that they always refer to a Gypsy married adult and can never be used for a non-Gypsy man or woman, who are called *gajo* and *gaji*. Even when a non-Gypsy woman marries a Rom and joins his household, she is referred to as *e gaji romni*, the non-Gypsy wife, and not as *e romni*. It should also be pointed out that the use of *o rom* to mean an adult married Gypsy man is not the same as *Rom* or *amaro Rom* which means 'The Gypsies' and is frequently translated by the Rom as 'the people' or 'the public'.

Marriage is not only a stage in the life cycle, it also creates a new set of relationships. Persons related through a marriage may also be related through kinship. They may even continue to use kinship terms after marriage, but regardless of their former relationship, marriage brings new obligations and rights to these relationships. Rom affinal terms may be divided into two groups. There are terms that indicate affines created by the marriage of a child or sibling (I) and terms that indicate affines created by one's own marriage (II).

I	II
1. *Xanamik* – child's spouse's parent	4. *socro* – spouses's father
	sacra – spouse's mother
2. *bori* – BW SW	
3. *Ẑamutro* – ZH DH	5. *kumnato* – spouse's brother
	kumnata – spouse's sister

1. *Xanamik* is the parent-in-law of one's child (see *Figure 11*). In an ideal marriage between second cousins the *Xanamik* will be

aunt or uncle to a nephew or niece, or they will be cousins. However, whatever the former relationship, the *Xanamik* relationship
adds a new set of obligations and duties to it, besides a mutual
respect and formality of relations between the four *Xanamik*.
These obligations are due not only to those who are *Xanamik* but
to some extent also to the families who are involved in the
Xanamikuria. For example, a family in Barvale was obliged to give
lodgings and hospitality to the brother of their *Xanamik* although
their *kumpania* (with whom they were sympathetic) was in the
midst of a fight with this man and his *familia*. Even though they
were furious about the behaviour of their *Xanamik*'s brother, they
were obliged to protect him from the wrath of their own *kumpania*
and show him 'respect' when he reminded them of their *Xanamik*
obligations. Everyone else in the *kumpania* agreed that this family
had no choice but to protect him (see 'Devil Incident', Chapter 4).
Similarly a woman who became *Xanamik* with her sister's son
remarked at the wedding that she and her sister had been such
good friends before, but 'now we don't know'. Their relationship
from that day on acquired an additional set of obligations about
which they felt a certain amount of ambivalence. *Xanamik*, who
are otherwise unrelated, have a more distant and formal relationship than those already related.

It should be noted that the term *Xanamik* does not distinguish
between the parents of the groom and the parents of the bride.
Cohn (1969: 479) attributes this to the symmetrical exchange that
is the basis of the relationship; one *Xanamik* gains a daughter-in-
law, the other gets the *daro* (marriage payment).

The *Xanamikuria* relationship is linked closely to marriage
arrangements. *Xanamik* are those two couples who arrange the
marriage of their children with the help of their respective families.
They negotiate the marriage payment, conditions of marriage, the
wedding feast, and post-marital residence. This procedure of
negotiation (*tomiamos*) is formally prescribed and from the moment
negotiations begin the future *Xanamik* adopt a new code of
behaviour. Although I shall discuss *Xanamik* roles and obligations,
the full implications of this relationship will only become clear
when marriage negotiations are discussed.

2. *Bori (Figure 11)* refers to the specific relationships, son's wife
and brother's wife[4] and in a general sense means 'the woman whom
my *vitsa* has acquired through marriage'. Anyone of the husband's

FIGURE 11 Relationship of Ego to *Xanamik*, *bori*, and *Żamutro*.

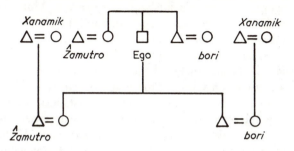

FIGURE 12 Model of uses of the terms *Żamutro* and *bori*.

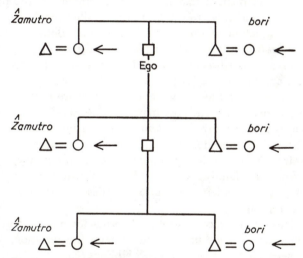

Żamutro: men at or below Ego's genealogical level to whom Ego's
     family gives a wife
bori: woman who has become the wife of a man in Ego's family

← direction of flow of women

vitsa may refer to a newly acquired bride as the *bori* regardless of
respective ages. For example, a child of nine once referred to her
brother's wife, who was nineteen, as 'my *bori*'. There is a strong
prohibition against sexual relations between a *bori* and her *socro*
(HF) or *kumnato* (HB) and in general with anyone in her husband's
vitsa. In terms of status a *bori* stands in a position of subordination
to her husband's family.

3. *Žamutro*, like *bori*, covers two genealogical levels and refers to the daughter's or sister's husband (*Figure 11*). More widely it refers to the man to whom I (and my family) have given a *romni* (wife) whereas *Xanamik* is the man and his wife to whom I have given a *bori* or from whom I have acquired a *bori*.[5] Just as the *Xanamik* relationship included the grandparents of a couple, *bori* includes a grandson's wife. This usage of the terms I have not found in other sources, and in the two instances where it was heard, the reference was to a son's son's wife when the three generations were also residing in the same *kumpania*. If this usage is general, then the model of the use of these terms would be as in *Figure 12*.

What we find then, is that in a very general sense, the terms *Xanamik*, *bori*, and *žamutro* extend to the families involved in the marriage transaction of one of their members. Both the terms *bori* and *žamutro* cross genealogical levels and include terms that in English are daughter-in-law and sister-in-law (respectively son-in-law and brother-in-law). If we ask why they should include these two genealogical levels, we find that they are related to the marriage payment (*daro*) and post-marital residence. *Bori* are women that a family makes a payment (*daro*) to obtain and who normally join that family's household upon payment of the *daro*. *Žamutro* are men from whom a family received a *daro* in exchange for a woman from the family, whether she be a sister or daughter. *Xanamik* are the elders who arrange these negotiations and conditions of marriage.

If we look at the second group of terms for affines, through ego's own marriage, we find another interesting question. Why are there separate terms for a spouse's siblings (*kumnato, kumnata*) and for brother's wife (*bori*) or sister's husband (*žamutro*), both in English covered by brother-in-law and sister-in-law? Again, this is related to post-marital residence and also to a prohibition on sexual relations between a man and his *bori*. A woman, at marriage, goes to live with her *socro, sacra* (father- and mother-in-law), *kumnato*, and unmarried *kumnata*. Because they have paid a *daro*, they now take responsibility for her behaviour and have certain rights to her services, but are prohibited strongly from having sexual relations with her, which is the exclusive right of the male relative for whom she was arranged. A man usually shares residence with his *bori*, but normally does not live with his *kumnata* (w z) or his parents-in-law. Similarly it is prohibited for him to have relations with his *bori* or his mother-in-law, but there is no such prohibition for his *kumnata*, and he may even marry a wife's sister.

There is a further use of these terms. According to Cohn (1969: 481) a woman calls her husband's brother *kumnato* and his wife *bori* (HBW). Similarly her husband's sister is called *kumnata* and her husband *žamutro* (HZH). Cohn thinks that this is a case of the woman using the terms her husband uses for these same persons since he would call his BW *bori* and his ZH *žamutro*. Certainly this usage is common. Women who were related to each other as husband's brother's wife (HBW/HBW) called each other *bori* and translated this as 'sister-in-law'.

Similarly a man's wife's brother is *kumnato* and his wife's sister *kumnata*; however there is another term which Cohn recorded for wife's sister's husband:

> Finally, there is a term, known now better by the older genera-
> tion than the younger, by which the only[6] fully symmetrically
> related affines (from the point of view of both generation and
> standing in regard to the buying or selling of wives) call one
> another. This is the term *pašo* which means wife's sister's
> husband. One would imagine that a special kind of solidarity
> exists between two *paše* – both men having obtained daughters
> from the same *socro* – but since the term is no longer widely
> used, I could not obtain sufficient information on its social
> meaning. (Cohn 1969: 481)

In Barvale I did not hear the term *pašo*; however, one young person explained that a man and his wife's sister's husband were *žamutro* 'which means they are related – it's just like brothers', indicating this special solidarity mentioned by Cohn between men who have taken sisters for wives. However, these two *žamutro* were also first cousins, a relationship which they may have felt was strengthened by affinal ties. *Žamutro*, therefore, may be the term currently used for wife's sister's husband. One would also want to know if *bori* is used for husband's brother's wife. In one tale of two women, who were in the relationship of HBW/HBW, they were called 'the two *bori*' and this was translated as the two sisters-in-law.

Behaviour between Relations

There are four factors that influence behaviour towards persons with whom one is related besides the category of the relationship itself. These are: sex, age, residence (*kumpania*), and *vitsa* (or *natsia*). The influence of *vitsa* (or *natsia*) membership is discussed in Chapter 6 in detail. The role of the *vitsa* and *natsia* in situations of conflict was introduced in Chapter 4. It is now important to explain the role of the *vitsa*, *natsia*, and *kumpania* in the general context of relationships and behaviour.

As a rule, members of one *vitsa* feel an obligation and desire to aid and protect each other in situations that involve opposition with another *vitsa* (or *natsia*). When a disagreement between persons of the same *vitsa* arises, as in the Easter *slava* conflict, then obligations to family members take precedence over *vitsa* membership. Similarly, residence or *kumpania* membership may also be a determining factor in behaviour since members of the same *kumpania* also feel a duty to each other beyond their duty to Rom of another *kumpania*. Of course this may not be so if the family's position in the *kumpania* is transitory. *Vitsa* and *kumpania* affiliations are overlapping in some cases, for example in a closed *kumpania*. Generally, allegiances to a relative are stronger than to a *kumpania* member. However, it would be difficult to say which obligation would come first, the one to a distantly related member of one's *vitsa* or to a friendly but unrelated member of one's *kumpania*. In any actual situation, other factors would be involved.

The implications of *vitsa* (or *natsia*) and *kumpania* membership with behaviour are directly associated with reputation.[7] The reputation of an individual cannot be separated from the reputation of his family: the reputation of an individual or family within a *vitsa* also affects the reputation of the *vitsa* as a whole. Behaviour that is shameful (*lashav*) or worse still, *marime*, creates a reputation for an individual and his family (since the family is considered responsible for the behaviour of its members) which ultimately must be borne by the *vitsa* and possibly the *kumpania* as a whole. This is not to say that every individual act taints the *vitsa* but that the general moral (and physical) character of persons and their families combined with the reputation of other families in the same *vitsa* creates a reputation for a *vitsa* (or *kumpania*, if this is the context). As we shall see later, this reputation is a major factor in determining the hierarchy of the various *vitsi*.

A good reputation is something that is built up over years, though one shameful or *marime* act can colour it quite suddenly. A girl and her family must have a good reputation in order to obtain a high bride price, and a man and his family must have a good reputation in order to be able to acquire a reputable *bori*. When a young girl left the community for one year, she and her family were tried and given thirty days *marime* after which she was immediately given in marriage to the son of a Kuneshti for no brideprice.[8] It was said of this Kuneshti: 'The Kuneshti cannot get good wives. Look at Nick, he can only get a *bori* who is *marime*!' This incident also illustrates the way individual reputations extend to the *vitsa*; in this case the whole Kuneshti *vitsa* was condemned (by a Kashtare), though of course such a sweeping statement was not based on fact. When I pointed out several marriages of reputable women with Kuneshti men, this Kashtare conceded the facts but added, 'but I don't know how they did it'. In one fight concerning adultery between families of two *vitsi*, the bereaved husband was satisfied to have his wife returned, but his brothers demanded payment for damage to their reputation. The taint of adultery concerned not only the individuals but the two *vitsi* as well. This particular incident was brought to trial in Barvale (amidst a certain amount of physical violence) though both families were from another *kumpania*. The people in Barvale were highly incensed at the flagrant attempt of these families to give the Barvale *Kumpania* a 'bad name' and protect their own *kumpania*.

Besides the *vitsa*, *natsia*, and *kumpania*, sex and age are the most crucial factors in determining the character of relations. These two factors, of course, extend beyond family relations and are basic to all wider units of social organization, but they can best be explained within the context of kinship.

Sex and Age

The male–female division is the most fundamental in Rom society. Men and women between puberty and old age are given entirely different status and role within a relationship category.[9] Actual physical separation of the sexes is very great, and this both exemplifies as well as reinforces the difference in treatment of men and women. Men and women are separate at all social functions. At a *pomana*, a marriage, *kris*, baptism, *slava*, *pakiv*, or in everyday conversation, the men sit on one side of the room and the women on the other. At a feast table, men sit and women stand behind getting what food they can. The Rom are avid conversationalists, but it is not mixed unless there is a specific incident or issue that involves both men and women at the same time. Women usually do not make political decisions in a *diwano* or *kris*, and they expect to be given orders by their fathers, brothers, husbands, fathers-in-law, and mothers-in-law. However, the superior status of the male sex is conditioned by age.

An increase in age brings an increase in status and power for members of both sexes until the peak is reached at very old age somewhere between fifty and sixty-five years of age. Men and women of the same age do not have equal status, men taking the superior position until they become grandparents, but then the power vested in the oldest people of either sex over their younger relatives is very great indeed. Old women may be very powerful and may take an active hand in running political affairs with the old men. They have not only outgrown the sexual stigma of being female, but they can cross sexual barriers as well. At a feast table, these women may sit with the men in strategic positions, and they may join male conversation by wändering between the two groups adding their opinion to the men (though they will not usually sit and join a male conversation). The men may resent this, but it is allowed. Conversely, a very old man may also join a group of females for a short time to discuss something though again they will not stay long, and the women are 'embarrassed' by his presence and restricted in their topics of conversation.

There is one other exception to the sexual barrier not determined by age, and this is for outsiders. Politically important *gaje* of either sex may be given a 'place of honour' next to the leader at a feast table. Of course this is to show his power and influence (with, for example, the social worker) as well as flatter, rather than honour the *gaje*. Thus in certain situations and contexts *gaji* and old women are classified as male, namely when they hold power, which is normatively a prerogative of the men.

Age is directly correlated with power and respect – the older one gets, the more power and respect one is given. The oldest person in the family, who is still physically and mentally capable, will be the final authority in all family matters and decisions. Older people are always given priority over younger ones when eating, sitting at a feast table, when visiting, or dividing money earned. This is, of course, conditioned by sex as has been explained so that a woman who is older than another woman has more status, but she may have less status than a man of her age.

Age is not measured in absolute years (which are not known

anyway) but in stages of the life-cycle (childhood, puberty, adulthood (marriage), and old age) and in the visible signs of age – greying hair, wrinkles, and usually obesity. A baby has very little social importance and if it dies, it is not given a *pomana*. In fact, it is such bad luck (*prikaza*) for the mother that she will have nothing to do with it, and in the past the grandmother buried the baby. Nowadays, burial of a baby is left to the social worker so that the bad luck is avoided altogether. A child (*shav*) is given a great deal of freedom from social obligations and is not expected to observe the rules of cleanliness or sexual separation.

A boy is called *shav* until he is about twelve and his parents begin seeking a wife for him when he is called *shabaro* (lit. big boy). A girl is called *shey* until she menstruates when she is called *sheybari* (lit. big girl). Menstruation brings a dramatic change to a girl, and she is introduced to shame (*lashav*) and cleanliness (*marime*) rules of washing and behaviour. She is not allowed to sleep with her younger sisters anymore, and her clothes must be washed separately from them as well, that is, with the clothes of her mother and older sisters. She is no longer allowed to wear *gaje* clothes (ready-made clothes from the store) but must wear Gypsy clothes consisting of a separate top and long skirts. These she must wear at least 'in public', i.e. in front of adult men. Her parents begin to keep a more careful watch on her and she is expected to help more in the house. She is also instructed on how to deal with her menstruation so as to keep clean personally and avoid polluting men. She must not pass in front of a man, nor show her legs, and is given a sense of shame (*lashav*) in her behaviour towards men. Finally she begins to fast on Fridays, and only if she is clean and careful not to touch menstrual blood, is she allowed to cook during menstruation. In one case, the mother slapped her daughter several times on her face when she told her mother of her menstruation, and then instructed her on what to do. This emphasized the shame that she must be aware of in future.

Marriage is the next important step in the life-cycle. A man is now called Rom and his wife *bori* and then *romni*. The man now participates fully in work groups (*wortacha*) and receives an equal share of the money earned. He is a fully fledged member of male conversations, and though he must defer to older men, he is an accepted adult. For the woman it is a very traumatic time. She goes from a fairly privileged position as a daughter (her *bori* having to do most of the work) to the lowly position of *bori*. She is

F

a virtual slave of her mother-in-law, and her husband's family give her orders, expect her to serve all guests, and assume a servile attitude. She lives in her parents-in-law's house and is expected to obey them in all matters. As she has more and more children, her prestige rises, and she ages very rapidly, partly because of the psychological attitude towards old age, which is coveted by everyone. By the time a couple have grandchildren and a *bori* of their own, they are in a very authoritative position. If they have a good reputation they will be respected and liked, and everyone will gather around them if they have troubles and support them, but it is when they no longer have parents or parents-in-law to give them orders that they are in command. The oldest person in the *kumpania* is invariably a very respected and powerful person until senility sets in. Death at a young age is considered very tragic; at a ripe old age it is natural and brings further adulation, prestige, and power. Old people plan very happily for their eventual demise.

Relatives and Affines

A consanguineous relationship implies cooperation, closeness, and trust. Affinal relationships imply respectful attitudes, obligations, and distance. In terms of sentiment, aunt/uncle, nephew/niece, and cousin/cousin relationships are somewhat in-between consanguineal and affinal relations, especially when they are potential affines.

Relatives are people one can trust in an emergency. For example, a man who was falsely threatened with arrest fled from Texas to Los Angeles where his relatives hid him, held a conference on the issue, and arranged for the solution. Relatives are also people one can ask for favours, and they will not normally refuse or expect to be repaid. When Spiro needed a spot to keep his caravan, he first asked his half-brother and then his wife asked her brother even though he was in the midst of a big quarrel with them both. Other factors, such as residence, may influence obligations of aid. Miller George helped his brother-in-law Spiro in the Easter *slava* fight even though it involved turning against his own brother. He explained that this was unusual but that he lives in this *kumpania* with his brother-in-law and not with his brother. In this case he decided to honour his weak kinship ties in the *kumpania* (which he was trying to extend through marriages of his children) to demonstrate his loyalty to his choice of residence rather than to his brother. He was also influenced by the lack of support from his brother when he tried to get the leadership of the Kuneshti San Francisco *kumpania*.

Relatives are not worried about eating each other's food though they may be wary of eating food from affines or strangers. They feel that they know their own relatives have the correct standards of cleanliness but cannot be sure of unrelated persons' washing habits. One Machwanka said she would not eat anything unless it was cooked by her father, mother, brothers, or sisters. She then asked a Kastelaka if she would eat Katherine's food, and when the Kastelaka said she would, she asked if Katherine was related to her.

Pomana obligations differ for relatives and affines. Close relatives observe mourning rules, such as no music or parties for up to a year, more distant relatives may avoid music and parties for six weeks, but affines almost never observe mourning beyond nine days. Residence is also a factor here since a *bori* who lived with her father-in-law until his death observed the same period of mourning as her husband and his relatives. Her mother (his *Xanamik*) did not, however.

Finally, it should be noted that behaviour between relations differs in public and in private. This is most noticeable between husband and wife, for the wife must show respect in specified ways for her husband in public. If she does not, he may become *marime* (polluted), but in private these precautions are waived. This section is primarily concerned with roles which are the expected and ideal behaviour of two relations in public. Individuals, of course, do not always observe ideal behaviour.

Parental Authority

Children must show respect (*pakiv*) to their parents at all times. In general, this means they must obey and care for their parents (and grandparents) and follow the social and moral rules of the society. Every action by a child, especially a grown son or daughter, reflects on the reputation of the parents; therefore, a breach of the rules is the shame (*lashav*) of the parents as well as the person who committed the breach. To break a moral rule is to lack 'respect' for one's parents and for adults in general. Dina covered her legs when several adult men walked in the room 'to show respect'.

When I asked her what would they do if she did not cover them, she replied, 'they would go to my parents and say I did not have respect for them'.

Until they become senile, parents have the right to make major decisions for a son or daughter unless their decision is overruled by their own parents. One old couple in their seventies still pool the income from their three sons, who are in their forties, and make the decisions on how it is to be spent. A married daughter who does not live with them visited them and bought them each a $500 grave plot and expensive clothing for their burial. Another son put a downpayment on their tombstone. Children who look after their aged parents, pamper them, and prepare for an expensive death are showing proper respect.

A man cannot claim true independence until he is a grandfather, and every man and woman looks forward to the day when he will have grand-children. Numerous children and grandchildren are desired because, as is said, they are needed to take care of their parents and grandparents when they are old. Boys are often preferred to girls since a son will most likely stay with his parents, and a girl will most likely leave when she gets married. However, a couple who have nothing but sons will 'be very sad' and will try to adopt a girl. A baby is not as important as an older child. One mother, when she left her husband and returned to her parents, left her new baby and took a three year old child with her. Her in-laws were irate at this action and stated that they would not have cared if she had taken the baby, but they were determined to get back the child. This is partly because a baby is *marime* for the first six weeks and in great danger of illness until baptized, whereas a child enjoys a rather privileged position characterized by the lack of sexual or pollution status.

Having many children brings great prestige to a couple. A woman who cannot produce children is considered a failure as a wife. One *romni*, who could not have children, adopted two, one from her husband's sister and one from her husband's brother. Another wife who failed to conceive in her first year of marriage was thrown out by her mother-in-law and called a 'useless whore'. When she did conceive, she was tolerated until the mother-in-law could get the baby for adoption. When speaking of one's ancestors it is frequently said, 'he fathered thirty children and weighed three hundred pounds', which shows greatness. The same may be said of a woman.

Dad/Shav

A father and his sons work together, travel and live together, and, if necessary, fight together. A man and his sons are a political unit, especially in times of trouble, when they always side with each other. A father helps his sons find work by scouting out a new place, arranging deals with the *gaje*, and generally setting up economic schemes for them or their wives. Stevan scouted out the welfare department before bringing all his sons to Barvale, and from Barvale he arranges farm work contracts for the summer. But a father's main responsibility is to find a good wife for his son, a wife who can earn money, has a forceful personality and will have many children. He also wants a *bori* who will entertain and serve her in-laws and who will enhance his prestige through her good reputation. The father, often with the help of his brothers, will pay for the brideprice and the wedding feast and will set up his son and new wife with some source of income once they are married.

In return, a son must be loyal to his father and show him great respect. He may give part or all of his income to his father, and he will usually work with his father. Later on he will support and care for his aged parents and pay for their funerals if necessary. He will also perform many duties for his father, often doing the major amount of work for a *pomana* or *slava* which his father gives.

Dad/Shey

The father–daughter relationship does not have nearly the close cooperation that exists between a father and his sons. A son usually takes precedence over a daughter and is given more privileges and preference. A daughter is expected to serve her parents and take care of them; however, she does not have to do the menial housework, which is left to the *bori*. She is expected to honour her parents in her behaviour, to be a virgin when she marries, and a good wife thereafter. But if her husband's family mistreats her, she knows her parents will always take her back, and will protect her from them, almost regardless of what she has done. It is very traumatic for a girl to leave her family at marriage and many come back because they are so unhappy. This pressure on the parents, to prevent the failure of their daughter's marriage, is bringing them more and more to choose marriages with cousins, especially cousins of the same *kumpania*, where they can exert some influence on their daughter's welfare.

On the other hand, a daughter who wishes to stay with her new husband cannot do so if her father orders her back home. When *Xanamik* fight, the daughter has no choice but to follow her father's wishes above those of her husband or father-in-law. When Laura wanted to return to her husband, she could not until her father's anger against his *Xanamik* subsided, and he decided to let her go. A father not only protects his daughter from her in-laws, including her husband (in this case, Laura had been kicked in her pregnant stomach by her father-in-law), but he will protect her from *gaje* authorities, police, or arrest. George Davis once paid several hundred dollars to his *Xanamik* to have his daughter returned because they were maltreating her. In Case 1, Appendix A, we saw that Stevan went to great lengths to get his daughter out of jail. John Marks had her arrested primarily to cause Stevan this expense and trouble. In Case 2, John Marks would not let Rita return to her husband and child for two years until he had sorted out his grievances with her husband's grandfather.

A father is also responsible for punishing his daughter if her behaviour is immoral in any way. Since this behaviour will affect his reputation, he must be the one to rectify it. Ted Wanko's daughter got pregnant, and he decided to marry her off as soon as possible to avoid disgrace. His cousin had a son, who is mentally sub-normal and therefore unable to get a wife, and Wanko arranged for this marriage. When asked what his daughter thought of the marriage, Wanko replied:

Who cares what she thinks. She needs a husband. I am mad at her anyway. She is pretty, blonde – my prettiest daughter. I taught her how to dance and sing, and I wanted her to become a movie star. Now she has done this to me. Who cares what she thinks. Danny's not perfect, but she's lucky to get a husband at all.

Needless to say, she married Danny.

Normally, a father is very concerned to find for his daughter a husband whose family will not mistreat her, but he is also interested in the value she will bring. Marko is always yelling at his daughter to dress better, or she will not get a good price. This is partially for her own prestige and partially for his prestige and financial gain. Marcia, who is concerned about her daughter's feelings towards her future husband, admits that her husband George is more interested in arranging a 'good marriage' from his point of view, i.e. one that will bring prestige to him. The father–daughter relationship is more one of distance and respect when compared with the mother–daughter relationship.

Dey/Shav

The mother–son, like the father–son, relationship is a very close one. Particularly when the father dies, the mother–son relationship is very strong, and the mother will live with one of her sons and will be looked after for the rest of her life. When a mother, who is not living with a son, has any problems her son will always come to her aid and protection immediately. Mothers often support their sons (in the absence of support from his wife) financially, but they will also expect support from their sons if they are financially successful.

A son is also expected to take his mother's side in any disagreement with his wife, especially in the first years of marriage, and in the only two instances in Barvale when a son sided with his wife, the outrage of the mother was very great:

> I born him, I raised him, I suffered with him. Does he 'preciate it? – No, he's no good. He don't know nuthin'. God will hurt him like he hurt me. God will kill him. I hope he dies in bed next to that whore (his wife). He'll get it from the God, don't you worry.

It is interesting that in both the above instances, the other Rom in the *kumpania* felt very ambivalent because, on the one hand, the son should agree with his mother and not 'talk back' to her, but on the other hand they did not sympathize with the mother who was trying to break up her son's marriage. In any case, it is not often a son will dare to defy his mother and defend his wife. A mother often favours her sons over her daughters and will allow them more freedom than the girls, more favours, and more leisure time. In one case a woman who was left destitute by her husband had to give her daughter away for adoption (to another Rom family) and kept the son. In another case, the parents slept on a double bed with their two sons whereas the girls slept on the floor with blankets.

Dey/Shey

Fathers give their daughters orders which must be obeyed immediately and require a more distant, respectful relationship. A mother's relationship with her daughter is more affectionate and based on respectful cooperation. She is responsible for training the daughter. She directs her in the household duties and teaches her how to serve food. She trains her in fortune-telling and other lines of work. She informs her of her moral duties and the outward signs of respect that she must show towards men and teaches her about cleanliness and pollution. When a girl first menstruates her mother explains what it means and how her behaviour and dress must change. Often when a woman has a baby, especially her first baby, she will go to her mother's home for help and midwifery, for she may feel more confidence in her mother than in her in-laws. A mother does not demand continual services of a daughter as she does from a *bori*, rather their relationship is one of close cooperation, often including economic cooperation.

Some daughters become so bitter about their experience with marriage that they return home to stay with their mothers for the rest of their lives. Though all women and men are expected to be married, an adult daughter may bring home a child and stay for years with her mother quite contentedly and often have to be coerced into accepting another marriage again. In Barvale several adult daughters had returned to their widowed mothers, and they, like most daughters, had a very protective and loving attitude towards their mothers.

A mother is often very upset at her daughter's marriage, partially because she understands the trauma of becoming a *bori* among strangers. Some mothers are hysterical at losing their daughters, and during the wedding try to prevent them from 'going to the other side'. Yana cried copiously when her daughter married even though she was going to Yana's sister's household which was only about two hundred yards away. The grief of mother and daughter at the latter's marriage is partly convention and partly genuine emotion.

The behaviour of a mother to her daughter contrasts so markedly from that of a mother-in-law to her daughter-in-law that in cases where a daughter-in-law is masquerading as a daughter for economic reasons, the true relationship between the two women is always obvious from their behaviour towards each other.

Papo/Mamo – Nepoto/Nepata
Although the term for grandchild is *nepoto* or *nepata*, grandparents often address their grandchildren as *shoro* or *shori* (diminutive of

shav and *shey*). Every grandparent in Barvale, whether single or a couple, had at least one adopted grandchild. This is a grandchild that the grandparent is raising as its own child, the parents of the child relinquishing any authority. These adopted grandchildren are called *shav* or *shey*, but they generally continue to call their grandparents by their true relationship. The children may refer to their mother or father but state that they were raised by their grandparents as this is a significant fact in determining the child's prestige.

Some grandparents are particularly possessive about their grandchildren and 'take over' the raising of several of them. Sonia Davis raised Nancy, her adopted grandchild, from birth but when she travels separately from her sons and daughters, she also takes other grandchildren. On one trip she took seven grandchildren with her. When I visited the parents of one child and enquired about him, the mother said, 'we don't know where he is. I guess he is in Texas with Sonia because he hasn't been home lately.' This was not a lack of concern on the part of the parents but a deference to the authority of their own parents to take their children when they please.

Adoption of a grandchild takes a specific pattern. A daughter whose marriage breaks up may come back to her parents pregnant or with an infant (it is the man's family's right to keep children, but a wife may take a nursing infant or keep a baby born after the breakdown of the marriage) leaving older children with her parents-in-law. She and her parents care for the child until she remarries, at which time she is not allowed to take the child with her as the grandparents will not part with it and say that her new husband will not 'feel it in the heart' for the child. In one case, a girl who remarried, blackmailed her parents with the help of her social worker into letting her keep the child, but mothers do not usually resort to American law to keep their children.

A husband whose wife has left him with small children will delegate the care of the children to his parents, and when he remarries, his new wife will not have much responsibility for the children, who are raised by their grandmother. For this reason, half-brothers often do not form the same bond as brothers since they are raised either in different households or by different women in the same household. If the husband leaves his parents' house with his second wife, the children of his former marriage will stay with his parents. Thus in general, children of broken marriages are adopted by their grand-parents. Grandparents who have not obtained a grandchild from a broken marriage will choose a favourite grandchild to adopt anyway.

Adopted grandchildren hold a very special position among children. They are the favourites of their grandparents who are more indulgent with them than with their other grandchildren. These grandchildren derive great prestige through their grandparents who are the most respected and authoritative members of the *kumpania*. Spiro indulges his adopted grandchild Sylvia and gives her everything she wants even to the point of taking things away from his son's children. His son and daughter-in-law cannot contradict this decision, and Sylvia is quite aware of her privileged position. Adopted grandchildren are given such an advantage over other children that they are often very powerful men or women in adult life, and it would seem that their advantage in status during childhood continues after the death of their grandparents. When recounting the glorious past of the powerful leader Tiny Bimbo, his relatives began by stating that he was raised by his grandparents and that was why he was so '*baro*'.

Having grandchildren also brings great prestige to the grandparents. Every *rom* and *romni* eagerly awaits the arrival of grandchildren because of the authority they will enjoy and because they are genuinely fond of their grandchildren. George, who is thirty-nine, stated at his son's wedding, 'I want them to get married because I want to be a grandfather'. Grandchildren, on the other hand, also have a special obligation to care for their grandparents. This is especially true of adopted grandchildren. One grandfather stated very openly that he adopted his grandchild to take care of him: 'I raised Louis and supported him all my life, and now it's his obligation to support me and care for me when I get old.'

A grandmother has a particularly special relationship with a granddaughter which is not unlike the mother–daughter relationsh p. She will often train the girl and if the grandmother is a famous fortune-teller, the granddaughter will bring a high bride-price because of her training. Teenage granddaughters often are responsible for the housekeeping for grandparents in the rare cases when they live alone. In Barvale, one very old couple said they could not stand the noise of their sons' large families and preferred to live nearby, but separately. Their teenaged granddaughters took turns living with them to do the housekeeping. Grandparents have the final authority over their grandchildren in matters of discipline and in determining their lives. A grandmother also will be the one to bury an infant who dies at birth, to be with her granddaughter or daughter at birth, and to bury the afterbirth. When a girl of five died, she was buried by her grandparents without further ceremony, and the parents were not allowed to participate as it would be *prikaza* (a very bad omen) for them.

Phral/Phral

Brothers cooperate economically either under the direction of their father, or of an older brother, if their father is deceased. Brothers often live in the same *kumpania*, or travel together, share work and share homes, their wives sharing the housekeeping. They spend much time together, both in leisure and working, and in general cooperate in day-to-day living. They also have a special obligation to help each other find wives or husbands for their children. If a brother dies, and there are no grandparents to take the children, another brother will raise them. They have a nearly egalitarian relationship unless one brother is very much older. If the father is alive, they form a male group to defend each other against other groups of brothers.

Brothers should not fight with each other, and there was no instance in Barvale of brothers whose relations were seriously breached, though as they get older they become involved with their own families. When the Easter *slava* fight broke out between the sons of half-brothers, Stevan and Spiro, who are elderly and vieing for the leadership of the *kumpania*, were quite shocked that their sons could come to blows. Naturally they sided with their own sons (not to do would be more shocking), but when they were together they were extremely amiable and joked about their 'little problem'. (Each was trying to get the other arrested at the time though later the proceedings were dropped.) In fact Stevan finally solved the problem by taking up a collection to pay for damages done to his half-brother's car.

Phral/Pey

Brothers have a closeness and equality which is one of cooperation and mutual aid. They work together and in recreation enjoy each other's company. The same can be said of sisters. The brother/ sister relationship is more concerned with aid and protection and is neither equal nor based on economic or day-to-day cooperation due to the difference in sex.

Brother and sister may have to face separation through the marriage of the sister, but the brothers are there to protect her if necessary. If her parents die a bereaved wife may return to her eldest brother's home, or she may call on her brothers to look after her and help her when she is in trouble.[10] When twelve-year-old Laura was unhappy with her new marriage her brothers arranged to get her home in spite of the opposition of her husband and his family. Sisters can also be a great help to brothers. During the Easter *slava* when George and Johnny were engaged in a fist fight, their respective sisters intervened, fought on their behalf, and sustained the most serious injuries.

An older sister may look after a younger brother, caring for him and feeding him. In large families she may completely take over the care of an infant brother and will be held totally responsible for his welfare by her parents, who simply direct operations and give instruction when necessary. Barbara Davis was seventeen, and the eldest of eleven children when her baby brother was born, and she was given complete responsibility for him by her mother who would only occasionally give advice.

Pey/Pey

The sister–sister relationship is very similar to that between brothers. Sisters chat together, sew for each other, exchange clothes, and have a very intimate relationship. They often sleep together, share housekeeping duties, and join together with their mother in making their sister-in-law perform her duties. Once a girl has her first menses, she cannot sleep or exchange clothes with a younger sister, and the relationship changes to one of care and instruction for the younger sister.

Sex separation is very great even in the household, and generally brothers spend their time with each other, separate from their sisters, who work and chat together. But unlike brothers, sisters eventually face separation when they marry and may spend a large part of their life separated. This factor inevitably changes their relationship. Many sisters manage to stay close together by marrying into the same *vitsa* or by living in the same *kumpania*, and in these cases they will remain very close and often share housekeeping. In one case, two old sisters who were both widowed within a year of each other joined households for the rest of their lives.

Kako Bibi–Nepoto Nepata

Relations between an uncle and aunt and their nephew or niece are generally characterized by respect and mutual obligations. These obligations are secondary to the obligations between a parent and child, and as might be expected, the bonds of affection are also not nearly so strong. Stevan and Spiro's children expressed respectful public behaviour towards their uncle and aunt, but between them there never was the loyalty and affection which one reserved for one's parents or children. When Katherine (age forty) took in her elderly Aunt Mary who had just left her son's home in some turmoil, Katherine explained, 'I must take her in, it's only right because she's my aunt, but I don't want her troubles.' She felt she had to explain her obligation which conflicted with her desire to keep out of Mary's family problems. This attitude is characteristic of the relationship and contrasts with the immediate support and aid for a parent or child's problems. Spiro was relieved when his niece (WBD) left his home, even though she had been doing housekeeping duties for him. She had had an illegitimate child previously, and he did not want her 'shame' to taint his family. Since she was a Kuneshti and he a Kashtare, this shame was not already shared because of *vitsa* affiliation.

The respect that a niece or nephew gives to an uncle or aunt is based on the difference in age and status. When their ages are equal, this respectful attitude is not necessary. Sylvia (age seventeen) was Helen's (age fifteen) aunt, but they often lived in the same household and behaved almost like sisters to one another, especially since neither had a sister of similar age.

Residence may also be a factor in the relationship. Annie (age twenty-five) and her mother's sister Julie (age fifty) had both married into the same *kumpania* and were both *bori* to the same person. Annie's mother-in-law (HM) was Julie's sister-in-law (HZ) and therefore Annie looked to Julie for advice and consolation in her relations to her in-laws. She and her aunt maintained an affectionate but respectful relationship, and Annie claimed that this affection was because 'Julie looks so much like my mother'. Then she burst into tears at the thought of her mother living far away.

Another important aspect of these relations is their potentially affinal character which is further reason for maintaining distance and respect. *Figure 13* demonstrates how marriages between cousins can mean the establishment of affinal ties between uncle or aunt and nephew or niece. Consistent with the use of *kako* and *bibi* for the brother or sister (and spouses) of grandparents as well as parents is the use of *Xanamik, bori*, and *žamutro* for several genealogical levels.

Cousins (*woro/vara*)

Cousins have mutual obligations of aid·and protection, and their relationship is basically egalitarian (unless there is a great discrepancy in age). This is a very flexible relationship which may be very close or very distant; cousins may grow up together, or they may never see each other. The cousin relationship is potentially the least close of all kin relations.

Cousins who grow up in the same household (for example, brothers may share a house) may be 'like brothers' or 'like sisters'. Young cousins in the same *vitsa* and *kumpania* formed play groups and chose their friends among each other. Older cousins often worked together, shared contracts for body and fender work, or worked in groups picking produce in the fields. At the Easter *slava* this also led to a fight between cousins. For cousins to fight is neither unusual nor scandalous, which indicates the rather competitive nature of the relationship. In any conflict between cousins, other persons invariably defend and side with their own siblings and families rather than the family of an uncle or aunt. In the Easter *slava* fight, each family took sides with its own family members and Shani, who was a cousin to both families involved, agreed to aid equally anyone who asked him and would not form an allegiance with either side. Because he was related equi-distantly to both families and had to take a neutral stance, it was proposed that the *diwano* to discuss the fight should take place in his house.

Cousins of the opposite sex, with the exception of first cousins, are not allowed to be together without supervision because they are potential spouses. First cousins are not considered potential spouses, therefore they are not guarded so closely, but even they have little opportunity to converse. The major exception to this is between first cousins of the opposite sex living in the same household who have the opportunity to form close relations. Since an unmarried girl rarely mixes or talks with men outside the home, apart from her brothers, her male first cousins living in the household are her only close contact with unmarried men. After marriage, contact between cousins of the opposite sex may even be expanded outside the household though no young woman should be seen conversing for a long time with any man.[11]

Cousins who become affines – *Xanamik, socro, sacra, žamutro, bori, kumnato,* and *kumnata* (see *Figure 13*) – invariably take on roles appropriate to these relationships. However, this is not seen

FIGURE 13 Kin who are potential affines.

a. When ego marries a cousin (*woro/vara*) his father and mother-in-law may be called *kako, bibi, woro,* or *vara.* Conversely a *nepoto/nepata* may become *bori* or *žamatro.*

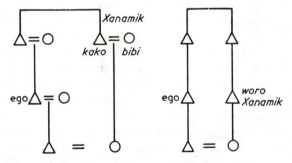

b. When ego's child marries a cousin, those he calls *kako, bibi, nepoto, nepata, woro,* or *vara* may become *Xanamik.* A *woro/vara* may also become *bori* or *žamatro.*

as a conflict in values – rather it is felt that the cousin relationship adds to and reinforces the new affinal ties and may take the edge off the rather unpredictable and easily hostile nature of the affinal relationship. In fact, it was felt that the most successful *Xanamik* relations are formed between cousins, and even unrelated persons call each other 'cousin' during marriage negotiations to show their good intentions for the future marriage and to express the egalitarian relations between them.

Affines

With the exception of a husband and wife, connection by marriage does not imply any endearment. Affines are not considered the same as relatives (*niamo*) or kindred, and when a Rom claims he is not related to a group of people he means by blood and not by marriage. Relations between affines always have an element of latent hostility and are conditioned by a series of stated obligations and duties that imply distance and avoidance.

Relatives who are potential affines (*kako/bibi, nepoto/nepata, woro/vara*) may have relationships of distance and stated obligations (as opposed to unstated ones with close kin). Among these same relatives, when the affinal potential is absent, and sex, *vitsa*, and *kumpania* are the same, then the relationship may be very close. These relatives have a wide range of potential relations depending on the context of the ties. Cousins, in particular, belong to the outer range of kin and have somewhat flexible roles.

In any discussion of expected roles between relations, it should be kept in mind that there is a strict division between private and public behaviour and between ideal and actual behaviour. Relations between husband and wife particularly emphasize this division, and my comments, as usual, are directed towards ideal, public expectations in behaviour and roles.

Before marriage ideally there is no courtship allowed between future spouses. In the past it is said they never saw each other until the wedding day, but this is generally not true now and the young *sheybari* and *shabaro* do get to know who each other are. They can eye each other at social functions even though they may not converse alone. The only way they could meet alone would be to arrange a clandestine meeting without the approval of their parents. The consequences of being caught are very severe. It will be assumed that they are having sexual relations, and either a marriage without brideprice will take place, or the girl's family will have to marry her off in shame to an undesirable husband.

As I have mentioned, sex separation is very strict. Young girls often pretend in front of their parents and elders that they do not want to get married, that they are not interested in men, and that the prospect frightens them. In groups of peers, sisters, and cousins, they discuss the available young men in great detail and their knowledge of male physiology and of sexual relations is quite remarkable. This contrasted with the almost complete ignorance of female physiology expressed by a man who had fathered seven children.[12] Being demure and embarrassed is strictly public behaviour for both young boys and young girls. Even boys dare not show too much interest in one girl, or her parents might suspect possible elopement, which could ruin his chances of marriage with her.

Boys and girls will not share activities or sit together as they would be 'embarrassed'. At the St Mary *slava*, however, they were allowed to stand together in one corner of the hall to watch individuals' dancing, while their parents talked on the other side of the room. This occasion was quite openly a time for arranging marriages, and at least four were arranged that evening. However, in general, it must be said that a newly married couple know very little of each other. If they are very young when they marry, they may not have sexual relations until several years after marriage. Most men agreed that the following are the ideal requisites for a good wife:

1. To be able to make good money, i.e. be a good fortune-teller, with an aggressive, forceful personality, and able to hustle. According to one father-in-law this is the major criterion. One old man boasted of his wife: 'Was she worth it (the high brideprice)? She was a bargain. She earned twice that in the first fortune-telling season, and she raised ten children. I did not have to make ten cents for the first several years of my marriage because she was such a fantastic money maker.'

2. She should have as many children as possible. But of course this is assumed at marriage, and it is not until later that this criterion matters. A wife who cannot bear children is considered a failure and may be sent home.

3. She should come from a respectable family and be respectable 'in her personality', that is, she should have a good reputation for being protected by her family.

4. She should be a good dancer and singer, be courteous, have good manners, and be able to entertain and serve men.

Adults seemed less concerned about what made a good husband, although young girls had personal preferences among the boys. In one instance, an old man was praised for being so kind and tolerant towards his wife who was ill and senile. However, a boy from a wealthy and respectable family would be coveted by a girl's parents.

In general, marriages become very strong once a couple has been married several years. A strong, forceful wife is a political asset to an ambitious man and can exert great influence on his behalf within the *kumpania*. A man with a meek, passive wife has little chance of assuming leadership in the *kumpania*. If a man dies, his widow can continue to wield a great amount of power on her own, but a powerful man who loses his wife will most likely seek another. One exception to this was the case of a powerful *romni bari* in her husband's *tsera*. When he died, other members of his *vitsa* blamed his death on her.[13] They claimed she was responsible because she spent all her time extending her power and neglected him. In this case she was reminded that she was an outsider to the *vitsa* and that her political position was not going to be tolerated after his death.

In public, a woman must obey her husband and show respect to his family, but if he mistreats her she can leave him. She is expected to earn the money for the family and handle it as a bank, providing him with money when he asks for it. Tilly's mother-in-law criticized her for not dressing her husband better and for not going out to tell fortunes and steal for her husband.

A wife is responsible for the purity of her husband, and she cannot allow him to become polluted by stepping over his clothes or mixing them with women's clothes when washing them. One wife said defiantly, 'I'll step over his clothes any time at home, but I could never do it in front of my father-in-law', emphasizing the difference between public and private behaviour.

Xanamik

The relationship between *Xanamik*, the parents of a married couple, is crucial for the whole institution of marriage. John Mark's said once, 'it's bad for first cousins to marry because then brothers will be *Xanamik*'. The contrast between the two relationships, brother/brother and *Xanamik/Xanamik*, illustrates the nature of *Xanamik* relations. Brothers are friends and equals, they aid and protect one another, and their affective bond is very strong. *Xanamik* must maintain distance and respect; they are bound by obligations and duties to each other, but they have no affective bond. Their first loyalty is to their married child.

Cousins, on the other hand, are said to make ideal *Xanamik* because they are related and yet not too closely related. A large number of *Xanamik* are cousins, and even those who are not, may call each other cousin during marriage negotiations.

Xanamik have several obligations. They must attend each other's *pomana* and observe the usual mourning procedure for at least nine days. They must show each other hospitality and give shelter, food, and aid if necessary; however, this is rarely requested since *Xanamik* prefer to keep a certain physical distance from each other. These obligations extend to the brother or parents of a *Xanamik* as well.

Xanamik obligations may be strong, but they do not override the loyalty of a parent to his child. The following case illustrates the kind of tensions that frequently arise between *Xanamik*:

> Mary Marks, an elderly widow, lived with her forty-five-year-old son and his recently married second wife, Laura. One day, Mary had a fight with Laura, and to her surprise her son defended his wife. This infuriated her, and she went to stay with her *Xanamik*. Laura's parents were at first willing to take her in and sent someone to get her clothes. However, Mary began cursing their daughter, and finally they lost their temper as well. Oaths (*amria*) were exchanged about each other's dead ancestors. That was the last straw, and Laura's parents told the old lady to go and stay with her niece who lived next door. Both Mary and her niece were furious that *Xanamik* obligations were being denied, and the niece claimed that her obligation to a great-aunt was not as strong as theirs to a *Xanamik*. This broke out into a full battle with pots of coffee being flung from one house over to the other, until the police were called in by both sides to stop the fighting.

Tension between *Xanamik* frequently breaks out into fighting, and this is given as one of the major reasons for the recent increase in divorces. The conflict cases described by John Marks in Appendix A illustrate the tenuous nature of *Xanamik* relations. Once *Xanamik* relations break down, the marriage is doomed.

The increase in marriages between cousins is also seen as an attempt to reinforce the *Xanamik* relationship with the bonds of kinship. This story told by John Marks about the problems between closely related *Xanamik* illustrates the role of *Xanamik* in creating and solving marital problems.

Johnny is my nephew (zs) and has a daughter married to my nephew Larry (bs) and a son married to my niece Laura (bd) whose father is Harry and mother Dina [see *Figure 14*]. Johnny lives on the West Coast with his son and Laura. When Laura and her husband Steve began having problems, they moved to Texas to stay with Harry and Dina. When they did this, their problems got worse because Laura's husband did not like being with his in-laws. He thought they were ordering him around too

FIGURE 14 Relationship between Marks and Mitchell *familiyi*.

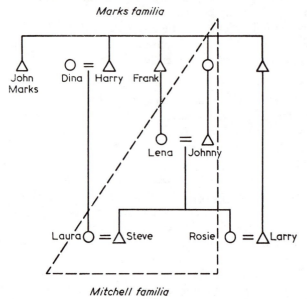

Marks familia

Mitchell familia

much and that his mother-in-law always took Laura's side in everything. So Johnny and Lena came to Texas, and Steve and Laura moved in with them.

One day Laura left her husband and brought her baby to her parents' house. I was there drinking beer with Harry and Dina. I phoned Johnny's house and spoke with Lena to tell them that Laura was at her father's house, and it would all be sorted out in the morning. You see, they might think Laura had been arrested. When Johnny heard about it he was furious and came over to beat up his *Xanamik* Dina whom he blamed for everything. Fortunately she was out, but he grabbed the baby and ran outside with it. Laura followed to get her baby, and he kicked her in the stomach. He shouldn't have done that because she was in the family way. When Laura returned and told us that, I got mad. It is a good thing we didn't see it at the time because we would have had to go out there and protect her. I phoned the police chief and told him a baby had been abducted from its mother. The police brought the baby back to us. Johnny was real mad because he knew that only I could have gotten the police to do that without arresting him. So he went to Larry's house and took back his daughter (Rosie) as a revenge. You know, a man can take back his daughter at any time. Larry came to me and said, 'Joe I don't want to have my home wrecked because of other people's problems', so there was nothing for me to do but send the baby back to its grandfather so Larry could get his wife back.

Then Johnny came and said he wanted to see his *Xanamik* Harry about getting back his *bori* (Laura). Harry was mad at Johnny hitting his pregnant daughter, so he refused. Harry said come back in a month or two. Johnny brought the baby back to Laura to look after as a sign of good will, and we arranged for Laura to meet with her husband to talk it over, and they agreed it was a minor spat. But she could not go back because Harry was mad. So Johnny has gone with Steve to Cincinnati to set up a place for the summer, and Laura will join them there in a few months.

You see, if you receive a daughter-in-law from far away from the family, nine times out of ten that marriage doesn't last. The heartbreak, the ordeal for your son – suppose he fell in love with this woman, and his home is broken up through his father-in-law. He would be very hurt. If the fathers-in-law are so strangers, so far apart that they could not get together like friends and relatives, that home would have a poor chance of getting back together. Even though the kids don't want their home broken or are in love, by Gypsy law and tradition, that home is broken. If the *Xanamik* fight, there is nothing they can do about it unless, as in a few cases, they have eloped together and stay away from both parents for as long as a year until the parents decide to make a go of it.

Xanamik relations are very tied up with the relations between a girl (*bori*) and her parents-in-law since most problems between *Xanamik* stem from the stresses in this relationship.

Socro/Sacra–Bori

Relations between a *bori* and her parents-in-law follow certain rules at all times though it is said that parents-in-law are stricter with a new *bori* than they are with her once she has proven herself, has had children, and is somewhat older. This, of course, depends on the individuals involved, but it is generally true that a *bori* has a harder time when she first enters the household of her parents-in-law. One woman explained her adjustment in this way:

> They (father and mother-in-law) are like father and mother to me now. I didn't know anything when I married. I was twelve, and all I knew was what my mother-in-law told me: cook, clean, and sweep up. They taught me everything, and they are the main family I know now.

When first married, a *bori* is made very aware that she is now under the jurisdiction of her parents-in-law and their family. The very marriage ceremony itself emphasizes this. The *zeita*[14] or, as the Rom translate it 'bringing the bride home', is the moment in the ritual when the bride is pulled across an imaginary line by relatives from her husband's *vitsa* with her relatives trying to stop the ceremony. From then on she is married and under the jurisdiction of her husband's family. Later she must entertain her father-in-law and his guests without the presence of her parents, which is the first time they are not allowed to participate in the wedding procedure.

A *bori* should remain quietly to one side at social occasions at the bidding of her mother-in-law. As a *sheybari* she can drink and talk boisterously, but as a *bori* a woman must be a model of submissiveness. One *bori* who got slightly tipsy at a party was told by her mother-in-law to stay with her children and stop drinking or go home. Another very self-willed aggressive young girl turned into a demure *bori* overnight with downcast eyes and hardly a word uttered. This behaviour did not last for long, of course.

The *bori* must obey her parents-in-law in everything, and she cannot expect her husband to help her or take her side against his mother. She is responsible for the major part of the housework, the cooking, cleaning, sweeping, and washing, as well as caring for her children. At any large social gathering the preparation of food and the table is done by the *bori* under the direction of her mother-in-law. She is also expected to support her husband financially and provide the basic financial support for the household. Kata Davis, for example, pays the telephone bill, although it is in her mother-in-law's name and is used by all her husband's relatives. Rachael's main complaint about her *bori* was that she was too ill to work or have children so that Rachael had to continue supporting her son. Of course a *bori* must also produce children and can expect one or more of them to be taken by her parents-in-law. If she decides to go back to her parents she does not have the right to take the children.

The parents-in-law are concerned primarily with the services that a *bori* will provide them. Miller said of his son's broken marriage: 'It's a shame Billy (age fourteen) and Laura (age twelve) didn't get along. Billy needs a wife, and it's nice to have a *bori* around who can do things for Mary (his wife).' But a mother-in-law also takes it upon herself to train and educate her *bori* and sometimes this can develop into an affectionate relationship. A mother also trains her daughter and training is associated with care and affection. The mother-in-law teaches the *bori* how to behave, how to run a house, have children, be a good wife, and be a better fortune-teller. The girl's relations with her father-in-law are much more distant and consist of performing duties for him. The prohibition against sexual relations between a *socro* and *bori* is very strong and even a hint of any liaison is a curse on the man (see Appendix A, Case 1). His strong reaction to the accusation is a measure of the severity of the crime. However, few *bori* would use this threat against their father-in-law.

The choice of a mother and father-in-law is sometimes more important for the girl than the husband. Dorothy had two unhappy marriages and in both cases she complained that her mother-in-law made a slave of her and her sisters-in-law terrorized her if she disobeyed her mother-in-law. In the second marriage, her husband beat her, and on these occasions her female in-laws took her side so she stayed with him for years. When she finally could stand it no longer and left, she had to leave her three children with her mother-in-law.

The parents-in-law do not always have the support of the community; there are limits to their authority. In one trial over marital problems in Barvale, it was decided to let a young couple with two children have their own house since the parents-in-law were interfering too much in the marriage. The father-in-law was amazed and irate at this verdict, 'because she's my *bori*. It is right for me to tell her what to do. Her parents use my son as an errand boy when they are over there so why should they tell me not to use my *bori*.' In this case the *kumpania* interfered to save the marriage and tempered the control of the father-in-law if only temporarily. However, everyone agreed that this was an unusual verdict, and I suspect that the whole story told by the girl was not revealed.

Not all relations with parents-in-law are bad. This case described by a social worker, seemed to fit the ideal:

> Upon first impression Diane appears to be very dull; however, this may just be her bride's manner which she feels is appropriate. She seldom speaks. She is very subservient towards her husband and extremely servile towards her mother-in-law and her other in-laws. She has taken over most of the housekeeping duties in the household. She may be overdoing it since she was not a bride selected by the family. As a result, Mrs. Mary Costello is extremely pleased with her and is very boastful about her new daughter-in-law's homemaking abilities.

In another case, old Rosie has a very good relationship with her *bori* with whom she has lived for about twenty years. She said, 'Katharine takes care of me and does everything for me. I don't know what I would do without her.' However, old Rosie's word is law; she is a firm disciplinarian and Katharine is unusually mild and unaggressive.

Socro/Sacra–Žamutro

Relations between parents-in-law and a son-in-law are quite different from a *bori*; first, because he does not live with them and can maintain more distance from them, and second, because he is not obligated to perform services for them. However, a *žamutro* is in a subordinate position to his parents-in-law and must obey them, but because he is a man it would not do to order him around too much. Usually relations are harmonious because he lives with his parents, but when he is in the same *kumpania* as his parents-in-law, a further strain is put on the marriage. One young husband came to ask his wife for money which she immediately gave him. When she asked for some back, he ignored her, and his mother-in-law who overheard this yelled, 'you want a wife, boy, you give it back'. He did. A powerful man will try to get his sons-in-law to join his *kumpania*, and of course if he is powerful, then it is also to their advantage to do so (though they will not live in the same house). Stevan has convinced two sons-in-law to join his *kumpania*.

In both cases the sons-in-law's fathers are dead, and their mothers are sickly and live with them. They join Stevan's sons as *wortacha* and work together.

A son-in-law who agrees at marriage to live in the same household as his parents-in-law is called a 'house *rom*'. A house *rom* has few rights and is under the domination of his parents-in-law. Consequently, he loses respect from the other men in the *kumpania*. No self-respecting Rom accepts this position unless he cannot get a wife in any other way, (e.g. he is mentally retarded) or suffers special unfortunate circumstances, as the following case shows:

> George and his half-brother agreed to a marriage between their daughter and son respectively. George set a very high brideprice, but the family only paid $300, and George felt cheated. Consequently he refused to let his daughter go to her in-laws family. Wally, the son, had no choice but to move in with his father-in-law. The parents-in-law completely dominate the young couple and make all their decisions for them. They even tried to get their welfare cheque put in the mother-in-law's name because the general opinion in the whole *vitsa* is that Wally is not 'bright' enough to handle money, that he is completely hopeless as a husband and a burden to everyone. They have all decided he is mentally retarded though his behaviour when he is not in the presence of his in-laws seems normal – they intimidate him. (Welfare Record.)

A house *rom*, like a *bori* must accept a life of being ordered around by his parents-in-law. One young man has refused to get married, though he is thirty, because he has no money for a brideprice and his only alternative is to become a house *rom*. He was also the most educated Rom in Barvale, and this added to his undesirability.

Kumnato/žamutro; kumnato/bori; kumnata/bori; kumnata/žamutro
Relations between these relatives are difficult to assess just as the use of the terms is rather ambiguous. A *bori*'s relations with her husband's brother (*kumnato*) and husband's sister (*kumnata*) are similar to her relations with her in-laws in general. She is subordinate to them, and they give her orders, though it is her parents-in-law who have the final say. The husband's sisters are given less work to do, and if they are lazy and domineering towards their *bori*, she will feel resentment, but if they are friendly and helpful to her, they may become allies. A new *bori* sleeps with her *kumnata*

until she is allowed to sleep with her husband. But now that her husband and parents-in-law are dead, Katherine is very disparaging of her husband's brother and his wife and shows great hostility towards them. *Kumnato/bori* (HF/BW) relations require avoidance and distance like the *socro/bori* (HF/SW) relations and have a similar prohibition against sexual relations.

Kumnata or *kumnata/žamutro* (WB, WZ/ZH) relations are based on more equality than a *bori* has with her brothers and sisters-in-law, but there is still an element of subordination for the *žamutro*. This comes out mainly between males (*kumnato/žamutro*) who have more frequent contact. When Stevan was making a speech his wife's brother began mocking him with 'oh king, oh king'. He was embarrassed but said nothing in retort. Brothers-in-law attend each other's *pomana* and will spend time conversing together although there is often an element of tension in their relations which is expressed in joking behaviour.

The relationship of WZH to WZH is slightly different. WZH/WZH relations were described as being just 'like brothers'. This is undoubtedly an equal sort of relationship lacking the tension of *kumnato/žamutro* relations since both men have taken a wife from the same family and stand in the same relationship (of *žamutro*) to that family. In one case the two men were first cousins anyway, and this further tie strengthened their friendly, drinking-partner relationship.

However, the HBW/HBW relationship seems to be fraught with more competition and hostility since both women are *bori* to the same parents-in-law and may compete for approval from them. This 'tale of the two sisters-in-law' exemplifies this competition.

Tale of the Two Bori

There were two *bori* (sisters-in-law) travelling with the family. The younger one was nicer and was favoured by her father- and mother-in-law. The older one worked hard, but the younger one got all the praises and was shown off in front of other people. The older one was jealous. One day her father-in-law told her to fix some food, and at the same time he was praising the younger one. So the older *bori* went out and got a snake and put it in the middle of the bread. She took the bread to her father-in-law, and he gave it to the younger *bori*. She ate it and the snake was inside her.

Soon her stomach began to swell, and her parents-in-law were so proud, and everyone crowded around expecting the baby. But nine months passed, and no baby, and then ten months and on and on. Everyone began to get worried. The older sister-in-law was grinning now. After two years they were frantic. Her belly got bigger and bigger, but she had no baby. She got sicker and sicker. One day an old man came to the camp and said 'I am hungry, please give me some food.' So they said 'all right old man, come and share our food with us.' When he had eaten he saw everyone was sad, and he asked why. They told him about the daughter-in-law. The old man told them to get some milk and heat it up in a huge tub. When it was steaming, he put the girl over the milk, and she breathed the steam. Soon, out came the snake, and the old man showed the people what had been making her sick. Even though he got the snake out, she died a few months later.

This tale shows little condemnation of the jealous sister-in-law's behaviour as the competition for the favour of their parents-law is considered natural and unavoidable. In fact the older *bori* should have had more privileges, but because the younger one was 'nicer' this was reversed. There seems to be almost a sense of 'justice' in the punishment of the younger *bori*.

Finally, there is one further relationship which I would like to mention here. This is the ritual relations established between godparents or sponsors (*kirvo, kirvi*) and godchildren (*fino, fina*). One of the striking features of Rom religion is that they have no religious practitioners. They often use the services of *gaje* priests and preachers when they need them, but it is the godparents who are the major ritual practitioners for each individual.

The *kirvo/fino* relationship is a ceremonial one which creates a kinship bond. The godparents may be chosen among relatives or non-relatives, and they may be Rom or *gaje*. In any case, the relationship creates a bond and a set of mutual obligations involving gift exchanges and ritual services. A *kirvo* is very respected by both his *fino* and the parents of the *fino*. As one girl explained, 'he is more than a father, he is more respected'.

Kirve (pl.) are normally chosen at the baptism of a child, and at this time they perform certain ritual services for the child and its parents and in return are given gifts from the parents. The *kirve* take the baby to be baptized in the church by a priest. It would be bad luck (*prikaza*) for the parents of the child to be present. When they come to collect the child, they lift it from its bed and leave a silver or gold coin under the baby. This will be saved for the baby and will bring it good luck. When they return with the baptized baby the family rejoices because now they can fondle it without fear of it getting sick. After baptism the baby will not have fear and cry at night, and they can remove the red band and *bujo* (amulet) which wards off sickness. The *kirve* buy the baby its christening clothes, but the parents of the child give the feast and party for the baptism. When the *kirvo* approaches the party of people he hoots his horn and throws candy to everyone. This brings good luck to those who catch it. As soon as they have eaten at the feast table, sponsors are presented with a complete set of clothing each, including underwear, shoes, and a handbag. When they wear these clothes, it gives them good luck.

Sponsors are also chosen at a wedding although one of the couple's sponsors from baptism may perform the 'honour'. Their duty is to take up the collection for the young couple. At Steve's wedding his *kirvo* from baptism argued that it was his right to do the honours (make the collection) since he was already 'godfather'. At the wedding the sponsors must be a couple who have never been divorced.

The *kirvo/fino* relationship involves other obligations besides that of ritual sponsor. When a child was sick it was often the *kirvo* who paid for the hospital bill. *Kirve* and *fine* will go to each other's side at a time of illness and must attend each other's *pomana*. At the Easter *slava* when people visited each other's home, it was also obligatory to visit the home of *kirve* or the *kirve* of one's child. On one occasion a woman gave a gift to another 'because she baptized my child'. In general, the *kirvo* is said to bring good luck (*baXt*) and good health (*sastimos*) to his *fino* whether at baptism or in marriage.

Uncles and aunts are often chosen to be *kirve* when they are particularly close to the family. This reinforces the affective bonds and prohibits the potentially affinal aspect. *Kirve* and *fine* are considered kin and are not allowed to marry. They also may not be allowed to enter into affinal relations. All of Tom's children are *fino* to their father's brother, Nick. The two brothers, Tom and Nick, often share their homes and work together as *wortacha*. George was *kirvo* to the children of his cousin through his *vitsa*, and his wife (who was their *kirvi*) was also related to the wife of this cousin. In another case the *kirvi* chosen was a great niece to her *fino*'s mother.

Conclusions

In general a close bond exists between relatives and a more distant one between persons related only by marriage. When ages differ, respect is always due to the older person, and when sex differs, respect is due to the male.

Certain relationships can best be illustrated by comparing them with other relationships both for similarity and contrast. The mother/daughter and mother-in-law/daughter-in-law relationships are similar in that they are characterized by economic cooperation, instruction, and authority from the elder woman to the younger. The younger woman must show respect and submissiveness to the elder. They contrast in that the first relationship is based on affection and intimate bonds, but the second is a distant and often resentful relationship. A girl experiences painfully the contrast in her role as a daughter and as a daughter-in-law, and it is only when she learns to adapt to her role as wife and mother that she begins to identify with her husband's *vitsa*.

Mother/son and wife/husband relations are similar in that the woman is expected to provide financial support for the man, and the bonds are expected to be intimate and strong and include mutual aid and protection. Either mother or wife, usually both, will raise a man's children. However, a man should show respect towards his mother and bow to her authority whereas with his wife it is he who can demand respect and authority. A man experiences great conflict between his role as son and husband and is constantly in the position of having to choose between one and the other.

The parent/child and grandparent/grandchild relationships are very similar. Both form very close bonds even though the child or grandchild is expected to show deference to the authority of the older and support them when he gets older. However, when he is still young, parents or grandparents care for and support the child and see to his education and moral behaviour. Parents and grandparents are in competition for a child and often share in the raising and education of the child. Even so, a child does not see much difference in his role as child or grandchild and will often be called *shav* or *shey* by both sets of adults.

As we saw, cousins are said to make good *Xanamik*. Both are relations of equality and lack of authority. Both feel more loyalty to closer kin than to each other, in the first instance, to brothers, and in the second, to the child. However, cousins have a very general, amorphous set of obligations and a rather flexible relationship in terms of sentiments whereas *Xanamik* have well defined roles towards each other. The *Xanamik* relationship is characterized by avoidance and respect and contrasts with the relationship of brothers which is close and affectionate but also equal. The relationship between brothers is like that between father and son in that they share a working economic relationship and aid and protect each other; however, in the first there is equality whereas in the second, the father has authority. The mother/daughter and sister/sister relationships contrast in the same way as father/son and brother/brother. Again there is economic cooperation and a lack of competition, with hierarchy in the first and equality in the second.

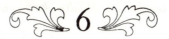

The *Vitsa* and *Natsia*

According to Yoors (1967: 134–5), and therefore the Lowara
Rom with whom he lived, the Rom are divided into four 'races'
(*rasa*),[1] the Lowara, Churara, Kalderasha, and Machwaya. Each
'race' or 'nation' is further sub-divided into *tsera* (or *vitsa* as the
Kalderash call them), and each *tsera* includes the descendants of
one ancestor and may be named after this ancestor.

Ronald Lee, whose information comes from Canadian Kalderash,
recognizes the same divisions – *natsiyi romaiya* (Romany nations)
divided into *vitsi*, and each *vitsa* into *familiyi* or extended families
(Lee 1967: 45). The divisions used by the Barvale Rom are basically
the same as those mentioned by Yoors and Lee. In Barvale there
are only three tribes or *natsiyi*: the Machwaya, the Kalderash,
and the Churara. There were no Lowara in Barvale as they are
quite rare in America.[2] The Kalderash, Machwaya, and Churara
are seen as intrinsically different 'races'. Personality traits,
physical appearance, status, morality, and intellectual ability are
generally attributed to the fact of belonging to a certain *natsia*.
However, all *natsiyi* are accepted as Rom, and they live together
in the same *kumpania* and may intermarry.

The Kalderash are divided into numerous *vitsi*, of which
several were represented in Barvale. How many Kalderash *vitsi*
exist today would be very difficult to determine since they are
spread over North and South America, Europe, Asia, and various
other parts of the world. The Kalderash are by far the largest tribe
of Rom. In Barvale the Machwaya did not sub-divide themselves
into *vitsi* as far as I could determine; however, I have heard of
Machwaya *vitsi* elsewhere in America,[3] and it may be that they
simply fail to use this sub-division because the Machwaya as a
whole are a small nation. Another factor in the disuse of the *vitsa*

names may be because of the prestige of calling oneself Machwaya. The Churara are represented by one very large *vitsa* in Barvale, the Kuneshti. When asked directly, informants were not certain that the Kuneshti were a Churara *vitsa*, and many said it must be Kalderash.[4] Lee (1968: 13) also calls the Kuneshti a Kalderash *vitsa*; however, there is considerable evidence, which I shall discuss later, to indicate that they are Churara. Again, one reason for the obscurity of their identity may be the very unfavourable moral and social position which other Rom ascribe to the Churara.

Each *vitsa* theoretically may include all the male and female descendants of a real or mythical ancestor, who also may be male or female. In practice the *vitsa* includes only those descendants who count themselves as members of that *vitsa*. In accordance with the cognatic principle of descent, any descendant of an ancestor has the right to belong to his *vitsa*, but actually, only certain people 'join' a *vitsa*, and most people eventually belong exclusively to one *vitsa*. The *vitsa* therefore is not a pre-determined unit of persons and involves an element of choice. Generally, a person chooses to identify with his father's *vitsa*, and this has led many gypsiologists to believe that the *vitsa* is a patrilineal descent group (see Cotten 1955: 21; Pickett 1966: 8). However, it is misleading to think of the *vitsa* as patrilineally determined since the Rom state that a person may belong to either his father's or his mother's *vitsa*, and even when he chooses his father's *vitsa* he may change this choice in later life and identify himself with the *vitsa* of an old widowed mother. The very word, *vitsa*, also gives no indication of a patrilineal tendency. *Vitsa* is from the Rumanian *vitse*, which means family or stock (G. & L.). The Rom translate the word *vitsa* as 'generation', members of one's *vitsa* being called 'the generations'. This does not refer to genealogical level but is being used in the sense of 'descendants' to indicate persons who have 'generated' from one source (see *shorter Oxford English Dictionary*).

It is also very misleading to think of the *vitsa* as a group in the way a *kumpania* is a group. The *vitsa* is primarily a unit of identification. The persons of one *vitsa* may never come together or function as a group in any way. Some *vitsi* are small enough to be a functioning group and a real body of persons, but most *vitsi* operate as a group only on two occasions. First, at a *kris*, it is said that the '*vitsi* get together'. This is not a literal statement, since each *vitsa* is merely represented by a man and wife. However, at an important trial involving possible expulsion (*marime*), the whole *vitsa* may attend since the situation gravely affects the *vitsa's* reputation. In this case the *vitsa* unites as a group. The second occasion when a *vitsa* may unite is at a *pomana*, especially the *pomana* of a very respected *vitsa* elder. *Vitsa* members share an obligation to honour each other by attending each other's *pomana*, and frequently almost the whole *vitsa* may be present. Part of the reason for this obligation may be that a *mulo* (spirit of the deceased) only plagues relatives and affines, and this includes members of a *vitsa*. However, even for an important trial or *pomana*, when a *vitsa* is very large, it is not possible for it to unite.

Each *vitsa* has a name which may be derived from a real or mythical ancestor (the descendants of Pupa will be called Pupeshti). A *vitsa* may also be named after an animal, object, or defining characteristic of the people in that *vitsa*. For example, Saporeshti comes from *sap* (snake), Kashtare from *kash* (wood, tree), and Bokurishti from *bok* (hunger, hence 'hungry people'). Some names are supposedly given in jest such as the Papineshti who were so named because they were adept at stealing geese (*papin* means goose).

Vitsi are born and die quite frequently. Some grow to be very large and famous, for the more prestigious a *vitsa* becomes, the more descendants who will ally themselves with the *vitsa*. When a *vitsa* becomes too large, several large sections of families within the *vitsa* may split off and begin calling themselves by a new name. Other *vitsi* may contain merely one large *familia* covering three or four generations. A small *vitsa* such as this will be forced to marry with other *vitsi*, and if they intermarry closely with one particular *vitsa*, they may eventually merge with them. The majority of *vitsi* are large enough to contain several large *familiyi*.

The *familia* is difficult to define in general since unlike the *vitsa* it does not have a *Romanes* name. Very rarely is one American family name used to indicate one *familia* within one *vitsa*. More frequently, out of a stock of American surnames a *familia* chooses one or two, sometimes, several, which are often used by their *vitsa*. However, several *vitsi* may use the same surname so even this method of identification is unreliable. For example, two Kashtare *familiyi* in Barvale used Davis and Costello respectively as *gaje* surnames, but on occasion they would change them around. Generally, a *familia* consists of a man and his wife (or one or the other) at the head, their grown sons and sons' wives, occasionally, married daughters and their husbands, but more often widowed or divorced daughters, and the children and grandchildren of these sons and daughters. A *familia* always covers three, and possibly four generations since a man or woman cannot be the head of a *familia* (*phuro*) until he or she is a grandparent. It may also include nephews, nieces, grandchildren, and other relatives adopted by the family. Occasionally, these adopted children are married adults with their children. The heads of various *familiyi* in one *vitsa* are brothers, sisters, half-brothers or half-sisters, first cousins, or the wives of deceased brothers or cousins. Several *familiyi* of one *vitsa* often live in the same *kumpania* or form travelling groups. Women who leave by marrying out join another *familia* and possibly another *vitsa*. Men who leave with a large family of their own eventually create their own *familia*. A woman who belongs to her husband's *familia* (and *vitsa*) may, when she is widowed, return to her father or mother, and she and her children may then form part of that *familia* (and *vitsa*). Residence is therefore a very important factor in *familia* membership.

In Barvale, for example, the Kashtare *vitsa* is divided into five *familiyi*. The Kashtare *vitsa*, which is reputed to be very large, also has several *familiyi* in other areas, mostly California, Texas, and Oregon. *Figure 2* gave the genealogical relationship between the five Kashtare *familiyi* in Barvale and demonstrated how *familiyi* within a *vitsa* divide, that is, along sibling lines. *Figure 3* showed how two *familiyi* might merge, that is, through marriage in the next generation. In *Figure 4* it was shown that when the same kind of intermarriage occurred between two Kashtare *familiyi* and one Machwaya *familia*, the descendants did not merge but choose the *natsia* affiliation of their father. The one exception was the case of the head of *Familia 6* (*Figure 4*) who first married a Kashtare and had a family, then married a Machwano and raised another family. Because she is an old and powerful widow, the head of several large nuclear families, and directs the instruction of her grandchildren in Machwaya customs, most of her grandchildren of both husbands are choosing to be Machwaya. One son by the Kashtare father, for example, generally lives with his (Adams) half-brothers and married a Machwanka himself. His children say they are Machwaya in most instances, but they have not yet chosen their *vitsa*.

In Barvale there are three *natsiyi*. Members of these three groups, the Kalderasha, Machwaya, and Kuneshti are considered by each other to be physically, morally, and socially different from one another. Their position in the general model of Rom social organization is unconscious for most people, though known by the elders. Nevertheless, everyone in the *kumpania* acts on the assumptions and beliefs implicit in the model, particularly in relation to the differences in the three *natsiyi*.

The *natsia* is not a 'group' but a category. Members of the same *natsia* never unite, may never know each other, and live in different countries throughout the world so that most do not know of the

FIGURE 15 Symbolic representation of the social status of the four *natsiyi*.

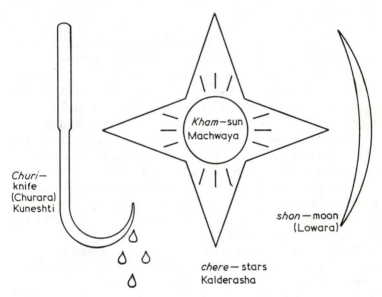

existence of the others. It is claimed that each *natsia* has a different dialect. Certainly in Barvale there are dialect differences between *natsiyi*, but whether all members of one *natsia* have the same dialect is extremely doubtful. The *natsia* is a category that determines status and behaviour between its members. This status is expressed in an origin's myth which the Rom in Barvale considered sacred and would never reveal. A search through the literature did not reveal any one myth dealing with the origins of the four *natsia*; however, the same symbols (*Figure 15*) appear again and again in Rom stories, myths, and beliefs.

It was through the school that the symbolism of the *natsiyi* emerged. We were looking for an emblem for the school to represent all the Rom in Barvale. One of the boys revealed that his grandmother had explained to him the differences between the *natsiyi* and how they are represented, and he immediately drew the picture given in *Figure 15*. He explained 'the sun is the Machwaya because they are more powerful. The Kalderash are the stars (though he drew only one big star) and the Kuneshti are knives.' He gave no explanation for the moon and could not say what it was. When the elders saw his drawing, they were furious that he had revealed this, and they said it was 'based on an old legend', and that we could not use it for the school because 'the Kuneshti would be furious since the knife represents hate'. They did not want the symbols mentioned again. The old lady who told it to her grandson said 'it is sacred information' which he must never tell even to other Rom unless he could trust them.

The sun represents the Machwaya; it is one and is powerful which is consistent with the superior status and power that the Machwaya possess over other *natsiyi*. It is also consistent with the apparent lack of Machwaya *vitsi*. The Kalderasha are the stars, and though he only drew one star, it surrounds the sun and is very large, just as the Kalderasha are very numerous. They also in a sense do have the position of revolving around the sun because their power (in Barvale at least) is always in relation to Machwaya power. The Kuneshti are the knife (more like a cutlass) which represents 'hatred'. This brings me to the reason for classifying the Kuneshti as a Churara *vitsa*.

Churara comes from the word *churi* which means knife and though no one knew what 'Kuneshti' meant they all agreed that they were 'knifers' and that the Kuneshti were associated with knives. The Kuneshti themselves claim to be descended from 'fierce turks who brandished cutlasses' (Tompkins 1967: 4) though they do not like the other Rom to mention the association with a knife. Cotten (1955: 26) also describes some 'killer gypsies' mentioned by her informants who were 'warriors' and decided they must be Churara.

Apart from the association with the knife which is the *natsia* symbol of the Churara, there are other indications that the Kuneshti might be Churara. Yoors describes the Churara as smaller and darker than other Rom and states that they were traditionally traders of horses and thieves. Certainly the Kuneshti in Barvale demonstrate this striking physical difference (smaller and darker), and several welfare records of occupations of the very old Kuneshti leaders mention that they were horse traders, although later they followed the same occupations as the other Rom in America.

The most important evidence is that the Kuneshti (like the Churara) are considered inferior to other Rom, and they are treated as if they were of another *natsia*. A Kalderash explains Kuneshti behaviour by referring to the fact that they are Kuneshti just as the behaviour of Machwaya is explained by referring to his *natsia*. The Machwaya are proud of being 'better' and think of the Kalderash as lowly, dirty, and ignorant. The Kalderash are suspicious of the Machwaya, resent their snobbery, and distrust them because they are often likely to take over and run things for themselves. Both of them agreed that the Kuneshti are the lowest of the three categories, that they are untrustworthy and will steal from or cheat 'even a Gypsy'. One Kalderash woman put it this way: 'The Machwaya are the highest. Their women are expensive, but they like to marry us because our families are stricter and more traditional. There are lots of us (Kashtare) and we are well known. But the Kuneshti, they can't get wives. Nick got three *bori*, and all three had run away from a *gajo* before. That's why he got them.' This statement is far from the literal truth but is interesting primarily as an expression of disgust towards the Kuneshti and as a way of singling them out as a group. I also heard from a Kuneshti that the Machwaya like to marry Kuneshti because the *bori* behave so well, that is, are completely subservient because of their lowly status.

The political implications of the three *natsia* statuses were manifest in both the Easter *Slava* and Devil conflicts, and from these examples it is quite clear that the Kuneshti are treated as being categorically different. At the Easter *slava*, the solution to the fight between members of one Kalderash *vitsa* was to shift the blame to an accepted culprit, the Kuneshti, and to oust all Kuneshti from Barvale. During the devil incident the possibility of Machwaya political domination was an additional threat. The Kalderash greatly resent Machwaya high status and despise Kuneshti low status, consequently conflict between these three for political ascendancy was a constant in Barvale.

Finally, a word about the crescent moon. Though the Rom in Barvale would not give any further information on the symbols in

Figure 15, it seems quite likely that the moon represents the Lowara. Since there were no Lowara in Barvale, I cannot say what their status might be; however, I suspect that it is quite high and only outshined by the Machwaya (represented by the sun). According to Yoors (1947: 1-18), the Lowara are trusted 'law-makers' (which is how their name is translated) and are very respected for their knowledge of laws, traditions, and *kris* procedure (see also Cotten 1955: 25).

The sun, moon, and stars are frequently encountered symbols in a religious context both among Barvale Rom as well as in the literature on other Rom. The blessing at a *pomana* death feast invokes the sun, moon, and God (*Kama, Shona, kai Devla, ashun ma*) to listen to the blessing which is given in honour of the deceased as if the Rom are calling on all *natsiyi romaiya* to preside over the *pomana* of one of their brethren. The staff of the political leader, which was common among European Rom but which has been replaced by a sheriff's badge in America, is described by Clébert (1963: 175) as an octagonal disc on a staff containing five figures: the battleaxe, the sun, moon, stars, and a cross. These figures are called 'the *Semno*' or authentic 'sign' of the Gypsies (Clébert 1963: 163). The moon is always a quarter moon, the sun is always on the right taking precedence over the moon, and the stars are always numerous and encircle the other two. Once when I showed the Rom in Barvale an amulet (from Leland 1891: 230) which contained these very symbols including a snake, they remarked: 'That looks like all the *vitsi*.'

The hierarchy of the *natsiyi* is a major factor in determining the hierarchy of the various *vitsi*. But whereas *natsia* hierarchy and status is immutable, the *vitsi* have more flexible status. Status may be gained through wealth, power, and reputation and may be lost in the same way. However, their status position only fluctuates within the framework of the *natisa* statuses, so that no matter how powerful or wealthy a Kalderash *vitsa* becomes, it is still felt to be inferior to the Machwaya.

Descent and the Vitsa

Descriptions of the *vitsa* in the literature are often sketchy and incomplete, and there seems to be little understanding of what a *vitsa* is. Part of the problem is the secrecy with which the Rom surround information on genealogy, *vitsa*, *natsia*, and family relations. Mrs Tompkins, the social worker who has spent six years trying to work out relationships, remarked:

> It took me approximately two years to figure out the division within the Gypsy community. I did not realize that there was more than one tribe (*natsia*) until I started to learn some of the Romany words and noticed that there were dialect differences in pronunciation. After I discovered the fact of tribal divisions, Gypsies would readily identify their tribal affiliations, whereas they would never do this before. (Tompkins 1967: 2)

Vitsa affiliation is even more difficult to discover since it is never so obvious as a person's *natsia* in appearance, behaviour, or conversation.

But perhaps a deeper reason for the ambiguity about the *vitsa* and *natsia* is the contradictions that the Rom themselves present in everyday conversation, combined with the fact that they are not actual groups but are categories. A *vitsa* is only very rarely united in one place, and large *vitsi* never are. Also, each person gives a different version of the relative statuses of the *vitsi*, his version being dependent on a number of factors, not least his own position in the hierarchy. Only a few elders knew all the *vitsi* in North America, and even they did not know their size, reputation, founders, mythology, power in the *kumpania*, etc. Consequently, it is very difficult to sort out information on the *vitsa*. Clearly a hierarchy exists, but it would take a massive amount of information about *vitsi* all over North America to sort out a reasonably accurate table of *vitsi* hierarchy. Unfortunately, most monographs virtually ignore the *vitsa* or have only very scanty information. For example, Coker describes his impressions:

> There seems to be a sense of hierarchy among the *vitsesti*. I suspect that the hierarchical sequence varies according to the *vitsa* of one's informant, but it was not possible to test this suspicion since only one informant could be induced to talk in some detail about *vitsa* hierarchy. There would probably be agreement as to the highest *vitsa*, for the one informant gave a name to that rank unhesitatingly (it was not his own), although he shifted the positions of the remaining *vitsesti* while making up his mind. The highest *vitsa* seems to be clearly delinated, with other *vitsesti* roughly grouped into two hierarchical ranks. (Coker 1966: 88)

Although Coker was not aware of the *natsia* division he does place the Machwaya at the top and the 'Mexican' and 'English' Gypsies at the 'lowest level' (88–9) which is consistent with statements of Barvale Rom.

Another confusion in the literature on the *vitsa* is the tendency to equate it with some kind of residential unit, either a *kumpania* (if it is a closed one), or a group of *familiyi* in one *vitsa* (if it is an open one). Only very small *vitsi* actually congregate in one place, and yet Cotten, for example, clearly thinks of the *vitsa* as a residential unit when she makes statements such as the following:

> Factors militating against large (*vitsa*) size include such elements as the negative correlation between *vitsa* size and the ability to support members within the non-Gypsy environment and increasing problems of household and equipment maintenance. In the days of outdoor camps, for instance, a very large *vitsa* was faced with problems of overgrazed pastures and over-rapid pollution of the campsite. (Cotten 1968: 1051)

It has also been commonly accepted among gypsiologists that the *vitsa* is a patrilineal group. Coker states correctly that 'there is no rule of unilineality in the inheritance of *vitsa* names. An individual has the right to both his father's and his mother's name' (1966: 87); but she thinks that the *vitsi* are merely 'name groups' and lumps together all names given to any groups of Gypsies: groups that are not Rom as well as *natsia*, *vitsa*, and family names used for the *gaje*. Cotten calls the *vitsa* a 'sib' and specifically a 'patrilineal band' and defines it thus: 'the men are related to one another consanguineally and the women affinally' (1955: 21). Later she adds, presumably because there are too many exceptions to this statement,

> just as a man belongs to the tribe (*natsia*) of his father, so he inherits his father's *vitsa* and *familia* affiliations. Theoretically a *vitsa* is a group of patrilineally related extended families; in practice, however, a man and his family have an absolute right to affiliate with any *vitsa* with whom consanguineal ties, either paternal or maternal, can be claimed. (1968: 1051)

This is a case of modifying an earler misjudgement by extending it rather than providing a new definition altogether.[5] The true situation is exactly the reverse.

The Rom have a cognatic terminology and cognatic principle of descent, that is, they trace their relatives through both male and female. Theoretically anyone has the right to belong to the *vitsa* of his mother or his father. In practice there is a preference for the father's *vitsa* and a preference for the father's *kumpania*. Residence and *vitsa* choice are related, and a person who grows up among relatives of his mother's *vitsa* will probably choose that *vitsa*. Since in most cases, residence of married couples is with the

FIGURE 16 Marriages among *familiyi* in the Bochesti *vitsa* and *vitsa* affiliation of wives and offspring.

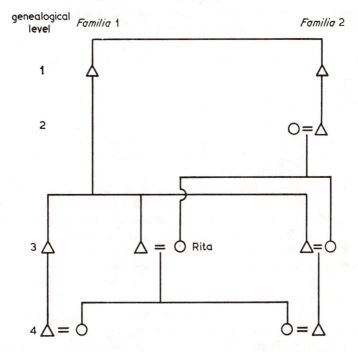

husband's father's *kumpania* and *vitsa*, their children will identify with their father's *vitsa*. In cases where both *vitsi* of a couple reside in the same or a nearby *kumpania*, there is genuine difficulty in making a choice of *vitsa* among children. In cases where the mother and father are of the same *vitsa* there is, of course, no choice.

As well as residence, marriage is a major factor in the choice of *vitsa* affiliation. Marriages endogamous to the *vitsa*, which account for as much as 50 per cent of all marriages, give no choice to the offspring for *vitsa* affiliation. *Figure 16* demonstrates how this can work over several generations. The children of those couples at the third and fourth genealogical levels can only be Bochesti since both their father and mother are Bochesti. In this case, the *vitsa* affiliation of Rita and her daughters did not change when they married since their husbands were all of the same *vitsa* as themselves.

When the woman is from another *vitsa*, there is a tendency for her eventually to identify with her husband's *vitsa*. This occurs only after long years of marriage and after having produced many descendants for the *vitsa*. Yana, who is a Machwanka, has been married to Stevan for many years and has numerous Kashtare grandchildren. She was very amused when I implied that she was Machwanka and not Kalderash and replied 'my children are Costello, my grandchildren are Costello, I am Costello'. Another Kastelaka who was only middle-aged was always referred to as 'that Kuneshti' because her husband, children, and few grand-children were Kuneshti. Sonia Davis, who was originally a Micheleshti, has, after her Kashtare husband's death, renewed many ties with the Micheleshti. Her children and grandchildren are Kashtare like their father, and they all spend a large amount of time in the Kashtare *kumpania*.

Even though older women usually accept their husbands' *vitsa* young wives, even with young children, still affiliate with the *vitsa* of their parents. If their parents die, and they lose contact with their brothers, they may adopt their husbands' *vitsa* more readily. However, a woman who is from a powerful and large *vitsa*, and who marries into a poorer and socially lower *vitsa*, will most likely maintain strong ties with her own *vitsa* throughout her lifetime. If she leaves her husband, or if he dies while she is still relatively young, she will return to her family, and her children will choose her *vitsa* if they are raised by their maternal grandparents. If she remarries, these children almost never go to their step-father's *kumpania* and *vitsa*.

However, *vitsa* affiliation is never an absolute choice, and in certain contexts a person emphasizes his ties through his mother even if he is considered to be of his father's *vitsa*. Again this is dependent on residence, and a man who is visiting his mother's relatives, fulfilling *pomana* or other obligations to them, will emphasize verbally his ties through his mother. 'My mother is Machwanka so I am Machwano.' But more often and more typically, the tie through the father is the important one.

kaski san?	'Whose' are you?
Me san de spiroski shey.	I am Spiro's daughter
Savo spiro?	Which Spiro?
O spiro le tinhasko shav	The Spiro who is the son of Tinha.
Anda save vitsa?	In which *vitsa*?
Anda le Bimbole	In the Bimbole (*vitsa*)

Vitsa Size

In principle a *vitsa* could be composed of every descendant of a famous ancestor as well as the wives of those who have come from another *vitsa*. Actually, no *vitsa* ever increases in this proportion since women leave when they marry into another *vitsa* and those who marry into the *vitsa* of their birth take the place of an outside woman who might have married into the *vitsa*. Also a *vitsa* that becomes so large that it ceases to be a meaningful unit of identification has a tendency to split along sibling or cousin lines. Nevertheless, because the Rom have large families and because there are advantages to belonging to a large and prestigious *vitsa*, the *vitsa* does grow very rapidly. The growth of a small *vitsa* into one large enough to split into two new *vitsi* can take place over a period of four to five generations. *Vitsi* that are very small, that have not reproduced enough children, may amalgamate with larger and more prestigious ones.

It is impossible to give an average size for a *vitsa* since population statistics are not available. The Kashtare *vitsa*, which was reputed by its members to be very large, could contain anything from one hundred to two hundred households. John Marks estimated his *vitsa* (Bochesti) at one hundred households (average household size in Barvale was eight). He personally knew all one hundred families, had regular news of them, and fairly frequent contact with all of them. It is likely that eight hundred persons was an optimum size for a *vitsa* because John Marks could summon all his *vitsa* relatives to a *pomana* fairly easily. However, in a few generations this *vitsa* would be too large. The Bochesti *vitsa* began sixty or seventy years ago when three brothers and their three wives immigrated from Europe, leaving behind six or seven brothers who presumably now have developed their own *vitsi*. Given that the Bochesti *vitsa* stems from three brothers, in seventy years it has grown considerably. John's mother, who was one of the wives to cross the Atlantic, is still alive; therefore the *vitsa* spans four generations at the moment and has not yet split.

The Mineshti are an example of a very large *vitsa* which has recently split into several new *vitsi*. There is considerable dispute about the origins of the Mineshti. One story is that they all descended from an old widow who rode on the back of a huge sow named Mina to transport her 'brood of ragged children through the Montenegran mountains' (Lee 1967: 45) to a better life in America. Her thousands of descendants now live primarily on the eastern seaboard. The dispute centres around the name Mina which is attributed to the widow or the sow, depending on the version one chooses. Another version is the following:

> It's named after a woman, Mina Demetro. Mina lived to be a hundred and twenty. I've never heard the exact figures on how big she was, but I've heard she had thirty children, the last one when she was sixty-five. Some say she died in the far-distant past, centuries ago, and some say she died around 1880; some say she died in Russia and some say Serbia and some say Poland: every old Gypsy in the Mineschti will give you a different story. Anyway, four brothers who were direct descendants of hers left Russia with their families in the late eighties and came to the United States via Canada and spread out and multiplied. Their names were Zlatcho, Groffo, Bortchi, and Wasso and I've arrested children of theirs and grandchildren, and great-grandchildren. (Mitchell 1955: 66)

The Mineshti have become so large that they have divided into at least three new *vitsi*. The Bimbalesti are all descended from the famous Tinya le Stevanosko who died in 1969.[6] The Markovitches and the Demetros, whose leaders are O Bab le Burtyasko and Wasso Russel Demetro respectively, are two other branches which have now split off (Lee 1968: 13). These two are also related by marriage since O Bab is married to Gutie Demetro, sister of Russel Demetro.

There are also families that are so small that they hardly count as a *vitsa*. These are usually recent immigrants who have left relatives behind and are just building their own *vitsa* in America. One group of Xoraxai, calling themselves Nichols (from North Africa) are an example of a recent and small *vitsa*. They have married with several Kalderash and exist as only a small core of sons and grandsons of the man who originally came to America.

They maintain different customs but eventually will lose their differences from other American Rom as they become part of other *vitsi*.

Vitsi are usually founded by a famous person. The Bimbalesti have branched off from the Mineshti because of the notoriety of Tinya le Stevanosko, who before his death had already become a legendary character. He is credited as a young lad with having wrestled with the devil who was trying to steal his hat. He is also credited with 140 arrests 'for everything from murder in the first degree to stealing an automobile jack' (Mitchell 1955: 48). He moved into New York to take over leadership after ruling Chicago for several years (Cotten 1968: 1053–4). His favourite pastime, or so the story goes, was to cash a $20 bill at a bank and by some sleight of hand keep the change and the original bill. The admiration expressed about this particular trick was that he did it not for the money, but to keep in practice. Bimbo practically waged war on the Machwaya and attempted to eliminate Machwaya power and wealth personally; consequently they have no love for him. His descendants, however, speak of him reverently as a latterday Robin Hood. In Barvale he was feared and despised, and it was only when he was dying that they could bring themselves to say anything in his favour, in case his *mulo* turned out to be as powerful as he was.

Usually a founder of a *vitsa* is either a very wealthy woman who had thirty-five children or a notorious horse thief who was eight feet tall, weighed four hundred pounds and had moustaches which touched the ground! Frinkulo Mikhailovitch, founder of the Frinkulesti, is described as: '... the biggest Gypsy in Russia. He was seven feet three, and one time when he was quite an old man, up around a hundred and ten, they put him on some scales in a hay market and he weighed four hundred and sixty' (Mitchell 1955: 65).

Not all *vitsi* are named after famous ancestors. The Meskesti (*meska*, bear) were so named because one of their ancestors had an incident with a bear (Coker 1966: 87), and the *Fusui Xari* 'Bean Soup Eaters' were presumably inordinately fond of this excellent dish. Most *vitsi* names seem to be either derived from the names of a person or the word for an animal, a metal or wood, or some eating or elimination habit. *Table 5* lists the *vitsi* names whose meanings could be determined. A complete list of *vitsa* names would, of course, expand the list and possibly the categories of

TABLE 5 *Vitsa names*[7]

eating	elimination
Bokurishti (*bokh*, hunger)	Khulare (*khul*, shit)
Fusui Xari (*fusui*, bean soup,	Kanereshti (*khan*, *kan*, fart)
Xari, one who eats)	PoXadeshti (*puterdea*, straddle
Lameshti ('lamb eaters')	the legs open)
	Guniareshti (*gunoi*, faeces)

metal	wood
Mihaiyeshti ('people of the	Kashtare (*kash*, *kasht*, wood,
mines')	tree)
Chokurshti (*chokesarav*, to	Rishtoni (*risho*, reed, cane)
forge)	
	Kuneshti ('knifers')
	Pikareshti (*piko*, spear)[8]
	Lampeshti (*lampo*, lamp)

people	animals
Frinkulesti (Frinkulo	Saporeshti (*sap*, snake)
Mikhailovitch)	
Pupeshti (Pupa Kaslov)	Papineshti (*papin*, goose)
Bimbaleshti (Tinya Bimbo)	Tut(k)eshti (*tutka*, turkey)
Adamovitch (? Adams)	Meskeshti (*meska*, bear)
Markovitch (? Marks)	
Cholteshti (Choldo)[8]	
	Mineshti (Mina, woman or sow)
	Yonkirshti (*yungxo*, young ox)

names (though it would not necessarily change what has been presented here). These names have been presumed to indicate some true ancestor or incident; however, they are just as likely to be mythical and symbolic rather than an historical fact.

Provisionally, *vitsi* names form the following six categories:

culture	nature
eating (food)	elimination (excrement)[9]
metal	wood
human	animal

Several *vitsi* names cross these categories. For example, the Guniareshti, a large and well-known *vitsa* on the east coast, were translated as 'garbage eaters'. This represents a joining of opposites: eating and elimination. Both the Pikareshti and Kuneshti are weapon users as opposed to people who are associated with a metal as a trade, and people who are associated with wood. Finally, the dispute over the name Mina is based on those who believe it refers to the sow and others who claim it is the name of the woman. The Yonkirshti also claim that there was a person named Yonko but it could also mean 'young ox'. Thus we could modify the table to the following:

culture		*nature*
eating	(excrement eaters)	elimination
metal	(weapon users)	wood
human	(human/animal)	animal

The organization of the three categories of *vitsa* names into a pair of opposites (nature/culture) and a liminal third (those names which combine elements of both) is not a unique system of categories among the Rom. This system of symbols will be discussed again in Chapter 8.

Not all families are called by *vitsi* names. Those who are recent arrivals in the United States may be called by the name of the place they last stayed. In some cases this name stays with them, and in some cases it is simply used in ignorance of their *vitsa* name or because the *vitsa* name means nothing to the American Rom. For example, there are the Zingareshti ('Italian' Gypsies), Xoraxai ('Turkish' Gypsies), Gurkwe ('Greek' Gypsies), Mesikaya ('Mexican' Gypsies), and Argentinos. There were several Gurkwe families in Barvale at one time who went by the *gaje* names Athanasso, Dennis, Tennis, and Tanasso. Mesikaya is a typical example of a place named used in ignorance of the *vitsa* name. There are several *vitsi* of Rom in Mexico, but since the American Rom do not know them well and look down on them because they are generally poor, they lump them all together under the term Mesikaya, which is not used by the Mexican Rom themselves (Pickett 1965: 85–7). These names based on places are often confused with *vitsa* names in the literature.

Vitsa Hierarchy

Just as the four *natsiyi* are arranged into a status hierarchy, the *vitsi* also have differences in status based on two factors: (1) the *natsia* it belongs to, and (2) a combination of wealth, power, and reputation. In other words, *vitsa* status is variable according to the fortunes of its members, but regardless of the fame and fortune of a *vitsa*, it is still bound by the status it derives as part of a *natsia*. In Barvale, even wealthy Kuneshti families usually have lower status than poor Kalderash families, and the poor Machwaya families always remind the more powerful Kalderash of their superior status as Machwaya.

Wealth and power are very important factors in *vitsa* reputation. A *vitsa* that becomes wealthy also becomes powerful and will attract many members who might have chosen other *vitsi*. The women will probably be expensive. (because of the benefits of marrying into a powerful *vitsa*), and sons-in-law may join their wife's *kumpania*. If the marriage dissolves, the women will be more likely to bring their children back to their *vitsa*. A wealthy and powerful *vitsa* can also enjoy more flexibility with general morals since it takes a more powerful *vitsa* to bring them to trial if they refuse. Machwaya, who are wealthy and powerful, have often avoided *marime* sanctions and trial even for very serious moral crimes, simply because the families making the accusation were poor and powerless.

Reputations change among *vitsi* and so do their positions in the *vitsa* hierarchy. However, their status derived from their *natsia* does not appear to change. The reputation of a *familia* affects the reputation of the *vitsa* as a whole, and therefore it is often *vitsa* members who are most indignant about the 'crime' of another *vitsa* member since their own reputation is at stake. In a very large *vitsa*, everyone cannot be held responsible for the behaviour of a few *vitsa* members, and this is one reason why *vitsi* tend to split when they become very large.

The Bimbaleshti were very powerful at one time and difficult to bring to trial; however there is a limit to the impunity anyone can enjoy, and at various times Tiny Bimbo was declared *marime*. Now that they are powerless and poor on the west coast they are particularly despised for the past crimes of their leader. In Barvale, when a Bimbiya family moved in, they were treated as *marime* and were completely ostracized by the *kumpania*. No one would visit them or invite them to any social occasions. When the wife went into the hospital, no one offered to look after her children or visited her, and when another Rom in the hospital talked to her by accident he commented, 'she is a nice person, not like the other Bimbiya'. However, the ostracism of this family by the *kumpania* was so strong that they soon left. According to the Barvale Rom the Bimbaleshti are one of the lowest Kalderash *vitsi*, and in status are 'next to the Kuneshti'. This they attribute to the very immoral behaviour of Tinya Bimbo who 'stole from the Gypsies'. Yet the Bimbos during the days of their power, thought of themselves as 'purer' than other Kalderash (Cotten 1950: 171).

The story of the Bimbos also illustrates the importance of knowing the position of the informant himself in determining

TABLE 6 *Framework for a scale of vitsi statuses*

Natsia	Vitsa
Machwaya	(apparently no *vitsi*) wealthy, powerful and reputable Kalderash *vitsi*
Kalderash	Poor or disreputable Kalderash *vitsi*
Churara	Kuneshti

vitsa status. Cotten's informants were Bimbaleshti whereas mine despised the Bimbaleshti. The Kashtare described themselves as a 'respectable' *vitsa* because 'we are large and well-known. The Machwaya like to marry us because we stay with our husbands.' However, the much wealthier Bochesti, John Marks, because of his trouble with Stevan (Appendix A, case 1), described the Kashtare as 'very dirty. They have no background for honesty.'

Since the status of any *vitsa* is constantly fluctuating and can only be gleaned from statements from several other *vitsi* as well as from its own members, it is very difficult to make a scale of *vitsi* statuses. The only certain factor is the *natsia*, but within *natsia* status, there is a hierarchy of *vitsi* which would have the framework given in *Table 6*.

Status positions are very touchy subjects, and a person will always defend his *vitsa* against the others. Whenever there is conflict between two persons of different *vitsi*, these relative

statuses are brought to the foreground. When the Kashtare and
Machwaya leaders in Barvale engage in conflict, their relative
status positions are a major issue. To the Machwaya, the Kalderash
Kashtare will always be ignorant and 'uneducated', and to the
Kashtare, the Machwaya are snobbish and always use their
'education' and position to dominate. To both the Kalderash and
Machwaya, the Kuneshti are unreliable, lowly, and often immoral.
They steal too much, get caught at it too much, and generally
spoil an area for others.[10] One Kashtare elder, whose Kuneshti
wife had been loyal and faithful for forty years, exclaimed when
she finally became senile, 'What can I do? She's Kuneshti. All
Kuneshti are crazy.'

Identity Among Vitsa Members

It should be clear now that the *vitsa*, unless it is very small, is not
a residential unit. *Vitsa* members may live scattered over the
United States and Canada and even in several continents, though
such long distances tend to provide a split in the *vitsa*. Such a
large *vitsa* as the Mineshti have been recorded in the North and
South American continents and in South Wales (Myers 1943: 85).
Irving Brown (1929: 161) states 'I have met members of the
Guneshti in Spain, France, Mexico and the United States.' Most
vitsi, however, have a much more restricted area. The Bochesti,
for example, are centred in Texas, Oklahoma, and Chicago, with a
few relatives in California and the Deep South. The Kashtare are
slightly larger and live generally in Texas, California, and Oregon
though many of them spend the summers in Alaska and Mexico
to get gold. However, although the economic and residential unit
is the *kumpania*, the *vitsa* is very important as a unit of moral and
political identity.

First of all, *vitsa* members are relatives (*niamo*) and are descended from one ancestor; therefore, they have ties and obligations which they do not have with non-relatives. These ties are
not only the ties of mutual aid which all relatives have, but are
political and moral as well. Like the *familia*, but less strongly so,
the reputation of the *vitsa* depends in part on the behaviour of its
members (and in part upon the status of the *natsia*), and the
behaviour of an individual or a *familia* implicates the whole *vitsa*.
For this reason, it is important to know a person's *vitsa* to be able
to 'know who they are'. Coker (1966: 88) declares that 'when an

individual becomes *marime* – polluted – all members of his *vitsa* also become *marime*'. In my experience the situation is actually not so clear-cut, though this may be an expressed ideal. A whole *familia* may become *marime* for the action of one person, and certainly the whole *vitsa* is implicated and must defend its reputation or rectify the wrong. According to Cotten (1950: 164) a person who is *marime* must have a trial to be reinstated *back* into his *vitsa* by a combination of the *vitsi* representatives, and in a sense it is his *vitsa* that is called to task and must assume some of the responsibility or at least some of the tarnish from his actions. A *marime* sentence does not cover a whole *vitsa*, as it might a whole family, but the other *vitsa* members feel shame (*lashav*), and they more than anyone else must make an effort to avoid the person and condemn his behaviour.

Similarly when a *vitsa* is powerful in one *kumpania*, its members share the prestige derived from its power and can depend upon *vitsa* support to extend themselves politically into other *kumpaniyi*. Like a bad reputation, wealth, prestige, and power eventually extend to most of the *vitsa* members. In any situation of conflict with other Rom, *vitsa* members will side together against another *vitsa* unless *familia* obligations take priority (as in the Easter *slava* fight). Once there is an issue where two people find themselves in disagreement, other Rom quickly take sides and line up along lines of closeness of relationship and *vitsa* membership. Often in a conflict, the man who had the most relatives (*vitsa* members) present, or who could swing 'unattached' votes was the winner.

Members of one's *vitsa* are 'relatives' even if one has never met them whereas members of other *vitsi* are '*streyino* Rom' (strange Rom) unless there is some other kinship or affinal tie present. Aid and protection in time of need is expected between *vitsa* members to an extent that *streyino* Rom cannot expect. For example, if a family trespasses on the territory of another *kumpania* and uses its resources, then the leader in the *kumpania* will be considered justified in informing to the authorities about that person's activities (though without enough information to get them arrested). However, if this family is of the same *vitsa* of a lesser member of the *kumpania*, that *vitsa* member will be expected to solve the problem by coercing his relatives to obey the rules of the *kumpania*. If he cannot, he may be expelled from the *kumpania* himself. A trespasser from a major *vitsa* of the *kumpania* is a very unlikely possibility because they will not want to jeopardize the position of their *vitsa* relatives and also because it is to their advantage, politically and economically, to enter the *kumpania* with the approval of their *vitsa*. In a strongly controlled *kumpania*, only *vitsa* members (or affines) join the *kumpania*, and in a loosely controlled *kumpania* anyone from any *vitsa* may attempt to enter the *kumpania*.

The *vitsa* is an important political unit as well. A political leader does not assume leadership for people outside his *vitsa*. Even the most important *rom baro* usually does not extend his leadership outside his *vitsa*. The very rich and powerful Joji Baro primarily ruled the Lee-Adams families of southern California, though many other Machwaya occasionally looked to him for the leadership. The *vitsa* is generally the outer limit of power.

Similarly a powerful leader recruits his support from the members of his *vitsa* and other relatives and affines. The *vitsa* is his main source of power and control, and the acceptance of his position by his *vitsa* is essential. No leader who loses the support of his *vitsa* will find political gain elsewhere. On the other hand, he must spread the advantages of his power to his *vitsa* and be generous with them. Stevan depends on the many Kashtare families in Barvale for the backbone of his support. Miller George, who has tried for years to get power through liaisons with the police in Barvale, has failed repeatedly because he cannot muster even the most basic support from his adult brothers and sisters.

At a *kris* each *vitsa* must be represented by a man and his wife who are leaders of a *vitsa*; consequently the *vitsa* is the political unit that is used to form the *kris*. This choice of jurors is also entirely consistent with the cognatic principle of descent in the *vitsa*. The wife is not an affine but a living ancestor (like the man) of the *vitsa*. It is interesting that just as the *vitsa* is in a sense on trial with the individual, it is also the *vitsa* which is the political unit trying the individual.

Two examples of the political importance of the *vitsa* as a judicial unit are given here. In both cases the various *vitsi* were called together to decide a matter of grave importance.

1. 'Gus, a Machwano, was arrested for a *bujo* in Del Hart, Texas that he and his wife did not commit. He was not allowed bail, but got out on a writ of habeas corpus and immediately fled to Los Angeles "to have a conference with the superiors of his

vitsa". In Los Angeles a "meeting was called from all the nations (*natsia*) to determine who was actually wanted in Del Hart".[11] Gus was afraid he would not be able to prove his innocence so several of his wealthy relatives called this reunion. Big Joe, Black Joe, and George were there, and I knew them, and I knew Gus, and although they are no relation, I knew they were respectable people. They decided I should be the one to go to Del Hart, but I had to think about it for a few days because they are Machwaya. Finally, I went with Johnny, Gus's son, and we made restitution to the old people for their money. We found out later who the guilty persons were, but we knew they were poor and these Machwaya did not care about the money, only about getting Gus off the hook.'

It should be noted that because these Machwaya were powerful, they were able to call 'all the nations' together. This was necessary because it was a matter that crossed into other *natsiyi*. John Marks was very cautious about handling a case that was not in his *vitsa*, but because he would be in the favour of the powerful Machwaya he decided to do it. The concern was not to persecute the 'guilty' parties, but to solve the problem with the law, and the first thing that Gus did when he was out on bail was to flee to his relatives and call together his *vitsa* to come to his aid.

2. In the Autumn of 1969 a meeting was called of all the *vitsi* and all *natsiyi* represented in Los Angeles to discuss the 'new rules' on the following issues: brideprice, informing to *gaje* authorities about people who trespass on a *kumpania*, and the kinds of *marime* sentences that will be effective. A man and wife from each *vitsa* were required to be present since the rules could not be effective unless accepted by all.

Again it should be pointed out that the *vitsa* is the unit within which political decisions on grave matters must be decided. The *vitsa-natsia* framework is the existing political and moral unit while the *kumpania* is the economic and residential unit.

Finally, the *vitsa* has important ritual ties. A man has a special obligation to attend the funeral and *pomana* of members of his *vitsa* even if this requires travelling long distances. *Vitsi* also have their own particular *slava*. The health and good luck enjoyed by each *vitsa* member is dependent on the health and good luck of other *vitsa* members. To assure good health and luck, members of a *vitsa* will all celebrate a certain *slava*, in their own *kumpania*. The Kashtare celebrate *Swetoyana* (St Anne's Day) on August 28 as a protection for the health of all their families. The Machwaya celebrate *Swetogiorgidan* (St George's Day) on May 6. The particular proclivity of one *vitsa* to give a certain *slava* usually starts because of an accident or illness from which the person recovers after the family has pledged to give the *slava*. This pledge eventually spreads to the whole *vitsa*, sometimes to more than one *vitsa*. The health, good luck, and reputation of all *vitsa* members are linked together. One powerful old *drabarni* claimed that her *vitsa* is exempt from serious disease because one of her ancestors aided *Mamioro* (the spirit who is the source of all serious illness). Another old lady said that her *vitsa* was dying out because 'heart trouble' ran in her *vitsa*.

Conclusions

For the Rom in Barvale people are categorized in a hierarchy that runs through several levels of organization (see *Table 7*). The most basic structural and moral division is between Rom (men) and *gaje* ('fools'), but they also recognize that there are people who belong to neither of these categories. These are the Gypsy groups who are not Rom and yet not *gaje*, and the moral attitude of the Rom towards these people is entirely consistent with their ambivalent structural position.

Within the category of Rom, there are further divisions: the *natsia* and *vitsa*. In Barvale there are three *natsia*, the Machwaya, Kalderasha, and Churara. The Machwaya have no *vitsi* as far as is known, the Kalderasha have numerous *vitsi*, and the Churara are represented in North America by at least one *vitsa*, the Kuneshti. Moral superiority is again delineated by these divisions. The Machwaya enjoy high status, and the Kuneshti suffer low status regardless of their wealth and reputation. The status of each Kalderash *vitsa* depends on its wealth, reputation, and power, but it is neither higher in status than the Machwaya nor lower than the Kuneshti. *Natsia* and *vitsa* hierarchy effects the status of the individual *familiyi* and partially determines behaviour between them. The effect of these statuses on behaviour was manifest in the Easter *slava* and Devil conflicts discussed in Chapter 4, when these categories were constantly referred to by the various contestants.

Finally, *vitsi* names are also divided into three groups: names associated with culture, names associated with nature, and names which combine elements of both. *Table 7* lists the social categories at various levels of organization.

Finally, these categories – Rom–*gaje*, *natsia*, *vitsa*, and *familia* – not only determine status but mark moral boundaries in a direct inside to outside line. Physical, financial, and moral support is

TABLE 7 *Social categories within levels of organization*

high status	middle status	low status
Rom	other Gypsies	*Gaje*
Machwaya	Kalderasha	Churara
culture	culture/nature	nature

given first to the members of one's own *familia*. Then there are obligations to *vitsa* relatives, to certain other cognatic relatives such as non-*vitsa* cousins, and finally to affines. Among non-kin, identity and obligations are very vague and depend on the *natsia* of the individual. The Rom as a people is the outermost moral boundary, for a Rom has no moral obligations towards, nor identity with, any person who is not Rom.

7

Marriage

Among the Rom only certain sexual relationships constitute a marriage,[1] and everyone must be married to participate fully in the life of the community. The ideal marriage is arranged by the families of the couple to be married who stand in the relationship of 'cousin' to each other. This is considered an ideal arrangement because the *Xanamik* who arrange the marriage will be cousins or uncle/nephew, and the bond of their kin relationship should help their relations with each other to be cordial and cooperative enough to solve any problems that arise in the marriage contract. When *Xanamik* are related in this way, a successful and stable marriage is likely, whereas marriage between families who are strangers is said to lead to the kind of conflict related by John Marks in Appendix A. However, the union of unrelated Rom is a legitimate marriage when it is arranged and sanctioned by the parents of the couple and when the usual brideprice negotiations have been carried out.

Certain sexual relationships are not only viewed as illegitimate but are *marime* and must be seen in opposition to legitimate marriage. These illegitimate unions are also important to an understanding of marriage. I shall begin this study of marriage with the structural principles, that is the marriage categories, and then relate them to marriage procedure, both ideal and alternative forms. Finally, prohibited (*marime*) sexual unions will be discussed with the view to establishing why they are prohibited, that is, why they contravene the structural principles.

Marriage Categories

In Barvale there was a preference for marriages between cousins. A cousin (*woro/vara*) may be a person of one's own *vitsa*, or of the *vitsa* of one's female progenitors, that is, the mother, mother's mother, or father's mother. When one of these female progenitors married a cousin as well, their natal *vitsa* may not be different from the *vitsa* into which they married, but usually each individual has cousins in several *vitsi*. In any case, this situation assumes that normal *vitsa* recruitment has taken place. This is, residence and *vitsa* membership with one's father, with women at marriage eventually taking the *vitsa* identity of their children.

Statements about marriage preference and arrangements are surrounded with secrecy, partly because marriage effects the welfare status of an individual and partly because kinship and marriage information establish a definite identity for a Rom with the *gaje*. Statements about marriage preferences include:

1. 'It used to be you got a *bori* from a different *vitsa*, but now it is better to get one in the family.'
2. 'It is more enjoyable to get a *bori* from a cousin.'
3. 'A wife can be no blood relation, and she can be from the same or a different *vitsa*; however, it's preferable to get a daughter-in-law from a man in your own *vitsa* or your mother-in-law's *vitsa*' (i.e. the informant's WM's *vitsa*).
4. 'Any one person, whether he is a Costello or a Mitchell, or an Evans, or a Stevenson, he tries to stay as close in the family as he can, not for the money (*daro*), but it has happened in the past where if you receive a daughter-in-law from far off away from the family, nine times out of ten that marriage doesn't last.'
5. 'If you marry out of the family group and give $5000 for a girl, the girl's father may come and take his daughter and you have no legal right. If there is a Gypsy trial there is still not much chance of getting her back because as a last resort the girl may say that her father-in-law has made a pass at her (*pedelas pala mande*) which puts a curse on him. Then the father-in-law is condemned, and there is nothing he can do even if everyone knows that it is not true. He may get about $1500 but the court will tell him not to go to church and swear on bibles that it is not true because the daughter-in-law has condemned you and you cannot. This is why you marry in the family. You try to get a woman from the mothers-in-law's group' (the *vitsa* of your own mother-in-law for your son; therefore father and son will have the same in-law *vitsa*).

As can be seen from these statements, ideal marriage categories are expressed in terms of the *Xanamik* relationship, with very little emphasis on the relationship of the couple. This is consistent with the importance of elders over the younger persons, especially in marriage negotiations. The ideal relationship for *Xanamik* seems to be 'cousins'. It was also stated that *Xanamik* could be uncle and nephew, but that they should not be brothers. Uncle and nephew is therefore a permitted and acceptable *Xanamik* relationship but is not the ideal. Of course, the parents of second cousins can be either first cousins or uncle and nephew.

Statistical Model

The statistical model for marriages indicates that approximately one-third of the marriages do take place between cousins. *Table 8* gives the percentage of cousin marriages in the Kashtare *vitsa* of Barvale, the Bochesti *vitsa* of Fort Worth, and the Kuneshti of

TABLE 8 *Percentage of cousin marriages*[2]

	cousin marriages	unrelated	possible cousin marriages	total marriages
Kashtare	(9) 31%	(13) 48%	(7) 21%	29
Bochesti	(13) 43%	(16) 53%	(1) 3%	30
Kuneshti	(6) 24%	(8) 32%	(11) 44%	25
	(28) 33%	(37) 44%	(19) 23%	84

San Francisco. The number of couples for whom I lack specific genealogical evidence, but who I suspect are related because of their *vitsa* names, have been recorded as possible cousin marriages. Couples recorded as 'unrelated' are those for whom there is no reason to suspect a cousin relationship. The unknown marriages could change the statistics dramatically except for the Bochesti where nearly complete information was available.

These statistics are more significant when broken down by generation to give a picture of the tendencies in marriages over three generations and thus to assess change over time. *Table 9* shows a remarkable increase in endogamous marriages in the last thirty years.

From *Table 9* it can be seen that in the oldest generation (living grandparents) cousin marriages were very rare. In the second age group, parents with several children, cousin marriages are very high and among the Bochesti it is over 60 per cent. Among the Kashtare it could also be that high since 25 per cent of the marriages are probably between cousins. In the youngest age group (this includes all recent and still unstable marriages during the two years of field work) the Kashtare cousin marriages went from 42 to 50 per cent but with the same amount unrelated. I do not think there is a significant change for age Groups B and C because, through observation, more complete information for marriages

TABLE 9 *Percentage of cousin marriages by age*

A. *group of siblings (ages 40–65)*

	% cousins	% unrelated
Bochesti	14·28	85·72
Kashtare	0	100·00
Kuneshti	0	100·00

B. *children of Group A (ages 20–39)*

	% cousins	% unrelated	% probably related
Bochesti	63·63	36·36	—
Kashtare	41·66	33 33	25·00
Kuneshti	42·85	57·15	—
Average:	53–57%	42–46%	

C. *grandchildren of Group A (ages 12–19)*

	% cousins	% unrelated	% probably related
Kashtare	50	33·33	16·66

in age Group C was available. In any case, Group C is too small, a number of marriages (6) to be conclusive. The change between age Group A, when very few marriages were between cousins, to age Group B, when at least half of the marriages were endogamous, is significant. This change is consistent with the informant's statement: 'it used to be you got a *bori* from a different *vitsa*, but now it is better to get one in the family.'

A breakdown of cousin marriages in *Table 10* reveals that second cousin marriages are by far the most common. This indicates that the stated preference to marry as close as possible, but not first cousins, corresponds with practice.

From *Table 10* it can be seen that there are four first cousin marriages which infringe the stated disapproval of marriages this

TABLE 10 *Degree of relationship in cousin marriages*

group	first cousin	half or step first cousin	second	third or more	adopted	total
Barvale *kumpania*	1	1	11	2	0	15
Bochesti	3	0	6	3	1	13
Kuneshti	0	4	2	0	0	6
total	4	5	19	5	1	34

close; however, it is interesting that there are as many half-first cousins or step-first cousin marriages as there are third cousin marriages and presumably they mark the fine border between a marriage that is too close and one that is good because it is endogamous. In two of the Bochesti first-cousin marriages, the marriage partners are first cousins through one set of parents and second cousins through another set. Whether these two couples are considered first or second cousins or both, is not known, but

TABLE 11 *Relationship of Xanamik*

	cousins	uncle, aunt nephew, niece	siblings	adopted	total marriages
Barvale *kumpania*	8	5	2	0	15
Bochesti	7	2	3	1	13
total	15	7	5	1	28

I have counted them as first cousins. Finally, there seems to be no preference for parallel or cross cousins as would be expected in a cognatic terminology.

Since the large number of second cousin and half-first cousin marriages corresponds closely with the ideal (they form about two-thirds of cousin marriages), the relationship between *Xanamik* should also correspond with the stated ideal. This is that *Xanamik* should be cousins, may be uncle/nephew, but should not be siblings. *Table 11* gives the *Xanamik* relationship for these same marriages among the Bochesti and the Barvale *kumpania*.

The case of the marriage of an adopted son who was unrelated to his adopted family is interesting. He married a granddaughter of his adopted mother, but this was not considered incestuous since they were not related by blood. It was considered that this marriage had no *Xanamik*, since his adopted mother was *Xanamik* to her own son. Among the siblings there does appear to be an avoidance of brothers becoming *Xanamik*. In only one case are the *Xanamik* brothers and their wives cousins. In another case, the men are cousins and their wives are sisters. Finally, two cases concern *Xanamik* who are brother and sister. In the one case of step-first cousin marriage, the *Xanamik* are a man and his sister's

TABLE 12 *Cousin marriages and vitsa preference*

	same vitsa	different vitsa	total
Barvale *kumpania*	9	6	15
Bochesti	9	4	13
Kuneshti	6	—	6
total	24	10	34

husband, his sister having only recently married the father of his *bori*.

In order to determine if there is a preference for marriage with a 'cousin' in one's own *vitsa* or in a different *vitsa*, the *vitsa* of the couple was tabulated in *Table 12* for the thirty-four marriages. There does seem to be a considerable preference for marriage with persons of the same *vitsa* when choosing a cousin marriage. Again this corresponds with the stated preference of marrying in as close as possible. It also helps to explain the statements about marriage with one's mother's natal *vitsa*. Cousins on the mother's side are an alternative form of endogamous marriage, and the ten cousin marriages with a different *vitsa* in *Table 12* reflect this alternative choice. When members of two different *vitsi* marry, their descendants may intermarry in perfect accord with the endogamous preference. Thus it is that two *vitsi*, once joined in marriage, may form several marriage alliances of which some will eventually be between cousins.

The tendency for certain *vitsi* to choose wives from certain other *vitsi* is described by Rena Cotten as a 'Special Gypsiological Problem':

> An intensive study of the *vitsa* would also involve interaction with and attitudes toward other *vitsas* of the same and of different tribes (*natsia*). For example, I have noticed that certain *Kalderaš vitsas* tend to get brides from a limited number of other bands. Why? (Cotten 1955: 34).

A suggested answer to her query is that several marriages with one *vitsa*, which will inevitably become cousin marriages over time, create the kinds of ties that are present in cousin marriages and therefore are an alternative form of endogamy. Let us see then exactly what happens between two *vitsi* who intermarry and how these ties are formed.

An alliance between two *vitsi* may begin with a single marriage or it may begin with sister exchange. The Kashtare–Machwaya alliances (*Figure 4*) began with the marriages of four brother/sister pairs. Consequently the marriages in the next generation are between second cousins. It is interesting to note that the marriage that ended in divorce did so because the couple were not the appropriate ages (she was twenty and he was ten); therefore, the pressure to bring about equal exchanges must have been great. There are frequent mentions in the literature and newspapers of double weddings between two families (sister exchange) and I suspect that these double marriages are seen as a way of creating strong enough affinal bonds between two *vitsi* to set off a series of marriages. The exchange of women between two *vitsi* guarantees the rights of each *vitsa*, since if one girl is taken back, the *vitsa* can retaliate and take back its own woman.[3] Sister exchange also eliminates the necessity of brideprice.

However, a double marriage is not the only way that a series of alliances begins between *vitsi*. The Bochesti have intermarried frequently with the Micheleshti. All four Bochesti cousin marriages with another *vitsa* in *Table 12* are with the Micheleshti family. Besides these there are five more marriages between Bochesti and Micheleshti where the relationship is unknown, and I suspect that some, but not necessarily all, of them are related as well. Furthermore these nine exchanges (*Figure 17*) are based on Bochesti genealogies alone; Michelesti genealogies would probably reveal more such marriages. Even so, these nine marriages represent 30 per cent of all Bochesti marriages. The exchange of women is relatively even (five Micheleshti women taken, four Bochesti women given), and all exchanges stem from the original marriage of the sister of a group of Bochesti siblings to the Micheleshti family. Through this marriage the Micheleshti have acquired three of her brother's daughters and have given women to four of her brothers' sons and a first cousin. Each marriage has added to the original tie until a network of marriage alliances between the two *vitsi* (see *Figure 17*) is formed.

Besides the marriage ties with the Machwaya in *Figure 4*, the Kashtare are closely intermarried with another group of Machwaya, the Marks of Kansas City. Again, from Kashtare genealogies

FIGURE 17 Nine Bochesti–Micheleshti marriages.

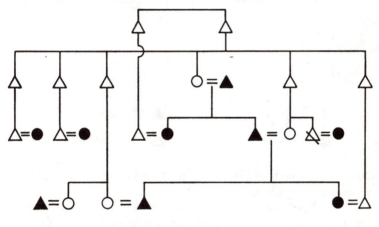

▲ ● Micheleshti   △ ○ Bochesti

alone there are ten Kashtare–Marks marriages (*Figure 18*). The total number of marriages cannot be calculated since some of these couples reside in the Marks *kumpania* (Kansas City), but six of these ten marriages are included in the twenty-nine Kashtare marriages in Barvale. Of the ten marriages, information on three indicates that they are cousins; however, all Marks married to Kashtare living in Barvale claim to be related to each other, having all come from the Kansas City *kumpania*. The number of exchanges in Barvale between these two *vitsi* is nearly even, but since there may be more Marks–Kashtare marriages in other places, this is not conclusive. *Figure 18* shows ten existing marriages in which the Kashtare gave four women and received five.

FIGURE 18 Ten Machwaya (Marks)–Kashtare marriages.

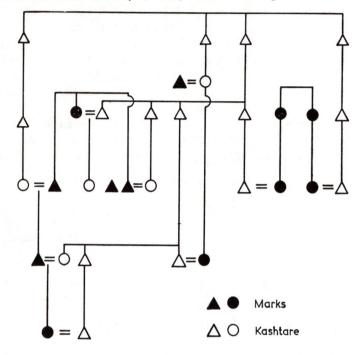

One marriage ended in divorce some time ago and cannot still be counted as an exchange.

In any *kumpania*, such as Barvale, which has several *vitsi*, a family that does not have strong kinship ties with other families will try to contract marriages with the dominant *vitsa*. Marriage is the only way of creating obligations between two families when they are unrelated. It is also the only recourse for a family in the *kumpania* that is isolated from its own *vitsa*. In most cases, the isolation from members of its own *vitsa* indicates that they have been involved in unorthodox behaviour, and if they are not acceptable to their own family, they are usually less acceptable to a *kumpania* composed of other *vitsi*.

The Kuneshti family in Barvale that occupies this uneasy position in the *kumpania* (and has been expelled many times) has attempted to establish marriage alliances with the predominant Kashtare. The head of the Kuneshti family, Miller, married his daughter to his sister's son's son, who is Kashtare (see *Figure 19, familia 1*). A second marriage was attempted with another Kashtare family (*Figure 19, familia* 2), and though not a cousin marriage, the couple are connected through marriage ties. In fact, the matriarch of the second family is *Xanamik* to the Kuneshti family in both marriages. This second marriage has had a rocky history because of bad will between the two families. During the Easter *slava* fight, the girl was taken home because the blame for the fracas was levied against her father-in-law, Miller, and he and his family left town for a certain time. It is no co-incidence that the more stable of these two Kashtare–Kuneshti marriages is the one with the closest kinship ties between *Xanamik*.[4]

If peripheral status families cannot arrange marriages with the dominant *vitsa* in a *kumpania*, an alternative method to reinforce

FIGURE 19 Kashtare–Kuneshti marriages in Barvale.

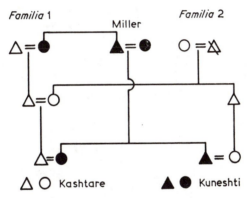

their position is to arrange marriages with each other. Three families that have low status in the *kumpania*, partly because they are small in numbers and partly because they are all connected with non-Rom Gypsy groups, have established several marriages with each other (*Figure 20*). This is both because it is difficult for them to marry into the Rom *vitsi* and because marriage with each other creates obligations of mutual aid and protection against hostility from the larger *vitsi*.

The practice of establishing marriages between certain *vitsi*, which I have been describing for Barvale, also exists in other northern California *kumpaniyi*.[5] In San Francisco, the Costa–John and George–John Kuneshti families are very closely intermarried, including several marriages between half-first cousins (see *Table 10*). The Marinos of San Jose and the Adams of Menlo Park are two Machwaya families who are also closely intermarried in the same pattern as exists in Barvale. These marriages stem from the original marriage of the head of the Marinos to a woman from the Adams family. Both are powerful and wealthy Machwaya families, and their intermarriages ensure the continuation of shared wealth from their respective *kumpaniyi.*

We have established that marriage should take place between persons who are as closely related as possible, but are not first cousins or closer. As we have seen, from one-third to one-half of marriages are between second and third cousins. Preferably, these

FIGURE 20 Marriage links between non-Rom Gypsy families in Barvale.

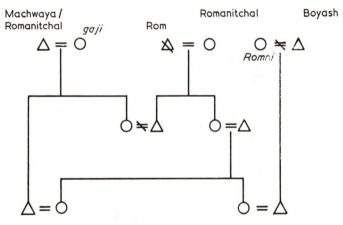

cousins should also be of the same *vitsa;* however, a cousin from the mother's *vitsa* is also acceptable. Again, in practice, most cousin marriages take place within the *vitsa;* however, those that do not usually are between Ego's *vitsa* and his mother's *vitsa.* When a marriage takes place between two unrelated *vitsi,* then their children and grandchildren will also be exchanged in marriage. Over several generations, this creates a number of marriage alliances between the two *vitsi,* and eventually these marriages will necessarily be cousin marriages.

Thus, in order of preference, marriages are arranged between cousins of the same *vitsa,* between cousins of different *vitsi,* between non-cousins of *vitsi* who may have marriage alliances between them, and finally between *vitsi* with few or no previous alliances. In the latter case, the first alliance may be a sister exchange as occurred between the Machwaya and Kashtare families

(*Figure 4*) or simply the marriage of a single woman to a man in another *vitsa* as occurred between Bochesti and Michelesti families (*Figure 17*). Subsequent generations will then attempt to make marriages with each other when they cannot make them with cousins and will therefore create increasingly closer ties between the *vitsi*. The advantage of creating a multiplicity of ties was apparent in the *Xanamik* fight when Johnny forced John Marks to return his grandchild by threatening to take back his daughter married to another Bochesti.

Marriage is not only a method of bringing *vitsi* into an exchange relationship requiring mutual obligations, but it is also a way of creating ties with members of a *kumpania* for families who do not have kinship ties. Kinship is the basis of aid and cooperation, but when this is lacking, marriage alliances are a good substitute. The low status Kuneshti in Barvale have attempted to improve their position, with only minor success, through marriages with Kashtare. Even lower status families from non-Rom Gypsy groups, who are unable to marry Rom (because of their status) have married with each other in order to create useful alliances. The preference for endogamous marriages is entirely consistent with general values that associate purity, good luck, and sympathy with closeness of relationship, and *marime*, bad luck, and hostility with distance of relationship. The furthest relationship (with the *gaje*) is both prohibited and *marime*.

The increase in endogamous marriages over the last thirty years reflects an expansion of the population combined with increased competition for territory and resources. *Kumpaniyi* have become more and more restricted to *vitsa* members. Marriages with strange *vitsi* threaten economic territoriality since a man would find it difficult to refuse an affine entry into the *kumpania*. Restricted *kumpaniyi* combined with endogamy ensure control of limited resources. Also there is an element of personal choice, since the more restricted the relatives in a *kumpania*, the less unrelated persons one comes into contact with for arranging marriages. A further factor is that political competition for the *kumpania* often takes place between *Xanamik*, and again endogamy decreases this competition since *Xanamik* are relatives and can share *kumpania* resources peaceably.

Finally, most Rom feel that endogamous marriages are potentially more stable. The increase in divorce is not only a moral issue, it is a threat to the authority of the elders, who appear to have turned to endogamy as an insurance that *Xanamik* must solve their problems without resorting to divorce. The connection between endogamy and divorce will be discussed later. First, we must explore the relationship of marriage categories to marriage procedure as this will clarify the social and ritual value of endogamous marriages.

Marriage Procedure

Descriptions of marriage arrangements (*tumnimos*) and wedding ritual (*abiav*) in the literature on the Rom are detailed and generally consistent with each other.[6] This consistency is unusual in written sources on the Rom, and I believe exists because these descriptions are statements of an ideal marriage procedure. Most are gathered from the statements of one informant or from a description of a spectacular wedding which lived up to the ideal. Unfortunately, it is not always made clear in the literature that this is an ideal and not an actual situation that is being described. Consequently, to those who read the literature and attend present day weddings, it often appears that these descriptions must be customs of the past and that the actual ceremony is a poor replica. I do not want to give the impression that marriage procedures and weddings have not changed; however, I find little evidence that the ideal has changed significantly. Whether adherence to this ideal is declining (as Cotten and Lee believe) is difficult to determine since there is very little statistical evidence on past practices. I think a clear distinction must be made between genuine changes (such as the increase in number of elopements), and marriages that simply do not live up to ideal standards.

Because there are several detailed and fairly reliable descriptions of how a betrothal (*tumnimos*)[7] and a wedding (*abiav*) should be conducted, I shall describe these only very briefly to provide the essential features and concentrate more on actual practices and statistical evidence since this data is lacking in the literature.

Among the Rom, marriage is arranged by the father of the groom and the father of the bride in collaboration with the other male members of their respective *vitsi*. Arranging a marriage for one's son (for it is the father of the boy who seeks a *bori* and opens negotiations) is a very important obligation of a father, and he may travel long distances in search of a suitable *bori*. One family came to Barvale from Texas to ask for a daughter-in-law (*mango bori*), and one family from Barvale, who went to Oregon for the summer to pick beans, came back with their eleven-year-old daughter betrothed.

These visits and marriage arrangements are accompanied by secrecy and excitement. Secrecy is maintained particularly in relation to the *gaje* since almost all Rom marry before the legal age, which in America is sixteen, and they fear prosecution. A further reason, of course, for secrecy from *gaje* is that they will be denied welfare money for a married child, or will be expected to declare brideprice money.

In theory, the couple themselves have no right to participate in the arrangements of their marriage though they do have the right to refuse consent to a union. In practice, they may be able to influence their parents to consent to a union and arrange it for them and may even threaten to elope if the parents are unwilling to cooperate. According to John Marks: 'Parents still arrange the marriage, but now some young people fall in love whereas they used to marry without ever seeing each other beforehand.' But from the point of view of the parents, love is not a prior considera-tion: One woman who was married at twelve remarked:

> We are married off before we know what is what, to a man we have never seen and don't like. I am lucky; I got to like my husband after a while, but I cried the first year the whole time. I wish I had been able to choose. That's Gypsy life, honey. My daughters, now I want them to choose their own husbands, someone they like, you know, but I guess they will get the same thing I did. We have to choose the man for them, but I want to make sure that they like the man we choose.

Another mother discussed what she considered a terrible wife for her son: 'She's no good. I know Tony loves Fatima. He's crazy about her, but I don't care. I do what's right for my boy. He wants a good wife – he can love another.'

The future *Xanamik*, in arranging a marriage, may discuss the arrangement for a few days before coming to a final settlement. Closely related families may well delay the formal betrothal for some time, perhaps up to a year, and will rely on an informal agreement that their two children will marry. But families who are less closely related or live in a distant *kumpania* will want to make a formal betrothal for fear that they will lose touch or that events will interfere with the arrangements.

In the first informal talks, the father of the boy sends an intermediary to visit the father of the girl and attempts to obtain his consent for the marriage and to get some indication of the *daro* (brideprice) he will ask. The *daro* is always discussed in terms of so many *galbe* ($5 gold pieces). This preliminary visit has two objectives: (1) to save the father of the boy the embarrassment of being turned down in case the father of the girl is opposed to the marriage, and (2) to get some idea of the price range he will be asking. The price is usually set high at first as a bargaining point and some compromise is agreed upon later. It would be an insult to the girl to begin with a low price, but on the other hand her father must not appear greedy for the money or ruin her chances of marriage by asking an outrageous price.

The actual amount of money asked varies and is based on several factors:

1. the ascribed status of the girl (i.e. which *vitsa* and *natsia* she comes from and the reputation of her family);
2. the acquired status of the girl (i.e. her reputation – morals, manners, ability to make money, whether she has ever been married before, etc.);
3. economic conditions of the families.

Prices fluctuate considerably, but at the time of this writing, they are high in relation to what most Rom are able and willing to pay. A Machwanka virgin of a well-known and successful fortune-telling family can expect to bring around $5000 for her *daro*. This is a price very few families can afford. Poorer and less prestigious, but respectable families, can expect to get from $1500 to $2000 for their daughter, and girls who have been married previously, or for some other reason have a dubious reputation, will bring only $400 to $600. In Barvale, where all the families are on welfare and do field labour, the most they could afford was in the range of $1500 to $2000. Many avoided this high cost by exchanges of women between families and in this case, no *daro* was asked. The Bochesti, who were financially well off, paid from $4000 to $5500 for a *bori*. John Marks himself claimed he paid Stevan $4000 for his daughter.

Once there is an indication that the father of the girl is agreeable to a betrothal, and he has named a price, the *tumnimos* ceremony takes place. The *tumninos* is a formal and public agreement between the two families in the presence of the *kumpania*, and it has the binding power of a legal contract. Once there has been a *tumnimos* and the marriage has become a matter of public concern, it is very difficult to dissolve the marriage without very strong reasons. After the *tumnimos*, the appropriate affinal terminology is used between the two families, and the couple are considered as bound as if they were married. Normally the wedding itself takes place as soon as possible after the *tumnimos*, sometimes in a matter of days.

Lee (1968: 19–20) describes the *tumnimos* ceremony:

> Once their consent has been obtained, the two fathers-in-law, or *Xanamícha*, arrange to meet with an assembly of male Gypsies who must belong to the local *kumpanía*. No Gypsy from another *kumpanía*, unless a relative, may attend and no *Gashó* can attend under any circumstances. They will choose a location, usually the home of a Gypsy of the community (though never either of the fathers-in-law), and here they will perform the ceremony of the *tumnimòs* or betrothal. The bride and groom cannot attend, and female Gypsies, unless relatives, are discouraged, though not actually proscribed.

> The father of the bride arrives first with his entourage of *Roms* and awaits the arrival of the father of the groom and his party, who then take their places at the table along with the others. The negotiations are then opened by the father of the groom who presents the father of the bride with the *daró* which is counted and verified by each and every male Gypsy present. I might mention that while this ceremony is proceeding, the curtains of the room are drawn, the door locked and a guard stationed outside.

> By accepting the *daró*, the father of the bride gives his approval of the marriage. The father of the groom now presents his opposite number with a ceremonial bottle of *rakíya*, or whisky, which is called *plótska* and to this is attached a *dikló*, or head-scarf, in which is wrapped the *kâpára* or betrothal present of the groom – usually a gold necklace.

> The head-scarf and the betrothal gift are intended for the girl, for in accepting the scarf which is the symbol of wedlock among my people, the girl gives her consent to the marriage. Should she change her mind, all she has to do is to return the gift and the scarf through an agent, and the *daró* will be returned and

the wedding called off. This seldom happens, however, since her father already knows in advance that his daughter has consented.

The two fathers-in-law then drink a small glass each of the whisky, saving the rest for the *abiáv* or wedding feast. The father of the bride now gives a certain sum of money to one of the Gypsies present, who goes out to buy food and drink for the whole party as a token of *pakív*, or respect, on the part of the father of the bride.

It is very common for marriages to be arranged less formally during a feast when young people can be observed in public. At one *slava* in Barvale, four marriages were discussed and arranged in a similar manner as this marriage arrangement described by John Marks:

At a large wedding in Oklahoma, one of the wedding guests decided to arrange a marriage for his son who is eleven years old. He went to the father of a ten year old girl with a bottle of whisky and said 'Cousin, I want to arrange to buy your daughter for my son'. The girl's father said, 'Let's wait three or four years until my daughter is fourteen or fifteen, and then we can discuss it. But I tell you what, I will guarantee that if nothing happens in between that time, you will have the first choice.' But the boy's father was not satisfied and wanted more guarantee. So he said, 'Let's arrange the engagement now and announce it so everyone will know that the girl is spoken for'. But the girl's father said, 'I don't like that because she may decide she prefers someone else and anything can happen', but the boy's father said, 'Well we can handle that when it comes'. The girl's father came to me [John Marks] and asked what he should do, and I told him that he had nothing to lose by making an engagement because anything can happen in the time being, but as long as he was doing that he should also set the price. So the girl's father went into conference with his brothers, and they said this: 'The wedding today will be our example. The price for the girl was $5500 and we will ask the same price. But if, when the marriage takes place, the price of a girl is more or less than the price today, we will both stick by this price set today.' Prices were high so the girl's father had nothing to lose there too.

Although this kind of publicly announced agreement is binding, because the couple were so young the possibility of intervening factors dissolving the betrothal were seen as great. The father of the girl would not allow his in-laws to take her for several years at which time the wedding could be arranged.

The Wedding

The couple to be married should be young, between twelve and sixteen years of age, and generally not over eighteen for a first marriage. If young, it is important that the girl be older than the boy since after marriage she must be able to perform her duties as a *bori* and make money for her husband; however, her husband need not take many responsibilities until he is fully mature. Virginity at the first marriage is also highly valued, and it is felt that this is more likely if a boy and girl are married very young.

The marriage ceremony (*abiav*) in its ideal form is only performed if at least the girl or the boy is a virgin, that is, if one of them has never married previously. If both have been married previously, a different version of the ceremony takes place. It is not uncommon for a first marriage, contracted at a very young age, to fail, and when this happens there is very little censure since it is generally agreed that the marriage failed because the child was 'too young'. Those who are older than sixteen or seventeen are expected to conform more to adult expectations and will be more strongly censured for failure to fulfil their roles. The result is that often a young person may try out one or two marriages before finding a satisfactory situation. Once they accept a marriage it usually lasts for life.

At a first marriage the wedding may take place either a few days after the betrothal or up to a year later, depending on the circumstances of the two families involved. For example, if the families are on the move, they may want the wedding immediately so that the groom's family can take their *bori* with them (see Appendix A, Case 2). If the families are closely related and live in the same *kumpania*, they may wait a year for the marriage until the couple are older and have become used to the idea that they will marry each other. Another factor in determining when a marriage occurs is whether a death has recently taken place or is expected to take place. Steve and Sylvia's marriage was carried out very quickly

because their Aunt Julie was going into the hospital for an operation, and if she died, they would be unable to marry for a year.

The wedding, in its ideal form, is a large and expensive affair.
After the betrothal, the groom's family arranges food for a feast
table (called a *baXt* table) in a hall. Whole roast pig, *sarme*, *pirogo*,
and other ritual foods are prepared. Excess of food and drink is
essential, and the lavishness of the display on the table brings
respect to the parents of the boy. The marriage ritual begins when
the guests arrive at the hall, have had some food and drink, and
have been given a flower to wear. The following is a description
of the wedding ritual based on a combination of statements and
observation. The order of the various aspects may vary from
wedding to wedding; some may even be left out, and each *vitsa*
has slightly different customary procedure.

1. The bride is dressed in a dress that has been made for her by
   her relatives from material purchased by the parents of the
   groom. A man and wife are chosen to sponsor the bride and
   groom (*kirvo/kirvi*) throughout the ceremony. This couple
   cannot have been married more than once. The *kirvi* dresses
   the girl and puts on her veil at the right time. When the girl is
   dressed, she is blessed.

2. The bride's veil (*diklo*) is put on a stick. The veil is either red
   or has red in it, and a red rose is put on the stick as well. These
   two items indicate that she is a virgin. The rose symbolizes her
   virginal blood which will be spilt, and the *diklo* is a symbol of
   married status. Red symbolizes happiness and good luck. The
   stick is carried around by unmarried girls (*sheybari*) who dance
   in a circle with it, holding hands. The men do not dance, and
   the groom stands to one side, embarrassed. The bride is brought
   onto the floor with no head-dress and must dance in a circle
   with the young girls, one of whom holds the *diklo*. They all
   hold hands and move in a circle with the bride in the middle
   weeping the whole time.

3. The bride is taken away, and the *diklo* is removed from the
   stick and put on her head by the *kirvi*. This is placed on her
   head with great care as the women gather around her, and she
   weeps the whole time. The women say that once it is on her
   head she is married.

4. Next is a ceremony called the *žeita* which is translated as
   'bringing the bride home'. At this point the bride becomes a

married woman. Everyone gets together at the end of the hall, and the sponsors bring out the bride. She is given a blessing from her immediate family, they kiss her and say goodbye with good will. There is a lot of shouting and confusion, and a group of boys and girls try to stop the *žeita*:

> They won't let her pass and demand some money to allow her to go home. They may demand five to twenty dollars. But these boys can stop the wedding and sometimes fights break out. Sometimes to get through, her clothes may be torn off, and I have seen weddings when the bride makes it to the other side naked. The bride may also be stubborn, and she may resist if she has no love for the man and is against the marriage. Her mother may be hysterical if she is sad at losing her daughter. But the price is paid, and she gets through to the groom's family and now she belongs to them.

At one wedding, the bride screamed and wailed and was pulled forcefully to the other side of the room by the groom's relatives: 'The groom never enters in any of these ceremonies, and all the *žeita* is done by the relatives present. The groom must be modest and keep to one side always. He must not look at his bride or be near her.'

5. The Collection

After this ceremony, everyone sits at the table and begins to partake of the feast. As soon as food has been consumed, the male sponsor hollows out a loaf of bread and with the bride and groom behind him in that order and each holding the end of a *diklo*, he goes to each older head of family at the table. A collection is taken from each man, usually a new $20 or $5 bill and is given to the bride to put in the bread. The man is given some beer by a boy who follows behind, and the sponsor makes a speech, each time exaggerating the amount given ($5 becomes $5000). Then a *diklo* is taken and put around the neck of the man, and everyone cheers and claps. To add interest to the ceremony, someone might refuse to give money, and a huge argument will ensue, everyone yelling and shouting, until he finally concedes.

6. The bride's father is also supposed to give back a *plutchka* to the groom's father from the brideprice, to help cover expenses of the wedding. In one wedding, the groom's father put out

$11 500 in all, and the bride's father gave him $500 from the brideprice.

7. After the feasting, the groom's family go home and give a further party for some of the wedding guests. *Gaje* who have been at the hall do not usually attend this. The parents take their daughter-in-law with them, and she is expected to entertain the group, dance, and serve food. Her parents are not allowed to come as this will 'embarrass the bride in front of her in-laws and her husband'. But her parents give a party at their house for other wedding guests. This emphasizes that she now belongs to her in-laws.

8. The partying lasts three days. On the second night, the bride and groom may sleep with each other. Before she must sleep with her mother-in-law or a sister-in-law. On the morning of the third day they 'put up the flag' to show to the people.

> This consists of the bride's nightgown. If there is blood on it, it indicates respect to the parents of the bride. On this third day, a party is given by the bride's family to celebrate her virginity. If she is not a virgin, the party still goes on, but virginity shows respects to her parents. Families going by old traditions always have a virgin, but most girls past sixteen nowadays are not. If the bride is not a virgin, it does not change the validity of the wedding, but it does make for more gossip. This third day party has to be very big and take care of all the people. It is for the public (all Rom). The larger the party, the more respect for the bride's parents.

According to Lee (1968: 21), the blood is verified privately by the two mothers and announced to the public. One old lady described this event with great emotion:

> Let me tell you about when I got married the first time. I was twelve years old and was a virgin. When my parents told me I was going to be married I cried and cried and didn't want to. But they said I had to and that my mother-in-law would be nice to me. My mother-in-law came to me and said 'we will soon see if you are a virgin' and I was so ashamed and cried and cried. I went to my mother and told her that I didn't want to have that mother-in-law because of what she said, and I was so ashamed but my mother told me it would be OK because she knew I was a virgin and that is what matters.

The wedding lasted three days and three nights. That is what it was in those days. It was a very big party, and there were about four hundred people there. Everyone danced and danced. The first and second night I was told to sleep with my mother-in-law, and on the third night she had a young married girl come to tell me that I was to sleep with my husband that night. She was too embarrassed to tell me herself. I cried and cried and scratched my face and pulled my hair, and said I didn't want to but she made me. She gave me a little white slip to wear to bed, and she told me to take it off in the morning and put it under my pillow. I was so embarrassed in the morning that I slipped out of the house and was gone for the day. She came to see my slip when I was gone. I would not believe it myself if I had not seen it myself years later for other young girls, but the blood forms a flower on the slip. It makes a rose.

My mother-in-law was so proud and she hugged me and said 'I will love you with all my heart now. You will be special to me, and I will always have you here' [clutches bosom]. If there is no blood the marriage still continues and the mother-in-law will love her new *bori*, but not as much as if she were a virgin. If she is not a virgin, the men at the wedding throw their flowers on the ground in disgust. Once the blood is found the mother-in-law takes it around and shows it to everyone so they will know she got a virgin for her son. And everyone praises the girl's parents for being so careful.

9. To conclude, the mothers of both of the couple comb the hair of the girl into braids and plait it with a *diklo*. They give her salt and bread to eat. Each mother gives it and a blessing. The girl wears the *diklo* from then on to show she is married. Lee describes the salt and bread ceremony, which according to him takes place at the wedding and is led by the patriarch:

The Patriarch then pronounces the benediction, which varies in its wording since it is unwritten. He then hands them bread and salt and wine which signify that the man promises to provide the bread of life, the woman the salt of love, and the wine that they will both share in the pleasures of life. Some more pragmatical Gypsies do not accept this romantic interpretation and say that the bread means that some days they will eat, the salt that some days they won't and the wine that sometimes they will get drunk together. (Lee 1968: 20)

The symbolism of the wedding ritual is an intriguing subject and will be dealt with in a general analysis of ritual among the Rom to be published later. For present purposes, it is the social implications of marriage that concern us. The wedding is quite clearly a *rite de passage* in the sense described by Van Gennep (1960). A young man goes from his status as a *shabaro* to a *rom*, and at marriage becomes an adult member of the *kumpania* and *vitsa*. He has the right to participate fully in the *kris romani* and in male economic groups of *wortacha*. The birth of his first child brings further prestige and confirms his status as an adult. A girl (*sheybari*), on the other hand, passes through a transitional period as a *bori* before she is given full adult status and respect as a *romni*. At her marriage she leaves the authority of her parents and passes to the authority of her husband's parents, and her role in the next few years is to provide housekeeping services for them and to produce as many children as possible. She is a newcomer to the family's household, and she has a lower status than the daughters of the house until she has at least one, possibly several, children of her own.

The *žeita* symbolizes publicly that the woman passes from the status of *sheybari* to *bori*, as well as from one group to another, from her own *familia* (and *vitsa*) to her husband's *familia* (and *vitsa*). In the *žeita*, each male of the bride's *vitsa* must give public approval of the exchange. They participate in the brideprice negotiations and in the *žeita*, and they give at the collection afterwards. At each of these three occasions, they may register publicly their approval or disapproval of the union. They may demonstrate that they are reluctant to hand over the bride at the *žeita* and that they value her highly. They may also make protestations at the collection and refuse to donate anything. In both instances the members of the two families crowd around the individual and shout their approval or disapproval of his actions. Of course, much of this display is a mock gesture, and there is also an element of amusement especially if these 'fights' cause *gaje* guests consternation. In the end the bride is allowed to pass or the protestor pulls out a fresh $20 bill which he had ready all the time.

This is the traditional and ideal marriage ceremony which still takes place today among families who have the money for such an elaborate ritual, are arranging a first marriage for their son to a virgin, and are traditional in outlook and want the elaborate wedding procedure. When these conditions are not present, several modified versions of the *tomniamos* and *abiav* may be substituted. A more informal brideprice negotiation may take place, and at the wedding the families may dispense with the *žeita*, the *diklo* on a stick, and proof of virginity. The ceremony may consist of a feast table, the blessing to the bride and groom, and the collection. Then the bride may go to her father-in-law's house where the partying continues. The whole wedding will take only one day, and the bride and groom will have sexual relations the first night.

For example, Steve and Sylvia, both seventeen years of age, have both been married twice before for short periods. They expressed an interest in each other to their parents who were glad to arrange this marriage because Steve's grandmother is Sylvia's mother's sister, both old ladies being prominent matriarchs in the *kumpania*. Their wedding was a simple feast table in the local park, a collection for the bride in hollowed-out bread sponsored by Steve's godfather from baptism, and afterwards a party at the groom's father's house. This wedding is just as legitimate as the full affair and was considered only proper for a couple that had been previously married.

Residence

After marriage, the couple live with the man's parents. The duties of a new bride are to care for her in-laws, perform all household duties for them, and produce grandchildren for them. Until she has fulfilled these duties, a couple cannot expect to set up their own household. Patrilocal post-marital residence is not only the ideal but the statistical norm, and most families in Barvale lived with the man's parents for many years. Marko and Kata Davis did not get their own house until their seventh child was born, though most couples in Barvale set up their own households after they have had fewer children. If the man's parents have a younger married son living with them, then a couple might leave the household soon after marriage, but if there is no one else to live with, a son will take care of his parents until their death. The actual living arrangements depend more on the desires of the parents than the desires of the couple.

Even when a man's son and daughter-in-law set up their own household, they frequently remain in the *kumpania* or travel with his parents until their death. At the death of their parents, siblings tend to disperse with their own large families. Occasionally daughters and their husbands remain in the *kumpania* with her parents, but not in the same household. This may be because his parents are closely related to hers and share the *kumpania* or because his parents are dead, and he has decided to take advantage of connections with his in-laws.

A man may also marry a woman, pay no brideprice, and become a house Rom. In this case he only has rights as a husband as long as she remains with her family, and he is at the beck and call of his in-laws. He loses respect among males in the community and in their eyes is neither a true man nor a true husband (*rom*). His children even belong to the girl's family. A 'house Rom', as he is perjoratively called, is only a last resort for any self-respecting man and usually the result of poverty or physical and mental disability. An old matriarch may try to find a house Rom if she has no sons to live with her.

Elopement

An alternative to the family arranged ideal marriage, which requires a brideprice and wedding expenses, is elopement (*romni nashli*). Whereas marriage is essentially a public exchange between two *familiyi* and, symbolically between two *vitsi* as well, elopement is an individual decision that represents rejection of parental authority.

In spite of the stated increase in elopements recently, it is still considered a scandalous event and though it rarely results in rejection of the family by the community (*marime*), it almost certainly brings loss of status and respect. Technically, elopement is not a marriage unless the families of the eloped couple discuss the matter and decide to let the couple stay together. If they do agree on this arrangement, usually because the girl returns pregnant, they may perform a wedding ceremony and exchange a much reduced brideprice. However, they may also decide to wait and see if the union is really going to work. Parents who decide to undermine an elopement union are supported morally by the *kumpania* and will almost always succeed, but they must then consider that they will not get a good brideprice for the girl.

However, respect may be a more important consideration than brideprice.

> If our daughter runs away with someone then we forget about her, but if she comes back (as they always will), we marry her to someone she doesn't like because she hurt us; she made us lose respect. If we lose respect with the people (Rom), we lose everything.

It is only after the first marriage that elopement becomes a more acceptable alternative to family arranged marriage. In six years in Barvale, there were only two first marriages that were elopements and both caused great shame (*lashav*) and scandal for the families involved. In one case, the girl's parents disowned her, and when her marriage failed three years later, they refused to take her back. In the second case, the parents of the girl kept her at home and in 'shame' with her baby for two years and only when it was obvious that she and her 'husband' (who they objected to entirely because he was a '*streyino* Rom') were not going to desist in their attempts to see each other, did they agree to the marriage.

More commonly, elopements take place on the second or third marriage when the parents' attempts to arrange a satisfactory marriage have failed repeatedly. Also, elopement is the only way to marry a person parents are strongly opposed to, such as a Boyash or Romanitchal Gypsy, and particularly a *gaji*. All unions between a rom and a *gaji* are elopements, and no marriage ceremony is performed. In some cases, the couple may choose to marry by American law in defiance of Rom tradition (*romania*).

Family arranged marriage is not only the ideal and the norm, but there is evidence that elopement is also used when a non-endogamous and therefore not ideal marriage category of person is sought. Of the thirteen marriages that took place in Barvale during my fieldwork, all but two were family arranged, though some of these were carried out with the fear of elopement in mind. Nine of these family arranged marriages were with cousins and two with unrelated persons. The two elopements were marriages of unrelated persons. Elopements between cousins is very rare unless they are first cousins, in which case marriage would not be approved of.

Elopement, therefore, takes place when a marriage is sought which does not conform to the ideal endogamous marriage. These may be marriages with '*streyino* Rom', first cousins, non-Rom

Gypsies, or *gaji*, and in the latter case, the union is not defined as marriage nor is a ceremony performed. Elopement is therefore a denial of parental authority in three ways: it denies them their role in arranging a marriage, it denies the girl's parents the bride-price, and it denies the approved categories of persons for marriage.

The Marriage Payment

The *daro*, or marriage payment, is a very complicated social institution that has important repercussions in every aspect of marriage. *Daro* is translated as 'gift, present' (from Rumanian *dar*) and although Tillhagen (1953: 117) used the word *daro* for the collection that the bride takes after the wedding, Lee (1968: 18) translates it as the 'dowry' or 'bridal price' given to the father of the girl by the father of the boy:

> This *daró*, is not, as some American writers have maintained, a proof that Gypsies buy their wives, since the girl must give her consent to the marriage and cannot be married against her will according to the *Romania*. It is actually a kind of present of respect from the family of the groom and something of a recompense to the bride's father for his loss of revenue from the daughter in his old age. (Lee 1968: 18)

I agree with Lee that the economic aspects have generally been overstated[8] and the wider social implications generally understated. In certain individual cases, the money gained was an important factor of consideration, and it is significant that these cases were labelled 'misuses' of the *daro* by my informants. Actually, often the amount of economic gain through the *daro* is very slight. One man who got $3000 for his daughter said that he spent two-thirds of it on the wedding feast, clothing, jewellery, and featherbedding for the bride, and used the rest to pay off debts (Tompkins 1967: 26). Some brides pay back the *daro* to their fathers-in-law in the first fortune-telling season or contribute to their own *daro* (Murin 1949: 32). Although the boy's father pays for the wedding feast, the father of the girl is expected to give back a certain amount (*plotska*) out of the *daro* to the father of the boy as a sign of good will.

From the point of view of the girl's family, the *daro* has traditionally been seen as a form of protection for their daughter from her husband's family. It has been stated that her situation with her in-laws will be easier for her if the price is high because she will be valued highly and her in-laws will not want to mistreat her and cause her to run home.[9] Although I still found indications that the *daro* given for a girl affects her status with her in-laws' *vitsa*, more and more families seemed to be dismissing the importance of this function of the *daro*. It appeared to me that the *daro* failed to provide any real protection for the girl in her marriage, and this was one of the reasons for the trend towards cousin marriages and a de-emphasis on the *daro* as a way to bind the agreement.

Yet it is true that when marriages take place between two un-related families, the *daro* is the only protection that a family can give to their daughter while she is married, though as a last resort she can return to her family. In cousin marriages, the girl is not going to a strange family, but remains among her own relatives. Her own family is able to see her more often and is available to come to her aid when problems arise. The *Xanamik* are more likely to be able to iron out any difficulties that develop between them since they are related anyway and therefore have a stake in friendly relations. In a sense, cousin marriage replaces the stated function of the *daro*. Therefore, as one would expect, with the increase in endogamy, there has been a decrease in the emphasis on *daro* transactions. There has also been an increase in alternative forms of marriage (elopements and sister exchanges), marriages that normally involve no *daro*. Elopement is a way of acquiring a bride who would either be too expensive or whose family would not agree on the exchange, as well as a way of acquiring a bride of whom the groom's family would not approve. Some families claimed to have dispensed with the *daro* altogether, though I have doubts about their statements which are often based on a desire to hide money transactions from *gaje* welfare workers or income tax authorities.

The increase in cousin marriages and the increase in elopements, both of which diminish the importance of the *daro*, are only two of the factors that are related to the change in *daro* policies. It is also felt by many poorer Rom that the *daro* is too difficult to raise in one lump sum; however, more wealthy families defend the system vehemently. Another reason given is that the *daro* causes too much trouble (*trubulo*) in cases of elopement or divorce, when brideprice negotiations become very difficult and often require a *kris* to be solved. For these reasons there was a general dissatisfaction with the *daro* system, and it was felt that more flexibility was needed.

One of the approved methods of handling the expense of a *daro* is to pay by instalments, and several families adopted this method of payment when they could. One man agreed on a $1500 *daro* for his daughter, took $300 as a downpayment, and the rest in monthly instalments. Meanwhile his daughter married and went to live with her husband. However, problems arose when the girl's father ran off with another man's wife, which meant he was *marime*, and naturally his son-in-law defaulted on the payments because he figured her father could not collect. In another case of delayed marriage payments, the boy's father defaulted on the payments, and the girl and her husband were forced to go and live with her father to remain married. This brought disgrace to the groom since he was forced to become a 'house Rom' and live among his in-laws.

Accepting residence with the girl's family (house Rom) is another way of getting a reduced *daro*. This alternative is not acceptable to most young men since they lose respect among the male community. One young man chose not to marry in these circumstances even though he was thirty, well beyond the usual marriage age, and his chances of getting another bride were very slim. He felt that the respect he would lose in the eyes of the community and the mother-in-law he would have to live with over-ruled the advantages of having a wife.

Elopement is a more acceptable way of avoiding payment of a *daro*, but again the scandal that it brings and the complications in agreeing on a settlement are severe drawbacks. For a first marriage, elopement usually causes too much scandal, and the girl's father feels cheated of his role and his *daro* and will probably not permit the marriage to continue. In a second or third marriage, he is probably more willing to accept the situation since it is unlikely that he would be able to arrange anything better or get much of a *daro* for his daughter.

There are, however, two legitimate methods of avoiding payment of the *daro* altogether. First, one may arrange a marriage between an adopted child (not a grandchild, but an unrelated adopted child) and a relative. I knew of two cases of this practice. In one case an old woman adopted the son of a poor Mesikaya family and raised him. When he was older she married him to her granddaughter. In the second case, a woman raised her niece (husband's brother's daughter) when the child's parents separated. When this niece grew up, the adoptive mother gave her to her own brother for a wife without asking for a *daro*.

The second method for avoiding a *daro* is to arrange an equal exchange of women, usually sister-exchange. This kind of equal exchange has been in practice for some time among the Rom. The Machwaya–Kashtare exchanges (*Figure 4*) were brought about between two poor families at least forty years ago. There were also rumours that several of the Marks–Kashtare marriages (*Figure 18*) were exchanges without *daro*. One of these marriages was referred to as a 'trade' although the informant would not reveal the other couple involved in the trade. As in the instalment method, this alternative to the *daro* has its drawbacks since if one marriage breaks up, the other may have to dissolve as well or pay a *daro* after all. Regardless of whether or not a *daro* is paid, it is considered desirable to have the number of exchanges between families even. One man remarked to his brother-in-law: 'Well, you got my sister, but now I have your niece [for his grandson] so we are even.'

Accusations are frequently made against persons who, it was felt, 'sold their daughters several times to make money'. These accusations are not new to the Rom. Irving Brown (1929: 50-1) quotes one Rom:

> 'They are worse than *gaje*,' he declared. '*Biken le borye trin star var*. They sell their daughters as brides three or four times. After a few months or a year they take them back and sell them over again. A fine thing for a Gypsy to do,' he snorted, 'worse than *gaje*.'

The very accusation 'worse than *gaje*' indicates what an unethical and immoral thing it is felt to be and implies that it is 'unclean' and defiling. John Marks' statements (Appendix A) reinforce this implication.

> It is more enjoyable to get a daughter-in-law from a cousin because there's been lots of dirty business. A man makes money giving a daughter-in-law by marrying her several times to different people. He does this by giving her (as a *bori*) for six months, then builds up evidence (against her in-laws) such as they beat her or her father-in-law made a pass at her, then her father takes her back and does not return the money. So it used to be you got a daughter-in-law from a different *vitsa*, but now it is better to get one in the family.

Part of the reason for the unethical quality of making money from 'selling' one's daughter is that the person is making money from another Rom. One man wrote in a letter to his rival's social worker: 'He is a fraud who makes his living by selling his girls to different Gypsies. He steals them back sometimes and re-sells them to someone else.'

These accusations are almost always made by the offended party who felt he had been robbed of a daughter-in-law or wife. It is difficult to know exactly how unscrupulous the actions were and whether the father is merely exercising his rights to protect his daughter or abusing the *daro* system.

A father has the right to take back his daughter from her in-laws if he feels she is being mistreated. In the ensuing trial, if a reconciliation is impossible, and if it is decided his action was justified, he will return either none or a small portion of the *daro*. If the *kris* decides he was not justified in his actions, he will be told to return a larger portion (the whole *daro* is rarely returned since she was a wife for a certain time and especially if she lost her virginity). However, a father's right to take back his daughter, if he feels it necessary, is not questioned. In a sense, the *daro* is a security for the groom's family since there is not much they can do to keep the wife; but they do have the support of the community in demanding a return of some of the *daro*, and they can call a trial for this. According to John Marks it is this very lack of security, and the desire to avoid trial and divorce that is stimulating more and more families to choose cousin marriages. It is interesting to note that Stevan, who he accused of making money from selling his daughters again and again, is, for the same reasons as John Marks, choosing cousin marriages for his daughters. Stevan's eldest three children are not married to cousins, but his youngest son, the recent marriage of an older daughter and his only two married grandchildren, are all married to cousins.

Divorce

Divorce should require a trial (*kris romani*) whereby the grievances of each family are stated publicly and the amount of brideprice to be returned is decided. The trial between John Marks and Stevan (Appendix A, Case 1) is an example of a formal divorce proceeding. The most crucial factor in divorce is the amount of the brideprice returned and if this can be agreed upon by the two families a trial may not be necessary; however, agreement on the amount returned is very rare since each family usually supports the actions of their own child and condemns the actions of the in-laws.

According to statements from many Rom, elopements and divorce were extremely rare in the past and are on the increase among young people.[10] It is claimed that young people now want to choose their own marriages, and this often means accepting their parents' decision in a first marriage and then later eloping with the person of their own choice. An elopement or divorce causes a scandal and requires a settlement of the brideprice. It may result in several arrests, a long *kris romano*, and *marime* sentences for the families. When they were rare, elopements and divorces were dealt with swiftly and harshly for the families; however, now that they are on the increase, it is felt that it is impossible to make so many people *marime* for so long. For this reason 'new rules' about marriage, divorce, and elopements have been discussed and generally accepted by the community.

These new rules were stated in the following way:

> We want to change the marriage. We don't want a *daro* any more. It's getting too expensive, and the young people are eloping too much. If there is an elopement, the parents get *marime* for not keeping the kids in line and you have to have a settlement of the *daro* which involves a long hassle, a *kris*, and everyone gets mad at everyone else, and then the kids would have to get divorced. So now the rules are changed. The boy can tell his parents who he likes and if they approve they can get together with the girl's parents just like always and arrange things. This way we can stop the elopements.

The only Rom who opposed these new rules were the really wealthy ones who can ask and pay high prices for their women. Most Rom agree that if the marriage breaks up irretrievably, it would be best to avoid a *kris* and return half the *daro*.

Adultery

Taking another man's wife is a serious offence and a scandal condemned by the Rom community. Though a woman cannot always expect exclusive sexuality in her husband, a man has exclusive sexual rights to his wife. If these rights are violated by another man, he can demand brideprice payment from the adulterer. This does not eliminate the immorality of the act, but it does legitimize the reshuffling of rights. When a man has received his brideprice back, he cannot make any more claims on his wife's sexuality. The following four cases give an indication of the importance of brideprice in creating and dissolving marriages.

1. Miller's married son ran off with Dorothy, who is the *bori* of a powerful Machwaya family. A *kris* was immediately called, and Miller was condemned by the court for his son's behaviour. He left the *kumpania* for six weeks, and when he returned he found that his welfare had been cut off by the other Rom. Miller felt that his son was wrong to do what he did and was as furious as everyone else, but he also felt that Dorothy's family should take some of the blame as well. Finally Miller's son and Dorothy contacted the *kumpania* by phone, and Dorothy promised to repay her *daro* to her in-laws, in instalments, so they could get another *bori*. This satisfied them more or less. It did not satisfy the in-laws of Miller's son who had now lost their house Rom; however, they could demand no compensation since the marriage had involved no brideprice.

2. Three months after 'Big Mick's' wife died, he ran off with Maruda, wife of Spiro. The whole community was outraged, not only at the adultery, but because he had not even waited until the year *pomana* for his deceased wife. They swore that if they could find him, he would have to return the wife and pay the husband damages. Of course, they never did find him. Spiro made several attempts to find his wife through the welfare department and the police. He claimed Maruda stole a fortune in jewellery and money and hoped the police would find her, arrest her, and bring her to California for trial. He said he would consider $3000 back from 'Big Mick' so he could buy himself another wife, and tried to get the welfare department to look for them by claiming 'Big Mick' was guilty of welfare fraud and of selling his daughters.

In the first case, the *kris* quickly condemned Miller for his son's behaviour and punished him by having his welfare cut. However, when Dorothy arranged to pay back her *daro*, her in-laws were satisfied since they did not, in any case, want her back as a shamed woman. The in-laws of Miller's son could do nothing about the loss of a house Rom since no brideprice was involved. In the second case, when a brideprice was not returned for Maruda, 'Big

Mick' could not reclaim his lost respect and Spiro was justified in using *gaje* police and welfare authorities to 'punish' his wife.

3. Mitzi was married to a Bimbaleshti, and when she left him, he demanded that her father return her or the brideprice. Her father offered to give him another daughter, Marie, for his wife, and he agreed to this solution.

4. Dino Christo claimed that his brother-in-law by his first wife, a Stokes, had an affair with his *gaji* wife. This caused a tremendous fight between the Christos and the Stokes families and they came to Barvale to have it out. The result of the *diwano* (during which pistols were brandished and several people hospitalized) was that the *gaji* should go back to Dino, but the Christos were not satisfied with this verdict and felt that they should get some financial compensation from the Stokes for the defilement of the adultery. They threatened the Stokes who had to leave town until things cooled off.

Cases 3 and 4 have different solutions. In Case 3, the original wife is exchanged for a sister, and in Case 4 the wife returns, but the family of the husband demand payment for the defilement of adultery and infringement on their rights.

There are many individual reasons for the failure of a marriage besides dissatisfaction between husband and wife. A breakdown in relations between two *Xanamik* or between a *bori* and her mother-in-law (the husband usually chooses to defend his parents against his wife) can result in divorce. The following two cases illustrate in-law situations that can result in the dissolution of a marriage. They also demonstrate how misleading divorce statistics can be.

1. Rita arranged for her fourteen year old daughter Ruby to go to the Miller family for $400. When she had done this she found that her welfare cheque was cut, since she was not supporting Ruby, and that she had lost a housekeeper, which she badly needed, so she regretted her action. She arranged to get Ruby back through her welfare worker (who pressured the other woman to return Ruby) and returned the money to the Millers. The negotiations were carried out in the welfare office with the social worker as witness.

2. Tony, an only son, married Fatima by pressuring his mother to agree to the marriage and threatening elopement. Fatima was ill the first year of marriage and did not conceive. Tony's

mother, who anxiously wanted a grandchild, became disgruntled with Fatima because she was too ill to fulfil her duties as a *bori* and because she had yet produced no child. She decided to dissolve the marriage and sent Fatima back to her parents. Then she told Tony she would find him another wife. But Tony ran off with Fatima to Los Angeles and finally contacted his mother when Fatima was pregnant. Tony's mother was furious that he had chosen Fatima over her, but hearing of the pregnancy she decided to make the best of it and kick Fatima out when she had the baby.

Conclusions on Marriage Category and Marriage Procedure

The increase in elopement and divorce, both of which are shameful acts, attacks the authority and respect status of elders and reflects a move towards more individual choice. Elopement and divorce are also related to each other since elopements rarely result in stable marriages and are quite self-righteously undermined by the parents. However, competition and hostility between *Xanamik* are also a cause of the increase in divorce.

In order to avoid the loss of respect and authority that elopements and divorce represent, elders have initiated several changes. First, they have turned increasingly to endogamous marriages and have chosen for *Xanamik* persons with whom they have a relationship of cooperation based on kinship. When relations between *Xanamik* are good, it is very difficult for the couple to get a separation. Similarly, endogamy reflects individual choice to a certain extent, since young cousins are more likely to see each other than are unrelated persons. Endogamous marriage also lessens the trauma for the girl in her new role since she will already know the family – a factor that will give her family some means of aiding her in her position. If they have more contact with their daughter and her in-laws, they can use their influence with them to help her. Second, elders have relaxed *daro* regulations so that poorer families can pay in instalments and related families can lower their prices or arrange equal exchanges of women without *daro*. Finally, they have simplified divorce procedure and agreed that half the *daro* should be paid back so that many divorces need not involve an expensive, bitter trial between *Xanamik* (see Appendix A, Case 1) as is usual.

Marriage is defined by the Rom as a union arranged by the couple's families in public view and sanctioned in a public ritual.[11] However, marriage by this definition is not the only kind of union that occurs. When individuals want to marry a person who is not of the ideal endogamous kinship category, they may choose elopement as an alternative; however, in doing so they not only express their rejection of the ideal marriage category and approved marriage procedure, but they also attack the authority, status, and purity (*wuzho*) of their families. This may be rectified when the *Xanamik* in the union decide to agree to the marriage and arrange a modified and simplified public wedding. In this case the union becomes an approved marriage. When the choice of marriage category is a non-Rom Gypsy, or a *gaji*, approved marriage does not ensue and divorce generally results.

Marime Sexual Unions

Until now we have discussed marriage categories and marriage procedure, and have mentioned briefly an alternative form of marriage, namely elopement and a modified marriage ritual after elopement. These are the only two forms of marriage that are socially acceptable; however, they are not the only social–sexual unions in Rom society. There are a number of sexual unions that are illegitimate or *marime*. For purposes of discussion, these unions are of two types: those that are between persons who are too closely related, by blood or marriage ties, and those that occur between persons who are too distantly related, Rom and *gaje*, and are seen as symbolic opposites.

Information on incestuous relations[12] is very difficult to obtain since they are extremely shameful, but this difficulty is further increased by misleading 'evidence' of brother–sister marriages in newspapers and official documents. Official documents, such as immigration, welfare and police records, and birth or death certificates, are not reliable evidence of consanguineal or affinal relationships unless cross-checked in some other (unofficial) way. Several 'brother–sister' marriages were brought to my attention during fieldwork, but when checked they always proved to be false.

In many cases the mistake was due to the common practice among American Rom of claiming that a daughter-in-law (*bori*) is a daughter (*shey*) to the welfare authorities. This is done to protect the husband from contact with the authorities. Officially, he is not receiving welfare (though his 'sister' is) and therefore they have no reason to contact him and no control over his movements. The family may prefer to have a 'daughter' with several 'illegitimate' children (in the eyes of the welfare department) even though the amount of money in her grant would be increased by including the husband on the application. Two examples of false brother–sister marriage illustrate this situation.

1. When Stevan and Yana came to Barvale they said that Rachael was their daughter who had had a child by 'a Mexican'. Her 'brother' Toma was not included in her cheque and was free to come and go as he pleased, seeking employment without having to report his whereabouts to the welfare department. However, Rachael had a child each year, and the social worker began to suspect that they could not be 'illegitimate' children because her status in the community was not diminished in spite of the protestations of shame and embarrassment which her family expressed to the social worker. Also, Rachael was always taking trips with 'her brother' and the rest of the community referred to them as a couple. Finally, when confronted by their social worker, after her fourth child, her parents claimed that Toma was really a nephew whom they had raised and that Toma and Rachael finally 'married'.

2. Marie is married to Katherine's adopted son, Danny. Although she claims to be Katherine's daughter, and Danny keeps well away from the social worker, she fulfils the traditional roles of a *bori*, all the housework falling to her. When Marie goes on her frequent trips, she always joins Danny, who is free to work and travel as much as he likes, without interference from the welfare department.

Sometimes, the Rom claim a *bori* is a daughter because the girl is under the legal age of marriage, and authorities who find out about a twelve- or thirteen-year-old bride often get very upset about child marriage and threaten the husband with prosecution for 'statutory rape'. The offspring of such a young couple may also be kept secret and may be registered to an older couple. Therefore the official complications can carry on for generations. Yoors describes a situation where this practice resulted in more difficulties than it prevented:

> I remember one case which turned out badly. A Gypsy woman had been arrested for stealing chickens and investigation into

her record seemed to prove that the man she was living with was her brother. The charge of incest, made more serious by the fact that the couple had several children, caused quite a stir in the European press. In actual fact there was no basis for it. Their respective families had, at different times, registered them both as children of the same couple, to whom neither of them was even related. Incest was as much against the moral and religious code of the Rom as against that of the *gaje*. Sometimes, because of the complications in trying to arrange the immigration status of a young bride joining her husband's group, it was found more expedient to let her assume the identity of the groom's sister. (Yoors 1967: 110)

There was another instance in Barvale in which a woman accused her husband's brother of sexually molesting her daughters. The welfare department and the police were worried by this incident, but as it turned out, she was trying to get her daughters returned to her from their uncle's house. The Rom had decided that he should have custody of them when her husband died as punishment for her anti-social behaviour.

Sexual relations between closely related persons, which are classified as *marime*, include: (1) all kin who are more closely related than first cousin. First cousins do sometimes marry though this is highly frowned upon; (2) the women whom a man calls *bori*, that is, relations between a man and his brother's wife or son's wife.[13]

Both of these sexual unions are prohibited, *marime*, and shameful (*lashav*) for the offenders and their families; however, there is a distinction between attitudes towards these two sets of sexual relations. The first is a relationship that is felt to be 'unnatural', invokes physical horror, and is said to 'come out in the children' or 'the children will be no good'. In Barvale, the child of an uncle-niece relationship was immediately given to an adoption agency, an act that is unthinkable to the Rom for other children, even children of a very shameful union such as that of a woman with a *gajo*. The difference seems to be that the *marime* of the former is bred into the child, but in other cases, the child can overcome this shame through living a model life.

Rosie ran away with her father's brother (*kak*) at age thirteen and travelled around with him for nine months. Her parents, when they discovered who she was with, were so horrified they dared not tell anyone in the community, since they would automatically be *marime* if the truth were known. When Rosie became disillusioned and 'ashamed' (*lashav*) at what she had done, she returned to her family pregnant, expecting to be beaten by her father and outcast from the community. Her father, who wished to protect his position in the community, instead, kept her situation secret and married her, without *daro* (brideprice), to the first man who would take her. Though she hated the man she married, and he mistreated her brutally, she considered this action by her father to be extremely generous and kind. She had twins by her uncle which her family immediately gave to an adoption agency (*gaje*). This action contrasted with her next child by her husband which was immediately adopted by her parents who adore it.

Several actions are unusual in this case. First, it is very unusual for parents to lie to the community about such a serious breach of morals, and they only did so because it would have wrecked their whole lives to admit such an offence. As I have said, it is also extremely rare for a child to be given to the *gaje*. Even twins are not adopted out normally; however, in this case the birth of twins may have also been seen as a bad omen.

Though sexual relations between kin are said to be unnatural, sexual relations with a *bori* are also felt to be a serious offence and are prohibited for social reasons. We have already seen that the very accusation of sexual designs on his *bori* induced John Marks to go to such extremes to defend his reputation. The severe consequences, the multiple arrests and *kris* that ensued, because of this accusation, are a measure of the attitude towards *socro–bori* incest. According to the accused, 'the worst thing you can say about a man is that he tried to make love to his daughter-in-law. Now that accusation would condemn any Gypsy to a judge and jury (*kris*) if his story were true.' Irving Brown describes another case of a *bori* who was arranged by her father-in-law for his son with an eye to possessing her himself (since he knew her father would not agree to his marriage with her), and the scandal that resulted when she escaped from her predicament (Brown 1924: 40-9).

Sexual relations with a *bori* are an infringement of the rights and obligations between a father and his son. A father arranges and pays for a bride for his son and has many rights to her services, including more housekeeping and entertainment services than the

husband himself. However, he is strongly prohibited from en-
croaching on the husband's sexual rights, which are exclusive.
This prohibition extends to the husband's brothers and in general
to all males of his *vitsa*. On the other side, a woman who joins her
husband's family, removed from the protection of her own family
and often among total strangers, is expected to provide certain
services for her father-in-law and mother-in-law, services that she
will later provide for her husband. She is protected from sexual
advances from her father-in-law and brothers-in-law who are the
first non-kinsmen she is allowed to be alone with and in whose care
she has been entrusted. Certainly residence is an important factor
in the prohibition. A man lives in the same household with his
bori (particularly his daughter-in-law), but he does not share
residence with his wife's sister (*kumnata*). Wife's sister marriage
is perfectly respectable as was seen in the case of the man who
married his wife's sister when his wife left him.

On the border-line between incest and permitted marriages are
marriages between first cousins. Like *kumnato/bori* and *socro/bori*
relations, marriage with a first cousin is considered undesirable
primarily for social reasons. These reasons are based on the
nature of the *Xanamik* relationship: 'You can marry a cousin, but
it is not good to marry a first cousin. That is, if your *Xanamik* are
uncle and nephew, it's all right, but not if they are brothers.'

This statement shows no disgust at an incestuous relationship
but is a statement about social problems that arise between *Xanamik* if they are brothers. *Xanamik* are expected to maintain a
respectful and formal distance from each other, combined with
an awareness of mutual obligations of hospitality. This distant
relationship is irreconcilable with the affection and close cooperation expected of brothers. First cousin marriage therefore
presents the individuals with two contradictory roles which cannot
both be fulfilled.[14] An uncle/nephew relationship contains an
element of respect and unequal status which is consistent with the
Xanamik relationship, and it can be easily adjusted to the new
status. Cousins also are kin, but more distant kin, and their
relations easily fit into *Xanamik* obligations and roles.

Statements that it is 'bad to marry a first cousin because of the
children' were common; however, children of first cousins are not
ostracized in any way, and it may be that these statements have
been picked up from the *gaje*. First cousin marriages do not seem
to be irrevocably shameful. One first cousin couple, who expected

me to be shocked, joked about being first cousins in front of other Rom. First cousin marriages are eventually accepted by the community though they are not arranged marriages. In every case, a first cousin marriage was an elopement.

Apart from the strong prohibition on sexual relations between close kin and a man and his *bori*, and the somewhat ambivalent attitude towards first cousin marriages, marriage with any other Rom is permitted. As we have seen, the preference is for endogamous marriages outside this inner circle of kin and affines. At the outer limit of permitted marriages, we also find negative attitudes towards three kinds of sexual unions or marriages: (1) marriage with non-Rom Gypsies, (2) marriage between a woman and a *gajo*, and (3) marriage between a man and a *gaji* (*gaji romni*).

Marriage with non-Rom Gypsies[15] is discouraged and considered socially inferior, but it is not prohibited. These marriages are very unsettled, and they rarely last very long because of the opposition of the Rom parents. The following examples of marriages with non-Rom Gypsies illustrate how these marriages are never fully accepted by the *kumpania* even when they are of long standing. The very low status of non-Rom Gypsies among the Rom is an ever-present factor in the unhappy situation of these wives.

1. Emma is a Boswell Romanitchal whose family travelled around the United States during the twenties. At one camp site, which they shared with some Gurkwe Rom, Emma and a young Rom 'fell in love at first sight'. He persuaded his parents to offer several thousand dollars for Emma, but her parents were insulted and told them 'we don't sell our daughters'. So Emma eloped with the young man, and the marriage lasted until his death. They have eight children and Emma says proudly, 'all my daughters married Rom'. Even so, Emma is not accepted in the *kumpania* and has little social contact with them.

2. Mary is an 'Irish Gypsy' (according to her mother-in-law) but is derisively referred to as a *gaji* by the rest of the community because she is light-skinned and has red hair. She eloped with a Machwano, and it is rumoured that their fights can be heard for miles. Her mother-in-law has almost completely taken over their only child, and it is quite clear that if Mary were to complain or leave, she would lose her baby. It is interesting that although she is called *gaji* by the other women, she is not treated

as one and participates fully in social events even though she suffers some discrimination.

3. Wanda is from a Rumanian Boyash Gypsy family which is settled and no longer speaks *Romanes*. She married into a Kuneshti family of some ill repute since it is rumoured that incest is part of their history. Wanda and her husband eloped, and since they returned, his mother has done everything in her power to undermine the marriage. She also plans to adopt their only child. Wanda has had such adjustment problems that she was referred for psychiatric care by her social worker. Then Wanda's 'mental illness' was used as another strike against her by her mother-in-law.

In all these cases, certain factors are held in common. The marriages are not pre-arranged as is normal but are elopements that force the marriage on the respective families. Even so, the families, quite self-righteously, do their utmost to undermine the marriage. The non-Rom wife is never fully accepted by the community as well as by the in-laws even though she conforms fully with Rom customs. In the only successful and long-lasting marriage, Emma completely accepted the Rom way of life and subordinated her own cultural background. Nevertheless, she has always suffered discrimination and ostracism from the Rom community, even though she and her family led respectable lives.

The negative prohibitory attitudes towards marriage with non-Rom Gypsies is entirely consistent with the stated preference for endogamous marriages within the incest prohibitions. I believe these marriages are frowned upon partly because they are equated with marriages between a Rom and a *gaji*, though slightly more acceptable, and partly because they are marriages with a person of low status and dubious cleanliness.

Marriage with Gaje

Marriage with the *gaje* is a denial of *romania* and is *marime*. The *gaje* are moral opposites to the Rom. They are unclean (*marime*) and lack a proper sense of shame, whereas the Rom are clean (*wuzho*) and understand shame. *Gaje* exist outside the social boundaries, and relations with them are intrinsically different from relations with one's own people, in some ways diametrically opposed. Behaviour which is wrong with Rom (e.g. stealing) is

I

appropriate with the *gaje* and that which is appropriate with Rom (cooperation, affection, and respect) is lacking with *gaje*.

Marriage with *gaje* is not only immoral but a contradiction in terms. The very words for husband (*rom*) and wife (*romni*) only allow for marriage with a Rom. Marriage is a bond that creates important ties between *familiyi* and eventually establishes a new family in the *vitsa*. The status of the families of the bride and groom in part determines the status of the children of that marriage and their place in the overall structure of social relations. A union with a non-Gypsy creates none of these ties and undermines even the very basic status of the children as Rom.

No Rom definition of marriage as a socially approved and socially arranged institution with a brideprice can include marriage with the *gaje*. As one elder put it: 'We don't like marriages with *gaje*. Gypsies marry Gypsies; *gaje* marry *gaje*. A Gypsy girl who has anything to do with a *gajo*, she's out. We don't want her and we don't want *gaji romni* either. Mixing leads to sin and trouble for our people.' The attitude is clear and absolute, but this does not mean that the situation never happens.

Over a period of six years (two hundred marriages), in Barvale there were eleven unions of Rom with *gaji* and these constituted 5·5 per cent of all marriages.[16] Of these eleven unions, three have endured long enough for the birth of many children. The other eight were ephemeral, some lasting only until the birth of one child. Cases 1–3 are the most enduring unions, and these all involve older persons who have a very stable relationship and have had many children. All three men live on the fringe of the community, have suffered strong ostracism, and have had much difficulty with their families and relatives because of this union. Only in Case 1 has the Rom actually remained a full member of the community, but his children have all had a high school education and occupy a very ambiguous position. His daughters wear *gaje* clothes and have all married non-Rom Gypsies.

Case 1

Joe is a fifty-year-old Machwano. He is literate (which is very rare) and is much more acculturated into American society than most Rom. He married a full-blooded Mono Indian, and she left her family, reservation, and tribe and has completely absorbed herself into Gypsy society, not only dressing like a Gypsy, cooking, and following all cleanliness laws, but she has learned some of the language as well. According to her, in the beginning, she had great difficulty in being accepted, but after many children she felt that she was accepted. According to the community, however, she is only tolerated. When she comes to social functions, she does not join into conversation with the other women and sits quietly on the side alone. When one of the old ladies got mad at Joe, she called him 'that *India*' with disdain and one of the biggest fights among the children at school was when one of the new girls claimed that their daughter should not be there because she is not 'a Gypsy but an Indian'. Nevertheless, this family speaks *Romanes* in the home, follows Gypsy custom, and accepts *romania*.

Case 2

Ted Wanko (45) is a Mineshti Rom who married a *gaji* and broke away from the Gypsies because of their discrimination against his wife. For twenty years he lived in one town in Missouri where he ran his own roofing and painting business from his garage. When his wife died, four years ago, he took to the road with his eleven children and two grandchildren and has been travelling since. The family speaks *Romanes* among themselves, and the three eldest daughters were all married to Gypsies by their father. One of the husbands was an 'English Gypsy' and when he deserted Ted's daughter, Ted said, 'he is an English Gypsy; therefore he is no good. I should never have agreed to the marriage. He never took any responsibility for his wife and child, and they often had to come home because they had no food or had been abandoned.'

Case 3

Richard (30) and Mary (34) have a very strong marriage and have eight children. He is very 'Americanized', his wife is a *gaji*, and their children speak English as well as *Romanes* in the home. They try hard to keep separate from the Gypsies because of the ostracism they get from Richard's relatives, but when they move away and hide the relatives always find them. On one occasion, some relatives saw them driving on the freeway, followed them home, and moved in with them. When this family has been destitute and appealed to his family for aid, however, they have not received any collection from the community because of the *gaji* wife. Nevertheless the relatives consider it their right to move in with the family whenever they can find them. Richard and Mary married by American law. They are not in good standing with the larger community and are separated from it at all functions. Their social worker described them as the 'least Gypsy-looking of all the Gypsies', and both their dress and favourable attitude towards schooling was unorthodox. Mary is an orphan, has a tenth-grade education, and her only relative is an aunt.

Jan Tompkins, who has observed many *gaji/romni* marriages felt that these marriages work if the *gaji bori* is willing to 'become completely absorbed in Gypsy culture'. She offered her own explanation of why they might do this:

> All of the *gaji* wives I have seen come from loosely organized families of migrant farm labourers or sharecroppers. They seem to respond to the close family life of the Gypsies. They are usually a little better educated than their in-laws, although they are not schooled enough to make their husbands feel inferior. They have a special status as they are literate and can act as secretaries and intermediaries with the *gaje* world. As a result, they feel needed and important. Since they were not born Gypsies they sometimes feel that they must prove themselves, and they become ultra-conservative. My fiercest argument over school attendance was with a *gaji bori* who was trying very hard to impress her assembled in-laws with her 'Gypsier-than-thou' attitude. (Tompkins 1967: 5)

One might suspect that men would want *gaji* wives because they need pay no brideprice. One young man, who was from a poor family and had for years tried unsuccessfully to get a wife, gave his considered assessment of the situation.

> I was once asked by a young Gypsy bachelor to give an opinion on a prospective bride who was offered for 'only $400'. This girl, a divorcee, was pregnant and had a broken jaw. I naturally advised him against the match since his only interest in the girl seemed to be her bargain-basement price tag. In the course of discussing this situation, I asked him why he was saving his money to buy a Gypsy wife when he could have a *'gaji'* for free. His reply went something like this:

> '*Gaji* wives are far from being free. It is true you can get an American girl for only the price of a $2.00 marriage licence. But this is only a down payment. As soon as she is married, the *gaji* girl becomes very demanding. She will not want to come home and live with my mother. She will insist that I buy her a

house. Then she will want new furniture and a washing machine. She will nag at me to work harder so she can buy more. By this time I will have spent thousands of dollars and will be in debt for the rest of my life. Even then, there is no guarantee that she will stay with me. And if she goes, she will take away my children, and the *gaje* court will force me to pay alimony payments even though I am left with nothing.

'I will admit that some of the *gaji* girls are very attractive. They are clean and interesting to talk to. However, I have given it a lot of thought and have decided that it is best for me to buy myself a Gypsy wife like my father did. She may not smell as nice as the *gaji*, but if I don't mistreat her she will stay with me and will be a good wife. She will take care of my house and my mother will be satisfied with me and will respect me no matter how poor we become. You are wrong when you say that *gaji* brides are cheap. In the long run, you could pay more than for the most expensive Machwanka. I would rather pay a bride-price in the first place and be assured of getting a wife I can live with.' (Tompkins 1967: 4–5)

To most of the women, the idea of marrying a *gajo* is practically unthinkable, and some have expressed physical revulsion at the thought. The only two women who expressed any desire to marry a *gajo* added that they could never do so because of the repercussions it would have for their families. Both women only mentioned a *gajo* marriage because they were suffering ostracism from the community for the repeated failure of their own marriages.

Of the two hundred marriages in six years in Barvale, there were three cases mentioned of *romni/gajo* unions. If these were counted as marriages they would represent about 1·5 per cent of all 'marriages'.[17] There were rumours of other cases, but these turned out to be non-Rom Gypsies whom the community spoke about as if they were *gaje*. The feelings about a woman marrying a Boyash or Romanitchal are almost as strong as a *gajo*; however the girl is usually 'shamed' but not *marime*. The difficulty, of course, in gathering evidence on these unions is that once a girl takes up with a *gajo*, she must disappear, and she ceases to exist as far as the Rom are concerned.

1. A *romni* married a *gajo* (Negro) and though she was *marime* and never had contact with the Rom, she taught her children

Romanes. One Rom who had known her before her marriage (and I suspect was closely related but would not admit it) visited her secretly and ate with her. This, of course, was kept secret from the other Rom since he would be *marime* if they knew about it. Finally, because of the danger, his wife made him stop the visits, and this contact with her was only revealed many years after his death.

2. It was rumoured that Lola married a *gajo* because she was working in a laundromat (a *gajikanes* job) and was considered *marime* by the community, though whether it was because of the job or a *gajo* husband was impossible to confirm. When I met Lola she was divorced and living with her family, and she claimed she had been married to a Boyash. However, I suspect that she and her family were *marime* for this period because at that time they seemed only to have contact with other Rom by telephone (which is the only contact they can have if *marime*). A year later they had been reinstated.

3. Helen ran a carnival in Australia for many years, was married to a Rom, and raised a large family of girls who all married Rom. After her husband died, when she was in her fifties, she legally married an Italian of thirty who apparently needed a way of immigrating to the U.S. When she came to Barvale with her *gajo* husband, the *kumpania* strictly avoided any contact with her, and though she was destitute at the time, they would not help or visit her. She wanted contact with the *kumpania* but did not seem to care much that she had married a *gajo*. Even when her husband was deported from the country, she was still not accepted by the community and eventually left.

Thus we see that only very rarely do unions with *gaje* occur. A man has more possibility than a woman of forming a relationship with a *gaji* and, in fact, these unions are frequent enough for the existence of the term *gaji romni* to express the relationship. However, only when he brings his *gaji romni* into the community and she accepts the life of the Rom may the union be tolerated eventually. It is never socially acceptable. In general, sexual relations with *gaje* are *marime*, and a man often fears syphilis and other proofs of *marime* and *prikaza* (very bad luck) when he has had sexual relations with a *gaji*.

A woman's position is much less flexible, and she is prohibited without exception from entering into a union with a *gajo* whilst a member of the *kumpania*. The consequences are *marime* expulsion from the group and shame for her, besides loss of reputation and status for her family, often with a period of *marime* as well. If she decides to leave the *gajo* and return to the group, she may do so. She remains *marime* along with her entire family for a period of time decided by a *kris*. If her behaviour during this period is exemplary, she and her family are finally reinstated. At this time, she is immediately married without brideprice to the first Rom who will accept her. Her reinstatement is not unlike a *rite de passage* (Van Gennep). The woman is expelled, then returns to the *kumpania* in a polluted state for a certain time until final re-acceptance into the community by marriage to a Rom.

The *marime* period for the girl and her family is extremely painful. They tacitly are members of the community, but they can have little social life and cannot eat with friends and relatives. Everything they touch is defiled, and they are avoided in their persons. Yet they are a topic of constant concern and example to the *kumpania*, and their behaviour must be respectful and demonstrate their sense of shame. The girl in particular must never speak unless spoken to, do all the housework without complaining, and keep to the house with downcast eyes.

Conclusions

Thus we have discussed several unions that are polluting (*marime*) and cross accepted social boundaries. These are sexual relations between persons who are too closely related by consanguineal kinship; sexual relations between in-laws and a *bori* who live together and share important obligations; sexual union with non-Rom Gypsies and with *gaje*. We have also examined sexual unions that are considered legitimate and can be called marriage and have looked at ideal marriage categories and procedure. We have found that marriage should be between closely related but not too closely related persons and that it must be family arranged to be legitimate.

Marriage is initially a contract between parents (or grandparents) for the young, unmarried members of their family, and the stability of this contract largely determines the outcome of the marriage. The institution of the brideprice is an essential feature of the legitimacy of the marriage which can only be dissolved when the two families agree on a fair repayment. Later, when the couple have their own children and grandchildren and arrange marriages for them, their own marriage is a creation of a *familia* and an extenuation of the *vitsa*. Marriage is therefore an institution for the benefit of elders who want to arrange the brideprice and have grandchildren. Elopement denies them this role in negotiations and sometimes denies them their own grandchildren.

The legitimacy of children is not an important issue except when the status of the children as Rom is threatened. This occurs when marriage takes place with an outsider. Illegitimate children are in fact favoured and are more valuable to a grandparent since he has an incontestable right to adopt them. However, the status of the children is an important consideration in arranging a marriage because the status of the families involved in part determines the status of the child.

But whereas the parents and grandparents of a man have important rights over his children and over the labours of his wife, only the husband has sexual rights with his wife, and the males of his family are expressly forbidden under penalty (*marime*) from having sexual relations with her. A wife does not have a monopoly in the husband's sexuality, but she must give her husband the sole right to her sexuality. The consequences of infraction of this monopoly are *marime* and shame for the man as well as the woman.

The wife is the main guardian of the cleanliness status of her husband and the most important potential source of pollution for him, especially since he has sexual relations with her. Her sense of shame (*lashav*), proper sexual cleanliness, and respect towards the man guarantee his cleanliness; if she fails in any of these respects, his cleanliness status is threatened, and he may be denied not only social contact with his fellow men but also a political voice in the community together with his respect status due him as a man.

Pollution, Boundaries, and Beliefs

Throughout this description of Rom social organization, I have referred frequently to certain concepts, such as *marime*, *lashav*, *prikaza*, and *romania*, which express important values and beliefs for the Rom and most of which have no direct equivalent in our own society. It now remains to draw these concepts together to see if they form a cohesive system of beliefs in relation to the social organization. What I intend to demonstrate is that pollution concepts are central to the whole belief system and are related to beliefs about the auspicious and inauspicious (*baXt*, *prikaza*), health and illness (*sastimos*, *naswalemos*, and supernatural beings. God (*o Del*), the Devil (*o Beng*), and the spirits of the dead (*mule*). Moreover, pollution ideas not only are the core of a system of beliefs that give order to the moral universe of the Rom, but they give meaning to social boundaries, both external and internal, and are the key to the survival of the Rom as a group.[1]

Details of religious beliefs and practices vary a great deal. Each *natsia* and *vitsa* has its own particular customs or interpretations of general rules. Even *familiyi* within one *vitsa* often observed different ritual practices, use of amulets, washing and eating regulations, etc. Nevertheless, the elders were generally in agreement on the overall rules, and in one enlightening session with four *drabarni* (female doctors) a striking degree of consensus emerged.

Most of the information in this chapter is the special prerogative of the elderly, especially the old women, some of whom are doctors (*drabarni*), without pay, for their own people. Although old and learned men may have general knowledge of medicines, their first concern is with political and jural matters. It is the women who carry on the medical traditions, who have knowledge of the

supernatural, whose curse is powerful (*amria*), and who safeguard
the group against pollution and bad omens (*prikaza*).

The most important single study of pollution on the American
Rom is a short thesis by Carol Miller (1968) on Machwaya
concepts of *marime*. Since hers is the pioneering effort in this
field, her work drew my attention to the sociological importance
of pollution and body symbolism,[2] and finally since it is unpublished, I should like to begin my discussion of pollution with
a short resumé of her conclusions.

Miller states that pollution ideas (*marime*) are more structured
than other beliefs because they are formally established in ritual
whereas beliefs about the auspicious and inauspicious, good and
bad luck, ghosts and dreams are for the most part 'intermittent,
fatalistic, short-lived and idiosyncratic . . . what the Gypsies,
themselves, call superstitions' (1968: 3). 'Beliefs and taboos concerned with pollution are less dependent upon individual or
situational experience. Pollution beliefs are formally exemplified
in ritual custom. All Roma Gypsies share a common tradition of
washing practices, of commensality ritual, of taboos that incur
rejection sanction (*marime*) and attendant patterns of belief'
(1968: 3-4). Although it is true that beliefs other than those concerned with pollution are less tangible because they are less
formalized in ritual, they cannot be dismissed as 'superstitions'
even if the Rom do so themselves. What I shall demonstrate is
that beliefs about health/illness/death, good/bad luck, god/
spirits/ devil, inside/outside, are not only related to each other in
a consistent way, but also to the social structure and to the more
formalized pollution ideas.

Miller further points out that *marime* is used in two senses:
'*marime* as the condition of defilement of the lower body (which is
rejected in washing and avoidance custom); *marime* as the publicly defiled condition which "rejects" the defiled from group
association' (1968: 4-5).

The Machwaya perceive no special distinctions between the
two senses, however. *Marime* is, to them, both pollution and
rejection. To say a person is *marime* means that he is rejected as
an unclean area or object is rejected. This lack of specificity
increases the effective use of the term in political contexts.
Beliefs about defilement add the element of disgust to the onus
of social disapproval. (1968: 5)

Miller concludes that *marime* has three important sociological implications. First, as a form of social control, *marime* (as rejection) arms 'the legal system with its single coercive authority – social ostracism by withdrawal of commensal privilege' (1968: 7).

Second, *marime* is an expression of what she calls the 'sex-status-respect' system. Specifically, adult women are required to show respect towards men and are considered more defiling than men. On the other hand, the pollution dangers which a woman presents are a protection for her. If she is maltreated, she can threaten a man with *marime* and bring him to court for trial. Also, although a woman is potentially more defiling than a man, she can by careful observance of washing rules and morality in a sense 'achieve' a cleaner status than a man (1968: 7).

Third, *marime* is instrumental during changes of status in the life cycle. 'Age-status in the life cycle – infant, child, adult, elder – is marked and ritually accented by discrimination in states of defilement' (1968: 35). Childhood is associated with *wuzho* status. 'At marriage the lower body becomes *marime* and hereafter the couple are liable to rejection sanction in a trial' (36). In old age 'old men gain moral importance (as do older women). They are regarded as good and clean, in contrast with their moral attributes as young men' (41).

My own discussion of *marime* is intended to develop on Miller's definition of *marime* and on these three sociological implications of *marime*, and in a sense carry on where she left off.

Pollution and Social Control

In Chapter 4 we discussed *marime* as a form of social control and punishment for persons who transgress important social rules. 'Rejection' from the community is the ultimate punishment of Rom society and can be enforced through gossip, avoidance, or by declaration in a *kris*. Even when declared by consensus in a trial, a *marime* sentence is not permanent, but may have a certain time limit. The person may also be reinstated in another trial if it is decided he has paid for his 'crime' and has led a model life since becoming *marime*. *Marime* is the single most important coercive authority of the legal system.[3] This meaning of *marime* can be represented in relation to its opposite, the social order or *romania*.

romania (social order)   *marime* (rejection from the social order)
wuzho (purity)   *marime* (pollution: defilement)

Marime, in the sense of defilement, can be represented as the opposite of that which is pure and clean, or *wuzho*. *Wuzho* implies purity of a physical and moral nature just as *marime* indicates physical as well as moral defilement and social rejection. *Marime*, as defilement, is associated in general with the lower half of the body and particularly with the genital and anal areas. The upper half of the body is *wuzho*, but in order for it to remain so proper separation of the halves of the body must be ensured. Co-mingling of the two halves is *marime*.

However, *marime* is not restricted to the lower body as Miller has suggested but has wider physical and social implications. *Wuzho* and *marime* as opposites are related to a large range of concepts only one of which is top/bottom body symbolism. *Wuzho* is also associated with persons inside the boundaries of the social group (Rom) and *marime* with persons outside these boundaries. In certain contexts, a man is associated with *wuzho* status and a woman with *marime*. As well as these basic oppositions of *wuzho* and *marime*, above/below, inside/outside, and male/female, *wuzho/marime* concepts have important implications for age, status, and sexual relations.

Before discussing these implications of pollution concepts, I must mention a third concept relevant to pollution, '*melalo*'. *Melalo* means 'dirty' but it refers to dirt which is more temporary and is 'clean' dirt compared with *marime*. Ronald Lee (1971: 244) has defined *melalo* as 'dirty with honest dirt' such as hands that are dirty with grease from working on a car as opposed to hands that have touched the genitals and are *marime*. If, as I am suggesting, *wuzho* and *marime* are related to a large range of concepts including sexual, social, temporal, and spacial boundaries, then we might also expect to find associations with the concept *melalo*. As we explore this range of boundaries, we will see how they are related to the three pollution concepts.

Inside–outside

We have seen that Rom and *gaje* are moral opposites and constitute the most important social boundary in terms of behaviour. Relations with *gaje* are restricted to economic exploitation and political manipulation. Social relations in the sense of friendship, mutual aid, and equality are not appropriate with them. Besides being social outsiders, the *gaje* do not maintain proper upper and lower body separation; therefore, physically they are polluted. Marriage, as a socially approved union sanctioned by a certain ritual, is prohibited with *gaje*. Sexual relations with *gaje* are *marime*, though when a man takes in a *gaji* and instructs her on proper cleanliness, he and his *gaji romni* will be tolerated after a certain time, though never completely accepted by the community. For a woman there is much less flexibility in the rules.[4] As long as a woman has sexual relations with a *gajo* she is totally outcaste and *marime*.

Not only the person of non-Gypsies but items that come into contact with them are *marime*. Any time a Rom is forced to use *gaje* places or to be in contact with large numbers of *gaje* (for example, in a job, hospital, welfare office, school), he is in constant danger of pollution. Public toilets are particularly *marime* places, and some Machwaya go to the extent of using paper towels to turn faucets and open doors (Miller 1968: 14). Houses occupied by *gaje* or clothes worn by them are also polluted but not in a permanent sense. A house, for example, can be improved by fresh paint and bleaching powder. Walls can be covered with tapestries and drapes and the floor with thick carpets.

Food that is prepared by *gaje* is avoided, and the Rom will not usually eat in *gaje* homes or eat food prepared by *gaje* and brought to their homes. If they must buy cooked food while travelling, they prefer food wrapped in clean paper or plastic rather than food served on plates. In restaurants, the Rom avoid eating utensils and eat with their hands, and they ask for a plastic or paper cup for drinks. Amid outraged stares from other customers and waiters, they are constantly worried about 'catching' something from the *gaje* around them.

The pollution danger from the *gaje* is also associated with illness and disease. The *gaje* are the source of many diseases, but the most feared is venereal disease. A man or woman who has sexual relations with a *gajo* is not only *marime* (both in the sense of polluted and rejected) but must be examined for venereal disease before being permitted back into the group.

Similarly, things or persons that become polluted are removed from the Rom community by giving them to the *gaje*. Special clothes reserved for the deceased during the series of funeral feasts after a death (and worn by a chosen person) become very unlucky (*prikaza*) when they are claimed by the soul of the person (*mulo*), and they are discarded by hanging them in the woods, leaving them at the cleaners, or giving them to a non-Gypsy (usually as a bribe, since there is no point in wasting an expensive gift). Children born of incestuous unions (which are *marime* and *prikaza*) are given to *gaje* adoption agencies. Finally, a person who has been formally declared *marime* is forced to live among the *gaje* and is denied social contact with other Rom.

The attitude towards non-Rom Gypsies is more ambivalent than the attitude towards *gaje*. Marriage with non-Rom Gypsies is frowned upon and must occur by elopement (that is, it is not publicly and legitimately arranged), but it is not prohibited nor is it considered as shameful as sexual unions with *gaje*. Marriage with a non-Rom Gypsy is conceptually *melalo* but not necessarily *marime*. Again the rules are more harshly applied to women than men. Furthermore, the cleanliness status of non-Rom Gypsies is also neither *wuzho* nor *marime*. Whereas the *gaje* are a constant source of pollution danger to the Rom, it is known that non-Rom Gypsies do have a better understanding of cleanliness and shame and there is considerable ambiguity about how 'clean' they might be.

Internal social hierarchy as well as inside/outside boundaries is associated with degrees of cleanliness. The hierarchy of the three nations of Rom in Barvale – the Machwaya, Kalderash, and Kuneshti – is partly expressed in terms of their purity and pollution. The Machwaya, who are considered superior, were described by a Kalderash in the following way:

> The Machwaya think they are better. They are higher class, but we dress just as well as them and look our best. Even though we look nice, when we go to their *slava* we are afraid to walk out on the floor because we might get it dirty and because they look at us like they are afraid we might touch them. They think they are cleaner. They are strange people. They're not like us.

The Machwaya are also in general wealthier than Kalderash or Kuneshti, and this is given as proof of their superior luck and cleanliness. Even those Machwaya who are poor always have their sense of superiority in cleanliness to hold over the Kalderash.

The numerous *vitsi* of Kalderash vary considerably in status, but they never are able to overcome Machwaya superiority. The wealthy Kalderash *vitsi* can attain a very high status and consider themselves cleaner than other Kalderash riff-raff.[5] One man from a wealthy Kalderash *vitsa* complained of some Kalderash who were 'dirtier than we are' and at the same time complained of Machwaya haughtiness and indicated that he felt they questioned his cleanliness and respectability. When Machwaya intermarry with Kalderash *vitsi*, they most frequently marry the wealthier and 'cleaner' Kalderash, as Miller (1968: 1) reports: 'The Machwaya occasionally intermarry with the other Roma groups, usually with upper middle-class Kalderasha who are thought to be most compatible by standards of language and custom.' The relative statuses of the Machwaya and Kalderash are symbolized in myth where the Machwaya are associated with the sun (because it is more powerful) and the Kalderasha *vitsi* are the stars (because they are numerous).

The Kuneshti occupy a low status compared with Kalderash and Machwaya and their nation, the Churara, is associated with hate (symbolized by a knife). The Churara have a reputation for spoiling areas of economic exploitation for other Rom by over-taxing the patience of non-Gypsies and bringing down the wrath of *gaje* authorities such as the police. Yoors, who lived with the Rom as a boy, described their horror when a Churara violated *marime* rules about drawing water (upstream to downstream, water must be drawn in a certain order, water to wash pregnant or menstruating women being furthest downstream) and risked polluting the whole *kumpania* (1967: 150). The Kuneshti in Barvale always occupy an inferior status to other *vitsi* and are considered 'dirty' and 'lack of sense of shame' even if they keep clean houses and observe proper body separation and washing rules. They are smaller, darker, and are said to have twitchy noses. These racial characteristics are provided as further proof that they are untrustworthy.

Thus we have the following pollution associations with social boundaries and social hierarchy:[6]

wuzho	*melalo*	*marime*
Rom	non-Rom Gypsies	*gaje*
Machwaya	Kalderash	Kuneshti
High status	Middle status	Lower status

Age and Marime

A very important aspect of pollution is its relationship to the stages of the life-cycle. The social status that an individual achieves at each stage of development in his lifetime is accompanied by a change in moral and pollution status.

At birth, a mother and baby are *marime* for six weeks and are isolated from adult men. At six weeks the child becomes *wuzho* and is thereafter considered innocent of defilement, shame, or social responsibility.[7] The child has freedom from most social restraints, and contacts defiling to adults are not necessarily defiling to children (Miller 1968: 35). Pre-puberty children in Barvale, for example, were free to eat food handled by *gaje* which post-puberty boys and girls would not touch. A child may be given its own urine for medicinal purposes, but after puberty this would be extremely defiling. A child's clothes do not have to be separated by sex or upper-lower body divisions for washing. However, certain rules of *marime* do apply to children. Pre-puberty girls can be contaminated by menstrual blood and do not wear the same clothes as post-puberty girls or wash their clothes in the same tub. In some households they are not allowed to sleep with their sisters who have menstruated. Boys are also separated from the potential defilement of contact with post-puberty girls. Consequently, the status of a child is neither clearly undefilable nor always potentially pollutable and remains rather ambivalent. Children can become *melalo* but not *marime*, and yet they are protected from certain *marime* contacts.

Miller (1968: 36-9) claims that the lower body becomes *marime* at marriage and remains so throughout adult sexual life. She supports this by asserting that only men and women who have been married are liable to rejection sanction (*marime*) in a trial. In Barvale the ambivalent status of childhood changed at puberty rather than at marriage. Girls who have menstruated are introduced to shame and are *marime* below the waist. Contact with their skirts and lower body is defiling to men and post-puberty boys, and they must wear the clothes and demonstrate behaviour that shows the proper restraint for their status. When they reach twelve years of age, boys often begin to experiment with sexual relations with *gaji*. This is encouraged by groups of young men as being manly, but it is also extremely dangerous and potentially defiling. If their sexual exploits became known outside this male group, they and their families would be *marime*. Miller (1968: 33) mentions a case of a man threatened with *marime* by a large and powerful *vitsa* because of his relations with a *gaji*. He counters by threatening all the boys of that *vitsa* with exposure, since they themselves had entertained *gaji* in his presence, if they continue with their case against him.

Furthermore, *marime* as a rejection sanction in a *kris* is applicable to post-puberty boys and girls, usually for a sexual offence. In two trial cases of post-puberty girls in Barvale, though they were not allowed to attend their respective trials (because they were not married adults) and had to be represented by their families, both received *marime* sentences along with their families. Since boys and girls usually marry shortly after puberty there is very little time lag between puberty and marriage so that in practice the distinction is not always real. Clearly the advent of sexual potency and sexual relations are both important aspects of the new *marime* condition of the lower body, and this condition lasts until sexual potency declines at old age.

Old age, which comes at the birth of several grandchildren, brings increased status and respect. Old people are highly respected and are regarded as intrinsically moral and clean compared to sexually active men and women. They are the protectors of morality and respectability and embody in their person the ideals of *wuzho* status. Premature death, besides the personal loss, is considered particularly tragic because the person never attained the respect, power, and *wuzho* status to which he was entitled in old age. It is said that a person who dies before reaching old age is likely to become a malevolent spirit (*mulo*), and this may be connected with his failure to reach *wuzho* status. At the menopause, women not only attain *wuzho* status, but they overcome the inferiority of their sex, and drop many of the behavioural rules required of adult women. For example, they no longer observe fasting on Friday, can eat at a feast table with adult men, and join male conversations. They also become extremely powerful and politically active.

We can now see how pollution concepts are a basic frame of reference for ordering important social divisions: categories of persons (Rom/*gaje*/non-Rom Gypsies), the status of the three *natsiyi*, and the status of the age categories (child, adult, elder). That these social categories form sets of three is not irrelevant. Three is a sacred and auspicious number most frequently used on ritual occasions. What I want to demonstrate is that this same frame of reference, the three pollution concepts, appear again and again in relation to a variety of beliefs and practices, which at first glance seem disconnected. In a more general sense, I shall demonstrate that this set of related beliefs, called *romania* and translated as 'religion' by the Rom, is the key to their unusual ability to face drastic change and remain Rom.

Body Symbolism

In any study of pollution we must determine how the body is divided and controlled in order for it to be pure. For the Rom, the body is divided at the waist, *mashkar*, a term which also means the spacial middle. The upper half and lower half have opposing pollution status, *wuzho* and *marime*, and must be kept separate.[8] The hands (*was*) mediate between the two halves and may become *wuzho*, *melalo*, or *marime*, depending on what they have recently touched. Hands which have just touched the genitals are *marime* and must be washed with soap and water before touching anything clean. Ronald Lee described how he postponed shaking hands with an old man until he could wash them because he had just touched his penis (1971: 105). Hands that are washing lower body clothes are also *marime* and must be washed with soap before handling upper body clothes. The custom of eating with the hands eliminates the need to ascertain the cleanliness of eating utensils.

There is no shame (*lashav*) associated with the top half of the body, whereas the lower half is associated with great shame (*baro lashav*), so that a woman may expose her breasts to anyone, but the sight of her legs is shameful and disrespectful. Women use their brassieres as their pocketbook, and it is quite common for a man, whether he be husband, son, father, or unrelated, to reach into her brassiere to get cigarettes or money. When women greet each other after a certain absence, they squeeze each other's breasts. They will also squeeze the breasts to show appreciation of a witty story or joke.

For women there is general freedom of attire above the waist. Breasts may be shown and blouses left unbuttoned or pinned in one spot only with a gold brooch. But from the waist down, a respectable woman must be well covered, preferably with floor length skirts. It is shameful to have too much leg exposed, and women who wear shorter skirts cover them with a sweater when they sit. A woman's skirts are polluting to a man and men avoid touching them.[9] A woman's skirts must never touch eating implements, a man's clothes, or objects he uses. Even exposure to her genitals is polluting. She cannot step over his clothes or pass in front of him face to face, unless she has a baby (which is *wuzho*) in her arms between him and her body. If this does happen inadvertently, she warns him to turn around or excuses herself with great embarrassment. One woman who walked in front of a seated man immediately stopped, squatted down so her skirts touched the ground, and asked his forgiveness.

The head is the most important area to keep clean and is the seat of power, especially for a man. If a woman throws her skirts over a man's head, theoretically he is permanently *marime* unless the woman publicly denies that it ever happened. A big head is a sign of good health and good looks and great care is taken to keep the face and head clean, to the point of using one soap and towel only for the face. Hair must be kept clean and is controlled with various rules. Hair cannot be combed on Friday (which is the Devil's day), when in mourning, or when ill with the measles, and a small amount must be cut from a woman's hair each Friday, supposedly for luck. Otherwise women should not cut their hair. In the past the head was shaved to indicate a woman has committed adultery. The eyes (*yakh*) and nose (*nakh*) are also controlled with ritual. Long eyelashes or hair between the eyebrows indicates that the person possesses the evil eye (*yakhalo*), and this must be countered with spittle placed by the person giving the evil eye on the forehead of the baby. At death, the nose is plugged with the ritually pure beeswax or with pearls to ensure no impurity enters.

Emissions from the top half of the body are also clean. Tears and spittle are clean, and neither crying nor spitting is considered an embarrassing or shameful act. Spittle is also used as a curative on cuts or scratches. It is put on a woman's shoulder to ease birth pains and as an antidote for the evil eye. One woman spat upon her breasts to protect herself from the 'dirt' of her enemy as she described his shameful acts. Blowing is also a curative and cleansing act. Blowing on cuts helps them to heal, and one blows on one's hands to prevent illness of the Adam's apple (*gusha*) if touched by the hands. Vomit is also a curative and clean emission; the most powerful medicine is *johai* (ghost's vomit).

The genitals are the area of extreme *marime*. Any disease or malfunction of the genitals is sufficient to prove a person is *marime*. One woman described how her daughter-in-law had a cyst in her vagina, how even careful scrubbing did not get rid of it, and she felt quite justified in breaking up her son's marriage for this reason. But, in general, emissions from the lower body are also polluting. There is great embarrassment associated with urinating (*Xin*). One old lady called off a visit to a friend because she was indisposed and felt it would be too embarrassing to have to urinate frequently. Men often go outside to urinate rather than urinate in their own homes, especially if guests are present.

Blood (*rat*) is only polluting when it is associated with female functions, and then it is dangerous to men. But clean blood, from the veins, is not polluting, and red is a colour associated with happiness and good luck. The blood in *johai* (ghost's vomit) is curative (*johai* contains the blood of regurgitated *gaje*), and when given to a person it cures convulsions, fear, and haemorrhaging. Another cure called *stradniki,* or Nine Brother's blood, is an important medicine and protection from illness when put in amulets.

There are two exceptions to the general *marime* of the lower body. I have already mentioned that the division of the body into upper and lower halves does not apply to children. The second exception is that in private (but only in private) a husband and wife do not pollute each other in the normal ways they do in public. In private a woman may step over her husband's clothes, pass in front of him, or touch him with her skirts, but she would be very ashamed to do this in public, and if she lapsed in her conduct several times her husband would risk becoming *marime.* Sexual intercourse is a polluting act even in marriage[10] (though more so outside marriage) and during their sexual lifetime, from marriage to old age, adults must observe strict washing and be-havioural rules in a sense to counter their condition.

Washing

Personal washing is extremely important. The face and head must be kept especially clean and pure, and even the lower half of the body can be improved by careful washing. The essential thing is to wash the upper and lower body separately. Ronald Lee (1971: 29–30) remarked:

> You can't wash clothes, dishes and babies in the same pan and every Gypsy has his own eating utensils, towels and soap. Other dishes and utensils were set aside for guests and still others for pregnant women. Certain towels were for the face and others for the nether regions and there were different coloured soaps in the sink, each with an allotted function.

In the days of camping, it was the rule among the Lowara not to speak to a person until he had washed his face and hands as if he were not a social entity until this morning washing ritual was accomplished. In Barvale today it is still the first thing a person does upon rising.

At ritual times washing is either more rigorous or prohibited altogether. On Friday, the day of fasting, Julie remarked that she does a special cleaning of the houses, washes her face, combs her hair, and puts on her *diklo*. She abstains from smoking or drinking coffee, and she lights a candle at her shrine where she prays for good health for her family. Immediately after death, close relatives indicate their state of mourning for three days by not washing their hands, face or body, nor can they shave, comb their hair, or change clothing. The defiled condition of the body which they must observe is accompanied by much wailing, tearing of hair, and beating the breast at the side of the coffin. This conventional behaviour after death all involves upper body flagellation which is undoubtedly connected with the enforced defilement of the upper body. On the third day at the first *pomana* table, they wash and change clothes, and must present a more happy appearance.

Not only the body but everything that comes into contact with the body is subject to pollution rules. In personal washing, certain towels and soap must be reserved for the upper body and certain ones for the lower body. Items that are used for handling food cannot be washed with items that touch the body. They cannot even be washed in the same basin. Even the house is divided into *wuzho* and *marime* areas. The front of the house is reserved for *gaje*, the back of the house for the family. The floor is *marime*, and any *wuzho* item that falls to the floor must be thrown away, cleansed thoroughly, or used only for *marime* purposes.

Clothes as well as other objects of personal use that are new are *wuzho* by definition. Since they have never had contact with the body they cannot have been polluted by improper separation. Conversely, used items are never so pure as when they were new, even when washed properly. Items used by *gaje* are particularly suspect, and most Rom, even when very poor, will not wear clothing worn by *gaje* unless they know the person to be 'clean' and of high moral standards. Wool jerseys from charities or rummage sales, for example, are often unravelled, the wool carefully washed, and crocheted into rugs or blankets. New clothes are essential for ritual occasions when purity is most important. Only new clothes are used to dress the saint at a *slava* or are given to the godparents at a baptism, or prepared for the 'wearer of the clothes' at a *pomana*. Every guest at a ritual should also have new clothes to wear. At the Easter *slava* in Barvale, every woman and girl made a new dress for the occasion, and men and children bought new clothes, including shoes, socks, and underwear. Also at the marriage of a virgin, the guests are expected to wear new clothes. For ordinary and not ritual use, clothes that have been used can be kept clean by careful washing. The ideal is to keep separate certain categories of clothes. Mixing these categories is not only *marime* but will bring bad luck (*prikaza*) and illness; however, each household differs somewhat from the others in the strictness of separation in washing. Basically, there are four divisions in washing:

top	bottom
male	female
food	body
adult	child

In this instance, food refers only to items used for food; regulations for cooking and eating will be discussed shortly. Given these four divisions, the following six categories for washing must be kept separate:

1. food (*wuzho/melalo*)   tablecloths, dish towels, and dishes; one soap is used only for these items

2. male top (*wuzho/melalo*)   shirts, ties, undershirts, handkerchiefs, sweaters, jackets, and men's face towels

3. male bottom (*marime*)   underwear, trousers, socks, men's body towels

4. female top (*wuzho/melalo*)   blouses, brassieres, scarves, apron, and face towels

5. female bottom (*marime*)   skirts, underpants, stockings, and women's body towels

6. children (*wuzho/melalo*)   all items

The *wuzho/melalo* or *wuzho/marime* qualification refers to the kind of dirt the clothes or items are allowed. For instance, if items in group one are used and washed properly, they may become *melalo* from use but not *marime*. If a dish towel or dish cloth falls to the floor, then it becomes *marime* and should not be used again as a dish cloth. Individual practice varies, of course, and it is possible that some families might not be so strict and would simply wash it carefully before re-use.

The apron (*katrinsa*) is the only exception to the top–bottom division. An apron is not *marime* because it is an outer garment and is always protected from the polluting areas of a woman by layers of skirt underneath. Also it is used to handle dishes hot from the oven and is associated with food; therefore, in some households it is washed with group one and in others with group four. This was the only example of an inner–outer division as well as top–bottom. Miller (1968: 13) reports a general feeling among the Machwaya that the closer the garments are to the body, the more defiled they become; conversely outer garments are 'cleaner'.[11]

Children's clothes do not have to be separated according to top–bottom or male–female categories, but they are always separated from food-associated objects and are usually separated from adult clothes. They do not necessarily have to be washed by themselves but may be washed for instance with bedspreads or towels. In some households, the adult–child division was strictly observed in wearing clothes so that a pre-puberty girl could not wear the same clothes as a post-puberty girl. However, there was often a certain laxness in the washing of children's clothes consistent with their ambivalent status.

Ideally, each of the six groups of clothes should be washed in its own basin or tub; however, few households lived up to this ideal. Most women avoided laundromats and had at least several tubs at home. 'We can't wash clothes in the laundromat but have to do it at home. We have to have special tubs for everything and separate the clothes.' A special basin for food items was present in every household; another bucket and cloth was used only for the floors and other *marime* surfaces. Besides these two basins at least one was used for *wuzho/melalo* items and one for *wuzho/marime* items, but several households also had male and female basins. Sandra commented: 'I can't wash everything together like some other Gypsy women. I have to do it all separate. I can't wash Nancy's clothes with the big girls, and I can't wash towels with the table cloth.' However, she had only one washing machine whereas her neighbour Rosie insisted on separate basins. Bibi went to the laundromat on the Friday before Easter (when everything in the house must be washed) and took only four separate bundles. These consisted of the groups two through five, food items (group one) being washed in a separate basin at home. Since each person has his own towel and face cloth, these may be washed in the appropriate category for each person's clothes.

Besides the washing of the body and items of personal use, a clean house is also an indication of moral and ritual purity. The Machwaya, who generally keep a neat and clean house, frequently point out this difference with Kalderash standards of house-keeping to prove their moral and ritual superiority. A clean house is thought to be conducive to good health. *Mamioro*, the spirit who brings illness, tends to visit houses that are dirty. But it is also felt that disease can be contracted from the *gaje* by living in their houses, and so these have to be scrubbed as much as possible, especially when recently occupied by *gaje*. A house that has had a succession of Rom families is 'cleaner' no matter what the house-keeping standards of those families.

To anyone who has visited a Gypsy home, this emphasis on cleanliness may seem perplexing. In some homes children discarded food on the floor when they had finished eating, along with cigarette ashes and butts, and all other rubbish. This is then all swept out of the back door once a day. Quite often old junk and rubbish is simply piled up in the back garden until the police threaten to have the place condemned if it is not removed. These houses, which were not unusual, are *melalo*. They are messy, untidy, and dirty, but they are not *marime* because the proper rules of body separation in washing and of cleanliness in preparing food are maintained. There is some stigma attached to a *melalo* house, but it is largely a matter of personal choice and generally not the concern of the community. However, it does not promote good health to have a *melalo* house, and there is a limit to how *melalo* a house can be before the *kumpania* begins to object and gossip mounts.

A house that is *marime*, that is one previously occupied by *gaje* or a family that has recently been 'rejected', presents an immediate danger and must be fumigated, the floors scrubbed with cleansers and astringents, and the walls painted with fresh paint. A person who kept a *melalo* house may or may not be condemned for this by individuals in the *kumpania* depending largely on their own house-keeping standards, but the attitude towards a *marime* house or area is always a matter of public concern, and the reaction is unanimous fear of pollution. Furniture that has been used by *gaje* is also suspect and must be cleaned thoroughly. Tables are not likely to be *marime*, but chairs and divans where *gaje* have sat are. The Rom prefer to get used chairs made of wood or plastic so they can be scrubbed. Some homes have one *marime* chair allotted for *gaje* visitors just as they may have *marime* dishes for *gaje* only (see also Lee 1971: 35–6).

The floor is a *marime* area of the house because it touches feet and shoes and is exposed to genitals but not because dust and food scraps collect there. Sitting on the floor or ground is quite common since only the lower body touches it, but sleeping takes place only on top of blankets or thick quilts (*perina*). Thick carpets, regularly cleaned, are felt to improve the cleanliness of the floor and may even be used outside on the ground. As I have mentioned, the toilet is permanently *marime* because of its function and may even be avoided in the home. Thus we can see that top–bottom categories are not only body divisions but extend to clothes, the home, and all items of personal use.

Food

Food must be especially pure (*wuzho*) and kept separate from contact with *marime* parts of the body, surfaces, or items. Food must be clean and pure because it enters the mouth and is associated with the pure half of the body. Before cooking, the hands must be washed carefully, and all items and utensils which come into contact with food must be kept *wuzho* by separate washing from items that touch the body. They are not only washed separately but in a separate basin kept exclusively for that use with a soap which is also kept for food only. Even then food cannot be cooked by pregnant women, women who have just given birth, and sometimes menstruating women. To ensure no female impurities come into contact with food at feasts and rituals, men generally handle the food. Food cooked by *gaje* is also *marime*. Rom usually will not eat in the house of a *gajo*, nor do they like to eat food prepared by a *gaje* in a restaurant or brought into their homes. Everyday food must be clean and guarded from *marime* contact, but food for rituals must be even purer and is carefully selected to obtain the purest condition. Fruit and vegetables are bought in unpacked crates so that they have not been handled by a retailer. Drinks are also bought in cases or beer in kegs, and meat is bought on the hoof and is butchered and prepared by certain elderly men. Again this ensures that the food has not been handled by *gaje* and has been prepared under clean conditions by clean persons.

Food at rituals must not only be different in quality or purity but in kind. Special dishes are prepared for these occasions. There are several dishes prepared only for rituals, but *sarmi*, a spiced rice and meat rolled in cabbage leaves is the most important ritual dish, and women must wash carefully before preparing it. Menstruating, pregnant, or women in mourning cannot prepare it. The ritual preparation of Easter eggs is also circumscribed by the same prohibitions.

At a feast table each person who sits down to eat (eating at a feast table is done in successive waves with the highest status persons – old men, adult men, and a few old women – eating first and then moving down to women and children) is given new plates of food, and dishes with food that has been touched are discarded, although this may constitute a considerable amount of waste.

New cups, plates, napkins, and tablecloth on a feast table are essential and therefore are generally made of paper or plastic and are discarded after use. The development of disposable table implements has greatly simplified the maintenance of *wuzho* conditions for the Rom. Disposable table implements and paraphernalia are always used on feast tables when large numbers of Rom will be present. Many of the guests may be from outside the *kumpania*, and many will not be relatives. For these people it is especially essential to provide obviously pure conditions lest they doubt the purity of the table, and embarrass the host by not showing up or refusing to eat at the table. At a table where only family are present, these precautions are not necessary since family members can be sure of their *wuzho* condition.

Not only the feast table, but other items associated with ritual must be clean. Money given in collections at a wedding, and especially money which is put into the hands of the deceased in the coffin, must be brand new. In Barvale, statues of the saints must be carefully washed and dressed in new clothes for each ritual. *Slava* candles are always new and as large as possible and must be of pure beeswax, this being considered purer than ordinary wax. Miller describes the Machwaya rules for washing these items.

According to ritual treatment, the icons, which include pictures and statues of Saints, and the *Slava* candle, are of even purer status than items concerned with the face. Only new or fresh face towels or paper towels are permitted to touch them during washing in conjunction with a soap that squirts or shakes from its container (i.e. never touches the hands). The hands must be exceptionally clean to perform this office. Some Machwaya do· not allow menstruating women to touch the icons or to light the candle. (1968: 13)

There is much more to food than the concern for its purity. Food and eating are an expression of the unity of the Rom, and this is denied to *marime* persons and to *gaje* in general. To eat with another person is a sign of friendship, equality, and respect. To refuse food in someone's home is a serious insult, for 'it means you think you are better then they are, that you don't think they are clean. If someone never offers you food or coffee it means they are no good. They don't respect you.' Of course, everyone must refuse to eat with a person who has been 'rejected' or risk becoming *marime* himself.

Eating together is a sign of mutual respect and faith in the cleanliness of the other person. Feasting is the ritual expression of commensality, and all Rom rituals – marriages, birthdays, baptisms, *pakiv*, *slava*, and *pomana* rituals – are accompanied by a *sinia* (feast table). Indeed the elaborateness and plentifulness of the feast table are major factors in the effectiveness of the ritual, whatever the purpose of the ritual may be. At the Easter *slava*, for example, the ritual is centred around commensality, and each family goes 'from tent to tent' (*tsera, tsera*) exchanges Easter eggs with a member of the household for *baXt* and eats something at each household that has prepared a table for their guests. This is an important *slava* for the *kumpania* since friendship and respect is reaffirmed between members of each household regardless of their *vitsa* or kin relationship to the others. Those persons who were conspicuously absent from certain households expressed their lack of acceptance of these families in the *kumpania*. For this reason, plus the quantity of alcohol that is consumed, Easter is an occasion of many fights.

Postiu, Mourning, and BaXt foods

Certain foods are called *baXt* foods (luck). These are black pepper (*kalo pipere*), red pepper (*lolo pipere*), salt (*lon*), vinegar (*chote*), and anything pickled in vinegar. Garlic is also considered a *baXt* food by some people. *BaXt* foods bring good luck to people who eat them, are used for curing various illnesses,[12] and are put in amulets to protect children from illness. Garlic and black pepper, along with other medicines, are often hung around a child's neck to guard against illness. One family even kept a piece of bacon impregnated with black pepper hanging outside all the time for good luck. It is said that the *mule* like *baXt* foods and other sour foods and will come for them at night. When a relative dies, some families put vinegar, lemons, and sour cream outside as it would be *prikaza* (bad omen) to have the *mule* come inside for them. *BaXt* foods are prohibited to mourners as well as the cooking of ritual foods.

Many families also observe *postiu*, which is abstention on Friday from all animal products (meat, eggs, lard, butter) except fish. *Postiu* is normally observed only by persons who can have sexual intercourse and is regarded as a cleansing act. It is not normally observed by pre-puberty children, by elders, nor by women in birth confinement. Women in birth confinement abstain from green vegetables and *baXt* foods, otherwise the baby will become sick. They are allowed *postiu* foods and are not allowed to observe *postiu* on Fridays. The observance of *postiu* is also said to promote good health, and many families would pledge a certain period of *postiu* for the specific purpose of improving the health of one person in the family. From the evidence, therefore, it appears that the good luck of *baXt* foods and the prohibition of *postiu* foods are reversed in the transition stages of certain rites of passage.

	normal	*transition*
BaXt foods	+	—
		(after birth and death)
Postiu foods	—	+
		(after birth)

BaXt foods and ritual foods which are normally good luck and purifying to eat are prohibited to eat or cook during mourning. *Postiu* foods which are prohibited on Fridays to bring good health must be eaten by the mother after birth to protect the child's health. *BaXt* foods and green foods (green is a *baXt* colour) also will make the baby ill if eaten by the mother but once the mother is past confinement, the baby is protected by amulets made with *baXt* foods.

We can now see that pollution rules are not only a framework for ordering social categories but have a deeper and more basic meaning. The body and the physical environment of the body are regulated by concepts of pollution. The body is divided into *wuzho* and *marime* areas, parts of which can become *melalo*, and items which come into contact with the body – food, clothes, houses, furniture, eating utensils, linens – are extensions of this division. But the implications of these pollution rules are also effected by other very basic factors – sex (male/female/child), age (elder/adult/child), and the inside–outside division of society. Pollution concepts are instrumental in almost every aspect of everyday behaviour as well as in the expression of status and social boundaries. There are further implications to pollution concepts which are relevant to a study of the belief system of the Rom. These include ideas about health and illness, the auspicious, and inauspicious, and the supernatural beings who play a role in determining these ideas.

Health and Illness

The most frequent toast, prayer, blessing, or greeting among the Rom is: *Devla BaXt hai sastimos* (God's luck and health) or some variant of that phrase. Good luck and good health are so commonly phrased together as to appear almost synonymous. Both are associated with God and may be considered to derive from God. Illness is feared by everyone and is a constant self-preoccupation. But illness is not only the concern of the individual; it is a social problem that assumes the same quality of importance for the wider group as problems of pollution. Most rituals are concerned with health in some way. Baptisms and *slave* are given for the stated purpose of ensuring good health and preventing illness. Marriage is often considered a cure for mental illnesses, and when a relative dies, weddings cannot take place and the series of *pomana sinia* begin their year long process. When any person becomes ill, relatives flock to his bedside and shower him with personal attention.

The *slava* is the ritual most concerned with health. Each *vitsa* has a special *slava* which it celebrates to promote the health of its members. The Machwaya give a *slava* on St George's Day (*Georgidan* – 6 May)[13] and the Kashtare and a few other Kalderasha *vitsi* celebrate St Anne's day (*Swetoyana* – 28 August). The Kashtare *slava* on 28 August was an especially elaborate occasion in Barvale in 1970 because 'so many of the family have been sick this year. We wanted to do it big.'

Much illness, particularly 'mental' illness,[14] physical deformities, mental retardation, epilepsy, genital infections, and repulsive skin diseases (e.g. psoriasis) are felt to be due to inauspiciousness (*prikaza*) or an infringement of pollution or sexual rules, both of which are *marime* and *prikaza*.

The mentally ill are usually deviants from *romania*. One young man was considered deranged because he 'talked back to his mother' and 'fooled around with *gaji*'. Another sixteen-year-old girl was judged to be mentally retarded because she took a $10 gold piece and bought $10 worth of goods. The coin was worth $40, and no one with 'normal' intelligence could have made that mistake. For these sorts of problems, marriage is thought to be the only sure cure, and parents often say that if they can only find a good spouse for the inflicted person, they will improve. One girl, who showed signs of mental disturbance, was committed to an institution because she would bring *prikaza* to her parents, but eventually when their 'luck' improved they brought her home and had her married. In the case of one mentally deficient man, he did improve considerably with marriage since he had someone to take care of him and was no longer a burden to his family. A woman cannot afford to be so lacking in intelligence since she would then be unable to earn a living. When a young epileptic's condition did not seem to improve after marriage, his parents were very surprised and stated that they could not understand why it had not helped. Marriage is considered a cure for any unusual behaviour, including homosexuality (Lee 1971: 30; 201–2). No 'normal' person remains unmarried. I knew three unmarried adults, and the rest of the community was very wary of them lest they bring bad luck to them. One girl of thirty was not only unmarried but contracted psoriasis as well and it was decided that she must have done something *marime* to be doubly afflicted.

Illness, therefore, is not only sometimes caused by social factors (e.g. *marime*) but may often be cured by proper social behaviour (e.g. marriage). Stories were often told of a person who suffered pain or illness for a long time, but through the 'help of his people' returned to a normal and healthy life. The story of Mike Marks illustrates this relationship between illness and social behaviour.

Mike Marks, a young Gypsy man at the age of twenty-two, suffered from a back injury and was in constant pain. The pain was so terrible that he hated the world. Mike's family, his wife, and three children, were very depressed and did not have a good life. They had to take constant care of him. Mike's only means of making a living for his family was by travelling with a carnival. This work got unbearable for him, and he got to the point where he wanted to leave his family. Some of the Gypsy families put some money together, so he could go to the doctor, but the doctors could not find anything wrong with him.

One cold rainy night when Mike and the rest of the people in the carnival were travelling to another town to set up for a new show, they passed by a cemetery. Mike's car had a flat tyre and he became very angry and started cursing the dead people who lay in their graves. His wife was trying to calm him down so his back wouldn't hurt. Suddenly he stopped and stared at the graveyard, for he was the only person who saw a man with a peg-leg coming towards him and five others. The peg-leg man asked him why did he use their names in vain. Mike was so shocked that he could not speak, but the look on his face told his wife that something was wrong. Then blood started coming out of his mouth, and his eyes were swollen up, and he was being thrown from one place to another. His wife was in shock. She thought he went crazy, and she and the others could not help him. When they stopped beating on him the man with the peg-leg told him that he and the other Gypsy people better get out of town when day breaks. But there was one important thing the Gypsy people had to do before they could get away alive.

They had to hold Mike in a circle for fifteen minutes, and if the ghost and peg-leg man got to him, he would die. But by some miracle the circle held its form, and they did not get to Mike. After that they were free to go. Everyone hurried to their cars and left as fast as they could.

But from that day on Mike has been cured, and is well and living. Today he is a very religious man, and every time he passes a cemetery he says, 'Can you forgive me?'.

This story, told by a relative, relates that Mike Marks is suffering from bad luck, bad health, and poverty. His fellow Rom try to cure his condition with a collection and *gaje* doctors, but this does not help. Then the 'true' source of his illness and bad luck emerges, his attitude towards the dead. Again his people must be the ones to save him from retribution from the dead, and their own lives are dependent on their actions as well. Only by joining together are they 'free to go' and is Mike cured. But Mike is cured not only of his backache but of his irreverent attitude towards the deceased.

Besides these mental and social problems, there are other diseases which can be divided into two kinds: Gypsy disease (*naswalemos romanes*) and non-Gypsy disease (*naswalemos gaji-kanes*). According to several doctors (*drabarni*), the *gaje* have different diseases from the Rom. *Gaje* diseases are caused by germs, and now that the Rom are living in *gaje* houses, they too are becoming susceptible to *gaje* diseases and must get treatment from *gaje* doctors. Almost everyone felt that they were sicker now than they used to be, and they attributed this to less travelling and to living in houses. When they lived in their own camps away from the *gaje*, they did not get sick so often nor did they need *gaje* doctors.[15] Many people would take a trip the minute they felt ill because it made them feel better. Travel is not only associated with health and houses with illness, but travel is also a way of 'out running' inauspiciousness (*prikaza*) which may be causing the illness. Illness is just one sign, though the most important one, of *prikaza*, and *prikaza* is only one cause of illness.

Germs, *gaje* (who transmit germs), and houses (which harbour germs) are the source of *gaje* diseases. The most horrible *gaje* diseases are syphilis and gonorrhoea, though 'flu, fevers, hernias, and haemorrhoids are also often attributed to the *gaje*. These diseases, especially venereal diseases, are contracted from the *gaje* and cured by them, and they are associated with *prikaza* and filth (*marime*). Miller found the same belief among the Machwaya although apparently she did not realize that this was only one source of disease.

> Gypsies used to believe and, in some degree, continue to believe, that all disease, including cancer, is caused by touching and eating *gadze* things. The Gypsy feels uneasy travelling by public transportation, for an example, and sitting in a seat 'all kinds of people have used', people with colds, fevers, skin disease or something more serious. Crowded situations among *gadze* are

claustrophobically *marime*, and public institutions, churches and schools are avoided for the most part. (Miller 1968: 16)[16]

To combat *gaje* disease, the Rom have turned to *gaje* doctors and hospitals. They have an uneasy feeling about *gaje* doctors since they are germ harbourers, but hospitals are even more feared as places of disease, germs, and death and are considered *marime*. While they are anxious to try any cure that might work, even surgery, which is greatly feared, many Rom suffer acute pain because they refuse to go to a hospital, and several in Barvale have died because they left the hospital prematurely.

1. Julie was told that she needed a heart operation and she and her relatives were in a panic for several days because they were convinced she would die in the hospital. Finally she refused to go and was taken on a 'little trip' for two months so she would feel better.
2. George died in a diabetic coma when his wife removed him from the hospital and fed him tea with strawberries instead of his insulin.

Hospitals, like all *gaje* institutions, are dreaded, but the Rom will make use of them when absolutely necessary. They are in general extremely knowledgeable of hospital procedure and know every service available and who the 'best' doctors are. They learn of famous clinics, know the ins and outs of hospital regulations, how to avoid them, and get what they want.[17] If they find that a doctor can cure effectively and that his 'medicine' works, they will flock to him. If a patient dies under his care, they never go to him again. Doctors have a special knowledge of medicine and curing techniques for *gaje*, much like the *drabarni* has knowledge of Gypsy cures. In serious cases, both may be used.

1. Yana told a story of the time that her son had a 'fit' and was rushed to the hospital. She went to the car where his 'fit' started and under the seat found two small *khandino drab* left by the devil who had caused the convulsion. She rushed these to him in the hospital, and to the nurse's astonishment, when he took it, he was cured.
2. 'Three Gypsies have died in our county hospital, and they now regard it as some kind of a slaughterhouse. Gypsies are very reluctant to get care at our Health centre, mainly because it's free. "Medical care couldn't be any good if they can't even

K

charge for it." Likewise prescriptions dispensed by the county pharmacy will be second-rate, or possibly even poisonous, while those prescribed by private doctors are nothing short of magic. In addition Gypsies are greatly influenced by the shape and colour of medications. Big, dark-coloured capsules are strong, while small white pills are ineffective. One heart patient told me that she was not going to take her orange medicine, because she could not believe that anything that was orange could possibly be good for her. Gypsies will often impoverish themselves taking up collections for private medical care. However, they often will pay only a deposit and then do their disappearing act.' (Tompkins 1965b: 7–8)

Gypsy diseases (*naswelemos romanes*) do not stem from germs or *gaje* (though they are susceptible to these diseases) but derive from several other sources. All serious diseases, such as polio and black plague, are caused by *Mamioro*. *Mamioro*, which means 'little grandmother', is a spirit (*muli*) though once she was a person.[18] When she appears she brings illness which can spread even to *gaje*. So just as the Rom are susceptible to *gaje* diseases, the *gaje* are also not immune from disease brought by *Mamioro*.

Mamioro appears only in filthy places and can be warded off by cleanliness (*wuzho*). If a person has a dirty house (*melalo*), and if there are dirty (*melalo*) dishes there, she comes to eat off them. If a place is clean, and the clothes and persons inside are clean, she will not appear to them. She often appears at rubbish tips and the sight of the filth makes her vomit. But as one old *drabarni* put it, 'what makes her sick makes you well', for this vomit, *johai*, which consists of regurgitated *gaje*, is curative.

Johai, translated as 'ghost's vomit' by the Rom, is their most powerful and valuable medicine.[19] As one person said, 'finding *Johai* is like finding treasure. Gypsies will pay a hundred dollars for it.' *Johai* cures fear from ghosts, haemorrhages, convulsions, and fits (such as epilepsy). It is a slimy yellow substance with red streaks (which are the blood of *gaje*), can be scooped from the ground and baked with flour to produce a hard white rock from which tiny pieces are chipped off for use. Any *drabarni* will have a piece of *johai* in her medicine bag (*bujo*) and is always on the lookout for a new discovery. The discovery of *johai* in a dump in Barvale caused great excitement, and when word of the discovery spread, women from all over California came to get a small piece.

Shrecha, Barvale's most powerful *drabarni*, always carried a piece of *johai* in her *bujo* which she keeps in the glove compartment of her car. She often sews *johai*, together with garlic and black pepper and/or *drarnego* (a special herb) in a bag made from a piece of her ancestresses' aprons (*katrinsa*, which is *wuzho*). This bag of *drab* (medicine) is sewn into an unbaptized child's clothes to protect him from illness. Shrecha is an effective healer not only because of her knowledge of *drab*, but because she has received special exemption from disease (and hence the power of her ancestresses' aprons).

> My great-grandmother was in a camp, and *Mamioro* came to her, but she was not afraid. She carried her around on her shoulders and bathed her until she was clean. She took care of *Mamioro*. And that is why my people don't get big illnesses – my whole *vitsa* – because my great-grandmother did this, and *Mamioro* said, 'your family will not have sickness'.

According to several *drabarni*, not all 'Gypsy' disease is caused by *Mamioro*. Certain diseases, such as *toska* (a disease evidenced by excessive worry or nerves) and convulsions (including epilepsy) are usually caused by the devil (*o Beng*). In these cases, a hard black lump called *khantino drab*[20] (literally 'smelly medicine' but translated as 'Devil's shit') will be found nearby. *Khantino drab*, of course, is very effective because when given to the 'possessed' person, it makes the devil *marime*, and he will go away. This stops the convulsions. If no *Khantino drab* can be found, some of an inflicted child's urine can be substituted. The threat of *marime* to the devil (*o Beng*) is effective partially because he is male. *Mamioro*, who puts out 'clean' vomit as medicine, cannot be chased away with this threat.

To summarize, *naswalemos* (disease) can be divided into several categories according to their causes, though there is overlap in actual diseases: (1) *naswalemos gajikanes* caused by *gaji*, germs, and *marime* associated with *gaje* (such as *gaje* houses) and cured by travel, *gaje* doctors, and general avoidance of the *gaje*; (2) *naswalemos romanes* caused by (a) *marime* condition due to some *marime* sexual act, demonstrated as unorthodox or unusual behaviour, physical deformity, etc., and cured by proper social behaviour such as marriage, (b) *Mamioro* who brings all 'serious diseases' and cured by *johai*, her vomit (consisting of regurgitated *gaje*) which is clean, and finally (c) *o Beng* who causes *toska* and

convulsions (both highly common ailments among the Rom) and
cured by *khantino drab*, his own excrement.

Health and illness are social conditions that are effected by
pollution rules, social behaviour, relations with *gaje*, and supernatural beings. In short, proper observance of *romania* and respect
for spirits (*mule*) and other beings (*o Del, o Beng*) will result in
luck and health (*baXt hai sastimos*). Infringement of *romania* is
not only *marime*, it is certain to result in inauspiciousness (*prikaza*)
and illness. Death is unavoidable and natural when it comes at old
age after a full life, but premature death is an inauspicious omen
and can be avoided by cleanliness, luck (*baXt*), observance of
romania, and being generous to one's people.

BaXt and Prikaza

Both *baXt* and *prikaza* are important concepts for understanding
the beliefs of the Rom, and both are associated with supernatural
beings. *BaXt* and health, which are practically synonymous, are
associated with *o Del* (God). One who has good health possesses
baXt, and one who is ill is suffering from *prikaza*. Certain objects,
spirits, foods, actions, and colours bring either *baXt* or *prikaza*.
As we have already seen, there are specific foods that bring *baXt*,
and other foods that must be avoided at certain times or they bring
illness. In general, living according to *romania* brings *baXt*, and
actions that deny *romania* are *prikaza*. *Marime/prikaza/naswa-
lemos* are as closely linked as *wuzho/baXt/sastimos*.

Generosity brings *baXt*, and to give generously at a collection,
to provide an elaborate *slava*, or to help one's fellow Rom when
they are in need will bring a person *baXt*. Wealth is also a sign of
baXt since making money is influenced by luck, and an unlucky
person will not be able to make a living no matter how hard he
tries. In the *lovoro* ceremony, when the day's take is divided, the
first action is to thank *o Del* for *baXt*. A fat, wealthy man possesses
baXt, and a thin, sick, and poor person has suffered from *prikaza*.
Miller confirms this belief among the Machwaya: 'Commercial
success, skill at swindling, large and healthy families are signs of
good luck; *o Del*, the god, is good if one's enemies suffer but,
otherwise, one's luck is at fault' (1968: 3). A fat, wealthy, and
generous leader is not only highly respected, but people flock
around him if only to acquire some of his *baXt*.

Cleanliness and the proper observance of *marime* rules also brings *baXt*. The head is the cleanest area of the body, and to eat the head of an animal brings *baXt*, health, and power. When someone wants to indicate that a person will suffer the consequence of their *marime* or immoral actions, they say '*Ka te shoro*' (over to her head) or '*ka te baXt*' (over to her luck). The head, *wuzho*, and *baXt* are closely associated.

Certain numbers bring *baXt*. Seven is a lucky number, but three is the number most associated with *baXt* and with purity. The most important ritual acts in rites of passage are done in threes to assure purity and protection from dangers. A brief description of the use of three and multiples of three in rites of passage illustrates the ritual value of this number.

1. *birth*

   During labour, a mother's pains are eased by touching her alternately for three times on the shoulder with saliva or a handkerchief (*diklo*) wet with saliva. Three days after birth, the baby is dressed in special clothes, called his 'three day clothes', which are made by three separate women of three different relationships to the child (e.g. mother, sister, and grandmother). This set of clothes brings good luck (*baXt*) to the child and is kept during his lifetime. On the third day of a child's life it is said that the *Trito Ursitori* (the three spirits, one good, one bad, and the other mediates for the two) appear to the child and decide how long he will live. In order for the *Trito Ursitori* to appear, three women must be with the baby: the mother, grandmother, and godmother, and the mother, baby, and house must be especially clean. The *Trito Ursitori* do not appear at each birth, but many mothers prepare for them in case they do. This myth was recorded by Maximoff in his novel *The Ursitory* (1945) and was known by every man, woman, and child in Barvale. A child also wears an amulet until baptism which includes three items. Confinement of mother and child lasts six weeks or nine days.

2. *marriage*

   A wedding traditionally lasts three days and three nights, and only on the third night should the couple consummate the marriage.

3. *death, mourning, and pomana sinia (death feast)*

   Immediately after death, close relatives must observe strict mourning for three days. This consists of keeping themselves in a polluted state. They cannot shave, wash, bathe, change clothes, comb their hair, or wear jewellery for three days.

Three days after death, the body is buried and a *pomana sinia* (death feast) is held. Thereafter a *pomana* is held at times in multiples of three for up to a year: three days, nine days, six weeks, and six or twelve months. On the third day after death, the spirit of the deceased may appear in the form of a black bird. At six weeks, the soul is released (called 'to clear the dead'). At the *pomana* each ritual act of purification is done in threes. Pieces of meat or pots of food must be cooked in threes, or if there are too many people, in odd numbers (three, five, seven, etc.). The table is blessed and purified with incense by carrying it around the table three times, and the ritual clothes to be worn by a chosen person are also blessed three times with incense. When people sit down at the table only one or two persons pass the drinks for the whole group, and they must start from one spot and go around the table three times only.

Colours also are associated with *baXt* or *prikaza*. Red is the colour of happiness and good health. It is worn as a protection against illness. It is put on unbaptized babies and is traditional for the bride. Green is also a lucky colour and associated with good health. Certain green plants, *nevala* and a resurrection plant, are kept in the house for luck, and green foods are eaten by a mother to protect her new born child.

Prikaza is attributed to the devil and to malevolent spirits such as *Mamioro* and *Martiya*[21] (the night) and associated with illness, *gaje*, *marime*, and untimely death. Black is a *prikaza* colour, and women never wear black clothes except in mourning. The place of death and funeral parlours are also *prikaza*. The night is very *prikaza*, not only because that is when the devil emerges from the water (no one goes near water after sunset), and when spirits of the dead are wandering around (a *pomana* is held at night so the spirit of the deceased can attend), but the personification Night (*Martiya*) brings death and illness, especially to new born babies. When a baby is born, windows and curtains are shut at night, and no member of the household should go out then lest they bring *Martiya* in with them.

Besides *Devla baXt* and *prikaza* there is a third kind of luck called *gajengi baXt*, or luck from the *gaje*. *Gajengi baXt* accounts for small misfortunes rather than serious ones. To be locked out of the house, have a flat tyre, or lose something is *gajengi baXt*. *Gajengi baXt* is of the same intensity of bad luck as *melalo* is of filth.

Whereas God is associated with goodness, good health, and *baXt*, the Devil is a source of evil, illness, and *prikaza*. On the other hand, the *mule*, the spirits of the dead, are much less clearly defined and may be beneficial or harmful depending on how many grudges they carried with them to the grave and how attentive their relatives were to their last days and to their *pomana sinia*. *Mule* can speak to relatives and friends in visions or dreams and may appear either to plague or protect them. The Rom have hundreds of stories about the appearance of *mule*, and no Rom goes to his grave without having seen one. There is general fear and apprehension with all *mule* since their intention cannot be known and the general reaction, as with many troubles, is to try and outrun them. However, they may appear to aid a relative. Rachael's brother appeared in his coffin once when she was embroiled in a fight with her *Xanamik* and convinced them that she should not be opposed.

The *mule* visit places where they have been during their lifetime and especially the places where they died or are buried. The place of death is considered *prikaza* for a certain period after death and is avoided by relatives who keep travelling until the six week *pomana* when they are less likely to be plagued by the *mule*. A place is laid on the feast table for the *mulo* at his own *pomana* though it is not expected that he will appear there. A spirit may eat food scraps, use the toilet, haunt houses where he lived or died, and will almost certainly use the food and money which is buried in the coffin with him. At the end of a year of wandering he comes to collect the clothes chosen for him and worn by a special person at the *pomana*. *Mule* are very vague wispy spirits who wander around for some time up to a year and are most likely to be dangerous the first six weeks after their death. But finally they go to 'heaven' or simply disappear. Although it did not appear that *mule* actually cause death, they can bring bad luck and jinx their enemies.

Conclusions

Though this discussion of concepts related to pollution ideas does not exhaust the range of beliefs that the Rom profess, it does indicate that pollution ideas are central to a larger system of classification that explains social behaviour and the natural environment. In the area of social relations, we find that pollution concepts are used in certain contexts to maintain boundaries between categories of persons.

purity	*wuzho*	(*melalo*)	*marime*
social control	*romania*		*marime*
social boundaries	Rom	non-Rom Gypsies	*gaje*
natsia	Machwaya	Kalderasha	Kuneshti
age status	elder	child	adult

Not only social relations, but the physical environment is demarcated by pollution concepts. The body, bodily emissions, body nourishment, and items of personal use and contact are ordered and bound by the *wuzho, melalo, marime* divisions. Furthermore, sex, age, and social boundaries in certain contexts are also associated with pollution status.

purity	*wuzho*	(*melalo*)	*marime*
body	top	(hands)	bottom
sex	male	child	female

The cleanliness condition of clothes, for example, does not only depend on whether they become *melalo* through use but on who uses them (male, child, or female; Rom or *gaje*) and on what part of the body they touch (top or bottom).

Physical and social life are ordered by pollution concepts, and good health is an expression of the correct maintenance of physical and social boundaries. But health is also affected by certain mystical states and beings. The quality of life depends on avoiding *prikaza, marime, naswalemos*, and *o Beng* and seeking *Devla baXt, wuzho, sastimos*, and *o Del*.

purity	*wuzho*	(*melalo*)	*marime*
health	*sastimos*		*naswalemos*
auspiciousness	*Devla baXt*	*gajengi baXt*	*prikaza*
supernatural	*o Del*	*mule*	*o Beng*

The importance of these interrelated concepts is not only that they order the lives of a group of people but that they order it in such a way as to provide moral security in a wider society that is alien, often hostile to them. They do not ignore the *gaje* world, but they regulate contact with it and place the quality of that contact within a fairly rigid moral system. This moral system, *romania*, which is based on divisions determined by degree of purity, is the key to their uniqueness.[22] At the same time, as with many societies and individuals faced with tensions and outside pressures, the continuation of their lives as they know it, lies with their belief system.

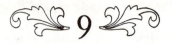

9

Conclusions

The aim of this book has been to describe holistically the social organization of a particular group of Rom. Although the literature on various Gypsy groups is vast, the paucity of sociological analyses of Gypsies is very striking, and rather than develop the theme of the mystery of the Gypsy 'soul' as seen by non-Gypsies, I have tried to deal with the Rom I knew as ordinary human beings with a comprehensible social life. At the same time, I hoped, perhaps unrealistically, that I would not fail to demonstrate the complexity of Rom character and the unique qualities of their way of life. I am convinced that whatever progress has been made in understanding the Rom, there is yet a long way to go.

My analysis has concentrated on important social categories, namely the opposition between Rom and *gaje* and the internal social categories, the *natsia*, *vitsa*, and *familia*, which are cross-cut in the *kumpania* grouping. The *kumpania* is the context within which social action takes place and therefore is the most flexible social unit. As members of *kumpaniyi*, individual Rom translate into action the social categories and beliefs that give meaning to their lives. The *kumpania* is flexible in the amount of political consolidation that may take place, and although basically a territorial unit, members of a *kumpania* can choose various degrees of mobility; economic relations are nevertheless based on the opposition between reciprocity between Rom and manipulation of *gaje*. Welfare, as a means of subsistence, has become an extention of the same economic behaviour as always. Thus I have tried to demonstrate how a particular group of Rom have handled the contradiction between continuity and flexibility in their own *kumpania* by adapting to a new economic situation (welfare) without compromising unduly social and moral ideals.

Both social form and social action, however, are ultimately related to a body of belief concerned with categories of cleanliness and pollution. These beliefs are not an aggregate of superstitions, as has so often been proposed in the literature, but form a system that gives meaning to behaviour both within Rom society and between Rom and *gaje*. Pollution categories play an important role in two areas of social structure. First, they are the key concepts for translating structure into action and for understanding the way action relates to structure. All action takes on a moral character which is explained in the language of relative cleanliness. Relations between members of different *natsiyi* and *vitsi*, choices involved in marriage arrangements, conflicts resulting from marriage contracts, manœuvres for political or economic gain, and choice of economic activities are all imbued with a morality, and this morality is always expressed in terms of the degree of relative purity. Secondly, pollution categories are the language of social boundaries. This includes basic social divisions on the basis of sex and age and the physical dimensions of the body; wider social units such as the *natsia* and *vitsa* and the world of the supernatural; and finally pollution categories are the means of determining the crucial boundary between the Rom and the *gaje*, so that their very identity as a people is expressed in terms of relative cleanliness. All these social boundaries are important, but the boundary between Rom and *gaje* is a constant preoccupation of their lives since they are always being confronted in unpredictable ways with an alien culture. Whatever the particular solution, theirs is always a precarious adaptation that is never resolved, never complete, because the threat of assimilation is never totally absent. It is not surprising, therefore, that when certain Gypsies have organized pressure groups to gain better conditions for themselves, one aspect of this movement has been to argue for a land of their own, Romanestan, as an ultimate solution to their problems (Acton 1974; Kenrick and Puxon 1972; Hancock 1973).

At this point it seems appropriate to conclude with some comments on the Rom as an ethnic group in America. The history of the Gypsies is, in a sense, the documentation of the survival of a group of people who have lived as outcasts in another society; thus from the point of view of many cultures, they are a pariah group. This status in the wider culture in which they live has had an important effect on their own social organization and, at the very least, has reinforced the rigid boundary between Gypsy and non-Gypsy. In America, where the very existence of the Gypsies is unknown or doubted by most non-Gypsies, they have not had to face so harshly as in Europe the consequences of being considered a pariah group. However, although no society develops in isolation, ethnic groups, and the Gypsies in particular, are by definition part of a wider social unit so for them the question of boundary maintenance between themselves and the wider society is primary, and a major concern of their social organization will be a response to this problem.

But although the Gypsies share with other ethnic groups the problems of determining inclusion and exclusion from the group, of determining the set of rules governing inter-ethnic social encounters, and of identifying another person as a fellow member, there are important differences between the Gypsies and other ethnic groups in America. The major ethnic groups in America are integrated into American culture to the extent that (a) an important part of their identity includes being 'American' as opposed to another nationality, and (b) they participate in a major aspect of structure; for example, stratification in America is partly based on ethnic relations between black and white Americans (see Barth 1969; Hannertz 1969; Suttles 1968). The Gypsies are less integrated into American society both in terms of structure and group identity. Second, and probably related, is that they have a more complex internal social organization than other ethnic groups, although at the same time it is oriented to the problems of living in an alien culture and to maintaining a strong distinction between themselves and others. This may be because historically they have had more time to come to terms with the problem of adaptation without assimilation than have other minority groups in America, and their mechanisms for doing so are highly developed.

Against these adaptive advantages, the Gypsies have certain more serious disadvantages than other ethnic groups. Blacks and Chicanos have suffered from discrimination in the educational system, but the Gypsies have hardly participated at all. Illiteracy may be useful in some instances for maintaining isolation, but as Gypsies become more known in America, particularly in welfare and police departments, they are at a serious disadvantage in their relations with such bureaucracies. Once Gypsies are officially recognized,[1] they are in danger of being unable to cope with American bureaucracy, and not everyone will be able to adopt the time-honoured solution of moving on to greener pastures. Related to this problem is the increasing demographic pressure among Gypsies in America and in the world generally. The fight for territories is intense precisely because, within their economic framework, making a living is becoming increasingly difficult. To combat this problem, some Gypsies, like other ethnic groups, have organized themselves politically into pressure groups. These groups are most vocal in England and France where demographic pressures are greatest. In America, the movement is embryonic and as yet marginal, but destined to grow as the numbers of Gypsies grow and as the economic situation there worsens.

Appendix A

These cases are the exact text of taped interviews with John Marks. Minor grammatical editing has been done only when the meaning would otherwise be obscure.

Case 1 *Kris romani* in New Orleans between *Xanamik* John Marks and Stevan

Case 2 *Diwano* in Wichita, Kansas, between *Xanamik* Yeso Nichols and John Marks

Case 1 – *Kris romani between Xanamik John Marks and Stevan*

'I am going to talk about a Gypsy trial. Now this story is based on a true trial, on a Gypsy trial which consists of judge and juries on a Gypsy marriage case which includes a divorce and a settlement not between bride and groom but between the father of the son and the father of the daughter. Now this is a case between John Marks[1] and the family of Stevan, who were engaged in a marriage between my son and Stevan who has a daughter that I wanted for a daughter-in-law. Now we arranged for a marriage between the parents of the bride and groom which is a tradition in the way the Gypsies go about marrying their son or daughter. Now the girl's father, Stevan, offered to marry his daughter to be the wife to my son, Danny. We agreed on a price to be paid the girl's father for her hand in marriage to my son. And some time after the wedding my son and his bride did not get along.

'It is more enjoyable to get a daughter-in-law (*bori*) from a cousin because there's been lots of dirty business. A man makes money giving a daughter-in-law by marrying her several times to different people. He does this by giving her for six months, then builds up evidence such as they beat her or her father-in-law made a pass at her, then her father takes her back and does not return the money. So it used to be you got a daughter-in-law from a different *vitsa*, but now it is better to get one in the family.

'When I got one for Danny she wouldn't sleep with him as a wife, only as a sister. Her father had put her up to it. So I got in touch with her father and said I wanted my money back. He said no, that I was trying to make love to my daughter-in-law, and he made his mistake when he said that. Now I knew that she had committed a crime before and was wanted for picking a man's pocket of $300. I went to the sheriff there and said that I would bring her in if he would bring her father down and cost him a lot of trouble and money. I drove her down to the sheriff because he agreed, and she was arrested and spent time in jail until her father posted bond. They fought the case on several occasions. Her father was in Reno and I had him picked up over there, and he had to pay bond to get out. I also had her arrested on charges in Fort Worth. She had an uncle in Beaumont who thought he could handle everything I did. They put her in the hospital on false charges (and I told the judge that) while trial had been delayed. He was furious that they had tried to make a fool out of him and sent two men down to see if she was really ill, and if not, to escort her to the trial. All this made a fool out of her father and her uncle. I had things pretty well arranged in Weatherford, and she had to plead guilty and was given a five year sentence on probation. We still had to have a Gypsy hearing to settle our differences. They tried to blackmail me in the same way but they had nothing on me so they failed.

'Now this takes us months later to New Orleans to a Gypsy trial. The Stevan family did not want to meet in Texas figuring that I was too powerful in Texas, and I had all my friends here in Texas, and they wanted a Gypsy trial by other members of the Gypsies from all parts of the United States. And that way I had to go to New Orleans for this trial to satisfy the company (*kumpania*), the public. In New Orleans there was about five hundred Gypsies there for this trial. So between John Marks and Stevan money-wise we arranged for a hall where the public can gather and listen to both sides of the story. And besides this would be the best way to settle the matter. We rented this hall, and we set a date the following couple of days to give everybody a time and chance to be there. The majority of the Gypsies was gathered at this hall; then they started picking out a judge and juries, which consisted out of different *vitsas* which is called 'generation' and families. This went on for several hours. There were two judges and twenty-five jurors at this particular trial. It doesn't ordinarily take more than one judge and ten or twelve jurors, but in this particular case, there was a lot of conflict. One judge was Alex Tan of Chicago, and one judge was Sonny Mitchell from Alabama. They are known to be honest and are well respected among the Gypsies for their honesty. At this trial, John Marks who is the father of Danny, the groom's father, was asked to take the stand and tell his story to the public, to the best of his knowledge. This took another couple of hours. Then Stevan was called to the witness stand. He gave his testimony to the judges and the jury and the public. His story was that my son wasn't old enough for his daughter. My son at the time was fifteen years old, and his daughter was twenty.

'Now I don't know where to go from there. All right. They're going to hang me for this. He said his daughter's complaint to him was that John Marks had bossed her a great deal in the period she was married to my son. Also, my wife disagreed to her behaviour and to her standards as a daughter-in-law. It was true, she wanted it that way. She was trying to make everything the opposite for us. It was all a set-up by her father and his brothers. He also accused me of trying to make love to his daughter which was my daughter-in-law. Now that accusation would condemn any Gypsy to a judge and jury if his story was true. He also accused the Boy's father of not giving them a large sum of money and setting them up on their own. But it was not promised as far as that goes. They were not living with us. I had bought them a trailer, a nice sixteen foot house trailer, and he had his own car, and he had his own money that I gave him. So that wasn't true.

'Then the judge and jury went to a secluded part of this hall to decide the true story of this case. They reviewed both sides of the story and found John Marks innocent of all the accusations. They found Stevan to be a fraud and to be in the business of making money on his daughter by marrying her at one place for three or four thousand dollars, getting her back and giving no money back, turning around and remarrying her again for a large sum of money and keeping the money again. So in review of the case they also reviewed the side of John Marks who had had this trial before a Gypsy court because he started his arrest on Stevan and his family to get even with them for the heartache he had caused his family. He would have been found to receive all his money from the Stevan family, but because of John Marks and the rage of madness which followed when he knew that he was being took by the Stevan family and also made a fool of – he was not really blamed for the action he took for the past several months – therefore, the juries agreed that the Marks family receive $2000 on refund. But through their conversation in the jury box they knew that the Stevan family did not have that kind of money, and the juries also knew that if they did not come to some decision where this case be settled at this time that this trouble could last indefinitely between the Marks and Stevan's family. Therefore, they agreed (along with the judges) to let Stevan pay $1000 and call it a final settlement on a divorce for both sides, the bride and groom. When the jury and the judges came back to the stand, they explained the money situation to the Marks family, and to show respect to the public they asked John Marks if he would do the public a favour and accept the decision of this court even though it wasn't quite fair to the Marks. But to avoid more trouble in the future, they had to come to this conclusion on account of the Stevan family, outside of this few thousand dollars they received for their daughter, they have lived from day to day not knowing the value of money, and they were actually not having more than a few hundred dollars at any one time. The Marks family wanted to get away from all this trouble and get their son properly married to some other woman, and they had to come to some conclusion at this time, so they did accept the court's verdict and gave their word that they would accept all responsibility of not creating any more trouble in the future. Stevan in return took the stand in his behalf and said that he would need three months to raise the thousand dollars, and at the end of three months he would send the money to John Marks. The court was asked if John Marks would accept Stevan's extension. He refused. The only way the Marks would accept such an extension was to have three people that was reliable to back Stevan as security so that Stevan would not double-cross John Marks at the end of the three months. So the court agreed to decide who would be the three men who would stand fully responsible for the thousand dollars in such a case. In another hour or so they came up with Sonny Mitchell as one respectable and reliable person and Alex Tan and Grover Marks. They are more or less my friends, and they accepted the responsibility and accepted the security that the money will be paid by the Stevan's, and they gave their word to the court that if the Stevan's side did not come across at the end of the three months with the thousand dollars that between Sonny Mitchell, Alex Tan, and Grover Marks, that I was guaranteed my money from them regardless. Ninety per cent of the time, there is no welshing. Once any family or any person, even without a 'background', gives his word to the public, they generally live up to it. But in this case, at the end of the three months, the Stevan family was in Witchita, Kansas, and John Marks contacted them for his thousand dollars. Then Stevan said that his daughter wanted to come back and remarry my son, and he was afraid to give me the $1000 because his daughter might elope with my son. I tried to explain to Stevan that we did not want his daughter, that my son did not want his daughter, there was no possible chance of the kids getting back together. Now or ever. That this was another way of Stevan to try to release the people that was responsible in the case and swindle me out of my thousand dollars which I had coming. I had a pretty good idea he was going to do that. I immediaately got in touch with Sonny Mitchell from Alabama and explained to him what Stevan was trying to pull. And I insisted on my money. He was one of the responsible persons to give me my money. In return, Sonny Mitchell from Alabama asked me if I could meet him by the following morning in Wichita, Kansas and if I would extend him that much time to see if he could get the money himself from Stevan instead of involving Alex Tan and Grover Marks and a further ordeal. But this was further expense to me so I went prepared. I got hold of six of my best muscle men of the family and got in the car, and we arrived in Wichita. The reason I gathered six of the Marks muscle boys was that Stevan (and there was a couple of his brothers in Wichita) himself weighed about 400 lb. He was a huge man. I knew there was gonna be a fight, and I went prepared for it. We arrived in Wichita and gathered at George Evans' home, who is a personal friend of the Marks. Sonny Mitchell arrived and if it wasn't for George Evans and his boys there would have been a large fight at this time because Stevan insisted that he could not give the money. Sonny told him that he promised the public that he would have to return that money. This went on for two days. Arguments were very hot. A lot of harsh words was relayed between the Marks and Stevan family. Finally after two days of a talking battle, Stevan did come up with the $1000 to Sonny Mitchell in return who did give the money to John Marks.

'Well he was a disgrace to the Gypsy tribe already when he refused, when he welshed on a promise that he gave his word, that he said in the Gypsy trial in New Orleans that he would give a $1000 which John Marks had coming. And of course like we mentioned before, Stevan was a very dirty man. In Wichita he was more or less forced to give the money up to the public which he did, you know what I mean, after a long ordeal and so forth. I never met him again. I have no relationships with him. My boy is married now. He has two fine daughters. He has a good wife. The first marriage of my son cost me about $15 000 which I carried to experience. There is no need to hold a grudge because it would just mean more trouble in the future. I just forgot about it.

'You see, that's why any one person, whether he is a Costello or a Mitchell, or an Evans, or a Stevenson, he tries to stay as close in the family as he can, not for the money but it has happened in the past where if you receive a daughter-in-law from far off away from the family, nine times out of ten that marriage doesn't last. Besides you might hurt your son or your daughter whichever might be implicated. The heartbreak, the ordeal, for your son – suppose he fell in love with this woman and for no reason at all his home is broken up through his father-in-law – he would feel very hurt. If a daughter got married, and the fathers-in-law broke up her home, and they were so strange, so strangers and so far apart that they could not get together and talk about this marriage like friends and relatives. If they were strangers, that home would have a poor chance of getting back together even though the kids are in love and do not want their home broken. But by Gypsy laws and traditions that home is broken. If the father-in-law breaks it up there is not much the kids can do about it unless in a few cases in the past the kids did elope, run away with one another, and got lost as long as a year from both parents from both sides and made a go of their marriage.'

Case 2 – Diwano in Wichita, Kansas between Xanamik Yanko Nicklos and John Marks

'In the year of 1952, my mother and family raised a niece of my sister's broken marriage. She had two kids, a boy and girl, which we raised. My father, my sisters and my brothers, we all helped to

raise the two kids. The girl was about ten years old and the boy
was about eight years old at the time their father and mother
broke up. She was married to a man by the name of Gus Adams,
Machwaya. Not the same one out of Houston. This was a young
man. The other is a man of about sixty–sixty-five now. And her
husband if he woulda lived today he would be a man about fifty-
four years. Now this niece of mine in the year of 1952 was a very
attractive girl, and the family of Kalumat City heard of her. We
were used at this time to camping at a Gypsy trailer camp which
was about twenty-five trailers and families, and one day this
family of Kalumat City arrived in Houston with the intention of
asking for the hand of my niece for the marriage of their son. He
was Nicklos and his *vitsa* was, I think, XoraXai. It means in
English, Arabian, he was one of those few Gypsies that arrived in
the United States from Arabia. His mother married an Arabian
who was called XoraXai and that started the *vitsa*. There was just a
handful of them, just him and a couple of two, three sons and a
couple of brothers and sisters, who was all his generation (*vitsa*)
put together. He was a very independent man. Nobody could
understand his way of living as Gypsies or as an American. He
was a very hard man to understand. He was a wealthy man. He
had a fortune-telling place, two of them in Kalumat City, which
is a very small town, suburb of Chicago. But from 1935 up to the
'60s the town was known as little Reno. It was quite open on
gambling and prostitution, and he made a lot of money there, all
rich people coming there for entertainment. They used to operate
their places from about four o'clock in the evening until four in the
morning. They slept through the daytime. The man just made a
lot of money there. They also operated in Wildwood, New Jersey,
at a park. See, they had the two places tied up in fortune-telling:
between Kalumat City in the wintertime and Wildwood, NJ.,
during the summertime in an amusement park.

'I did not know the background of the family, and I was in
charge of the marriage of my niece. They came to Houston and
went off and got a bottle of whiskey, as the tradition goes, and
asked my niece to be married to Miller Nicklos' son, who was the
son of Yanko, who was the originator of the family. After a few
days – the boy was a very good-looking boy on the Nicklos side,
and my niece was for a Gypsy a very beautiful girl. She was very
light skinned. She was a beautiful woman – we agreed, the Marks
to the marriage to the family.

'However, we did not know their background at the time. A few days later the wedding took place, and a few days after the wedding the Nicklos family along with their daughter-in-law, my niece, left for Kalumat City. We kept corresponding once in a while, not too close, for a couple of years.

'Then I went to visit some Gypsy friends in Dallas. This was July, 1954. My younger kids and my mother went with me. On the way back to Fort Worth, I went to buy strawberries for my mother, and we were hit by another car. My son was slightly injured and my daughter too, but my mother was critically injured. We took her to Dallas by ambulance. She had broken legs, fractured pelvis, face torn, bad cut on right leg. At her age, the doctors didn't think she would pull through. So according to the Gypsies' tradition I notified the immediate family to arrive as fast as they could to the Methodist hospital in Dallas. This was brothers, sisters, nieces, nephews, cousins from all parts of the United States. I called my niece's family in Wildwood, New Jersey and advised her of her grandmother's condition. When the girl heard of the condition, she immediately made some arrangements with her husband to come to Dallas leaving her year old baby girl behind with her mother-in-law. When she arrived in Dallas, her grandmother remained in critical condition for several weeks and the immediate family kept vigil around the clock at the hospital. We slept there, ate there, kids, wives, husbands camped on the lawn at the hospital.

'After about three weeks my niece's husband decided that this was not his troubles and that he was away from home long enough. Even though my mother was in critical condition he wanted to go back to Wildwood. My niece wanted to remain with her grandmother until she could know the outcome of the case. She and her husband got in an argument over whether to stay or leave. I was advised about this misunderstanding, and I immediately decided to avoid further trouble in the future. I knew how the Gypsies operate and in particular the Nicklos family. The grandfather of this boy would be furious if he went back without his wife. I had a very close friend in the detective department. His name was Chick Mattalock. He understood the Gypsies. I wanted him to come in my home and interview the boy and the niece before the boy went back to Wildwood. When the officer came into my home that afternoon, Tom Nicklos and his wife Rosie, my niece, who was pregnant, I introduced them to the officer. I had the officer

take notes, where they were from, who they were, why they came
to Fort Worth, and for what purpose they came. They told the
officer that Rosie's grandmother was in the hospital and that they
came to pay their respects, that they were not forced, that they
were very happy being in Texas and that they were on their own.
At the time of these notes, they were here in Texas for two weeks. I
asked the officer to interview Tom Nicklos alone to see that he was
not staying in Fort Worth by any stress by the Marks, that if he
needed police protection for any reason the officer would give it to
him. He told the officer that he was very happy that he was going
to fly back home and leave his wife behind and would come back
in a few days. The following day, Tom took the flight from Love
Field to Wildwood, New Jersey and arrived back with his family.
Rosie did not go back with her husband because her grandmother
at this time was still in the wards and wasn't expected to live or
die. She knew her husband's grandfather who was the leader of
the family. She knew that she would not be able to come back to
her funeral and that as long as she was in Texas, and it was a
matter of a few days to learn the outcome, she wanted to stay
and see the ordeal of the whole thing. Her husband wanted to stay
with her, but he was advised by his grandfather, not his father, to
come home and leave his wife in Texas because he had a way to
force his wife to come back to New Jersey. The man was entirely
a Gypsy of his own. He was an individual. He had wealth, and he
needed nobody as far as trouble was concerned.

'When Tom got back to Wildwood, his grandfather went and
made some false charges against Rosie, saying that she had stolen a
large sum of money in diamonds and that John Marks was present
at the robbery and he, John Marks, was the driver of the car. He
managed to get some warrants out on Rosie, his daughter-in-law,
and on John Marks. The warrants were grand larceny. He had the
warrants sent to Fort Worth to pick up John Marks and Rosie.
When the warrants arrived, I was advised over the ordeal, the
warrants that came on bogus charges. I immediately got hold of
Mattalock, and we then went to the District Attorneys' office and
gave him our view of the story that it was nothing but a Gypsy
feud and that Nicklos was using American law to get even with
the Marks family. The District Attorney relayed the message back
to the District Attorney in Wildwood, New Jersey, trying to avoid
a lot of embarrassment and ordeal to the Marks family as well as
to the law on both sides. After months, Nicklos demanded an

arrest be made. The law in Fort Worth ignored these warrants as they had enough proof to show they were bogus. After more months, Nicklos did not give up. So he took a plane from Wildwood to Texas and hired a lawyer in Forth Worth, and he had copies of the warrants of Rosie, and through the law he managed to come over to John Marks' house and make the arrest. Rosie immediately posted bond and got out of jail within the hour. He filed a procedure on extraditions, but of course that took another year or so.

'In the meantime the Nicklos family knew of a *bujo* in Silver City, New Mexico. He went to Silver City and got the law officers there and guaranteed the officers that he knew who got this *bujo* (which is known as switch-the-bag) for approximately $5000. The officers were very interested as the case was about three years old. They had nothing to go by. When Nicklos came and guaranteed them that he knew who had got the money there, they were very interested. He immediately gave the name of John Marks and Steve who is a brother to John. The warrants came in from Silver City to Fort Worth for the arrest of John and Steve Marks. In return, John went to the District Attorney in Fort Worth along with the sheriff, Marlin Wright. We called up the District Attorney in Silver City and demanded a description of the people that was wanted. The description of John was 5′ 11″ and approximately 180 lbs. John Marks is 5′ 5″ and 160 lbs. Steve and John Marks were automatically dismissed by the District Attorney. When the District Attorney in Silver City found out that the Nicklos was in a feud with the Marks and was just trying to cause the family of Marks a terrible trouble, they withdrew the charges. After about two years of the Nicklos family throwing everything at the Marks and accomplishing nothing, Rosie was later dismissed of the charges of her father-in-law's father.

'John Marks in particular was more powerful than Nicklos himself, and he thought I was nobody from nowhere and he could play ball with me. He could arrest me on false charges and Rosie on false charges, bring us back to New Jersey and play ball with us down there. I was too educated for him. When I had this lieutenant in my house, I knew that Nicklos was going to try this thing. Knowing the background of various Gypsies and this Gypsy in particular, I knew what he was going to do – how to hurt me, damage me, and to get his daughter-in-law back – but I played his hand all the way through. I was one step ahead of him in every field.

'Then after about two years of American laws, they asked me if I would meet with them in Kansas City on a Gypsy trial. I agreed. They called a trial because Rosie was still home. She wanted to go back, but she was mad at them too for arresting her and trying to force her hand. She knew that I would not stand for it. She knew that I would not let her go back by force. Until we came to some understanding at the Gypsy trial that she could not go back. So I went to Kansas City, and it was not exactly a Gypsy trial (*kris*), it was a Gypsy conference (*diwano*). I would not stand for a Gypsy trial because I thought I had done no injustice, and therefore I did not want a Gypsy trial, but I would listen to a group of Gypsies to see what the outcome of the case would be. We met in Kansas City with a party by the name of Grover Marks not related to the one in the first conference. This is something very usual. The Gypsies got just a few American names. There can be ten John Marks, ten Grover Marks. They do have different Gypsy names. This Grover Marks was an established Gypsy, property owner, well-to-do. Broko is his Gypsy name. When we met in Kansas City at Grover Marks' residence, we had an agreement to let Rosie come back, and Grover Marks was to pay part of the expense that was caused to John Marks for large fees for bond. This was a total of $1500. The father-in-law to Rosie Nicklos agreed to pay. Now this money was supposed to be put up in a fund to Grover Marks for a period of thirty days until all charges were dropped on both sides and all madness, feud between these two tribes was settled. Then that money was supposed to go to John Marks who was the rightful owner of this money at the end of the thirty days. John Marks was to bring Rosie into Kansas City the following week. Grover Marks and Miller Nicklos and father would be present and Steve Marks to receive the daughter-in-law. These Marks was very good men, and they were good friends of mine. You base this choice on friendship, on people you know are reliable, that you know are your friends, that you know they won't go as friends against the truth. You can know a person for life, and you can ask him to a Gypsy trial, and he can be sworn in to give nothing but the truth, and he would do so even if he condemns me.

'So I came back from Kansas City by plane. I done all this by flying. The following week I got Rosie who wanted to be united with her family and was happy that I did get together with her in-laws, and we flew to Kansas City. We got to Kansas City, and we got around the conference table with Grover Marks, and we come to an understanding of the ordeal. While we was at the conference table a long distance phone call came in at Grover Marks' residence from Chicago from the Nicklos family that there was an accident and Rosie's child had been burned by a pot of boiling water and that they were on their way to the hospital and for the Nicklos family to come home as soon as possible. I and Grover Marks never dreamed that this was a fake telephone call and a trap towards the Marks. At this time Rosie went back with her husband to Kalumat City. I hopped the next flight to Fort Worth. When I got home I was under arrest for blackmail, for extortion by telephone, and also by threatening the Nicklos family that I would come to steal the baby. I was placed under arrest on a federal warrant in Fort Worth, Texas. Boiling the case down, and the F.B.I. settling the stories out on both sides, we decided that if there was any extortion, it had started in Fort Worth and we demanded a hearing on a certain date. Therefore they subpoenaed all the people involved in this case – the main people were Miller Nicklos and his father and they were the complainers. The F.B.I. started their investigation in Kansas City, how Rosie had re-met her husband there, how Grover Marks was a reliable Gypsy, and stood behind the Marks and told how there was no blackmail, no kidnapping, and no extortion, and that he happened to be a judge at the hearing. Grover was also subpoenaed to come to Fort Worth to testify on behalf of John Marks which he agreed to do. And I may add that the pleasure was his because he did not know that he was doing business with such a scum on the other side, the Nicklos. The trial was set for about a month after this meeting in Kansas City and the arrest. Everyone was looking forward to the outcome of the case. But Miller Nicklos and his father knew that they had a bogus warrant when they arrested John Marks, and they implicated a lot of good people amongst Gypsies. And he knew that they would all back John Marks at the trial. Therefore how he managed it, what he done, he went to the District Attorney in Chicago and withdrew the charges against John Marks, and we were very disappointed that we did not have a hearing to see the outcome of the case. But I guess you go by the law and when they both managed to withdraw his charges that ended all the case. A few years later, Rosie's got more kids, and she is very happily married. Her husband on occasion comes to Fort Worth, Texas with his wife and kids to visit with the Marks family and thank them for the good wife they have given them However this all happened since his grandfather died because until then they had to obey all laws by him.

'Even if you weren't guilty in American law, you have won nothing as far as a Gypsy trial is concerned. You see he done it by force. He didn't do it legally according to Gypsy laws. He over-forced everything. He overdone everything. The Gypsy court's decision is about 90 per cent followed. I told you about Stevan who did not, but usually the decision is abided. If I went against the Gypsy trial, I would lose my life before I would lose my name. Honour . . . A few of them, not very many, could be dirty. Even if I thought the decision was unjust I would go by it. You take an oath before the Gypsies, get together, and in a lot of cases you have to put this money security. Your word is not your bond, but your money is. I mentioned the $5000 the income tax people want, but it was given to me as security money and was not mine. In a lot of cases the person is known for welshing and therefore in a public hearing you would have to have money to back his word because his word isn't worth a dime. If he went against his word he loses his money. The oath is swearing to God that you are telling the truth and will accept the decision. There is always a fine or a dis-grace – (*marime*) – they could be expelled from the race of Gypsies for a period of six months or a year. Well that's another story (*marime*). That's something that no human being in the world can understand, that particular part of the style of the Gypsies. A crazy ordeal. A crazy ordeal.'

Appendix B

Relationship Terminology – Male or Female Speaking

1. *pápo*	FF	MF					
2. *mamí*	FM	MM					
3. *kák(o)*	FB	MB	FZH	MZH	FFB	MFB	FMB
	MMB	FFZH	FMZH	MFZH	MMZH		
4. *bibí*	FZ	MZ	FBW	MBW	FFZ	MFZ	FMZ
	MMZ	FFBW	FMBW	MFBW	MMBW		
5. *dad*	F						
6. *dey*	M						
7. *phral*	B						
8. *pey*	Z						

9. *wóro*   male children of those ego calls *kako, bibi, woro*
vara FBS FZS MBS MZS FFBS MFBS
FMBS MMBS FMZS MMZS FFZS MFZS

10. *vára*   female children of those ego calls *kako, bibi, woro*
vara FBD FZD MBD MZD FFBD MFBD
FMBD MMBD FMZD MMZD FFZD MFZD

11. *shav(o)*	S, pre-puberty 'Gypsy' boy, male child			
12. *shey*	D, pre-puberty 'Gypsy' girl, female child			
shavé	plural, 'children'			
shabaró	post-puberty, marriageable boy: groom			
shebarí	post-puberty, marriageable girl: bride			
13. *nepotó*	BS	ZS	SS	DS
14. *nepáta*	BD	ZD	SD	DD

TERMS FOR RELATIVES THROUGH MARRIAGE

15. *Xanamík*	SWF	DHF	SWM	DHM
16. *sócro*	WF	(HF)		

17. *sácra*   WM   (HM)
18. *rom*   H, adult married male, 'Gypsy' man
19. *romní*   W, adult married female, 'Gypsy' woman
    (O Rom =   the 'Gypsies')
20. *śamutró*   DH   ZH
21. *bori*   SW   BW
22. *kumnáto*   WB   (HB)
23. *kumnáta*   WZ   (HZ)

TERMS FOR RELATIVES THROUGH A RITUAL RELATIONSHIP

24. *kirvó*   'godfather'; 'sponsor' at a wedding or baptism
25. *kirví*   'godmother'; 'sponsor'
26. *fíno*   'godson'
27. *fína*   'goddaughter'

TERMS FOR OUTSIDERS

28. *gajó*   adult, married non-gypsy male
29. *gají*   adult, married non-gypsy female (pl. *gaje*)
30. *rakló*   young, unmarried non-gypsy male
31. *rakli*   young, unmarried non-gypsy female

TERMS OF ADDRESS

papío   'grandfather'
mamío   'grandmother'
káko   'uncle'
bibío   'aunt'
mámo, dále   'mother'
dáde, táte,   'father'
móva
shoṛó   'son'
shoṛí   'daughter'

NOTES

Terms in brackets indicate meaning for female ego.
Other terms have been recorded: *pašo* – WZH; *naika* or *bratsa* (female speaker) for *kumnato* (Cohn 1969: 481); *teteisa* – *kumnato* (female speaker) (Cotten 1950) but like Cohn, I was unable to obtain any information on them, and they do not seem to be in current usage.

Notes

Introduction

1. Gypsy is a generic word used to refer to any Gypsy group, whereas Rom refers only to those Gypsies who call themselves Rom.
2. Influences in language and custom indicate that either their ancestors spent a long time in Rumania or else 'Rumanian' influence has spread far and wide.
3. The *vitsa* (pl. *vitsi*) is a large unit of cognatic kin composed of several branches headed by siblings or first cousins called *familiyi* (sing. *familia*). Each *vitsa* has a name and identifies itself with one or another *natsia* (*natsiyi*) which can be translated loosely as nation or tribe. See pages 181–205 for a complete description and analysis of these categories.
4. The same problems have arisen, and the same sense of confusion remains when other ethnic groups are approached superficially and from the outside. Interestingly, the conclusion in these studies is very similar, and the impression is one of social disorganization. Valentine (1968) gives an excellent critique of the pitfalls of this approach and its disastrous consequences for the Blacks in America when the results of these studies are used by social administrators.
5. Personal Communication from Miss J. Okely.

Chapter 1

1. In Britain, English Romanies or travellers are often distinguished from Irish and Scottish travellers, sometimes called Tinkers or Tinklers. This distinction is based on certain characteristics such as accent and customs, but is not very significant sociologically since they do not form distinct groups. The term tinker is the latest in a series of scapegoat terms (others include diddicai, posh-rat, etc.) used by local authorities to push on unwanted Gypsy families by claiming they are friendly to 'real' Romanies but not to 'dirty tinkers'. (For a discussion of this issue, see Acton 1974.)
2. According to Yoors (1967: 133–135) the *Manush* or *Sinte* (*manush* means man in the sense of 'human being' or 'person') may be

considered a fifth related though distinct tribe. (See also Cotten 1955: 20.)

One comes across other terms that they use to classify themselves, such as *Rom Tanesko* (town Gypsies) as opposed to *Rom Dromesko* (travelling Gypsies). John Marks explained the difference. 'The *Rom Tanesko* stay in larger cities, they live high, eat with spoon, fork and knife, buy furniture, trade and don't travel all the time. The *Rom Dromesko*, in Mexico for example, have the *cine ambulante* and live in tents. They are on the road the whole time.' Ronald Lee (1968: 12–13) and other Gypsies I have met refer to the *Rom Serbiyaiya* (Serbian Gypsies) and the *Rusuria* (Russian Gypsies), which simply differentiates the country of origin before immigrating to the United States and consists primarily of a difference in pronunciation in *Romanes*. Serbian Gypsies use *k* and *g* sounds where Russian Gypsies use *ch* and *j* – *kinav*: *chinav*; *lulugi*: *luluji*. They are still Rom and must fit into the tribal classifications. For example, Kalderash Rom may be Serbian or Russian; however the Machwaya are always Serbian, since the Machwaya come from Serbia. All these terms often confuse the truly important organizational divisions of the Rom.

3. Except in certain rare cases when they are adopted (but not stolen!) as a child. Jan Yoors is a good example and typical in that when it became time for him to participate as an adult, he did not marry a Gypsy girl and left the group.

4. In the languages that I read. These are French, Romany, Spanish, and Portuguese, and, of course, English, which is the language used for most important sources.

5. For an introductory book that presents a fairly critical recapitulation of the literature, see Clébert (1963), *The Gypsies*, or Esty (1969), *The Gypsies: Wanderers in Time*.

6. Rena Cotten (1950), *The Fork in the Road: A Study of Acculturation among the Kalderaš Gypsies*, which is based on the *Bimbulesti vitsi* in New York City; David Pickett (1962), *Prolegomena to the Study of the Gypsies of Mexico*, which is a description of some aspects of the nomadic Rom of Mexico; Carol Miller (1968), *Machwaya Gypsy Marime*; and Harper (1951), *Family Organisation of the Portland Gypsies*, on Rom living on the northwest coast of America.

7. Bonos (1942) and Coker (1966) on Rom households in Philadelphia; Rena Cotten Gropper (1954–5; 1968) on New York Kalderash; and Cohn (1969; 1970; 1972) on Northwest Canadian Rom. Also helpful are Mitchell's articles 'The King of the Gypsies' (1942) and 'The Beautiful Flower' (1955) and Irving Brown's *Gypsy Fires in America* (1924) and his other articles in the *JGLS* (1929; 1936).

8. Bruno is mentioned as a major source of information on Gypsies for Mitchell's *The Beautiful Flower* (1955: 46).

9. The Rom 'like' those that they 'respect'. The two concepts are inseparable.

10. Bhatia (1963), *A Gypsy Grammar*; Ackerley (1912–14), 'The Dialect of the Nomad Gypsy Coppersmiths'; Sampson (1926), *The Dialect of the Gypsies of Wales*; and, particularly, Gjerdman and Ljungberg

(1963), *The Language of the Swedish Coppersmith Gypsy Johan Dimitri Taikon* (hereafter referred to as G. & L.).

Chapter 2

1. *Kumpania* (plural: *kumpaniyi*) comes from the Rumanian, *kompanie* meaning 'company', or *'gesellschaft'*, or family group (G. & L.: 273).
2. There is insufficient information on these families to give a statistically significant influx–outflux figure.
3. A *bujo*, translated as 'switch-the-bag', is a swindle involving a large amount of money from a gullable fortune-telling customer.
4. This is not borne out by medical records in Barvale which, over a period of six years, show an improvement in health due to more regular medical care.
5. The Lowara use *tsera* (or *tserha*) to mean *vitsa* as well as 'tent' (Yoors 1967: 135). This usage of *tsera* was not recognized by the Kalderash in Barvale and throughout this book I shall use *tsera* to mean 'household' or 'tent' and *vitsa* to refer to the unit of restricted cognatic kin, following Kalderash usage.

Chapter 3

1. Recently in Oakland a Black leader suggested that it would improve the situation of the Blacks if each person would invite a policeman to dinner. He was hooted off the rostrum.
2. There is no word in *Romanes* that I know of to describe this technique. In English the best word is 'to hustle'. Hustling is a time-honoured technique and even the earliest accounts of Gypsies describe the same methods of making a living.
3. For example, they are allowed to have as much wealth in jewellery as they like, but they are not allowed to have new cars. The *Rom*, who put their savings in gold and cars, consider this absurd, but accept the practical consequences of being seen with a new car.

Chapter 4

1. This is a good example of how regular employment would conflict with their values.
2. I never heard a word for loneliness and I suspect it is a concept and feeling that rarely arises.
3. In certain contexts *romania* is translated (for the *gaje* who have no equivalent word) as 'religion', in such statements as 'it's against my religion to inform upon another Gypsy'.
4. In a time of transition of leadership, several *phuro* may be vieing for the position. In Barvale, when 'Big Mick' left, three or four men tried for several months to take his position, until Stevan emerged victorious.
5. Gypsy Project, 1970 – Vocational Rehabilitation Division, Salem, Oregon.

6. She was a one-eyed dwarf, psychotic, and paranoid, the only case of genuine mental illness I ever encountered.
7. Turner 1957; Gluckman 1965; Swartz 1968; Bailey 1968; Nicholas 1965, 1966, 1968.
8. Police records did in fact reveal a warrant for Wanko's arrest under another name. This police report indicated that Wanko had 'abducted' his own daughters and was thought to be having sexual intercourse with them. Of course, such a report would normally be ignored by the Rom since it obviously dated back to some trouble with Wanko's *Xanamik* (co-parent-in-law) at the break up of his daughter's marriage; but in this instance it was used as corroboration of gossip.
9. This is not unlike problem-solving in a tropical forest tribe where dissenters and people disliked in the village are forced to move to another village. There, as among the Gypsies, mobility is a major form of social control.
10. For further information on *kris romani* see Tillhagen 1958-9; Yoors 1947; Pickett 1966, especially pages 6-8.
11. Called *krisatore* (masc. plur.) according to Yoors (1947: 3). The arbitrator is called *o krisako rom p'uro kai Xal sere* (Yoors 1947: 16), that is, the one who brings about the downfall of the guilty party. This means literally 'the elder of the *kris* who eats heads', and refers to the importance of a man's head in both power and cleanliness status. See also Brown (1929: 171) who says the arbitrator is called '*o baro*'.

Chapter 5

1. The relationship is abbreviated by the first letter in the term, except Z = sister.
2. Origins of the terms are from Gjerdman & Ljungberg (G. & L.) 1963 as established by Cohn (1969).
3. These are the terms as given by my informant. It may be, however, that the *w* in *woro* is a peculiarity of his pronunciation and that *voro* is used as well. Some Rom had the habit of substituting *w* for *v*.
4. According to Pickett (1966: 9), the Mexican Rom use '*phraleski bori*' to indicate brother's wife.
5. According to Cohn (1969: 480), *žamutro* 'is complementary to *bori*, covering the man, whether of one's own generation, or the descending one, who made a *bori* out of a woman from the speaker's family'. This statement is confusing as he could be using *bori* in the second instance, to mean 'bride'. It should be remembered that one gives a *bori* to one's *Xanamik* and one's *žamutro* receives a wife for himself and a *bori* for his family and *vitsa*.
6. Other than HBW/HBW, of course.
7. The word for reputation given in G. & L. is *hirea* and by Yoors (1947: 2) is *hiro*. The Rom are very concerned with their reputation (or 'background').
8. See pages 137 for a description of this case.

9. Children have indeterminate sexual status as well as rather ambivalent cleanliness status (see Chapter 8).
10. There is a very moving song about a girl who is unhappy in marriage because her in-laws beat her, but she tells them that she is not alone in the world – she has two brothers who will protect her.
11. These relations are not unlike cousin relations among the cognatic SaraKatsani (Campbell 1964: 99–106) though this relationship extends beyond first cousins.
12. Of course, it is impossible for me to generalize about discussions on women in male groups.
13. A woman can curse (*amria*) or pollute (*marime*) a man and cause his illness or death. All old women are suspected of being witches (*choXani*), but this was the only accusation of witchcraft that occurred during my field work.
14. This is probably a noun deriving from *žavtar* – to depart; hence 'the departure'.

Chapter 6

1. The Kalderash use the word *natsia* instead of *raca* and *vitsa* instead of *tsera* (which they use to mean household). They translate *natsiyi romaiya* as 'Gypsy nations' (see also Lee 1967: 45) but refer to a person's 'nation' or 'race' interchangeably. Tribe would be a better translation, but I shall employ Kalderash usage.
2. The Kalderash that I knew swore that the few Lowara they had met (all recent travellers from Europe) were 'true Rom'; yet in most instances they were unwilling to accept as Rom any 'Gypsy' who was not like themselves. Even those who had never heard the name Lowara agreed that these Lowara must be another *natsia*, and there was a general fascination about Lowara dialect and customs.
3. John Marks mentioned the Pikareshti as one Machwaya *vitsa* with whom he was in frequent contact; however, he never referred to them as anything but Machwaya. Irving Brown (1936: 72) also mentions that the Machwaya have *vitsi*.
4. According to Derek Tipler (1969: 27–33) the Colteshti are another Churara *vitsa*. He states (30) that many Churara are mistaken for Kalderash, notably, he suggests, the Swedish Kalderash whose dialect forms the basis of the Gjerdman and Ljungberg (1963) dictionary.
5. Hocart (1970: 173–84) describes lucidly this common malpractice in anthropology.
6. For the history of Tiny Bimbo, see Brown 1936: 74–6; Gropper 1968: 1053–4; and Mitchell 1955: 48.
7. The following names have also been suggested by Ian Hancock (personal correspondence): Bochesti (*bok, box*, avarice); Chukuria (*tusknari*, hangman); Groneshti (*groino*, ugliness); Jaikurshti (*dzai*, freeze; *kur*, heels).
8. According to Tipler (1969: 28, 32–3), the Cholteshti are a Churara

vitsa; according to John Marks, the Pikareshti are a Machwaya *vitsa*; the rest are Kalderash.

9. Excretion traditionally took place outdoors away from camps. Even today the Rom prefer to relieve themselves away from their homes, outdoors if possible, or in *gaje* (public) toilets. It is extremely bad form to use the toilet in someone's home especially if other persons present must necessarily be aware of this act.

10. Yoors (1967: 148–59) has a good description of these same accusations by the Lowara towards Churara in their *kumpania*.

11. This is a case told by John Marks in his own words.

Chapter 7

1. The view of marriage ascribed to here is that proposed by Leach (1961: 107–8), and lately Riviere (1971: 57), namely that marriage is a 'bundle of rights' and that these rights must be established in each case under consideration, hence any universal definition of marriage is an illusion.

2. Cotten (1950: 89) quotes 33·3% endogamous marriages for all ages, but counts as endogamous only marriages within the same *vitsa* since she believes *vitsi* are 'patrilineal bands'. Consequently her statistics exclude cousins of a different *vitsa*.

3. See pages 170–171 for an example of this procedure.

4. Recent news indicates that this marriage, after three years of negotiation, has finally stabilized, and the couple now have their first child.

5. Cotten (1950: 89) also found the same pattern: 41·7% of the marriages between the two *vitsi* she studied were with each other and a further third were within the same *vitsa*. The marriages between the two *vitsi* stem from the marriage of the leader of one *vitsa* to a woman from the other *vitsa*.

6. For the most reliable descriptions, but not necessarily identical to American Rom, see Tillhagen (1953), Brown (1924), Lee (1968: 18–22), Cotten (1950: 85–101), Pickett (1966: 96–9), Maximoff (1960), and Petrović (1936). Tillhagen's information is primarily from one informant and only three pages are devoted to present day marriage procedure. Cotten and Lee deal specifically with Kalderash Rom in America.

7. According to Ackerley (1913–14: 207), *tumnimos* comes from *tomnipe* and means 'bargain'; hence, *tumnimos* means 'I betrothe' or 'I bargain'.

8. See Cohn (1969: 479) who speaks of the 'considerable economic stakes that are involved in the practice [of] buying and selling wives'.

9. Cotten (1950: 90–3) gives several statements to this effect.

10. It has not been possible to verify this and calculate the percentage of marriages that result in divorce, partly because of the secrecy surrounding divorce, since it is shameful, and partly because of the problem of finding out about marriages that take place before the legal age. When these marriages are discovered, the Rom will not admit that they are marriages, but claim they are betrothals, and when they dissolve, they are not called divorces.

11. In both ceremonies, *tomniamos* and *abiav*, the presence of the *kumpania* as well as the families is essential, for the *kumpania* is the basic public group.

12. I never discovered a word for incest either from informants or in any dictionary of *Romanes*. The difficulty in discussing these matters and the shame associated with them could be obscuring any mention of the word. Therefore it is impossible to say if any such word exists.

13. This probably also includes the father's wife and extends, though less strongly, to all wives of a man's *vitsa*. Adultery is shameful and *marime* in any case, but can be rectified with a resettlement of the brideprice, except in cases of adultery (or incest) between a man and his *bori*. In these cases, the shame and the *marime* cannot be solved through court procedure.

14. I suspect that when first cousins marry, their fathers are quite old and have already drifted apart considerably. Their first loyalties being to their own large *familia*.

15. I do not know how the Boyash feel about marriage with the Rom. English Gypsies in America seem to seek marriage with the Rom when they wish to remain 'Gypsy', and they marry *gaje* if they wish to leave the Gypsy life; however, I imagine they would prefer marriages with other Romanitchal when these could be arranged.

16. Of the fifty marriages compiled for Barvale between 1969 and 1970, three were with *gaji romni* which would be 6%.

17. This percentage is approximate; it is compared against the total number of marriages I came across and not against the *kumpania* since only one allegedly occurred in Barvale.

Chapter 8

1. My debt to Mary Douglas (1966) for her inspiring work on pollution is very great.

2. My first reaction to her thesis was disbelief, but when I tested many of the beliefs and practices among the Kalderash, they would discuss it quite openly whereas before they had simply replied, 'Gypsies don't do that.' Also once I myself began observing 'proper' cleanliness I was no longer as *marime* as other *gaje* and was treated quite differently. One woman even complained that I became fanatically clean.

3. However, it is not the *only* coercive authority as Miller claims (1968: 7). Fines are also levied for less important crimes.

4. The harsher interpretation of rules for women not only in marriage but in all cleanliness has to do with the purity of the group. Yalman (1963: 43) has also found that 'it is through women (and not men) that the "purity" of the caste-community is ensured and preserved'.

5. See Rena Cotten 1950: 171, for further examples.

6. *Vitsa* names also formed the following categories consistent with pollution ideas, but since they are not linked with any behaviour (as

far as I know), and the evidence is still tenuous I have not included them:

culture	culture/nature	nature
metal	wood/metal weapons	wood
food	excrement eaters	excrement
human	human/animal	animal

7. Cotten (1950: 123) claims that 'children are thought to be holier and purer than adults'.

8. Yoors (1967: 150) and Cotten (1950: 202) confirm this body division among the Rom. Regulations for controlling the lower body and keeping the upper body pure do not normally apply to children and old people.

9. Yoors (1967: 150) reports the same prohibition among the Lowara: 'A woman was considered *marhime* from the waist down and she must avoid letting the bottom of her skirts touch a man not her own, or anything he used. If her skirts should brush against plates, cups or drinking glasses, these were immediately destroyed, so as not to "soil" the next male user.'

10. I have heard from two separate informants that oral intercourse is a very popular method of sexual intercourse, but this was difficult to verify. Oral intercourse represents a dramatic reversal of the usual boundaries and the most common expressions of contempt were those referring to it (e.g. *Xa miro Kar*). According to Irving Brown (1929: 165) public knowledge of such an act is sufficient to make a person *marime*. 'One of the most serious cases of being *maXrime* was that of a Gypsy of whom it was said "*Čumidel leski romni*", the words "*ande miš*" being understood. It has already cost him hundreds of dollars to try to clear himself, and it will cost him many more before he is pronounced *uzho*, according to predictions.'

11. Like incestuous relations, this reverses the usual inside (*wuzho*), outside (*marime*) division for obvious reasons. Garments that have closer contact with *marime* areas are more polluted.

12. Eggs, garlic, potatoes, vinegar, and black pepper are common medicines for various illnesses. I am presently preparing a pamphlet on Rom remedies and recipes and do not intend to go into illnesses and their cures in any great detail here.

13. These dates are closer to the Orthodox church than the Roman Catholic, but are picked from their own memory rather than a dictate from the church.

14. Any serious denial of *romania* or unorthodox social behaviour is felt to be due to mental illness (*dilo*).

15. I had no way of verifying any increase in the amount of sickness since the Rom began living in houses; however, all Rom firmly believed that the two were connected. For the six years they have been living in Barvale there has been no increase in illness; on the contrary, due to the availability of free medical care, many illnesses which they arrived with have been checked or cured. However, one

doctor felt that perhaps the diet, which is suited to a strenuous life on the road, is unsuited to a more sedentary life.

16. She adds in a footnote: 'Western disease theory does not conflict with such precautions. Gypsies are few, the *gadze* are numerous; sick *gadze* must outnumber sick Gypsies, in all likelihood. Crowds, in any case, increase the possibility of contagious disease' (42). It is easy to see why venereal disease is attributed to *gaje* since its appearance among the Rom is directly attributed to relations between young boys and *gaji*. Cancer was unheard of until *gaje* doctors told them about it, and the same can be said of hernias and diabetes.

17. See Salloway, Anderson, and Ginafortoni (1971) for a description of the efficient use of medical facilities by Boston Rom.

18. *Mamioro* is not unique to American Rom. In Serbia, 'Bibi' was thought to be the source of cholera (Petrović 1937: 115–37). G. & L. list for Swedish Gypsies that *Mamioro* means 'little grandmother' and 'cholera', and the Rom in Barvale translated it as 'grandmother' or 'flu'.

19. *Johai* is possibly a slime mould or wood rot. Yana saw several hundred slime mould cultures at the University of California in Berkeley, but she said they were not similar, and anyhow 'how can you grow vomit'.

20. According to Shrecha you could buy 'Devil's shit' in a chemist in East Oakland, but since she never showed me where this was located, I never had the pleasure of asking the pharmacist if he had any 'Devil's shit'.

21. Lee (1971: 244) calls Martiya the 'angel of death'.

22. In this sense, there are parallels between Rom and Indian social structure, which at one time the Rom may have been part of, and which, according to Dumont (1970), is based primarily on the opposition of the pure and the impure.

Chapter 9

1. In August, 1972, the United States government declared the Gypsies an official minority.

Appendix A

1. When speaking into a tape-recorder, John Marks often referred to himself in the third person to indicate, presumably, that he was just another character in the story. This technique gave his narrative a sense of objectivity that would be lost with the use of the first person.

Glossary

Stress is not needed when writing Romani as it is usually on the final syllable; however, as an aid to pronunciation I have included stress in the glossary. I am indebted to Lee (1969 a) for English equivalents of Romani sounds:

Phonemes

a	as in l*a*st, but shorter
e	as in p*ai*n, but shorter
i	as in t*i*n
o	as in g*o*t
u	as in bl*ue*
ch	as in *ch*urch
sh	as in *sh*ip
r	trilled as the Spanish *r*; also a gargling sound as in Parisian French; however, many Rom do not distinguish between the two.
X	as in Scottish Lo*ch*
ẑ	as in trea*s*ure
k, p, t	as distinguished from the aspirated sounds, kh, ph, th.
y	as in *y*et
g	as in *g*ot
s	as in *s*it
b, d, f, l, m, n, v, w, z	as in English

Glossary

abiáv	wedding feast
amriá	curse; oath

baró	big, large
báXt	good luck; auspiciousness
o Béng	the Devil
borí	bride; daughter-in-law, sister-in-law (BW)
Boyásh	non-Romany speaking Rumanian Gypsies
bujó	bag; medicine bag; a swindle called 'switch-the-bag'
Churára	a nation of Rom, from *churi*, knife
daró	brideprice
o Del	God
dikló	headscarf, indicating a married women; handkerchief
diwanó	a group of adults convened to discuss a matter publicly
drab	medicine
drabarní (f)	a female who has knowledge of medicines, a doctor; a fortune-teller
família (pl. *familiyí*)	an extended cognatic family
gajó (f. *gají*, pl. *gajé*)	an adult non-Gypsy
gajéngi baXt	bad luck; luck of a non-Gypsy
žéita	(p.p. of Zavtar; to depart); the moment when a girl passes from her family to that of her husband's
Gúrkwe	a group (or *vitsa*) of Rom supposedly from Greece
iohaí	a medicine translated as 'ghost's vomit' which is regurgitated by *mamioro*
Kalderásh(a)	a tribe or nation of Rom traditionally coppersmiths
kar	penis
Kashtaré	the major Rom *vitsa* in Barvale
katrínsa	a woman's apron
kidemós	a collection
krís romaní	a trial composed of adult Rom.
kumpanía (pl. *kumpaníyi*)	a group of Rom travelling or living together in a territory, an economic and residential association

Kunéshti	a Churara *vitsa* of Rom
lasháv	shame; honour
lovoɽó	a ceremony to divide money earned (from *lové*, money)
Lowára	a tribe or nation of Rom, traditionally horse traders
Machwáya (m. Machwáno f. Machwanka)	a tribe or nation of Rom supposedly from the Serbian province of Matsva
mamioɽó	a spirit or ghost who is said to bring serious illness (from *mamí*, grandmother)
marimé	polluted, defiled; rejected or outcast by trial
Martiyá	'the night'; a night spirit who brings illness and death
melaló (adv.)	temporary or honest dirt
Mesikáya	'Mexican Gypsies'
miɽó (m. sing.)	my
mish	vagina
mulé (pl.) (m. *muló*, f. *mulí*)	the spirit or soul of a dead person; ghost
naswalémos	illness, sickness
nátsia (pl. *natsiyí*)	a nation, tribe, or 'race' of Rom
nav	name
nav romanó	'Gypsy name'; *nav gajikanó* – non-Gypsy name
ófisa	fortune-telling establishment
pakív	(v.) to honour, respect; (n.) a feast given in honour of a visiting guest
patragí	Easter
periná	feather eiderdowns
phuró (f. *phurí*, pl. *phuría*)	an elder or patriarch of a *familia*
pomána	a death feast given three days, nine days, six weeks, and six months or one year after death
(*pomána siniá*)	death feast-table
postíu	a fast; to abstain from eating certain foods on Friday
prikáza	very bad luck or omen, inauspiciousness

o Rom	a group of Gypsies divided into four, perhaps five nations
ρom	an adult married male Rom; husband
ρomni	an adult married female Rom; wife
ρomanés	the language of the Rom
ρomanía	the laws and traditions of the Rom; social order
Románitchal	a Gypsy from Great Britain, 'English Gypsy'
rom baró	a leader, the 'big man' in a *kumpania*
(f. *romni bari*)	
sármi	a ritual dish of stuffed cabbage
sastimoś	good health
sláva	a feast given in honour of a saint to bring good health, good luck, etc.; a feast on a religious holiday
streyíno Rom	a Rom whose family or *vitsa* one is not familiar with
tséra	tent; household
tumnimoś	the betrothal
(*tomiála*)	
vítsa (pl. *vítsi*)	a category of cognatic kin
wortácha	partners in an economic enterprise
wuzhó	clean, pure
Xá	(voc.) eat
Xanamík	co-parents-in-law (spouse's parents)
XoraXaí	'Arabian Gypsies'
źamutró	son-in-law, brother-in-law (ZH)

Bibliography

This Bibliography contains only works to which reference was made in the text, and is by no means a bibliography of the subject.

The Journal of the Gypsy Lore Society (T. & A. Constable, Ltd., Edinburgh) is abbreviated *JGLS*.

ACKERLEY, F. G. 1912–13. The Dialect of the Nomad Gypsy Coppersmiths. *JGLS* **VI** (4): 303–26.

—— 1913–14. The Dialect of the Nomad Gypsy Coppersmiths. *JGLS* **VII** (2): 116–49; 161–214.

ACTON, T. 1974. *A Sociological Analysis of the Development of Attitudes towards the Changing Place of Gypsies in the Social and Cultural Structure in England and Wales from the Moveable Dwellings Act Agitation to the Romanestan Controversy.* D.Phil. thesis, Oxford University.

AYRES, G. 1966. Seers Confirm it – He's Fouled up. *Oakland Tribune*, Metropolitan News Section, August 21: 11, 15.

BAILEY, F. 1968. Parapolitical Systems. In M. J. Swartz (ed.), *Local-Level Politics*. Chicago: Aldine.

BARTH, F. 1955. The Social Organization of a Pariah Group in Norway. *Norveg*, Folkelivsgranksking 5, Oslo: 125–44.

—— 1969. *Ethnic Groups and Boundaries*. Boston: Little, Brown and Company.

BHATIA, R. G. 1963. *A Gypsy Grammar*. Unpublished PhD dissertation, University of Pennsylvania.

BLACK, G. F. 1914. *A Gypsy Bibliography*. Gypsy Lore Society Monograph, I.

BONOS, A. H. 1942. Roumany Rye of Philadelphia. *American Anthropologist* **44**: 257–74.

BROWN, I. 1924. *Gypsy Fires in America*. New York: Harper.

—— 1929. The Gypsies in America. *JGLS* **VIII** (4): 145–76.

—— 1936. The Mačvaya in California. *JGLS* **XV** (2): 72–8.

CAMPBELL, J. K. 1964. *Honour, Family and Patronage*. Oxford: Clarendon Press.

CLÉBERT, J.-P. 1963. *The Gypsies*. Trans. by Charles Duff. Harmondsworth: Penguin Books.

COHN, W. 1969. Some Comparisons Between Gypsy (North American *rom*) and American English Kinship Terms. *American Anthropologist* **71**: 476–82.

—— 1970. La Persistance d'un Groupe Paria relativement Stable: Quelques Réflexions sur Les Tsiganes Nord-Americains. *Études Tsiganes* **16** (2–3): 3–23.

—— 1972. *The Gypsies*. MS.

COKER, G. 1966. Roumany Rye in Philadelphia: A Sequel. *Southwestern Journal of Anthropology* **22**: 85–100.

COLEMAN, A. 1962. *Gypsy Families in Hawaii*. Unpublished report to the Department of Social Services, Welfare Division, Honolulu, Hawaii.

COTTEN (GROPPER), R. M. 1950. *The Fork in the Road: A Study of Acculturation Among the Kalderaš Gypsies*. Unpublished PhD dissertation, Columbia University, New York.

—— 1954. An Anthropologist Looks at Gypsiology. *JGLS* **XXXIII** (3–4): 107–20.

—— 1955. An Anthropologist Looks at Gypsiology. *JGLS* **XXXIV** (1–2): 20–37.

—— 1968. Urban Nomads – The Gypsies of New York City. *Transactions of the New York Academy of Sciences*, series II, 29: 1050–56.

DOUGLAS, M. 1966. *Purity and Danger*. London: Routledge & Kegan Paul.

DUMONT, L. 1970. *Homo Hierarchicus*. London: Paladin.

ELIADE, M. 1956. *Forgerons et Alchimistes*. (Collection *Homo Sapiens*) Paris: Flammarion.

ESTY, K. 1969. *The Gypsies: Wanderers in Time*. New York: Meredith Press.

EVANS-PRITCHARD, E. E. 1940. *The Nuer*. Oxford: Clarendon Press.

FARON, L. 1961. *Mapuche Social Structure: Institutional Re-integration in a Patrilineal Society of Central Chile*. Illinois Studies in Anthropology, no. 1. Urbana: University of Illinois Press.

GJERDMAN, O. and LJUNGBERG, E. 1963. *The Language of the Swedish Coppersmith Gypsy Johan Dimitri Taikon*. Uppsala: A-B Lundequistska.

GLUCKMAN, M. 1965. *Politics, Law and Ritual in Tribal Society*. Chicago: Aldine.

GRAHAM, R. 1965. Stars Fall on Gypsy Queen. Gypsy Queen – a Clouded Future. *San Francisco Chronicle*, 2 October: 1, 10.

HANCOCK, I. 1973. *Mutrás-Amen Andé Tiri Pirí Le Bilaréngi – Some Aspects of Gypsies and Gypsy Nationalism*. Unpublished manuscript.

—— 1974. Gypsies in Texas. In, F. E. Abernethy (ed.), *The Folklore of Texan Cultures*. Austin.: University of Texas Press (in press).

HANNERTZ, U. 1969. *Soulside: Inquiries into Ghetto Culture and Community*. New York: Columbia University Press.

HARPER, E. B. 1951. *Family Organisation of the Portland Gypsies*. Unpublished B.A. thesis, Reed College, Portland, Oregon.

HOCART, A. M. 1970. *The Life-Giving Myth* and other essays. London: Methuen & Co (first published 1952).

HOSTETLER, J. A. 1968. *Amish Society*. Baltimore: Johns Hopkins.

HOSTETLER, J. A. and HUNTINGTON, G. E. 1967. *The Hutterites in North America*. Stanford University case studies in Cultural Anthropology: Holt, Rinehardt & Winston.

JONES, G. 1970. Crime Fighters or Extortionists? *The Houston Post*, Sept. 24, 1970. Page 1/SW.

KENRICK, D. and PUXON, G. 1972. *The Destiny of Europe's Gypsies*. London: Sussex University Press.

LEACH, E. R. 1961. *Rethinking Anthropology*. London: Athlone Press.

LEE, R. 1967. The Gypsies in Canada. *JGLS* **XLVI** (1–2): 38–51.

—— 1968. The Gypsies in Canada. *JGLS* **XLVII** (1–2): 12–28.

—— 1969. The Gypsies in Canada. *JGLS* **XLVIII** (3–4): 92–107.

—— 1969a. *Learn Romani*. Edited by Donald Kenrick. Published by *Romano Drom*, the Educational Committee of the Gypsy Council, London.

—— 1971. *Goddam Gypsy*, an autobiographical novel. Montreal: Tundra Books.

LEEDS UNIVERSITY. 1962. Catalogue of the Romany Collection formed by D. U. McGrigor Phillips. Edinburgh: Thomas Nelson & Sons.

LELAND, C. G. 1891. *Gypsy Sorcery and Fortune Telling*. London: T. Fisher Unwin.

LEVY, J. DE BAIRACLI. 1962. *A Gypsy in New York*. London: Faber & Faber.

LIVERPOOL UNIVERSITY. 1936. Catalogue of Gypsy Books collected by the late Robert Andrews S. Macfie, Liverpool.

MACDONALD, J. C. R. 1939. *Crime is a Business*. Stanford: Stanford University Press.

MAXIMOFF, M. 1949. *The Ursitory*. London: Chapman & Hall (originally published in Paris, 1946).

—— 1957. *Savina*. Paris: Flammarion.

—— 1960. Naissance, Baptème, Enfance, Finançialles et Mariage chez les Tsiganes Kalderash. *Études Tsiganes* **6** (1) Jan.–March: 11–21.

MILLER, C. J. 1968. *Mačwaya Gypsy Marimé*. Unpublished M.A. thesis, University of Washington, Seattle.

MITCHELL, J. 1942. King of the Gypsies. *New Yorker:* **18** (August 15): 21–35.

—— 1955. Profiles – 'The Beautiful Flower'. *New Yorker* (June 4) **31**: 39–89.

MURIN, S. 1949. Hawaii's Gypsies. *Social Process in Hawaii* **14**: 14–37.

MYERS, J. 1943. The 'Greek' Nomad Gypsies in South Wales during August 1942. *JGLS* **XXII** (3–4): 84–100.

NICHOLAS, R. W. 1965. Factions: A comparative Analysis. In M. Banton (ed.), *Political Systems and the Distribution of Power*, ASA Monograph no. 2. London: Tavistock Publications.

—— 1966. Segmentary Factional Political Systems. In M. J. Swartz, V. Turner, and A. Tuden (eds), *Political Anthropology*. Chicago: Aldine.

—— 1968. Rules, Resources and Political Activity. In M. J. Swartz (ed.), *Local-Level Politics*. Chicago: Aldine.

PETROVIĆ, DR. A. 1936. Contributions to the Study of the Serbian Gypsies, no. 8, Marriage. *JGLS* **XV** (3): 107–26; (4): 182–93.

—— 1937. Contributions to the Study of the Serbian Gypsies, no. 10, Feast Days. *JGLS* **XVI** (3): 111–37.

PICKETT, D. W. 1962. *Prolegomena to the Study of the Gypsies of Mexico*. M.A. thesis, Syracuse University, New York.

—— 1965. The Gypsies of Mexico. *JGLS* **XLIV** (3–4): 81–99.

—— 1966. The Gypsies of Mexico. *JGLS* **XLV** (1–2): 6–17; (3–4): 84–99.

—— 1967. The Gypsies of Mexico. *JGLS* **XLVI** (1–2): 60–70.

Richmond Independent 1966. Palm Reader Fee Slashed in Martinez. September 1: 3.

—— 1968a. Warning on Theft Team given by Richmond Police. May 22: 35.

—— 1968b. Gypsy Woman Hit Run Theft. May 20: 21.

RIVIERE, P. G. 1971. Marriage: A Reassessment. In R. Needham (ed.), *Rethinking Kinship and Marriage*, ASA Monograph no. 11. London: Tavistock Publications.

SALLOWAY, J. F., ANDERSON, G., and GINAFORTONI, R. 1971. The Urban Gypsies and the Medical System: Lessons. Paper presented to the Society for Applied Anth., Miami, April (mimeograph).

SAMPSON, J. 1926. *The Dialect of the Gypsies of Wales*. Oxford: Clarendon Press.

San Francisco Chronicle 1966. Gypsy Case Cop Demoted. January 3.

SUTTLES, G. 1968. *The Social Order of the Slum. Ethnicity and Territory in the Inner City*. Chicago: University of Chicago Press.

SWARTZ, M. J. 1968. *Local-Level Politics*. Chicago: Aldine.

TILLHAGEN, C.-H. 1947. A Swedish Gypsy Investigation. *JGLS* **XXVI** (3–4): 89–115.

—— 1949. Gypsy Clans in Sweden. *JGLS* **XXVIII** (1–2): 1–17; (3–4): 119–134.

—— 1950. Gypsy Clans in Sweden. *JGLS* **XXIX** (1–2): 23–39.

—— 1952. Funeral and Death Customs of the Swedish Gypsies. *JGLS* **XXXI** (1–2): 29–54.

—— 1953. Betrothal and Wedding Customs Among the Swedish Gypsies. *JGLS* **XXXII** (1–2): 13–30; (3–4): 106–24.

—— 1956. Diseases and Their Cure Among Swedish Kalderasha Gypsies. *JGLS* **XXXV** (1–2): 49–62.

—— 1958. Conception of Justice Among the Swedish Gypsies. *JGLS* **XXXVII** (3–4): 82–96.

—— 1959. Conception of Justice Among the Swedish Gypsies. *JGLS* **XXXVIII** (1–2): 18–31; (3–4): 127–34.

TIPLER, D. 1969. The Colteshti. *JGLS* **XLVIII** (1–2): 27–33.

TOMPKINS, J. 1965a. *Gypsies in Richmond*. Report to the Welfare Department, Richmond, California. Part I – 1–10.

—— 1965b. Part II – 1–11.

—— 1967. Part III – 1–16.

—— 1971. Gypsy Attitudes Toward Medical Care: Theories of Disease, Magic, Healing and Cure. Unpublished lecture to the San Francisco Children's Hospital.

TURNER, V. W. 1957. *Schism and Continuity in an African Society.* Manchester: Manchester University Press.

VALENTINE, C. A. 1968. *Culture and Poverty: Critique and Counterproposals.* Chicago: University of Chicago Press.

VAN GENNEP, A. 1960. *The Rites of Passage.* Trans. by Monika Vizedom and Gabrielle Carfee. London: Routledge & Kegan Paul.

VOCATIONAL REHABILITATION DIVISION 1970. *Gypsy Project.* Unpublished report on rehabilitation of Gypsies, Salem, Oregon.

WEYBRIGHT, V. 1938. Who Can Tell the Gypsies' Fortune? *Survey Graphic*, March.

—— 1939. Letter to Mrs McGrigor Phillips, March 27 (Romany Collection, Brotherton Library, Leeds: 131).

—— 1945. A Nomad Gypsy Coppersmith in New York. *JGLS* **XXIV** (1–2): 2–8.

WOOD, M. F. 1973. *In the Life of a Romany Gypsy.* London: Routledge & Kegan Paul.

YALMAN, N. 1963. On the Purity of Women in the Castes of Ceylon and Malibar. *JRAI*, Part I, **93**: 25–58.

YOORS, J. 1947. Lowari Law and Jurisdiction. *JGLS* **XXVI** (1–2): 1–18.

—— 1967. *The Gypsies.* London: Allen & Unwin, Ltd.

Author and Subject Index

Index of *natsia, vitsa,* and individuals' names